A CULTURAL HISTORY OF MEMORY

VOLUME 5

A Cultural History of Memory
General Editors: Stefan Berger and Jeffrey Olick

Volume 1
A Cultural History of Memory in Antiquity
Edited by Beate Dignas

Volume 2
A Cultural History of Memory in the Middle Ages
Edited by Gerald Schwedler

Volume 3
A Cultural History of Memory in the Early Modern Age
Edited by Marek Tamm and Alessandro Ancangeli

Volume 4
A Cultural History of Memory in the Eighteenth Century
Edited by Patrick Hutton

Volume 5
A Cultural History of Memory in the Nineteenth Century
Edited by Susan A. Crane

Volume 6
A Cultural History of Memory in the Long Twentieth Century
Edited by Stefan Berger and William Niven

A CULTURAL HISTORY
OF MEMORY

IN THE NINETEENTH CENTURY

Edited by Susan A. Crane

BLOOMSBURY ACADEMIC
LONDON • NEW YORK • OXFORD • NEW DELHI • SYDNEY

BLOOMSBURY ACADEMIC
Bloomsbury Publishing Plc
50 Bedford Square, London, WC1B 3DP, UK
1385 Broadway, New York, NY 10018, USA
29 Earlsfort Terrace, Dublin 2, Ireland

BLOOMSBURY, BLOOMSBURY ACADEMIC and the Diana logo are trademarks of
Bloomsbury Publishing Plc

First published in Great Britain 2022
Paperback edition first published 2024

Copyright © Bloomsbury Publishing, 2022

Susan A. Crane has asserted her right under the Copyright, Designs and Patents Act, 1988, to be identified as Editor of this work.

Series design: Raven Design

Cover image: A street photographer at work on Clapham Common, London, with a mobile booth. Original Publication: From *"Street Life in London"*, pub. 1877 (© John Thomson/General Photographic Agency/Getty Images)

All rights reserved. No part of this publication may be reproduced or transmitted in any form or by any means, electronic or mechanical, including photocopying, recording, or any information storage or retrieval system, without prior permission in writing from the publishers.

Bloomsbury Publishing Plc does not have any control over, or responsibility for, any third-party websites referred to or in this book. All internet addresses given in this book were correct at the time of going to press. The author and publisher regret any inconvenience caused if addresses have changed or sites have ceased to exist, but can accept no responsibility for any such changes.

A catalogue record for this book is available from the British Library.

A catalog record for this book is available from the Library of Congress.

ISBN: HB: 978-1-4742-7350-3
PB: 978-1-3504-0862-3
Set: 978-1-4742-7384-8

Series: The Cultural Histories Series

Typeset by RefineCatch Limited, Bungay, Suffolk
Printed and bound in Great Britain

To find out more about our authors and books visit www.bloomsbury.com and sign up for our newsletters.

CONTENTS

LIST OF ILLUSTRATIONS vi
GENERAL EDITORS' PREFACE viii
   Stefan Berger and Jeffrey Olick

   Introduction 1
   Susan A. Crane

1 Power and Politics 21
   Matt Matsuda

2 Time and Space 39
   Nick Yablon

3 Media and Technology 55
   Elizabeth Edwards

4 Knowledge: Science and Education 79
   Thomas Dodman

5 Ideas: Philosophy, Religion and History 95
   Stan M. Landry

6 High Culture and Popular Culture 115
   Kathrin Maurer

7 The Social: Rituals, Faith, Practices and the Everyday 135
   Cecilia Morgan

8 Remembering and Forgetting 157
   Stéphane Gerson

NOTES 175
BIBLIOGRAPHY 183
NOTES ON CONTRIBUTORS 209
INDEX 213

ILLUSTRATIONS

INTRODUCTION

0.1	Photographer at Work, 1877.	10
0.2	The Historical Family Album, *c.* 1910.	16
0.3	Mother and Baby in Blue, *c.* 1850.	18

CHAPTER 1

1.1	Transplanting of the Bread-fruit Trees from Otaheite by Thomas Gosse, 1796.	24
1.2	Opium War memorial, Humen, China.	30
1.3	Anthropometric data sheet of Alphonse Bertillon, 1893.	37

CHAPTER 2

2.1	Mosher's Memorial Offering to Chicago.	41
2.2	"Beef Depot Monument" in *Leslie's Illustrated Newspaper*, 1862.	43
2.3	Brennan Farm House, 1879.	46
2.4	A copy of a life mask of Abraham Lincoln, 1860.	48
2.5	Chest of drawers by Michael Allison, *c.* 1800–20.	51
2.6	Writing desk, *c.* 1830–60.	52

CHAPTER 3

3.1	"A Post Office in an Indian Tea District" in *The Queen's Empire*, 1897–9.	62
3.2	Ruins at Pollonanaru, Sri Lanka.	64
3.3	"Raising the Flag" in *Illustrated London News*, 1884.	66
3.4	"Hoisting the Flag at Port Moresby" in *Narrative of the expedition of the Australian squadron to New Guinea*, 1885.	67
3.5	"Raising the Flag" in *The Graphic*, 1885.	68
3.6	"Raising the Flag" in *The Queen's Empire*, 1897–9.	69
3.7	Statue of Captain Cook, Sydney, in *Illustrated London News*, 1878.	70
3.8	Stereocard of the memorial at the Cawnpore massacre site, by James Ricalton, *c.* 1900.	71
3.9	Engraving from a photograph of the memorial at the Cawnpore massacre site, India, in *Illustrated London News*, 1874.	73
3.10	Postcard of Cawnpore massacre site memorial, *c.* 1905.	74
3.11	Sites of colonial memory in *The Queen's Empire*, 1899.	75

CHAPTER 4

4.1	Front cover of *American Phrenological Journal*, 1849.	82
4.2	*La Tâche noire* by Albert Brettannier, 1887.	90

CHAPTER 5

5.1	The Walter Scott Monument, Edinburgh.	97
5.2	*Voltaire Nude* by Jean-Baptiste Pigalle, 1776.	105
5.3	Bust of Voltaire by Jean Antoine Houdon, 1778.	106

CHAPTER 6

6.1	Liebig's Meat Extract Company trading card.	116
6.2	*The Sedan-Panorama*, 1885.	121
6.3	Postcard from the Boxer Rebellion, 1900–1.	123
6.4	Image of Napoleon at the Battle of Embabeh, 1827/1839.	125
6.5	*History of Frederick the Great*, 1842.	127
6.6	The Hermann Monument, Teutoborg Forest.	131

CHAPTER 7

7.1	Langton Family Home, Toronto, 1856–57.	139
7.2	Australian Garden in New South Wales, *c.* 1872.	140
7.3	The Piano in the Parlor, Ontario, *c.* 1880s–90s.	141
7.4	Elizabeth Johnson Clench. Sampler, *c.* 1830s.	142
7.5	Mae Hagen's Christening Gown.	144
7.6	Mrs. Harris's Wedding Portrait.	145
7.7	Wedding in Tasmania, 1875.	146
7.8	Post-mortem photograph of a small child, *c.* 1880s–90s.	148
7.9	Tsimshian Tea Party, *c.* 1890s.	151
7.10	Naneebahweequa/Catherine Sutton portrait, *c.* 1860.	153

CHAPTER 8

8.1	*The Black Eagle of Prussia* by Gustave Doré, 1871.	160
8.2	*Puteaux–Monument de la défense* by Ernest Barrias, *c.* 1900.	162
8.3	"Quatrième fête historique de la Société de bienfaisance de Douai".	163
8.4	*Promenades dans la Forêt de Fontainebleau* by Claude-François Denecourt, 1844.	164
8.5	Statue of Victor Schoelcher, 1896.	167
8.6	Postcard of the Grand Hôtel et Fontaine Adam de Craponne, 1914.	169
8.7	"Souvenir historique. Déclaration de la Guerre", *c.* 1870s.	172

GENERAL EDITORS' PREFACE

STEFAN BERGER AND JEFFREY K. OLICK

Any project titled *A Cultural History of Memory* begs a number of questions from the very beginning. For instance: What does it mean that this project is a *cultural* history, rather than some other kind of history? (What other kind of history might it have been?) In turn, what makes memory a feasible and interesting topic for such a history? (It certainly isn't immediately obvious that it would be.) Finally, why a cultural history rather than *the* cultural history? (After all, with forty-eight chapters spread over six volumes, how many more cultural histories of memory could one imagine?)

CULTURAL HISTORY

A Cultural History of Memory is but one entry in a series of cultural histories already and soon to be published by Bloomsbury, including cultural histories of Animals, the Human Body, Food, Gardens, Women, the Senses, Dress and Fashion, the Theatre, Work, Law, Money, and Hair, among many others. The publisher has taken a light hand in prescribing the orientation of these projects, leaving the definition of cultural history to each project's senior editors. And this is very well, as there are many different ways to inflect the idea of cultural history, and different approaches are likely appropriate to the different subject matters. In turn, we have not imposed any particular definition on the editors of the six volumes in this current project, nor have they on the authors of the forty-eight chapters that comprise the total product. That being said, we have relied on a broadly shared understanding of the purposes and tools of cultural history in framing this particular entry in the series, and it is clear that its many authors have as well, though perhaps with occasional divergences.

Namely, contemporary cultural history, at least as it has been practiced in and on the West (and this is one of the important limitations on the project we will discuss below), has defined itself in contrast to at least three other approaches (on the historiographical developments sketched in the following pages see in greater detail Berger, Feldner, and Passmore (2020)). First, there is a broadly defined "traditional" political historiography, dominant in the nineteenth century, that wrote the story of states, their leaders, and their wars. These "high politics" approaches, of course, fully advanced the claim to "objectivity," particularly since the matters they studied—states, their leaders, and their wars—have been quite well documented. These approaches, nevertheless, not only studied the world of nation-states and their high politics but were often part of defining the claims of those states and glorifying the achievements of their leaders, so their claims to be value-free and scientific were obviously dubious ones.

Following this, though at different times in different parts of the world, and only partly under the influence of Marxist perspectives, there developed a vibrant interest in "economic" and "social" history alongside, and sometimes in contrast to, the traditional political histories: the stories not of the "great men" and the great achievements, but of economic processes and social structures. Like political history, this was often presented in national containers and sometimes served the purpose of highlighting the particular "achievements" of nations in the economic and social spheres. Only later did a nascent Marxist historiography, often relatively weak in the universities before the 1970s, come to understand this study of history to be part of a struggle not merely to interpret or understand history, but to change it, as Marx famously put it in his eleventh thesis on Feuerbach.

A stronger concern for ordinary people in social history, however, only occurred with the turn to "history from below," sometimes also referred to as history of everyday life, micro-history, or historical anthropology. This was largely a development that gathered momentum from the 1970s onwards. "History workshop" movements that often became supporters of this new, more human-agency centered understanding of social history, critiqued older forms of social history for being too focused on structures and processes and thereby for ignoring human agency. Furthermore, these approaches criticized the adherence of much of social and economic history to modernization theories and teleologies of progress that appeared to many practitioners of historical anthropology as outdated. The interest of these historians in the everyday had made them turn to anthropology and, inspired by anthropological methods and theories, they set out to change understandings of the social and cultural. As Robert Darnton has put it, "The anthropological mode of history [. . .] begins from the premise that individual expression takes place within a general idiom" (quoted in Hunt 1989: 12). In other words: history had to start from individual human agency and then locate it within a wider collective field.

More difficult to understand is the next form of "traditional" historical interest that was always a lesser strand when compared to political and economic/social history: namely, intellectual history or the history of ideas. Like "traditional" forms of history that focused on states, wars, and high politics, intellectual history has often focused on a narrow slice of life as well: the thoughts and ideas of other great men than politicians (though sometimes them too), mainly artists, scientists, philosophers, and others whose writings are seen to have captured, defined, and led the "spirit" of an age. To be sure, intellectual historians are quite interested in the contexts and structures that enabled the great thinkers to produce their great works, as well as in how those great works affected the less great thoughts of the cultures and societies that produced them. The recent influence of the so-called "Cambridge school" around Quentin Skinner and J.G.A. Pocock is a good example of such contextualization of great thinkers. Internationally even more influential has been the "history of concepts"—shaped seminally by the German historical theorist Reinhart Koselleck. Conceptual history is now a truly global undertaking and one that takes seriously the belief that we need to thoroughly historicize our key concepts in order to understand how people made sense of the world and how they consequently acted in the world.

Next to political history, economic and social history, historical anthropology, and intellectual history, cultural history now forms one of the great traditions of historical writing, reaching back to the very beginnings of professional historiography. Jacob Burckhardt and Johan Huizinga are just two examples of classical representatives of cultural history that can still be read with great pleasure and benefit by contemporary cohorts of students. However, older cultural history often had a strong emphasis on studying "high culture" and thereby distinguishing what was "true" and "worthwhile" culture from "popular culture" or simply "trash." When a "new cultural history" began to conquer history departments in the 1980s, it democratized older forms of cultural history by redefining culture in broader and more inclusive terms. Furthermore, many of its practitioners were much influenced by the "linguistic turn" and theories associated with poststructuralist approaches (Toews 1987: 879–907). Like historical anthropology the new cultural history was dissatisfied not only with an older political history interested mainly in "high politics" but an older social and economic history reducing the past to structures and processes. Unlike an older intellectual history, it was also not so much interested in "great ideas" but instead in ordinary thoughts and practices. Whilst the initial interest in language led cultural historians to study discourses, many soon realized that discourses had to be related back to practices. Furthermore, practices had much to do with things and objects, in other words, materials that needed to be considered to have an agency of their own in history. The history of material culture could thus build on the linguistic turn and practice theory, but it carved out a niche of its own in a field of cultural history that became increasingly compartmentalized as we enter the new millennium after 2000.

Marxist social historians like E.P. Thompson and Geoff Eley spearheaded new understandings of the history of society that took on board many of the insights of the new cultural history without ever abandoning an appreciation of the Marxist understanding of social developments. Thompson, for example, focused not only on the economic condition that made the English working class, but on "the way [. . .] material experiences are handled . . . in cultural ways" (Merrill 1972: 20 f). This happened, according to Thompson, through "cultural and moral mediations." In turn, however, Gareth Stedman Jones moved the discussion even farther afield from economic reduction when he declared that "We [. . .] cannot decode political language to reach a primal and material expression of interest since it is the discursive structure of political language which conceives and defines interest in the first place" (Stedman Jones 1983: 21-22). For the "new cultural historians" in this tradition, then, what they, in part following Emile Durkheim among others, called "representations" became of primary interest. And, as Roger Chartier put it, "The Representations of the social world themselves are the constituents of social reality" (Chartier 1982: 30). This is because, as Lynn Hunt writes, "All practices, whether economic or cultural, depend on the representations individuals use to make sense of their world" (Hunt 1989: 19). The goal of cultural history is thus, as again Chartier defines it, to show "how, in different times and places, a specific social reality was constructed, how people conceived of it and how they interpreted it to others" (Chartier 1998: 4). In this, Chartier followed Lucien Goldmann, who had defined worldviews—the true subject for intellectual historians who were interested in culture more broadly—as "the whole complex of ideas, aspirations and feelings which links together the members of a social group [. . .] and which opposed them to members of other social groups" (Goldmann 1967: 17). And this is indeed the approach that most of the authors in these six volumes have taken, though in an obviously wide variety of ways in and for a wide variety of contexts.

MEMORY

The turn toward memory, especially understood as a collective or cultural phenomenon, can in fact be seen as—though not only as—another inflection of the new cultural history (Berger and Niven 2014). Its interest in representations and discourses encouraged an interest in memories as constituting those representations and discourses. Whether it was written in pursuit of a nostalgic longing for a great national past, as is evident in some of the contributions to Pierre Nora's seminal seven-volume study on the realms of memory of France (Nora 1981–7), or whether it was conducted in the search for understanding and possibly overcoming the consequences of traumatic events in the past, like genocides or wars, memory history has linked contemporary memories to processes of sense-production in the present that gave rise to very different and always contested understandings of the past.

It should already be obvious, then, that the cultural history of memory undertaken in the forty-eight chapters that follow is not just about recall or other basic cognitive processes. Though the concept of memory employed across these six volumes is sometimes the lay understanding of memory as what and how people can recall in different times and places, the majority of the chapters take memory to be something broader. Memory may seem to take place within individual minds, yet for most of the last century numerous scholars both within and beyond cultural history have understood memory more broadly (Olick, Vinitzky-Seroussi, and Levy 2011). Individual memory always takes place within social contexts, with social materials, from social positions, and in response to social cues. So whatever neurological or mental processes it involves, these are obviously deeply embedded in structures and contexts that extend far beyond the individuals whose minds engage in remembering, traditionally understood. Individuals, moreover, employ many technologies of memory—for instance, chanting or writing—which exist outside of themselves and are not part of their brains, and which vary across social settings and in their impacts on individual mnemonic processes. In this way, it becomes perhaps clearer why memory is such a rich terrain for cultural (and other!) forms of history.

However, many of the chapters that constitute this cultural history of memory take yet another step beyond the mind—that is, beyond what Maurice Halbwachs, one of the key figures in contemporary thinking about memory, called the social frameworks of memory, to see memory as an inherently social activity (Halbwachs 1950). We often—even most often—remember together. Social psychologists understand that there are significant differences between remembering alone and remembering in a group, whether this is a matter of simple recall (e.g. when a group of individuals can reconstruct memorized lists more completely than the sum of individuals alone via cuing and other social processes) or in narrative process (e.g. when a family retells a story of an experience they have shared, and the complete narrative emerges from the many voices involved, which bring different pieces than everyone necessarily would have recalled). However, some scholars argue that groups themselves remember; for instance, they build libraries and fill them with materials, they curate representations of the past in museums and elsewhere in ways that transcend the resources of individuals, and they preserve knowledge that very few individuals recall (Assmann 1992). As such, scholars often refer to social, collective, or cultural memory—the forms and traces of the past that transcend the capacities or even interests of individuals—and many do not believe these forms of memories are merely metaphors (see Erll 2008). The field of memory is thus a vast one, and it is clear that understanding all the different forms of memory—from the neurological to the museological—requires, and is an appropriate subject for, all the resources of cultural history.

Having said that, the development of memory studies since the 1980s has been characterized by the gradual constitution of a new discipline that was self-consciously transdisciplinary. Of all the disciplines that constituted this new field, historians were arguably in a minority. Literary scholars and sociologists were far more numerous, and, as all six volumes in this series demonstrate, a cultural history of memory cannot do without referencing a range of literary, sociological and other disciplinary approaches to memory.

Apart from its characteristic transdisciplinarity, which had a major impact on memory history, however, the latter also remained, for quite some time, tied to the national container that, as we have already discussed, had been so strongly established in the historical sciences in the century roughly between 1850 and 1950. The move of memory history to *transnational* forms of memory has only been a relatively recent development, following a general trend in historical studies to criticize "methodological nationalism" and move to more transnational forms of historical writing, emphasizing interlinkages, adaptations, and transfers. However, as a perusal of any of the hugely successful conferences of the Memory Studies Association will show, most scholars today still focus on national memory.[1] Transnational, let alone global memory is not practiced very widely,[2] which also reflects a major difficulty for a cultural history of memory; there are simply not enough scholars who can truly synthesize vast amounts of work on a particular theme in a global perspective. Here we can only trust that our failure will be an inspiration to future generations of scholars to move to more global perspectives on memory history.

Where our six volumes have hopefully been more successful has been in moving histories of memory away from their fixation with trauma, especially national trauma. The huge body of work on the memory of genocides, in particular the Holocaust, and the equally massive amount of work on the memory of wars, especially the two world wars, but also the Vietnam war and a range of civil wars, is an indicator of to what extent memory scholars have homed in on traumatic events in the past. Undoubtedly, much of this work has been incredibly valuable and inspirational, but the six volumes that we introduce here, whilst not ignoring genocides and war, also intend to highlight a range of other areas in which memory history can be usefully applied.

If *A Cultural History of Memory* tries to escape memory history's bias toward "methodological nationalism" and toward traumatic events in the past, it also deliberately—and structurally—seeks to introduce a longer-term perspective and to show how memory history is a relevant and intriguing exercise for older periods of time. Once again, looking from a bird's eye perspective over the field of memory history, we see a massive concentration of work in the modern period, basically from the late eighteenth century to the present day. But the first four of our six volumes underline to what an extent the history of memory benefits from considering older time periods. As general editors, we particularly hope that modernists (of whom we are culpable examples) may delve into the writings on pre-modern times, as it will reveal not only substantial differences, but also, and certainly more striking to us, amazing similarities when considering the role of memory for cultural sense-production.

A CULTURAL HISTORY

Finally, what of the definite article "A" Cultural History of Memory. In the first place, across a work as extensive as this one (or these ones), it is obvious that there are many different approaches to the subject matters. Though all contributing to this cultural history, the authors come from numerous different disciplines and specialties, have different foci, bring to bear different interests and expertise even within this "one" work. We do so, moreover, from numerous different countries, languages of origin, and periods of study, though the list, however extensive, is still limited in significant ways. In the second place, however, much as the publishers did not lay a heavy hand on the forms of cultural history to be employed, they did determine that all the volumes should have the same structure. Hence, we came up with eight themes that had to be the same across all six volumes. In choosing broad themes—power and politics, media and technology, knowledge: science and education, time and space, ideas: philosophy, religion, and history, high and popular culture, the social: rituals, practices, and the everyday, and remembering and forgetting—we sought to give the volume editors the space to adapt those themes to the particular foci appropriate to different times and geographies. As any reader of the six volumes will realize, the editors made good use of that leeway, but this also leads to the phenomenon that different authors have put the emphasis of their respective chapters differently and usually in line with their own specialisms.

The publisher also dictated the epochal labels we employed, and they determined that the eight topics addressed in each chronologically constituted volume should be nominally the same as the topics in the other volumes. Much as we appreciated the reasons for this—for instance, so that a particular theme could be followed across the epochs, or that someone interested in a particular epoch could recombine the history of memory we have produced for that epoch with the history of something else addressed in other entries in the series—this constraint did raise concerns for us and our colleagues. For instance, no single chronology labeling applies uniformly for different areas of the world (e.g. not every society or culture identifies the same antiquity, or an antiquity at all). And the present chronology is a very Western one indeed. Moreover, the application of these labels can be anachronistic. After all, the people whose forms of memory we are studying in a particular age did not understand themselves as having that particular place in history (e.g. the people in the antiquity we have studied did not think of themselves as inhabiting an ancient world). Finally, had we not understood the imperative of recombination of themes and periods, the editors of each epochally-defined volume might have wanted to label the eight chapters differently from the editors of the other volumes, since the same relevances did not necessarily obtain in the same ways in different periods.

Nevertheless, much as the ground we have collectively covered here is vast indeed, we might still hope—if not for other, at least for additional work in this vibrant field on this fascinating subject. We hope that, despite the additional works that might be possible—and that we hope will be produced—what we have to offer here will be of use to as many as possible. The field of memory studies is a relatively new one. But the sophistication of the chapters (and volume introductions) we have the pleasure of presenting here shows that much as the field has a long way to go, it is well on its way.

Introduction

SUSAN A. CRANE

How was memory understood and experienced in the nineteenth century? What has it meant to remember "the nineteenth century," then or later? These related questions provide the foundation for the present volume's cultural historical enterprise. They invoke our relationships to a past that we label "nineteenth century" in both scholarly and emotionally resonant ways. There is no way to think about any historical past without some kind of desire—to know, to experience, to understand, to remember and not to forget—motivating the inquiry. This became clear to me in a new way when a student asked me whether I had ever met anyone "from the nineteenth century." I had, but she had not, and with that knowledge, she looked at me new eyes. I had become a living connection to a past that she was interested in (and, yes, I felt instantly older). Historical consciousness—an awareness of the fascinating ways in which the present is crucially related to and yet distant from the past—can trip up even historians. And by any definition, the nineteenth century was an era of abundant historical consciousness.

Memory is timeless, in that we all have it, use it, depend upon it, lose it. But "even memory has a history," as one of the premier scholars of nineteenth-century memory observed in the opening line of his book, *Present Past* (Terdiman 1991). Richard Terdiman went on to characterize a particularly French "memory crisis" in the *fin-de-siècle*, vividly articulated among that culture's elites. Iconic figures in modern memory studies, such as Sigmund Freud, Henri Bergson, and Marcel Proust, emerged during this "crisis." From the perspective of a modern European historian such as myself, a cultural history of memory in the nineteenth century without reference to these turn-of-the-century writers is unimaginable.

If a crisis of memory can be said to have concluded the nineteenth century, what were its origins? And whose crisis was it? Was it only an elite minority of French intellectuals? Did it resonate within French culture, or transnationally, or globally? What other kinds of memory persisted or resisted crisis? The cultural history of memory situates ideas—often considered more properly the subject of intellectual history or philosophy—in their multiple, material contexts of production and reception. Answering these questions requires attention to connections among disciplines, communities of memories, sites of memory, and memory objects: the places and practices of memory. For all that individual thinkers sought to conceptualize "memory" and discursively form that object in distinct disciplines in the nineteenth century (such as history, psychology, archaeology, or sociology, all of which became distinct disciplinary identities in this era), memory practices have always eluded strict confinement to categories of analysis for the simple reason that they originate in a human brain and in a human body dependent upon memory for its daily biological functions as well as higher order mental capabilities. A longer durée of memory study must involve the incommensurate temporal orders of an individual's mental lifespan and social existence, the natural past (astronomical, geological, cyclical; "time immemorial" and diurnal), and the remembered past (see Nick Yablon's discussion of "Time" in this volume). Memory studies look less at the functions of the brain than at the externalization of remembering, the sites of memory which individual historical actors and social collectives imbue with meaning. The very definition of "modernity" may be laced with a "crisis of memory," but this is only one aspect of memories in the nineteenth century.

A cultural history of memory thus requires not only evaluation of intellectuals' contributions, but also of the multimedial circulations of ideas and their forms of representation. The published work of authors exists as tangible memory objects. Books, magazines, newspapers, and other forms of textual reproduction offer audiences physical contact with formats for memory discourse. Readers take in printed words and images (and words as images) and, in reading, remember what someone has written or made; readers acquire knowledge but also the visual experience of reading which they then remember, share, discuss, and, just as often if not more often, forget. Recirculation of ideas in all their mediated (remembered and forgotten) forms then cultivates popular culture imagery, including myriad forms of mass media and marketing, which also implicates the sites of their consumption in the public sphere, from cafés and shops to museums and commemorative celebrations, as well as the intimate spaces of the private sphere (see Cecilia Morgan's chapter in this volume). Institutionalized sites for the preservation of memory objects—libraries, archives, museums, academia, and schools—proliferated in nineteenth-century cultures, and all of these offer rich realms for historical inquiry. However, domestic interiors and migrant's suitcases offer equally compelling spaces for more mobile memory objects and discursive formation of nostalgia and commemoration. The market for memories encompassed global trade networks and privately sequestered mementos, as intimate as a lock of hair requiring its own locket (Batchen 2004b).

A cultural history of memory looks not only at definitions or invocations of memory; it also inquires into the meanings associated with remembering and forgetting in the daily lives and cultural output of historically contextualized societies. We are thus concerned with both discursive and material cultures, with technologies and forms of representation that reflected and engaged nineteenth-century sensibilities about the past. In part, this is a logical consequence of the externalization of memory functions from the brain into interactive social networks of meaning making: When we refer meanings to sites of memory, we engage history and memory in the presence of their artifacts (which include published histories like this one) and memorials. A pioneer in the field, historian John R. Gillis, sagely noted how this process of remembering is encoded in a language that retains the object status of material culture even while referring to ideas, symbols and abstractions:

> That memories and identities change over time tends to be obscured by the fact that we too often refer to both as if they had the status of objects—memory as something to be retrieved, identity as something that can be lost as well as found.
>
> —Gillis 1994: 3

The nineteenth century characteristically proliferated these objects of memory discourse, in part as a direct consequence of the rise of modern nation-states, new entities that sought to portray themselves as having unique and significant histories. Gillis postulates the distinctive character of national self-formation, as "nations came to worship themselves through their pasts, ritualizing and commemorating to the point that their sacred sites and times became the secular equivalent of shrines and holy days" (Gillis 1994: 19). What Eric Hobsbawm and his colleagues termed "the invention of tradition" served the formation of national identity through claims to native historical practices (Hobsbawm 1983). But while dominant discourses of nineteenth-century identity prioritized the nation, they coexisted with contestations of local, imperial, colonial and subaltern identities with different memory claims. For every national holiday celebrated around the flag or national monument, there were communal commemorations; family, clan, or tribal anniversaries; religious pilgrimages; and other socially significant sites of memory that embodied minority and dissenting collectives' claims about remembering and forgetting.

A cultural history of memory thus emerges at the intersections of history and memory, where memories are created, stored, exchanged, and created anew. As cultural historian Ann Rigney suggests, memories are not stable entities or fixed objects; rather, they are themselves generative:

> To the extent that engagement with acts of remembrance can in turn generate new acts of remembrance in the form of embodied acts or new artifacts, it has become logical to speak of "productive reception."
>
> —Rigney 2016: 68

Engagement with memories, performances of remembering and forgetting, and contestation over meanings occur as embodied interactions with material culture and discursive formations. Rather than accept the artificially constrained distinction between history and memory which perpetuates disciplinary boundaries, this collection of essays considers how histories are about memories and how memories participate in historical cultures. Histories and memories are made and unmade by multiple individuals and collectives continuously, but they are also made and unmade by the objects themselves.

This volume's cultural history of memory in the nineteenth century begins not in 1800, since the designation of calendar years and centuries is itself a historically contingent convention. When does any history—much less a history of memories—begin? Rather, it continues a history dating from antiquity, conducted in the preceding volumes of this series with identically titled chapters. Contributing authors discuss modernity's concerns with time, chronology and progress; the establishment of disciplinary boundaries around professional identities and methods associated with history, geology, natural history, psychology, archaeology, and anthropology; and the creation of media technologies such as cameras and photography, film, lithographs, and other forms of mechanical reproduction. Nineteenth-century memory objects, created or recovered with intent to foster recollection, featured innovations of their kind, ranging from monuments and memorials to souvenirs, tattoos, time capsules, photo albums, postcards, christening gowns, and more. Sites of memory (*lieux de mémoire*) were located in intimate and public places alike, from homes to museums, across generations and at the intersections of imperial and colonial, national and domestic spaces.[1] Locating memories within their complex temporal, social, and geographical frameworks, we consider the practices and places in which memories were created, sought, retained, and forgotten by individuals and their constituent collectives.

The contributing authors in this volume explore "the realms of memory" (an alternative translation of Pierre Nora's *lieux de mémoire*) across realms of historical inquiry formulated by the chapter headings. Each has successfully engaged distinct historical-cultural formations. There are many more which could be considered: memorization as a required educational learning tool, say, or arts of memory practiced in oral traditional cultures. In what follows, I offer further examples of intersections formed within nineteenth-century historical cultures, featuring visual and material cultures of memories. Images provide a vital illustration of object-driven memory work, and photography emerged in this era as a powerful new medium for documentation, commemoration, and preservation, as one among many new and internationally resonant media technologies.

HISTORICAL CULTURES OF THE NINETEENTH CENTURY

Jürgen Osterhammel's monumental work *The Transformation of the World: A Global History of the Nineteenth Century* opens with a long chapter entitled "Memory and Self-Observation: The Perpetuation of the Nineteenth Century." It is striking that a book whose scale is global and whose length exceeds 1,000 pages devotes inaugural concern to memory. Osterhammel argues, "Today's perceptions of the nineteenth century are still strongly marked by its own self-perception" (2014: 3). The remembered past has imprinted on the present because "the nineteenth century was an age of well-nurtured memory . . . The collecting and exhibition institutions that it created continue to prosper, without being tied to the goals set at the time when they were founded" (Osterhammel 2014: 17). The era's diverse devotions to remembering and forgetting produced institutions and institutionalized practices whose reach has exceeded their grasp, to paraphrase a poet of that century, Robert Browning. Nineteenth-century historical cultures were highly self-conscious: in their intentions to record, reflect, recall, and recirculate, they animated themselves and created forms for self-sustaining membership, whether in national cultures, families, imperial networks or migrant diasporas.

Memory and membership are inexorably linked. When nineteenth-century Americans responded to exhortations to "Remember the Alamo!" or, later, "Remember the Maine!" they honored the memories of martyred defenders of patriotic causes (some Texan, some American; the latter largely forgotten now, the former having acquired mythic status). The calls to memory went out both in text—as newspaper headlines, pamphlets and books—and verbally—in speeches, songs, and performances. Insofar as they resonated across time, these rallying cries became shorthand for larger political commitments; they also inspired counter-memories and resistance in similar formats, such as the *corridos* written and performed in post-Alamo Texas (Flores 2002). Invoking historical events in order to motivate political action in the present is not new; what was particular to modernity in these cases was the rapid, multimedial circulation of claims and counterclaims to knowledge about the past and the expectation that a large-scale public would respond with recognition to the mere mention of the past event.

Memory-as-slogan proved remarkably effective in modernity. It was also quickly perceived by professionalizing historians as a challenge to their recently developed standards of ethical practice. As philosopher Avashai Margalit distinguished, "Memory, then, is *knowledge from the past*. It is not necessarily knowledge *about* the past" (2002:14; original italics). Public reference to a historic event—as opposed to its citation in a written history—testifies to its fame. Notoriety is not reliant on fact or accuracy but rather on salience. Becoming famous transforms the ordinary place into something remarkable, such as a battle site like the Alamo or Waterloo, as Stuart Semmel observes:

> Waterloo, John Scott wrote in 1816, had "been raised to a par with the most famous names of the world, never to be forgotten until some interruption happens to the human race." The invocation of historical fame demanded the language of cataclysm.
>
> —Semmel 2000: 17

Nothing less than catastrophe could alter the historic significance of what had once been so ordinary as to be unremarkable. Poetry, songs, and slogans offered meter for memorizing what it meant to "meet your Waterloo," referencing the past quite adequately without footnotes.

Slogans circulated materially as well as orally, on posters, in public protests, and in advertisements. In this sense they present a classic case of the cultural history of memory, at the intersection of visual and verbal. Technologies of vision were deeply intertwined with contemporary thought. As J.D. Braw demonstrates, even the doyenne of modern historiography, Leopold von Ranke, argued that "the aim of history-writing [*Historie*] is to bring past life before one's eyes" and thus "History" was something to be *seen* (Braw 2007: 48). Ranke chose to write history, and thus has typically been understood to have represented the past verbally rather than physically; but writing is published and read in book form, and thus consumed visually and tactilely. Ranke's entire oeuvre was likewise characterized by an emphasis on the visual nature of historical consciousness (see Kathrin Maurer's discussion in this volume). The precocious professional discipline of history, situated within academia and designated by name for the first time in the nineteenth century, was thus not as distant from popular cultures of memory as its ivory tower location might imply. As David Lowenthal delineated in his now classic inventory of memory cultures, *The Past Is a Foreign Country*, academic disciplines of memory emerged as coevals to literatures (fiction, memoir, poetry), theater, music, song, fashion and design dedicated to recollection of the past:

> Scott's historical novels, Gothic Revival architecture, neo-chivalric fashions of dress and conduct, classical standards of beauty, successive passions for all things Roman, Greek, Egyptian, Chinese, early English—all this betokened a people besotted with their past. John Stuart Mill thought his fellow countrymen all "carry eyes in the back of their heads."
>
> —Lowenthal 1985: 97

Lowenthal thought these historical obsessions were typical of Victorian Britain; while it was not true that everyone in that society was a "crazed medievalist," predilections for the past were found across class, gender, and economic divides. Given the pastiche and variety of the popular pasts, it's worth considering which pasts were *not* revived or were being actively forgotten: it was never "all things Roman, Greek, Egyptian, Chinese, early English" but rather fascinations and fetishizations focused on a particular era as representative of the glories of that chronotope, the conceptual conflation of time/place that signified essential value. Inherently excluded, for instance, were the non-elite cultural heritages and memory practices of these places. An Egyptian mummy of a pharaoh had aesthetic and archaeological interest that the clothes of the ordinary Egyptian of the same era did not. Not *all* things ancient were valuable or worthy of memory, but all were newly seen to be potentially so by the emerging social sciences.

Popular forms of memory in the nineteenth century ranged across a broad spectrum: the panorama, pantheon, and museum for visiting; novels, plays, opera, poetry, song for consumption; ruins, historical sites, and natural wonders for contemplation of the past. Stephen Bann provocatively stated that "no one reads the histories of the nineteenth century" the way readers have continuously consumed much of the historical fiction of that era. But he said this in order to problematize the distinction between "truth" and "fiction" which was being so productively challenged by "the proliferation of new forms in which the historical understanding sought to express itself in the Romantic period"

(Bann 1995: 25). Romanticism exerted a huge influence over popular as well as elite forms of memory, even if its hegemony in the historical profession was short-lived.

The sentimental and emotional tug of relics and ruins appealed to a generation that produced *The Keepsake* (1828–57), an English annual publication of illustrated poetry and prose, in which Leigh Hunt inscribed their resonance:

> What renders a book more valuable as a keepsake than almost any other is that, like a friend, it can talk with and entertain us ... where such an affectionate liberty can be taken either in right of playing the teacher, or because the giver of the book is sure of a sympathy in point of taste with the person receiving it, the said giver should mark his or her favorite passages throughout (as delicately as need be), as so present, as it were, the author's and the giver's minds at once.
>
> —Piper 2009: 128–9

Books were still relatively expensive in this era; the invocation to write in it is a mark of ownership (even if it is to be done delicately). Reading opened up a new form of historical understanding as mutuality, an exchange of ideas and opinions among like-minded individuals, membership in the literary circle. If reading fomented shared historical consciousness, writers emerged in the nineteenth century as a collective of idea-transmitters, and all books were potential souvenirs—keepsakes "to remember me by." As Andrew Piper notes, inscriptions appeared frequently in books as dedications exchanged between readers in the collections of the American Antiquarian Society (2009: 132–3). The network formed among readers, authors and the published book extended Romantic circles beyond their immediate users, creating collectives while preserving emotional ties via historical artifacts. The book as souvenir preserves Romantic sensibilities.

It's worth recalling, as Benedict Anderson noted, that a generational cohort of influential nineteenth-century historians was born in the Revolutionary crib: Leopold von Ranke in 1795, Jules Michelet in 1798, Alexis de Toqueville in 1805, both Karl Marx and Jacob Burckhardt in 1818 (1983/2016: 197). The French Revolution produced a generational-historical consciousness, registered by transnational contemporaries as absolute change. Literally displaced by warfare or metaphorically "stranded in the present" by dispossession and confusion, Europeans experienced losses that accumulated into a new understanding of the past as lost (Fritzsche 2004). The violence committed across the continent was mirrored by the violence rendered to the calendar, time, and the clock by revolutionaries who declared that national chronology restarted with their Republic (see the chapters by Nick Yablon and Stéphane Gerson in this volume). History was no longer solely the interpretive domain of religious or secular rulers, or solely comprising important political events in the past. Peter Fritzsche suggests that, in this era, more and more people began to visualize history as a process that affected their lives in "knowable, comprehensible ways.... The emerging historical consciousness was not restricted to an elite, or a small literate stratum, but was the shared cultural good of ordinary travelers, soldiers and artisans" (2004:13). What contemporaries shared was a sense of loss and longing, nostalgia and a desperate optimism about progress which reflected the depths of their despair. Historical consciousness thus measured the presence of traumatic memories. While "conservatives, monarchists and emigres were more apt to see the events of 1789 in revolutionary terms, as a fundamental break with the past," a "collective singular of generic revolution" emerged within publics across Europe and its empires, impacting as well new nations founded on some of the same principles as revolutionary France (Fritzsche, 2004: 44). This strong sensibility of dislocation within one's own lifetime and experience was shared across social and cultural boundaries and produced a generational cohort. Their children and grandchildren then inherited both loss and nostalgia, expressed as remembering and forgetting how a generation lived through traumatic historical events (on nostalgia, see Thomas Dodman's chapter in this volume).

A modernity that perceived itself as cut off from the past also felt itself, perhaps in consequence, deeply rooted in both natural and historical antiquity. The nineteenth century witnessed foundational discoveries in geology (fossil records and the age of the earth) and archaeology (translation of the Rosetta Stone, the "discovery" of Troy and many other sites). Classically-trained scholars, architects, artists, and tastemakers alike fostered appreciation for Greek and Roman cultures, but also recovered a pre-history that antedated the great civilizations. Graecophilia and admiration for Rome affected how they understood the legacy of the French Revolution. Consider Karl Marx's famous observation in *The Eighteenth Brumaire of Louis Bonaparte* (1852) that "the Revolution of 1789–1814 draped itself alternately in the guise of the Roman Republic and the Roman Empire." Although educated by German scholars to venerate classical learning, Marx was perhaps referring not only to the political rhetoric that was classically inspired or the historically themed paintings of Ingres and David, who depicted revolutionaries in togas. As Simon Goldhill points out, Marx's observation makes literal sense if we consider how revolutionaries themselves claimed to be inspired by conflated classical references such as those in Christoph Willibald von Gluck's operas, where Greek—not Roman—political ideals and myths dominated, and which were staged to very different political purposes throughout the century (Goldhill 2012; 42). It is no coincidence that Osterhammel's inaugural chapter on memory, discussed above, opens with an "overture" about opera as a global phenomenon in the nineteenth century. From Brazilian rubber barons' opera houses to Chilean obsession with Rossini in the 1830s; from Beijing to the capitols of the Ottoman empire; and above all in Paris, opera was celebrated as a vital, visual, and aural form of remembering antiquity (Osterhammel 2014; 5–7). Nostalgia and politics melded with appreciation of antique civilizations in high and popular culture.

As a child in the late nineteenth century, the sociologist Maurice Halbwachs would later recall, he experienced a living connection to French historical events through his family. His grandparents linked him to the Revolution and *fin-de-siècle* Romanticism; his parents represented the world that Halbwachs was born into and formed by, which he only came to learn about later as a historical era: the Paris Commune, "the Paris of 1860," the Franco-Prussian War (Halbwachs 1980: 67–8). Halbwachs deduced the "frameworks of collective memory" from his experience as a member of a family. Citing his impressions of his aunt's salon or of opening books and albums in his home, Halbwachs noted the sensation of feeling the presence of the past inadvertently; unlike the scholar who seeks out the past in order to understand history, Halbwachs noticed how everyday life was permeated by the past. Some experience this historical consciousness as nostalgia; others, like Halbwachs, as a way of being. The theory of collective memory that has become so influential in today's "memory boom" thus emerged from a practitioner of one of the new social sciences and was based as much on his personal experiences of family life in the nineteenth century as on his scholarship. These kinds of intersections between personal life and history, between lived experience and social scientific understanding of them, offer an essential insight into the cultural history of memory in the nineteenth century.

HISTORY, MEMORY AND ERASURE IN NINETEENTH-CENTURY PHOTOGRAPHS

One of the deans of modern cultural memory studies, Raphael Samuel, vividly remembered his first exposure to nineteenth-century photographs as happening around 1965. Although he had been studying that era of British history for three years and "had even begun to teach it," he hadn't considered photography at all, either as a historical subject or as a historical source:

> Worse (I remember thinking guiltily), it had not even occurred to me to wonder what nineteenth-century people looked like. Nothing had prepared me for any resemblance to ourselves.
>
> —Samuel 1994/2012: 317

Samuel was struck by the ordinary humanity of the people depicted, so like "ourselves" and yet so distinctly different in their period costume. The two photographic exposures he recalled happening in 1965 concerned mug shots which his professor, Keith Thomas, had uncovered in a records office, and "some reproductions from Thomson and Smith's *Street Life in London* . . . a book then hardly known, but subsequently reprinted, and today one of the sources of those atmospheric prints to be found on the walls of the 'period' pub" (Samuel 1994/2012: 316). The publishers of our current volume selected an image from John Thomson and Adolphe Smith, *Street Life in London* (1877) as the cover illustration before any of the chapters had been written. While this is unremarkable in terms of contemporary publishing practices, it raises the crucial issue of how photographs are reproduced as historical evidence and how historians understand photographs as historical evidence. A cultural history of memory in the century that created both the historical profession and the photograph cannot ignore either topic, which is why Samuel devoted a considerable section of his path-breaking *Theatres of Memory* (1994/2012) to "Old Photographs." Indeed, the camera's relationship to the "memory crisis" cited by Terdiman, above, has been the focus of significant, subsequent scholarly inquiry (Batchen, 2004b; Shevchenko, 2016).

In the vast virtual archive of images, historical photographs represent a subset of available sources: those that have been preserved and, a further subset, those that have been digitized. The digital-historical photography archive, while enormous, is itself still only a subset of the photographs made, circulated, saved and lost or destroyed in the nineteenth century, the era in which "the camera as historian" offered heretofore unavailable and exemplary documentary capabilities, to reference a publication created by a British photographic survey project, *The Camera as Historian* (1916). Not only could the new technology preserve the present as instantaneous past, it was also understood at the time to have something like a purely objective ability to "mirror" what was in front of it. It could be a "mirror with a memory," as Oliver Wendell Holmes famously coined it, and could represent its mirrored subjects in an immediate, unmediated, and permanent fashion (Shevchenko 2016). From mid-century onward, amateur photographic surveys as well as professional studios produced historical records purposefully (Edwards 2012). While photography also flourished as an aesthetic medium, museums of the period were more likely to use photographs for background information, such as recording materials in collections, or as background illustration providing context for more valuable museum artifacts, than they were to exhibit photographs (Crane 2020). And while the popular photography market boomed within the souvenir craze of the nineteenth century, creating portraits and memorabilia, photography also served as an archival tool. Given that a third of *The Camera as Historian* was devoted to "questions of storage, the relative merits of boxes, drawers, and vertical files . . . the label . . . the decimal system of classification," etc., the book could just as easily have been titled "the filing cabinet as historian," as the photography historian John Tagg quipped (2009: 221–3). In short, photography in the nineteenth century served a variety of functions within the marketplaces of memory.

Cultural histories of memory, as well as of photography, may be illustrated with famous and familiar photographs; see, for example, Mary Warner Marien's *Photography: A Cultural History*, which features a famous image from *Street Life in London* known as "The Crawlers" (fourth edition 2017; Thomson and Smith 1969: 116). "The Crawlers" presents a single destitute woman, whose downcast gaze and grim demeanor evoke the plight of those so enfeebled they must crawl to get a cup of tea. It is atypical of *Street Life* photos in being so closely focused on one person. Widely circulated or well-known photographs, having appeared in many publications, may become iconic through familiarity as much as through any instantaneous perception of their aesthetic qualities. Recirculation of "The Crawlers" began shortly after the volume was published, and continues in the 1969 reprint I am holding, which features this image imprinted directly on the cover of the book; it was seen as an icon of Victorian poverty as well as a reminder of the humanity of those whose suffering is greatest. Mid-century critics hailed Thomson as "the first photojournalist," and "The Crawlers" was featured as an early example of "modern" photography in the influential *History of Photography* published by Helmut Gernsheim (1955) (Morgan 2014: 21).

But in their very familiarity, iconic photographs also provide evidence of erasure. They are often reprinted and recirculated without caption, provenance, or context and, for that matter, without the identity of the woman in the photograph (a fact essential to photojournalism as well as "period-typical" historical photographs; see Crane 2020). Instead of requiring contextual information or caption, iconic photographs are expected to be "worth a thousand words," silently providing sufficient visual evidence to support some kind of recognition, while relinquishing specifics. Well aware of this phenomenon, Raphael Samuel noted that "we have little patience with pictures which keep their secrets: the whole point of using them is to show history 'as it was'" (Samuel 1994/2012: 328). Iconic images trade on communicating something that is already known. The poverty of the familiar image—that is, the lack of contextual information that travels with the image—is thus its most salient feature. Critical analysis of famous and familiar images, or those chosen as representative of an era or a topic, is incumbent upon the cultural historian.

The photographer John Thomson had been working in Asia for ten years and publishing diverse photographic projects dedicated to representing cultural heritage and exotic locales, such as *The Antiquities of Cambodia* (1867) and *Illustrations of China and Its People* (1873) before he produced the body of work featured in *Street Life in London* (Morgan 2014: 22 ff). He brought an interest in ethnology and imperial travel experience to his partnership with the socialist activist Adolphe Smith, who authored the essays that accompany Thomson's photography but are not typically cited when the photographs are recirculated. Emily Morgan has surveyed the literature on Thompson and Smith's work and suggests that their combined efforts to document the plight of the London poor and workers as well as depict the "charm" of the cityscape failed to find a public because they didn't play up to popular demands for depictions of delightful "street types" and offered too much surrounding (unattractive) context. An internal tourist market, in other words,

FIGURE 0.1: Photographer at Work, 1877: A street photographer at work on Clapham Common, London, with a mobile booth. Original publication: From *Street Life in London* by John Thomson and Adolphe Smith, pub. 1877 (Photo by John Thomson/General Photographic Agency/Getty Images).

had created a demand for photographs of "the natives" at home. Initially published serially, the photos and their captions did not sell well, however, and the authors resorted to combining their work into a book, which also sold poorly (Morgan 2014). Its afterlife as a resource for visualizing the nineteenth century has made it much more familiar than its initial publication could have accounted for.

The photograph gracing our cover initially appeared as half of a pair entitled "Photography on the Common—Waiting for a Hire"; the second half depicted two men and a saddled donkey (Thomson and Smith, 1877/1969: see p. 9 of the unnumbered plates at the beginning of the book, and p. 40). Ironically, both the photographer and the donkey's minders are "waiting for a hire," but the caption is hyphenated in a manner that indicates separate photo titles. Smith's essay for this pair of images is entitled "Clapham Common Industries" to highlight the intersection of labor and leisure in the healthful fresh air of the park, not necessarily the role of the photographer. Thomson's photograph (Figure 0.1) sets the photographer to advantage, in full light but not at the center; rather, the photographer's gear and portable studio is in the middle, dividing the photographer from the three adults and child at right. Smith's essay highlights a memory market driven by the desire of the absent parents to see photographs of their children, for the adults in the image are not related to the child. Instead, it is a nursemaid, who becomes "an advertising medium" for the photographer, bringing the children back again and again (not coincidentally, the photo and essay which precede this pair depict "Street Advertising"). The photographs made in the park are

... cherished in the homes of the poor, and are often found in the nurseries of the wealthy. They serve to recall the past, to revive latent affection for the absent; they never do any harm and sometimes awaken the better and more tender instincts of our nature.

—Thomson 1877/1969: 41

Smith indirectly hints at controversy ("they never do any harm") regarding memories of children and photography in general, in the name of recalling the past. For Smith, photography trades in affection and desire, in making absence present, regardless of class—while making the working woman the medium of exchange.

In what ways, then, does this photograph inform a cultural history of memory in the nineteenth century? The historical information in the photograph "speaks" only to the informed viewer, who already knows it and recognizes it; the uninformed viewer can only project their partial and suppositional knowledge onto it or react to it aesthetically. The identities of all of the individuals in the photograph have been erased (if they were ever recorded, which is unlikely; they have not been transmitted). The writer Smith labels the photographer Thomson's subject not as photography or family desire for memory, but as Clapham Common, an outdoor place where there is a photographic market and healthful air to breathe, which also cannot be seen: the subject (air; or an entire park) is invisible, while the visible subjects (photographer, photography patrons and one presumably impassive child) are presented as representing the past in a photo made during their present, rather than themselves. Children are most often rendered voiceless in history, but in photographs, all human subjects are voiceless.

In discussing photography and *Street Life in London* this way, rather than allowing a photograph to illustrate "the nineteenth century," the cultural history of memory approaches the intersection of past and present, a moment of extended present, where all memories happen. A parallel case is made by Krista Thompson in her discussion of the problematic use of nineteenth-century historical photographs to represent slavery in Jamaica (Thompson 2011). Another cover photograph, this time of Jamaican cane cutters working in 1891 and therefore long after emancipation in the British West Indies, was chosen for the book edited by Michael Craton, James Walvin, and David Wright, *Slavery, Abolition and Emancipation: Black Slaves and British Empire, A Thematic Documentary* (1976). Thompson shows how the book's ahistorical repurposing of the photograph created portraits of "slaves" out of free black cane cutters, a trend in the photographic representation of slavery that has been fairly typical over the past fifty years of historical scholarship. Unrepresented in these histories: the cane cutters' identities, their fears of re-enslavement and the "overseeing presence" of the camera (Thompson 2011: 58, 60; for further discussion of "erasure" see Stéphane Gerson's chapter in this volume). Thompson also highlights how those same workers were in fact being represented in a new type of nineteenth-century labor: "working as a photographic subject," being posed for the camera (2011: 54–5). "Working as a photographic subject" demonstrates how photography will feed entertainment, tourism, and advertising markets of memory, and facilitate the creation of new memory objects: postcards, photographs, and photo albums.

TOURISTS, COLLECTORS, AND PILGRIMS IN PURSUIT OF RUINS AND RELICS: MATERIAL CULTURES OF MEMORY

The proliferation of public museums in the nineteenth century was a noteworthy phenomenon of the era, a source of national competitiveness and imperial aggrandizement that also stimulated scientific and intellectual knowledge creation. Following the innovations of the Prado, British Museum, and the Louvre at the end of the eighteenth century, art, historical, and natural history museums emerged as platforms for public enlightenment and entertainment. If the nineteenth century may be characterized as obsessed with museums and archives, ruins and relics, monuments and memorials, it is worth noting that the compulsions to preserve, restore, and memorialize were multifaceted. As Stuart Semmel reminds us, "the squabbling muses of decay and preservation should each be heeded by the cultural historian" (2000: 15). Advocates of restoration such as Antoine Chrysostome Quatremère de Quincy (1755–1849) and Eugène-Emmanuel Viollet-le-Duc (1814–79) hoped to prevent letting the age of historic monuments show, preferring to enhance the impression of longevity, while legions of admirers of Romantic ruins clung to the vestiges of the past in all their fragmentary appeal. These competing trends were never restricted by national borders but rather emerged in tandem around the globe (Swenson, 2013b).

The explosion of interest in creating new monuments added "statue mania" to "monument mania." Tourism sprang up around both types of historical monuments, ruins as well as restorations. As George Mosse showed, by the later nineteenth century, gargantuan public monuments were being erected on sites commanding large vistas, designed to facilitate visitors and mass spectacles—in Germany, by venerating Hermann the German and Otto von Bismarck (Mosse 1975). Pilgrimages, traditionally rooted in spiritual memorial, expanded to include trips to historic battlefields and authors' homes as well as ruined cathedrals, with a "pilgrimage mania" emerging in the 1870s.

The late Ottoman era (1799–1917) witnessed a revival of pilgrimage to the holy lands, while at the same time a "mania" for Napoleonic war battlefield pilgrimage emerged on the European continent and battlefield tourism took hold in the United States, complete with guide books (Bar and Cohn-Hattab 2003; Semmel 2000: 11). Impulses to commemorate through monuments, to preserve and protect historical sites and ruins, and to visit all of these as well as sacred pilgrimage destinations, intersected in this era to create lively cultures of memory. And as the historian Teresa Barnett reiterates (based on the predictable frequency with which interlocutors have felt it necessary to point it out to her), there are indeed similarities between sacred and historical relics, but this is precisely because of the connections that nineteenth-century collectors and tourists made between them (Barnett 2013: 50–3).

Memories of war lived on in multiple collectives following the Napoleonic wars, such as veterans' associations, patriotic women's associations, student fraternities, and patriotic gymnasts' associations (in terms specific to the German context: *Burschenschaften* and *Turnvereine*)—while memories of the Thirty Years War came back to haunt the same countryside.[2] Fervor to honor and remember previous conflicts led to developments in modern commemorative practices, such as the tomb of the unknown soldier, after the First World War, national cemeteries with marked graves for soldiers following the American Civil War, and the creation of public memorial monuments around the globe. Collective public performances of mourning and memorializing only grew in extent and fervor throughout the era. Just as personal ambitions stimulated collective historical collecting in this era (see Crane 2000a), markets for memories that collectively produced collectibles fed personal desires for antiques, mementos, relics, and keepsakes. In the nineteenth century, a mania for souvenirs emerged (see also the discussion by Nick Yablon, in this volume).

Nineteenth-century tourists were notorious for engaging their memories in the inspiring landscape by chipping away a piece of whatever they could not carry. This trend in the market for authenticity was observed throughout the century, troubling critics who wanted to keep the past and its ruins intact. It was far from a new trend, and it has in no way disappeared. No less a statesman than Thomas Jefferson couldn't resist cutting off a piece of William Shakespeare's chair during a visit to the Stratford-upon-Avon house in the 1780s (a relic that currently resides at Jefferson's historic Virginia home, Monticello). "Tangible memories"—that is, pieces of the original relic or something touched by a famous person or entangled in a famous event — were in demand. Semmel notes branches stripped from the "Wellington tree" before the tree itself was uprooted and carved into keepsakes (2000: 29). Manufacture of souvenirs out of authentic relics and ruins may be a form of reverential interaction with the originals; it may serve the consumer by providing a tangible connection to the desired past. It also intervenes against potential destruction. The collections of the Smithsonian in Washington, DC, include several bits of wood from historical sites such as Mt. Vernon, the home of George Washington, which were fashioned as souvenirs and sold in order to discourage enthusiastic visitors from "wanton chiseling," carving their own bits out of walls, plants, and furnishings; and other bits of wood that attested to the touch of a famous person or event, such as "the fence rail split by Abraham Lincoln" or a wooden chip cut from a railroad tie at Promontory Point, Utah, site of the transcontinental railroad conjunction (Bird, 2013). Nor was the "chiseling" restricted to wood; Samantha Matthews details the macabre demolitions, and partial reconstructions, that literary fans made of various authors' corpses, or their "poetical remains" (2004).

Tangible memory objects filled museums, where they were locked away in glass cases or storage rooms, preserved but untouchable, calling into question the nature of historical preservation's relationship to the desire for the tangible—for touching the remains rather than merely viewing them. The inimitable Stephen Bann drew attention to the oral, tactile, and olfactory aspects of the "amor vetustas" or love of antiquity, suggesting that they were implicated in many expressions of historical consciousness related to the fragmentary remains and relics of the past and should not be denigrated in favor of the sense of sight.[3] The tangible memory could take on the form of literal imprint upon the skin: Tattoos, which had long served sacred, memorial, and social functions among the peoples of Oceania as well as among pilgrims to holy sites, became for seafaring Westerners the souvenir of their travels and travails. The problematic use of tattooing for convict marking, with its dehumanizing implications and the creation of social ostracization, highlights how institutions of incarceration understood the perpetuity of the tattoo, its permanence, and uniqueness as a record (Caplan 2000).

Sailors and soldiers were and are inveterate collectors of souvenirs; tourists are the same, and their desires intersected on the nineteenth-century field of battle. Battlefields were littered with human remains, and visitors were delighted to find and claim thumbs, teeth, and skulls from Waterloo and other sites of "famous victories." A purported tooth from the site found its way into a Briton's mouth as a dental replacement; Sir Walter Scott possessed a former Life Guardsman's skull (Semmel 2000: 9, 12). The Smithsonian also possesses a lock of Sir Walter Scott's hair, preserved in a glass vial and donated in 1878, forty-six years after his death (Bird 2013: 94). Ironically, Scott was himself a site of memory for fans of his novels. Literary tourists flocked to his home at Abbotsford, which (irony atop irony) was itself a faux medieval structure, renovated to evoke the era that inspired Scott's stories. As Stephen Bann formulated it, Scott's architectural ambitions mirrored his literary ones: He built "air castles," which became solid as books and an estate (Bann 1984: 101). Filled with historical artifacts and recreations, Scott's Abbotsford fulfilled both his own and his fans' historical desires. Ann Rigney suggests that the layers of Scott-memory tourism can be understood as evidence of

> . . . a radically modern relationship between memory and place that fitted the changing conditions of his age, being based on a combination of portability (memory can be re-located and re-assembled) and hyper-locatedness (the past can be re-experienced in an immediate way by going to particular places).
>
> —2012: 131

Visitors to Scott's manse could see his writing desk and steal a seat in his chair, if no one was watching (see also Stan Landry's discussion of Scott and Romantic historical consciousness, in this volume).

Scott's fame resonated around the world after his death, shaping communities of memory in vastly disparate locations: witness the number of streets named "Waverley" (Rigney 2012). As an exemplar of international fame and mnemonic resonance, Scott was perhaps only rivaled by his contemporary, the explorer and polymath scientist Alexander von Humboldt, for the number of places named after him (Rupke 2008). And in contrast to the public pantheons of Europe, which honored famous men but were largely restricted in access to the elites who sponsored them, the worthies who had thoroughfares, towns, and counties named after them remained accessible to cultures of memory, as it were, on the street level (Bouwers 2012: 218). Naming, more generally, has always been a memory practice, from children's names to cities and their streets. Fame perpetuated memory, from patriotic slogans and songs to the street signs of the burgeoning metropolises, and no fame arrived without its collectible counterpart. Indeed, many objects acquired their desirability through connection to fame, so much so that a market for fake memorabilia ran parallel to the authentic. While this is not unique to the nineteenth century, it is remarkable how new technologies facilitated the production of fake antiquities, antiques, and relics to meet the demand (see Gillingham 2010; Rosenstein 2009).

Visiting locations from Scott's fiction likewise kindled memories of the stories that blended with visions of the natural and historical landscape. Fictional landscapes were recalled and envisioned in real places. Natural landscapes were also claimed as sites of national memory in the nineteenth century. After Henry David Thoreau (1817–62) famously spent his time at Walden Pond, nature attracted more attention as a place that inspired reflections on the past as well as the present. Alpine hiking clubs joined forestry experts in designating mountains and forests for preservation. The forest of Fontainebleu in Paris found its hero in Claude François Denecourt, whom Simon Schama wittily designates "The Man Who Invented Hiking" by inscribing blue arrows onto the pathways through the forest, creating marked trails for fellow urban nature-lovers (1995: 547). The world's first wilderness park was created in California in 1864, amid the horrors of the American Civil War, to protect the giant and wondrous sequoias which, at the time, were believed to be the oldest living things on earth (Schama 1995: 185–201). If "age value" determined whether a ruin was to be preserved, it figured equally prominently in early nature preservation.

SHOWING ITS AGE: PATINA AT HOME AND ABROAD

Among French Revolutionary émigrés, and migrants more generally, "family circles cultivated memories of the emigration and guarded the handwritten letters and journals. . . . The household was thus both the focus of and the point of transmission for memories of exile. . . . The domestic sphere . . . preserved and made visible the souvenirs of the *ancien regime*" (Fritzsche 2004: 79). If the household and its attics were domestic archives, we may also speak of "memory à la mode" in fashion and design. What else motivates the demand for reproduction furniture or daily wear which references that of another era if not a desire to remember a past as presence, to invoke its authority and, perhaps, to imbibe an elite's prohibitively expensive culture through cheaper reproduction? The nineteenth-century proclivity for adopting a hodgepodge of styles from across millennia caused some consternation among aesthetically sensitive observers. As midcentury poet and critic Théophile Gautier (1811–72) observed, "it is fashionable to buy antique furniture, and any bank clerk now feels obligated to have his own *Medieval-style bedroom*" (Maleuvre 1999: 116). In his discussion of the ways that nineteenth-century bourgeois interior design ambitions mirrored those of the new museums, Didier Maleuvre suggests that the French domestic interior space was decorated in a manner which reflected lack of self-confidence as much as nostalgia. Or, as David Lowenthal cynically puts it regarding Britons of the same era, "Made abject by their borrowings, Victorians sought an identity to gain self-respect" (Lowenthal 1985: 100). Critics like Gautier shuddered equally at the lack of taste as at the public's unwillingness to be guided by more aesthetically sensitive tastemakers. By the end of the century, writer Paul Bourget (1852–1935) looked down his nose at the accumulative effect of interiors cluttered with bibelots that put

> . . . something of the Far East, a taste of the Renaissance, a whiff of the French Middle Ages or of the eighteenth century on the corner of a table! . . . Our nineteenth century, by collecting and surveying all possible styles, has forgotten to create a style of its own!
>
> —Maleuvre 1999: 119

Bourget notes ironically that originality has been forgotten in favor of historical copying, but this was also trending in the museums of the period. Artists visited museums to learn by copying the masters; when they could not afford or obtain sufficiently impressive originals, museums were happy to purchase or commission plaster casts of antique sculptures. What appears forgotten is likely only too expensive to acquire: Original art must be commissioned or discovered. Memory and forgetting mix in the critic's analysis as well as in the bourgeois interior.

The complaint that the nineteenth century's inclination for borrowing outstripped its own creativity was frequently heard toward the *fin de siècle*. Philosopher Friedrich Nietzsche (1844–1900) likewise deplored that "we moderns have nothing of our own" (Lowenthal 1985: 101). But if nineteenth-century critics were unimpressed with bibelots, the objects may be said to have the last word, for they have themselves become the subjects of historical study.

Across Europe and its empires, in the Americas and beyond in the nineteenth century, homage to historical architecture flourished in public spaces and domestic exteriors: Greek columns on presidential homes, Roman arches on capitol buildings, Gothic spires on college dorms, Tudor tweaks on suburban houses—all competed for pride of place. Builders in German states debated "in what style should we build?" by reviewing the nature of "German" architecture in all of its historical styles. In his 1828 essay of the same title, architect Heinrich Hübsch (1795–1863) concluded that debts to Hellenic architecture in no way prohibited Germans from breathing unique life into ancient forms, imitation being the sincerest form of flattery and emulation the sign of deepest admiration. In her discussion of the British photographic surveys cited above, Elizabeth Edwards includes an image from a *fin-de-siècle* photograph album that demonstrates the fascination with historical styles of architecture in an unusual way (Edwards 2012: 21). Each album page is distinctively labeled by period (e.g. Saxon, Norman, Tudor) and richly illustrated with chromolithographs of that era's architectural styles and historical landmarks (Figure 0.2). The album, which Edwards found in an Oxford flea market, appears to contain a family's portraits. Each page features one or more family members, photographed professionally but in different studios and at different times, created by a solicitor from Oldham.[4] Slots in the page indicate where photographs are to be inserted, although not which photos to add where (one wonders how the creators of this album chose to match family members to different heritage eras). The background images present both ruins and historical architecture in use, and the family assumes its position within those images as potential

FIGURE 0.2: "Saxon" page from the "Historical Family Album," *c*. 1910. Collection of Elizabeth Edwards.

guardians of the past, or as respectful consumers of the historical landscape as tourists, residents, and inheritors of the legacy. Each family portrait photo is surrounded by glimmers of the past.

The patina of age has long been a hallmark of historical desire, but even a connoisseur of patina such as John Ruskin (1819–1900) could be seen adjusting its shine. Ruskin wrote, "the greatest glory of a building is not in its stones, or in its gold. Its glory is in its Age . . . in its testimony of durability"; patina, or "that golden stain of time," was a mark of authenticity and longevity (Ruskin 1849). However, in transforming a daguerreotype of his own, depicting St. Mark's in Venice, into a mezzotint, Ruskin removed the existing gas lamps, whose presence offended his historical sensibilities. "One imagines him," writes Jennifer Green-Lewis, "working of course by gaslight—carefully scouring away the present. . . . For Ruskin, St. Mark's was better served by the erasure of the present, because what was real, and *where* it was real, was the past" (2016: 57). Ruskin erased the offensive technology of the present in the name of remembering the past as it really "is." Using the newest technology to create a vision of the past for the future, he extinguished gaslight in the name of modern memory. As with the photo album, elements of the past must remain intact behind the images of the present.

ANXIETIES OF MEMORY: EXTINCTION AND MOURNING

The American scholar Kirk Savage, writing about memories of the Civil War and slavery in the nineteenth century, suggested that "[t]he increasing tendency in the nineteenth century to construct memory in physical monuments—to inscribe it on the landscape itself—seems symptomatic of an increasing anxiety about memory left to its own unseen devices" (1994: 130). These anxieties, like Terdiman's "crisis of memory," may have been reactions to the rapid onset of modernity that resulted in "statue mania" and "monument mania," and the post-Napoleonic historical consciousness described by Peter Fritzsche. But they may also reflect the extraordinary appearance of multiple new media and technologies of memory in the same era that produced the material cultures of memory discussed here, all of which faced the natural process of decay and ruin with renewed stamina and a desire to resist forgetting and oblivion. And as new technologies aided memorial practices, new directions in science led to a conceptualization of extinction, which had direct bearing on those same anxieties.

Mourning rituals are public forms of memorial that pre-date and set precedent for nineteenth-century funerary practices. Not coincidentally, the first example of a public collective memory event featured in Halbwachs' essay, "Collective Memory and Historical Memory" (1950/1980), is the public funeral procession of the French writer Victor Hugo in 1885, which the sociologist remembered witnessing as a child. Cemeteries of the period featured tombstones and grave markers, memorials that could be maintained and visited. But the recently invented daguerreotype and later the camera offered new and highly valued means to "secure the shadow" that had previously only been accessible through commissioned paintings. "The shadow" was common parlance for the spirit of the deceased; securing the shadow meant capturing a likeness of the dearly departed, without gruesomeness. In this era, living in close proximity to death was part of everyday life, and mortality rates were high among children. As art historian Stacey Hollander explains, posthumous painting's popularity was not completely eclipsed by the new media; initially, daguerreotypes served as copy sources for posthumous paintings (2014: 122). Indeed, they could supplement each other quite powerfully, as in a daguerreotype featuring both

FIGURE 0.3: Mother and Baby in Blue by William Matthew Prior (photographer unidentified), New England *c.* 1850. Sixth-plate daguerreotype. Collection of David A. Schorsch.

a posthumous painted portrait and the mother of the dead child holding that portrait (Figure 0.3). Symbolism works on multiple levels in this image, presented in a recent exhibition amid an extraordinary, moving assemblage of posthumous portraiture from the early American republic. In the painted portrait, artist Matthew Prior depicted a toddler girl with "one shoe off," a symbol understood at the time to indicate that the subject was deceased (Hollander 2014: 122). In the daguerreotype, the child's portrait is held by her bereaved mother, as if to reanimate her desired presence on the maternal lap. The identities of both females are unknown (again: erased). Hollander notes that midcentury Americans were likely to commission both photography of the deceased and posthumous portraiture: one to record the inanimate corpse "in all the solemnity of the passage from this world to the next," the other to preserve an approximation of the living likeness (2014: 122).

In addition to remembering, memory serves as an anticipation of oblivion, the fear of not remembering. Compounding loss and fear, the daguerreotype of the Mother and Baby in Blue memorizes the child's beloved face in anticipation of forgetting what she looked like. The anxieties of loss and forgetting took on specific form in the anticipation of extinction as framed by nineteenth-century writers and scientists. The "salvage paradigm" which emerged in anthropology applied to a perception that indigenous peoples around the world were vanishing and must be documented before they disappeared (Pinney 1997: 45). Fiona Stafford chronicles a ubiquitous "myth of the last man" through nineteenth-century English-language literature, which depicted "the last of the Mohicans," "the last days of Pompeii," "Roderick, the last of the Goths," and many more (Stafford 1994). Charles Lyell (1797–1875) transformed understanding of geology in 1830 by demonstrating that the visible strata of the earth represented its history, the slow transformation over time rendered in distinct lines. Dating the earth's layers countered existing notions of time and duration, challenging religious authority and centuries of belief. But as the scholar Patrick Brantlinger shows, Lyell also wrote about extinction in ways that influenced Charles Darwin and reflected their society's racism: ". . . few future events are more certain than the speedy extermination of the Indians of North America and the savages of New Holland in the course of a few centuries, when these tribes will be remembered only in poetry and tradition" (cited in 2003: 28). Extinction was to be anticipated, since it had already happened — and not only to flora and fauna but to human communities, and in the same way: through competition between them.

As Stafford's authors inscribed their last men, Lyell anticipated remembering last men only in literature. In the *Voyage of the Beagle*, Darwin wrote, "no fact in the long history of the world is so startling as the wide and repeated extermination of its inhabitants" (Brantlinger 2003: 166). The nineteenth century almost witnessed the extinction of "perhaps the first human race which was breathing its last": the painful story of William Lanney (1835–69), also known as "King Billy," the last Tasmanian, testifies to the appalling way in which science, photography and literature combined in anticipating and erasing "the last man." Like his few remaining community members, Lanney posed for tourist photos. Following his death, Lanney's body was sought by the Royal College of Surgeons in London and the Royal Society of Tasmania; in the name of science it was dismembered, with parts going to each institution. Brantlinger drily concludes, "no advance in scientific knowledge came from this grisly fiasco" (2003: 128–9). Instead, Brantlinger demonstrates, a discourse of the "self-exterminating savage" emerged, a dystopian twin of "the noble savage," whose races were "doomed" to extinction (2003: 33). Anthropology's mission was to study them before they disappeared. The camera facilitated the creation of photographic subjects for science and posterity: "the last men" posed, and their shadows were secured.[5]

If we continue here a cultural history of memory inaugurated in antiquity, which concludes in this series' next volume on memory in the twentieth century, it cannot be said that this volume completes either the study of memory or the study of memory in the nineteenth century. The "long nineteenth century" arguably ended with the First World War, but in fact its history continues. To borrow an image from Terdiman's era of "crisis," this history might be appropriately imagined in a shell-shaped pastry called a *petite madeleine*. In the novel *A la recherche du temps perdu* (1913–27), the aroma of this delicacy dipped in lime-blossom tea famously evoked in Marcel Proust's hero a deep nostalgia, specifically for Sunday mornings spent in his aunt's home, Combray, but metaphorically for the past in general as an ineluctably distant place to which he could never return.[6] Proust grappled with the ways in which memory was present—to be experienced as such, but also as a disturbing and insistent ghost. Madeleines are still being consumed today and indeed are more accessible than ever, on sale now at globally ubiquitous Starbucks coffee houses and in the vast warehouses of Amazon and Costco. Because we are still smelling madeleines today even though most of their consumers are probably unaware of Proust's fictional version, I would suggest that the cultural history of memory in the nineteenth century does not end in 1900, because it is being remembered and imagined—produced and consumed—by historians in the present. Even obliviousness, like memories, like madeleines, has histories.

I would like to thank Elizabeth Crane for volunteering her excellent copyediting services and Nitza Cabral for her assistance in creating the volume bibliography.

CHAPTER ONE

Power and Politics

MATT MATSUDA

On April 28, 1789, HMS *Bounty*, of the British Royal Navy, approached the waters near the island of Tofua in the South Pacific, west of Tahiti. The first mate, Fletcher Christian, broke out weapons from the ship's hold and mutinied against the captain, William Bligh. Taking control of the ship at sword point, Christian set Bligh adrift in an open longboat with officers and loyal crew members. Bligh navigated his party to the Dutch colony of Coupang before finding a ship back to England. Christian and his mutineers returned to Tahiti, and then set off to find an island of refuge, eventually alighting on Pitcairn, where they were undiscovered for a generation.

Just twelve weeks later, July 14, on the other side of the world, the governor of the royal prison in Paris also faced violence: riots by crowds against symbols of royal power of which his charge—the Bastille, was the most visible. They were reacting to word of possible stored arms, or plots of military actions against their popular movement. It was a time of political and social unrest in France. Just months earlier, King Louis XVI had opened the Estates General of the realm and by July erupted this world-famous moment of violence: the storming of the Bastille, commemorated as the signal moment of the French Revolution.

The alignment of these two tales may seem an odd juxtaposition, yet they contain within themselves the elements necessary to consider histories of memory at a moment that, arguably, marks the dawn of the nineteenth century. The double framing here, however, is more than just an argument about how memorializations take place or do not. It is also about artifacts representing particular theses characterizing the "memory" of a time, and we must first define that time. I am beginning "the nineteenth century" with these figures from 1789, as exemplary moments when new mnemonic regimes were deployed, especially in the particular shapes of that memory as articulated in terms of *power and politics*, across a globe-spanning geography that became connected with the nineteenth century: Tahiti and Hawai'i, China and Haiti, the United States, Columbia, and France.

How then, does memory manifest through power and politics? One way historians have approached this question is "traditional," to look at states and parties and institutions of governance and to understand how they celebrated themselves, created their own legitimating ancestors, and constantly recycled their newly articulated "traditions" of revolution and transformation (Hobsbawm and Ranger 1983). Yet, more broadly, the nineteenth century is where and when historical consciousness emerged in so many new and vital forms, when "arts of memory" as classical mnemotechnics were dispersed into disciplines as varied as psychology and history; when museums, cameras and photography, world expos and mass communication created ways to share and collectivize the experience of remembering the past (Yates 1966; Nora 1989).

In the register of power and politics, the historian Eric Hobsbawm set forth his classic reading of the nineteenth century as an Age of Revolution, which he dialectically drew out as organized around the figures of the social and economic upheavals of the Industrial Revolution, and the political turmoil of the French Revolution. As a relentlessly unfolding saga, he also argued that both ultimately became intertwined and inextricable from a nineteenth-century Age of Capital and an Age of Empire, with vast, colonial impacts across the entire globe. The memory of power and politics in this era is defined by the intersection of upheavals in the reorganization of labor and production, revolution destructuring entire social orders, the birth of institutions that will embody new nations, and the waxing and waning of global hegemony from the collapse of old colonies to the new imperialism (Hobsbawm 1962–87).

Thus, a way to grasp how power and politics are manifested in memory is to look at apparently disparate moments, and conjure their connections. Here, our two sites—the mutiny on the Bounty, and the storming of the Bastille—frame the transition to the nineteenth century by connecting to other events and mnemonic markers: commemorations of revolution against global empires built on slavery and commodity extraction; genealogical practices as counter-memories and historical contests; an Age of Revolutions recorded in the rise and consolidation of nationalist and administrative institutions.

These are embodied in moments that may seem initially far afield such as the Haitian Revolution, or the Opium Wars in China, the rise of the Napoleonic state, Atlantic consolidation of nations as exemplified in Europe, South America, and the United States. Yet all are strongly remembered and disputed as historical memory. That is, the boundaries and meanings of "the Revolution," or "the Wars," or "the State" are subjects endlessly debated, celebrated in memorials and chronicles that are then rebuilt or rewritten, and continue to be contested. There is no singular history of a nation, people, or community, only a constant cycle of dialogues between the past and the present. We see this in commemorated places such as the Cabildo in St. Louis, the words and actions of diplomatic exchanges in Port-au-Prince, Haiti, the exhibitions of a museum in Guangdong, China, and the twenty-first century dance movements of a performer in Papeete, Tahiti.

By first evoking Tahiti, we can begin our investigations by thinking about a domain where multiple contests over memory and history occurred on a globe-spanning scale just at the end of the eighteenth and beginning of the nineteenth centuries: the South Pacific. These contests took place between local, indigenous mnemonic practices, European narratives of historical time as Enlightenment replacing reputed primitivism, and the place of a legendary maritime tale in shaping world-wide narratives about an entire Oceanian world.

What does the Bounty case teach us? HMS Bounty was sent from England, circling the globe, all the way to the island of Tahiti in the South Pacific on a singular mission: to harvest cuttings and plantings of *uru*—the starchy breadfruit tree indigenous to the islands. Unlike earlier navigational, strategic, and prestige science explorations under captain James Cook and botanist Joseph Banks, the Bounty mission stands out for the encompassing logic of its voyage: the breadfruit plants were specifically requisitioned to be transplanted in the Caribbean, as a plentiful food source for slaves working on British West Indies sugar cane plantations.

In effect, a Royal Navy ship was sent around the world to transfer a tropical plant from a Pacific Ocean island to another in an Atlantic-facing sea, for the benefit of settler colonialism in the name of commercial profits. The *Bounty* tale has been endlessly reimagined and newly narrated so that the original events, such that they can be known, are increasingly obscured and remembered principally through their dramatic representations.

In one version, popularized in Hollywood filmmaking by the actors Trevor Howard and Marlon Brando, Captain Bligh is an arrogant and arbitrary tyrant, abusing his crew, while First Officer Christian is the courageous seeker of liberty and expression, giving up the oppressive naval life he knows in favor of one where he is free to imagine his own society, composed of loyal sailors and Tahitian men and women. In writing his own narratives of the events, the historian Greg Dening was acutely self-aware that such "histories" are in fact partial perspectives, adoptions, and remembered inventions. "I have my own re-enactments, of course. What historian does not? I re-text the already texted past. I have no experience of the past that I re-present other than that past transformed into words, symbolized ... my files of notes taken after hours of chasing old newspapers, reminiscences and letters" (Dening 1992: 5). Dening would demonstrate that every event and chronicle is a deep layering of multiple times and transcriptions.

From a European perspective, in fact, such recitation of stories and images already shaped by an earlier generation held extraordinary power to shape entire perceptions of worlds leading into the nineteenth century. In Tahiti, these representations and selective chronicles were characterized by narratives of an alternate, elysian, prelapsarian world, shaped by encounters with the Tahitian islands first by the English navigator Samuel Wallis in 1767, and then more resonantly a year later with the Frenchman Louis Antoine de Bougainville made landfall. Greatly influenced by the prevailing temper of Rousseauist natural philosophy, Bougainville wrote famously "I thought I was transported to the Garden of Eden ... as numerous people there enjoy the blessings which nature flowers liberally down upon them."[1]

This imaginary was adopted by the *philosophe* Denis Diderot, whose own literary accounts of "noble savagery" as a corrective to the decadent ills of overly civilized Western societies located the Tahitian islands in a virtuous, if indolent and timeless idyll. Thomas Gosse's 1796 illustration captures this peaceable vision. Scholars have studied this image in detail, noting its depiction of the "traveling nature" of the nineteenth century, and the "translation of an insular plant into a globalized commodity" (Bewell 2008, Ch. 2 passim). More, it "memorializes" the moment that colonial histories connect Tahiti with St. Vincent, Jamaica, and Britain, transplanting not a foodstuff for universal consumption and adoption, but for subsistence to slave populations. Nonetheless, Gosse's popular mezzotint captures only radiant Maohi peoples assisting Captain Bligh's crew with the transplanting and transport of the breadfruit plants, absent any signs of political or imperial tension.

Such narratives and depictions would prove a staggeringly oppressive fiction as Tahitian histories of voyaging, complex hierarchical social development, sophisticated cultural and religious practices, and dynastic politics pursued by warring chieftains and clans would be subsumed by an encroaching European presence that emptied the islands of their own pasts. These narratives were expressed across the nineteenth century as missionary and trader influence was succeeded by direct imperial seizure of Tahiti and the Society Islands by French naval forces under the Admiral Abel DuPetit Thouars in 1843. The Admiral claimed abuses against French missionaries and interests by a supposedly scheming Queen Pomare—who was, in fact, defending her sovereignty—and the virtues of French rule in

FIGURE 1.1: Transplanting of the Bread-fruit Trees from Otaheite. Painted and engraved by Thomas Gosse. London (1796). Alexander Turnbull Library, Creative Commons License http://mp.natlib.govt.nz/detail/?id=9175&l=en.

an otherwise uncivilized territory. Islanders resisted in violent military confrontations (Newbury 1980).

The real "memory work" of colonialism, however, took place not through political, but cultural erasure. The languorous imaginary of the South Seas imposed a cultural timelessness upon the islands, strongly reinforced by the painter Paul Gauguin's sensual and mythical images, especially of Tahitian women, flowers, deity and spirit figures, and metaphysical landscapes, beginning in 1891. Despite his own written anti-colonial laments disparaging local officials, it was Gauguin's art, along with the tropical romances of writers like the naval officer and highly popular Pierre Loti, that evacuated Tahitian history of political struggle, French gunboat diplomacy, and anticolonial guerilla warfare against outlanders, and replaced it with exoticism (Matsuda 2005: 91–112).

In this way, the assertion and disruption of memory is foundational to understanding the experience of colonial politics in the Pacific, and genealogical contentions are once again the key. In the Polynesian islands, the past—and thus knowledge of the present and future—was held by *ariki*, trained memory-men whose roles were shaped around flawlessly recounting chronicles and lineages of ancestors as defined by genealogies. These genealogies are called *whakapapa* in the New Zealand Maori instance, a literal and figurative layering of times, ancestors, and cosmological connections linking the present to the past. In the Hawaiian islands, the *moʻokuauhau* incorporates memory within the evocation of ancestral bones, and a place for them to stand tall and protect a living culture (Metge 2013: 1–12; Selwyn Te Rito 2007: 1–5; Sanford Kanahele 1986).

These cultures came under threat in the nineteenth century as imported and imposed mnemonic regimes—settler colonialism as commercial progress, the Christian faith as enlightenment, cultural eradication as the extinction of barbarism—encroached upon Islander worlds. Victor Segalen's mysterious, exotic novel, *Les Immemoriaux* (1907), traces exactly this moment in literary form, as his Tahitian Maohi protagonist, Terii, recounts the lineage of creation and ancestors to his group one evening when—suddenly and unthinkably—he cannot remember the next name in his genealogy (Segalen 1907: 6–7). Amid cries of reproach and terror at this offense against the order of ancestors, he flees from his people. At the same time, European missionaries are landing in the islands.

This initial rupture would become forced erasure under colonial regimes. To the present day, genealogical tracings identify and situate Islander cultures, anchoring histories, and ethical and political commitments to community and land in confrontation with forgetting and disappearance under outlander colonials. These indigenous historical traditions are manifested in embodied mnemonic practice. Often called resistance, more useful is the Foucaultian notion of counter-memory, that is, a form of assertion of temporal location and legitimacy not only as a space of pushing back against power, but a claim upon the past in the name of the present and future that is fundamentally drawn from genealogies (Foucault 1977: 139–64). It is an alternate history, one that denies the logic of Progress led by some to dominate and lead others, in favor of deeply rooted and embodied local knowledge drawn from ancestors.

The nostalgic sentiments for a lapsed Edenic idyll from a European perspective are not the only survivals and assertions of contests over memory. If memory is not the record of what happened, but what is re-membered—that is, embodied and transmitted to subsequent generations, then expressions of Tahitian culture as a form of politics and memory, rather than erasure, become profound anti-colonial narrations.

The histories and lived recollections of Tahitian culture that were subsumed by French gunboat power—but more importantly, by cultural rewritings of colonized peoples into picturesque ciphers—were never wholly erased, and have shown resilience across the generations. Speaking of memory-history as an "enactment," in 2016, the sixth edition of the literary program "Pinaʻinaʻi" was staged in the Tahitian capital of Papeete, combining authors, speakers, and dancers in reenactments of Tahitian history from a local and indigenous perspective through the media of poetry, music, and dance.

Unsurprisingly, the performances were dedicated to "The holes in our collective memory," a powerful invocation of alternate memories embodied in non-academic chronicles and printed histories, instead remembering personalized struggles of self-determination: from holdings in land to survival of the local language, dating back across the nineteenth century of European influence, colonial settlement, and military seizure.[2] These remembered pasts are then implicated in twentieth century legacies of continued metropolitan French domination, and nuclear testing in the local atolls. By chanting, reciting, versifying, and dancing, artists capture the reverberation and echo of ancestors and forebears.

This stands as a powerful, traditional mnemonic suggestion: the centrality of embodiment as a site of memorial understanding as indivisible from lived practice. This is true across Oceanian island groups. As Hawaiian scholar of the hula dance, Amy Kuʻuleialoha Stillman, has noted, "Hula is inherently a site of cultural memory, not only in the performance, but in the entirety of its practices of archiving knowledge of the past" (2001: 188). Far from merely folkloric, or expressive of cultural representation, such dance forms are local expressions of the tensions between power and politics in the context of Western colonial systems.

The hula, in particular, was banned in the Hawaiian islands by Queen Kaʻahumanu under the influence of missionaries dedicated to containing indigenous bodily storytelling—and historical consciousness—in 1830. Practice continued under restrictions and edicts until 1883, when King Kalakaua reasserted the primacy of indigenous culture by proclaiming, "Hula is the language of the heart and therefore the heartbeat of the Hawaiian people." That moment of bodily expression and transmission of heritage was, however, once again marginalized by global imperial politics (Stillman 2007: 221–34). Seized by the United States in 1893 by American Marines landing from warships, the Kingdom of Hawaiʻi was annexed during the Spanish-American War of 1898, and hula—as with Tahitian culture—was subsumed into a picturesque exoticism, and then a touristic entertainment, until reasserting itself as an expression of historical survival, living culture, and embodied memory in the 1970s during a time of indigenous identity revival and anti-colonial activism.

As the historian and activist Jonathan Osorio has put it, remembering is an obligation to act and restore continuity to history. "The contemporary sovereignty movement does not distance itself from the monarchy, though a few of the movement's supporters advocate a return to monarchy itself. We commemorated the passing of the kingdom as a day of mourning and commitment to the restoration of our nation" (Osorio 2002: 253). The overthrow of the kingdom by American military forces is here an unresolved struggle for Hawaiian political independence, and for Hawaiians seeking a return to Hawaiian sovereign rule. These claims remain largely unrecognized as Hawaiʻi was taken as part of another country—governed as a territory by administrators sent from Washington, DC, and then subsumed as the fiftieth state of the United States beginning in 1959 as a tourist paradise.

Struggles in the Oceanian Pacific underscore that memory is politics. These struggles embody tensions between indigenous and Western mnemonic regimes, ancestral genealogies, embodied practices, and claims for self-determination against imposed imperial narratives of enlightened progress and exoticized, pacified representations of primitivism erasing sophisticated, living cultures. The *Bounty* legend did much to generate, and then reinforce this representation of the Oceanian Pacific Islands and their paradisical—not political—place in world history.

The legacy of the *Bounty* also contains within itself another narrative fundamentally tied to islands and their role in the politics and power regimes of the eighteenth and then nineteenth centuries: that of natural resource exploitation chains. The *Bounty* saga was, in itself, less a colorful and tragic drama about personalities and principles, and more an illustration of colonial capitalism, and an entire industry—in this case sugar—seeking to maximize and extend profits through slave labor. Here, tensions between the logic of commercial profit and labor exploitation sparked epochal political conflict. The lives on Caribbean plantations, and the oral histories that captured them through genealogies and tales of everyday life, compose the foundations of memory growing out of harsh experience. In Jamaica, some recollections became printed memoirs, such as those of James Williams, who shaped histories of experience through personal chronicle:

They keep us at work till between four and five o'clock, then take us back to the workhouse—take the chains off we all, and make us go upon the mill again, same fashion as in the morning. After that them put us into the bar-room—put the chain and collar on again, and our foot in the shackle-bar, to sleep so till morning. All the woman put into one room, and all the man in another; them that have any of the breakfast left from morning, them eat it after lock up, but them that eat all the allowance at breakfast, must starve till morning.[3]

Scholars have significantly debated the role of such "memories" like Williams' and—especially when rendered and published in written form as his were—how broadly the individual voice can and should then speak for a general experience (Aljoe 2004: 1–14). Such are the questions raised by memory. This was true at both ends of the Bounty trajectory, from the genealogical traditions maintained by Pacific Polynesian peoples, to the remembrances of enslaved populations in Jamaica, Haiti, and on other Caribbean islands where breadfruit, sugar, and political economy were linked. These memories are encoded in recountings and reports, through the creation of escaped maroon colonies, and through the preservation of ancestral knowledge.

At the close of the eighteenth century, however, those lived memories would soon take on the character of nineteenth-century political change: narratives of heroic, revolutionary nationhood. In the Caribbean planter colony on Santo Domingo, an entire world would soon be convulsed by violent, rebellious upheaval, demands for liberation, and renamed Haiti. The questions of commercial and labor exploitation were front and center, and the politics of the French Revolution were a proximate motivating cause.

The planter class and often prosperous freed blacks on the island had long been agitating for more autonomy from the metropole, much as the Third Estate had been doing on the Continent. With the French Revolution, and an idealized proclamation of Liberté, Egalité, and Fraternité, the new Assemblies in Paris abolished slavery and precipitated uprisings in the colony. Major figures such as Toussaint L'Ouverture, Jean-Jacques Dessalines, and Dutty Boukman, led first slave revolts and then militias and former-slave armies, working for and against French and British militaries, forcing settlement and stalemate, driving out planter colonial control, and ultimately proclaiming the independent nation of Haiti.

In Haiti, mnemonic formations have been built around integrating and shaping—sometimes uneasily—the heroic, nationalist, and everyday registers of lived experience. Michel-Rolph Trouillot has been one of the key theorists of the means by which the past is silenced or extolled, and how narratives are selected—a process indivisible from the power and politics of historical knowledge. As Trouillot notes, historical work is founded upon archives, and archives are themselves repositories composed of survivals and silences (1995). Haitian history is rich in such examples, and is a particularly salient case, for memory-practices on the island intersect with histories of slavery, revolution and nation-building identities, global commodity exploitation, and a direct collision between ocean and island histories and those of the French Revolution.

The particular figure of the fugitive slave—the maroon—is central to Haitian historical identity. The heroic Fathers of the Nation—L'Ouverture, Dessalines, and Boukman—are exemplars of the Haitian Revolution, and understood as embodiments of a genealogy that connects nation and sovereignty in their lives and acts with a broader reverence for the ancestral maroon, the survivor, the one who defied and resisted, and escaped to form a free community on the margins of an unjust society. This underscores an understanding of the Haitian Revolution as a proud, stunning moment of great heroes and grand principles in struggle, but more importantly—as an incarnation of the thousands of unknown and unremarked men and women who defied masters, and risked death, understood to be acting in the name of liberty. Dessalines framed a Haitian identity not as a universal principle, but a distinctive community by exhorting, "We have dared to be free. Let us dare to be so by ourselves and for ourselves" (Dessalines 2006: 189).

The shaping of memory culture in Haiti at the beginning of the nineteenth century is exemplary of the challenges and contests resonating around the world in terms of narrating historical time. If royal houses and aristocracies had legitimized the order of societies for generations, new forms were necessary to give structure to the politics of a revolutionary era. Who was an ancestor? Who was a hero? What roles did fame and commemoration play? What elements of the past provided foundations and lessons for liberty and sovereignty, and which were to be discarded and eradicated as symbolic of oppression and injustice?

These questions were not internal to the historical narratives that founded Haiti as a nation. They were entangled, as with many memories, within complex webs of global meaning and responsibility. In 2010, Nicolas Sarkozy became the first French chief of state to visit Haiti—since independence in 1803. The President, visiting historical sites, intoned, "Our presence here has not left only good memories ... the wounds of colonization and, perhaps even worse, the conditions of separation have left traces that are still fresh in the memory of Haitians."[4] Sarkozy recognized—or was compelled to acknowledge—that the legacies and felt pains of the nineteenth century could not be bounded by chronology or dismissed as having receded or faded with the experience of previous generations. Rather, questions of justice, perpetually denied or deferred, continued to animate the past as a living present, and memory as a vital force.

It is important, then, to understand the resonance that nineteenth-century conflicts have well into the twenty-first century, underscoring the ways in which the "memory" of a century is not, by its very definition, specifically located in or contained by the chronology of that period. Many of these mnemonic questions issue from unresolved matters of justice. In some cases, this evocation of "justice" can be quite literal—as in clashes over jurisprudence. In 2009, the Chinese embassy in Britain issued strong warnings that the British government was damaging diplomatic relations by condemning the execution of a British citizen, Akmal Shaikh, for heroin smuggling in China. Gordon Brown, the British Prime Minister, released a statement that he was appalled by the judgment, and appealed for clemency based upon disputed details about the case, including the competency of the accused. Embassy spokeswoman Jiang Yu responded, "Nobody has the right to speak ill of China's judicial sovereignty." The controversy was not uniquely a struggle between states about the protection and rights of foreigners and national governments. As the Chinese embassy's official statement made clear, the sentence was representative of "strong resentment" toward drug trafficking with foundations in "the bitter memory of history."[5]

That the case of Akmal Shaikh had been tied to a deep narrative of historical memory was lost on no one. In this domain, few histories are so resonant as the Opium Wars between China and Western powers led by Britain from 1839 to 1842, and again from 1856 to 1860. The ostensible causes of the wars have been history textbook material for generations. The adoption of tea as a part of British culture, especially in the eighteenth and nineteenth centuries, evolved into a national addiction, incurring a ruinous balance of trade between Chinese tea exporters, who demanded payment in silver, and the

British state and trading companies, which faced limited Chinese interest in their own goods.

In search of profits, British traders began to import opium from their colony in India into China, creating an equally addictive market and public health hazard. Strict Chinese officials like Lin Zexu (1785–1850) became key figures around which to organize commemorations, laudatory historical accounts, and memorials dedicated to using his figure to symbolize Chinese resistance to foreign exploitation. Lin was noted for his confinement of foreign merchants and threats of capital punishment against Chinese collaborating agents. "Let the Barbarians deliver to me every particle of opium on board their store ships. There must not be the smallest atom concealed or withheld" (Gelber 2004: 63). Destruction of the merchant's opium stocks by Lin triggered a British military response in the name of fair trade, open markets, and treaty concessions. Landing troops, securing fortifications, and destroying Chinese coastal defenses on both land and water, the British and allies emerged triumphant. From this, Britain imposed treaty ports, established extraterritoriality, and gained Hong Kong island. French forces also demanded and were awarded similar concessions.

Supported by the Emperor for his unwavering stance against the British merchants and military, and iconically breaking the opium smoking pipes of Chinese addicts themselves, Lin Zexu soon came to embody the vagaries and fates of shifting regimes and changing political fortunes. Admiration of his hard measures against the Western trading houses and their agents turned to blame as China entered into military conflict and was humiliated in the Opium Wars by Britain and France. Subsequent cessions of territory and sovereignty, through unequal treaties and loss of ports like Hong Kong, forced Lin out of favor, and he was exiled to Xinjiang in western China.

A generation later, as China faced new political struggles at the end of the Qing Dynasty—especially during the Boxer Rebellion against external influence in China (1899–1901)—Lin once again became a stalwart symbol of Chinese authority against foreign incursions. His home in Fuzhou was dedicated as a memorial during the Qing era in 1905, as the government wrestled once again with opium and imperial invasion questions, and his statue and story adorn multiple commemorative and monumental locales, including sites in Macau, and a statue in Chatham Square, Chinatown, New York.

His legacy also includes the 1957 Opium War Museum in Humen town, Dongguan, where murals, mannequin dioramas, reliefs, and exhibitions relate the human cost not only of wars, but the cost in lives of drug trafficking—a clear and formalized message entwining Chinese history, personal and national humiliation and rehabilitation, and contemporary politics. A number of historical and commemorative sites have been built around nearby military fortifications that figured prominently in the conflicts, and a regional monument makes the point emphatically, with a towering representation of an opium-pipe being snapped in half by two massive hands. Of many images possible to symbolize the Opium War events, this one underscores strength, defiance, and a breaking of colonial bonds through remembrance as much as an evocation of Lin Zexu and his campaigns. It also bears an internal message: after the 1989 student protests and occupation of Tiananmen Square in Beijing, the Chinese leadership underscored the importance of state-managed political and economic change to avoid the dangers of "foreign contamination," and the risk of repeating the "century of humiliation" (Flath 2005: 180–1).

The case of Akmal Shaikh was prosecuted under twenty-first century Chinese law and justified and upheld as a remembered grievance of one nation against another dating back

FIGURE 1.2: Opium War memorial commemorating the Chinese destruction of British opium stocks in Humen, China. Alamy Stock Photo.

to the nineteenth century. In fact, historians like Julia Lovell have argued that Opium War memory has been critical to the formation of the modern Chinese state. "Mao [Zedong], in his essays, was careful to keep the history of the Opium War, imperialism and China's Century of Humiliation at the front of Chinese memory. For him, it was a crucial way of building Chinese nationalism and of mobilizing the populace . . ."[6]

The histories from China—as with those of Oceanian peoples in Tahiti and Hawai'i, or unresolved injustices in Haiti, exemplify how memory—whether in genealogies, dance, slave rebellions, wars, monuments, museums, juridical decisions—can be understood as struggles over power and politics emanating from an Age of Empire. They are linked together through a common set of mnemonic references and struggles: evocations of "memory" and of past injustices as foundations for claiming sovereignty and grievances against nineteenth-century imperial systems, globalized commodities, and an encroaching Western domination over other parts of the planet.

Just as Hobsbawm broadly narrated this nineteenth-century as an Age of Empire, so the global contests that I have assayed by using the *Bounty* tale as a figure to unpack connections between mnemonic regimes, commodity chains, plantation economies, and gunboat diplomacy can be even better understood by more closely examining the states that exerted such imperial powers around the world. These states can be directly connected to the second figure I've evoked to locate memory in the nineteenth century: the famed Bastille violence in France.

The Bastille events were sparked by general unrest and specific concerns about royal military actions. They are important in that they materialized in a resonant fashion through protest, organized action, and popular defiance of aristocratic authority, the shifting landscape of political legitimacy in 1789. They introduced a flashpoint of urban violence participating in the general ferment about taxation, representation, and privilege, and debates around the clergy, nobility, and third estate of the realm that precipitated a crisis of the kingdom.

The Bastille was attacked as both a tactical measure, and as a symbolic assault on the authority of royal law: the insurgents sought weapons, feared the royalist forces, sought to liberate prisoners, and proclaim a new epoch of popular sovereignty. The fortress was torn down to erase the presence, symbolism, and memory of the regime. In its place was the articulation of a nation and people. Arguably, the nineteenth century launched with this political "event," one that directly framed the upheavals in Haiti and, soon, in the rest of the world, from Europe and Russia, to North Africa, to North and South America: the French Revolution, from the new declarations of rights through the state violence of the Terror and the Napoleonic era. The Revolution, by issuing a Declaration of the Rights of Man and Citizen, aimed at transforming not only political regimes, but social orders. In Europe and around the world, the Revolution set itself as a champion for republican and democratic forms of government emanating from popular actions, powering what would become "modern" political ideologies and institutions, especially (nineteenth century) liberalism and nationalism.

Scholars such as François Furet and Lynn Hunt, commenting on the originary moments of the French Revolution, point out that the particular new form of politics that would mark the nineteenth century was in fact not something to be described, but something to be defined. Without the traditional legitimacy of a royal house, and an aristocratic estate under siege, it was in fact "political culture," a contested and conflicting assertion of rival discursive practices, that defined the meaning of politics in symbology, claims to leading and speaking in the name of The People.

Furet's fundamental contribution was to ask where sovereignty would reside in a revolutionary situation, if not in the person of a monarch. Without inherited authority and the legitimacy of dynastic bloodlines, the seat of political authority would be effectively vacant. In such an instance power transferred to whatever individual or party could control, in the French case, *la parole*—the Revolution expressed in words that captured and incarnated the general will of the new body politic. Lynn Hunt anchored this to civic rituals and public, mass practices of dedication to a "mythical present" of solidarity, manifested in banners and festivals. Politics became the expression of everyday social relations, informal styles of speech, a leveling of sartorial distinctions, a furtive changing of the calendar into rational ten-day cycles rather than biblical seven-day weeks (Furet 1981; Hunt 1984).

One of the key commentators on this apparent de-structuring of social organization through political violence from the storming of the Bastille through the radical Jacobin bloodshed of the Terror and rule by guillotine, was the aristocrat and shrewd observer of nations in historical transformation, Alexis de Tocqueville. His essay on the relationship between the *Ancien Regime* and the middle nineteenth century, *The Old Regime and the French Revolution,* published in 1856, argued for an understanding of politics that says much about memory and power.

In spite of the powerful appeal of a narrated rupture from the past presented by Jacobin revolutionaries claiming to give birth to a new world, Tocqueville argued the opposite: while the legal and representational authority of the monarch and aristocracy had, indeed, been shaken, real political power had only been reinforced institutionally. This was because of the relentless continuity of the State. As he famously suggested, "I am willing to admit that centralization was a noble conquest, and that Europe envies us its possession; but I deny that it was a conquest of the Revolution. It was, on the contrary, a feature of the old regime, and, I may add, the only one which outlived the Revolution, because it was the only one that was suited to the new condition of society created by the Revolution" (Tocqueville 1856: 50). In effect, the assaults on authority through violence manifested from the fall of the Bastille delegitimized the monarchy, while encouraging a new, popular state, organized around serving, protecting, and administrating the populace in the name of liberty, equality, and fraternity.

But what was this supposed to look like? Formerly located in the king, state power was reimagined and appropriated by Napoleon Bonaparte as part of a bureaucratic behemoth that reorganized former local domains into administrative departments, promulgated a civil code of uniform, authoritarian laws, installed concierges in residential quarters and established a far-seeing police order, obedient to Napoleonic decrees and dictates. It was as a function of this Napoleonic "system" that a Bonapartist imaginary took on such a resonant and pervasive presence in nineteenth-century history. Napoleon was well aware of this as an intentional project of legacy-building across generations, as he told the diplomat and chronicler Louis Antoine Fauvelet de Bourrienne, "There is no immortality but the *memory* that is left in the minds of men."[7]

Political theorist Sudhir Hazareesingh has studied the impact of this self-fashioning as appropriated by subsequent regimes. "Napoleon Bonaparte became the object of a veritable popular cult, in which his memory as a warrior, ruler, and upholder of the values of the French Revolution was celebrated—first by Bonapartist and Jacobin republican groups under the Restoration, then (after 1830) by the official institutions of the July Monarchy and the Second Empire" (Hazareesingh 2004: 463).

Even after Napoleon's defeat and exile in 1815, this continuity of State authority persisted and came to define nineteenth-century institutions of ruling power through the Restoration, which saw the return of conservative leaders overthrown by Bonapartist armies in Europe, and particularly the identification of the State as the embodiment of peoples with new, nationalist histories with which to understand and narrate their own lives. This first required a rupture from the past, a new nation and polity in place of an old regime. The impacts and memories of the revolutionary era are found, expectedly, all across France, in monuments, commemorations, and symbolic locales such as Place Louis XV, where the king himself was executed in central Paris, renamed Place de la Revolution, and then Place de la Concorde in a shifting narrative of remembered and asserted meanings—from monarch to moment of rupture from the past, to idealization of a national people (Nora 1984–92).

The nesting of these names and narratives within each other intentionally identifies the nation with memories and legacies of revolution. From the violent protests around the Bastille, revolution became encoded in a language and imagery of populaces—The People—rising up against old masters. The Atlantic upheavals beginning in the late-eighteenth century in the American colonies, during the French Revolution, and in Haiti also ignited and consolidated their own legacies: wars of independence in the nineteenth century across North and South America.

The revolution in Haiti compelled Napoleon Bonaparte's decision to conclude the Louisiana Purchase with the United States and the government of Thomas Jefferson, who feared both French influence and the inspiration of a slave-led revolution in North America. Having lost Haiti, Napoleon pulled back from plans to land troops and build up a sizeable military and trading entrepot under direct French control in New Orleans;

instead, he determined to "sell" the French claim to the United States. Jefferson, the American president, shortly sent Meriwether Lewis and William Clark on an expedition to discern the outlines and extent of the western territory. The agreement was signed by an American delegation in Paris in 1803, and the formal transfer took place in the council chamber, or *sala capitular* of the Cabildo building in New Orleans in 1804. The Cabildo is an edifice of columns, arches, and Mansard roofs, and a classic site—like the Place de la Concorde—of overlaid historical memories. That is to say, it materially incarnates in its construction and employments as a location, a series of overlapping narratives of new nations.

As a place of French authority during much of the eighteenth century, the location housed the prison of the *corps de garde* police force. With the Louisiana territory coming under Spanish control in the late eighteenth century, a brick and stucco Cabildo—or meeting place for the illustrious council—was built. Over the generations, the Cabildo burned down in subsequent New Orleans city fires and was rebuilt. Each reconstruction imbricated brick and mortar from the original prison foundations, and subsequent structures, becoming an overlay of multiple eras and uses from council to court (Yakubik 1997). That the Cabildo would become a museum and national historic landmark in the twentieth century only reinforces its particular status as a place of historical memory. Like many such mnemonic locales, it is resonant for not embodying only one past or narrative, but many—French, Spanish, French again, then American. The latter most famously marks the moment—with the Louisiana Purchase—that designated the near-doubling of the territorial United States. Similarly, in the nineteenth-century history of the United States, the same chamber is noted for also hearing and ruling on a canonical legal case having much to do with politics and deployment of juridical power—Plessy v. Ferguson (1896)—which ruled that racial segregation was legal under a doctrine of "separate but equal."

What began at the Cabildo became an inextricable part of the American national narrative, as celebrated at the 1904 World's Fair in the United States, also known as the Louisiana Purchase Exposition, marking the hundredth anniversary of the Purchase. The nineteenth century saw the rise and popularity of such expositions as singular contributions to national self-representation and commemoration, and memory-fashioning entities. Organizers commemorated the Purchase as a signal moment in the U.S. history, aligning their own civic glory in St. Louis, Missouri with that legacy of the early American Republic. Exhibitions focused on commercial and industrial developments, as well as "native" structures from reconstructed adobe villages to thatch-roofed huts from the Philippines. These colonized evocations of cultural styles elided the histories, labor, and lives of colonized peoples, held under political and military exclusion in the United States. This pacification was itself a form of forgetting, just as violence became a mnemonic for historical change—ideologies of nations aligned with military conflict—that dramatically transformed the global political map of the nineteenth century.[8]

From the early century, revolutionary forces were unleashed both in Europe and across the Atlantic. Thwarted in the Caribbean and overextended in North America, Napoleon's regime turned its energies of conquest from the New World to Europe, but the political effects nonetheless resonated across the hemisphere. By invading and overthrowing or forcing into exile the crowned heads in Spain and Portugal in 1808, restive Spanish Creoles in Spanish America were forced to question their own obeisance to Seville. Initially forming ruling juntas to ensure continued political authority, the collapse of royal authority emboldened independence movements across what would become Latin

America. The Portuguese monarchy, equally threatened, relocated itself to Brazil, with Prince Regent Pedro ultimately declaring himself ruler of an independent country. New nations of Colombia, Mexico, and Chile declared independence in 1810, Paraguay and Venezuela in 1811, Argentina in 1816, and ten others in the early 1820s.

The case of Colombia is illustrative of how politics, power, and memory intertwined and strained against one another in the nineteenth century. In a progressive narrative, the overthrow of Spanish rule is equivalent to the liberty of a people and the founding of their nation. Colombian history, however, suggests nothing so simple. After Napoleon's incursions, Colombian towns declared independence—and immediately fell to fighting with one another for paramount control of regions. The former soldier and then legendary military and political leader, General Simon Bolivar, won, and then lost, military challenges with Spanish troops and the territories of Colombia were reconquered by 1817. Bolivar regrouped and returned to the battlefield, finally ousting Spanish forces and ensuring Colombia's independence in 1819.

The Gran Colombia of Bolivar's dreams—integrating Venezuela, Colombia, Panama, and Ecuador—fragmented by 1830, however, and the remaining territories of Colombia and Panama were riven by scores of insurrections and at least eight civil wars. Still, his heroic and commemorative legacy was not undone, as scholar Matthew Brown points out, "Bolivar's memory became part of the everyday landscape of national imaginaries: Bolivar statues, squares, cities, bridges, cafés, political alliances and bus companies are common across the continent, not to mention the country, Bolivia, which has borne his name since its creation in 1826" (Brown 2016: 320). Notably, the legacy of Colombian history as a memory struggle continued to mark politics into the twenty-first century. In 2016, the Colombian government signed a peace accord and amnesty with guerillas of the Revolutionary Armed Forces of Colombia (FARC) after fifty years of violence, kidnappings, and displacements that killed a reported 220,000 victims and forced millions from their homes. Colombian voters rejected the agreement, which was implemented over the objections of slightly more than half of the population. Many denounced as injustice the apparent forgiveness extended. In a news piece, the scholar Camilo Gonzales Posso spoke of establishing a Center of Memory and Peace of Bogota, and reflected: "memory is always a process, subjective, full of passions, of illusions, of partial recollections. Because of this, memories are traumatic, implanted, and always exist with the risk of not being just."[9]

Among those memories would be not only personal losses and victimizations on both sides of the conflict, but deeply rooted differences dating from the nineteenth century over the meaning of the past. One of those episodes involved a coup d'état by General José María Melo in 1854. His movement was defeated militarily, and he himself charged with rebellion. As historian Joshua Rosenthal has pointed out, the national governments were loath to carry out extensive legal proceedings and often addressed political unrest with decrees of *indulto*—effectively pardoning challenges to the state. Individual appeals for clemency by erstwhile combatants ran into the thousands.

While the governments tried to reconcile the body politic through these dispensations, the very consideration of almost endless requests served to underscore the constant tensions between accountability and a will to move past the conflicts in the name of stability and unity. This raised questions: how much memory should a state maintain, and when and what should it attempt to forget? What is the imperative, and also the price of reconciliation in history by recognizing, remembering, but also forgiving the past? In the nineteenth century, claimants kept these questions alive while disavowing their own culpability. More, *indultos* raised questions about "the complex relationship between law, memory, and peace as acts of amnesty can be perceived as legitimizing amnesia—that the crimes of those receiving amnesty have been wiped from legal memory."[10] Memories of justice served or denied inheres in individual cases and decisions, and how they are retold by those who have brought claim, sought redress, or found themselves in the status of victims.

As indicated here however, memory can also inhere in institutions, as with legal records and precedents. In such cases, the intertwining of power, politics, and memory in the nineteenth century became more subtle and complex than adjudicating challenges against governments. Nineteenth-century *power* was gradually disarticulated from rulers and statesmen and resituated into professional and expert roles allied with, but not formal parts of, the ruling circles. In this way, institutions of governance became integrated with the management of knowledge and expertise, as with law as a profession rather than a simple judicial extension of state policy. Thus, the famous expression of the modern world by the social and industrial theorist Henri de Saint-Simon that society would pass "from the government of men to the administration of things" (Rabinow 1989).

Michel Foucault articulated this cogently, though examining the deployment of discursive practices, the ways that power and politics—often synonymous—became disbursed into evidence of micro-power and bio-power: that is, gatekeeping control over what was or was not knowledge, practice, and accepted behavior. Institutions of knowledge, jurisprudence, and medicalized regulation of bodies and learning became the sites of what could be recognized as legitimated power regimes, often in the form of expert authority or institutionalized normalization. Power continued to be an authority to speak—as in the domain of revolutionary political discourse—but also now to heal, train, educate, the provenance of a select group, reinforced by institutional practices in law, in medicine, in the sciences, public policy, and higher learning.

Scholar Jeffrey Olick has pointed out that since the nineteenth century, memory and something called "nation" have come inseparable, such that "political elites invented and propagated legitimating traditions" and historians "objectified the nation as a unitary entity with a linear descent." In dialogue with Rogers Brubaker, he argues that while nations pursue this self-aggrandizing narrative of origin and progress, in fact "nations are not entities that develop; they are practices that occur, institutional arrangements that are continually enacted and reenacted" (Olick 2003: 1–5).

In this context, the elaboration of administrative structures of governance through everyday engagements with schools, clinics, courts, and managers frames a particular understanding of remembrance practices. These might be called embodiments and expressions of memory, though unlike Polynesian dance, they were expressions of technologies of institutional memory. As Elizabeth Loftus has argued, in an elaboration of the dictum set forth by Saint-Simon, through highly administrative settings, "memory is possessed not only by humans but by a great number of things as well." The materiality of such memory is located in any number of "documentary and numerical records, official forms, databases, libraries, archives, contracts, authorized biographies and histories, and scriptures," according to historian Charlotte Linde, who further notes the integration of transmitted knowledge and protocols as institutional memories in "operating procedures, budgeting, marketing, administrative systems . . . physical structure and design" (Linde 2008: 11).

Power as administratively defined by the control of institutional memory came to define the mnemonic practices of nineteenth-century states. In defining national borders and controlling the movement of populations, certifying laborers, and defining undesirable behaviors and estates like vagrancy and homelessness, governments issued identification papers, work permits, and documents that would evolve into national passports.

Such documents were themselves indicators of a particular ideal of individuals and communities, as debated by French scholars of legal and social policy. As the Paris lawyer Alfred Lagresille argued, nineteenth century societies were organized around presumptions that described a formalized bourgeois class standing, "A family situation created by marriage, offering company and relations of affection; an establishment, a habitation, a place of habitual residence which will constitute for him relations of friendship and neighborliness."[11] To ensure this, the State should have its own institutional memory—a means for not only identifying, but locating those who lived, or transgressed, within its borders. Another attorney, P. Le Roy in 1889 averred, "Among the new measures, the most important is the creation of identity cards. It is the most radical and surest means: one avoids long searches, false allegations, and suspicious declarations."[12] This memory of the state placed the archive, the file, the identifying document at the heart of defining citizenship, as well as legal and extra-legal activities.

To track criminal actions, forensic investigators developed standard evidence analysis techniques to reconstruct crime scenes, and adopted photographic portraits and mnemonic standards pertaining to facial features and physiognomies to identify suspects. In courtrooms, judges turned to trained medical-legalists, who used their clinical and laboratory experiences to pronounce on the credibility and reliability of witnesses purporting to recount from memory the details of disputed incidents.

Alexandre Lacassagne, medical-legal studies dean in Lyon, notably underscored exactly this point in one of his publications: "The witness, whether he be a savant or an ignorant pupil, can inform Justice. It is sufficient for him to have memory. The expert on the other hand, must have made special studies and above all demonstrate intelligence and judgment."[13] The testimony of "the expert," buttressed by professional authority and extensive reliance on staged experiments and case studies, increasingly supplanted the recollections of the witness. The criminologist Alphonse Bertillon created an entire visual-measurement system to aid police inspectors in their work identifying, cataloging, and memorizing the faces and features of suspects. The example of his own portrait demonstrates how the technology of photography, with an allied reliance on numerical, physiognomic measurements, deconstructed the face of a suspect into component elements through dimensions, proportions, and colors. Collected together, such cards formed an institutional facial recognition archive to remember, recall, track, and allow surveillance of individuals and groups.

Across colonial possessions, governors and military commanders also administered their settlements through memos, images, and briefings sent to ministries and officials. These were correlated with field studies and expeditions, where reports reduced cultures to administrative writing and representation, and budgetary allocations. Suggests scholar Richard Thomas about British practices, "The various civil bureaucracies were desperate for these manageable pieces of knowledge. They were light and moveable. They pared the Empire down to file-cabinet size" (Richards 1993: 4). All of these structured the discursive and institutional practices that conferred authority, acted as gatekeepers, and set in motion the administrative and coercive mechanisms of state power and politics, drawing upon the memory of archives, records, data, practices, and expertise.

The historian Richard Evans has argued that the nineteenth century was, broadly, an age consumed by the pursuit of power, whether domination and exploitation through commercial and imperial authority, or liberation and sovereignty through nation-building

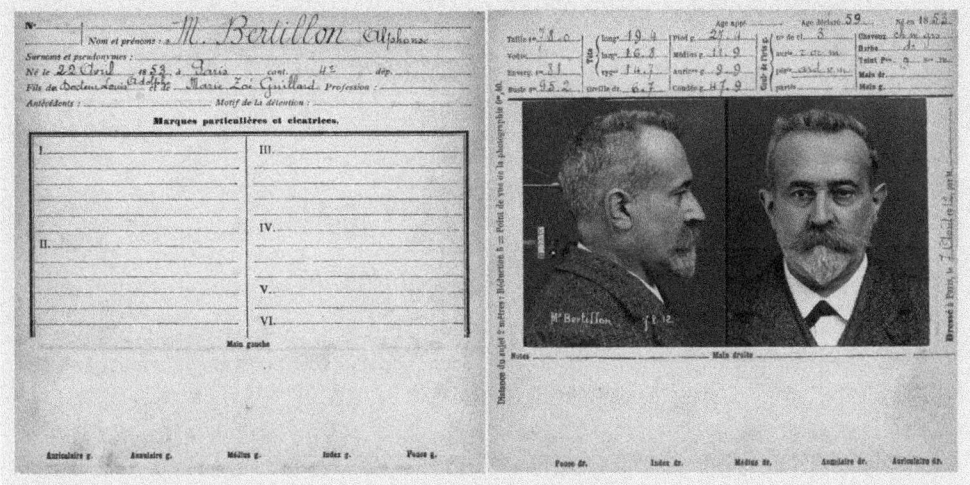

FIGURE 1.3: Anthropometric data sheet (both sides) of Alphonse Bertillon (1853–1914), a pioneer of the Scientific Police, inventor of anthropometry, first head of the Forensic Identification Service of the Prefacture de Police in Paris (1893). Wikimedia Commons.

and assertion of a people's rule. The *Bounty* and Bastille tales we began with hinge on a changing century and align a multiplicity of other mnemonic sites: customary cultures challenged by imperious and imperial ambitions; old colonial possessions warring to become nations, subjects to become citizens; traditional communities struggling with new forms of political legitimacy; nations constructing themselves by displacing power into institutions and disciplining entire societies through regimes of knowledge. These historic shifts manifest themselves in tales of slave colonies in revolt, ancestors remembered, speakers of revolution, gunboat diplomacy, disputed legacies of justice and forgiveness, and the institutionalization of authority.

As described here, the "nineteenth century" began in 1789, a moment to mark the beginning of vast shifts in political power around the world, captured in conflicting memorial traditions from Tahiti and Hawai'i, to China and Haiti, the United States, Colombia, and France, and their continental and Oceanian domains more largely. They remained entangled across generations by commercial and political transformations that aligned nineteenth-century national struggles and authority with imperial rule.

As the nations came to contest one another for dominance, they would open new chapters in histories of memory through power and politics, in the places, commemorations, monuments, and lingering questions that would mark the beginning of the twentieth century in a cataclysmic rupture, the Great War from 1914–1918.

CHAPTER TWO

Time and Space

NICK YABLON

For several decades, the category of memory has productively liberated historians from fixing events or regimes in their respective periods, allowing them instead to explore the ways in which they have been fluidly remembered, or forgotten, across time. We now have a rich and varied body of work on how—to take just three examples from US historiography—antebellum abolitionists invoked memories of the American Revolution to galvanize opposition to slavery; white Southerners formulated a nostalgic vision of the Confederacy as part of a strategy to roll back Reconstruction; or recent groups have conflicted over the significance and legacy of an 1864 massacre of Indians (Minardi 2010; Brundage 2000; Kelman 2013). Yet, too often such studies tacitly assume that memory itself is transhistorical. They show that different groups remembered (or forgot) certain aspects of the past and what ideological uses they made those memories serve, without necessarily attending to the historical changes in *how* people remember the past—and how they *understand* how they remember. It is not just our specific memories of events that have changed over time, but also the very faculty of memory.

Fortunately, a growing cadre of scholars has begun this task of historicizing memory. Several have considered how this mental (yet always socially embedded) faculty came to be mediated by modern institutions such as museums and archives, and by various technologies of dissemination from the printing press to digital media (Nora 1996–98; Crane 2000a: esp. 105–42; Landsberg 2004). Others have explored the history of attempts (whether by poets, philosophers, or scientists) to understand how memory works—and how it is related to other mental faculties such as reason or creativity, to the bodily senses, or to the unconscious (Winter 2012; Matsuda 1996: 79–110). Some of them have focused on the changing metaphors (from memory palace and writing slate to filing cabinet and screen) that these various analysts used to convey the workings of memory—metaphors that subtly came to influence *how* people remembered (Assmann 2011: esp. 137–68). We can draw on histories of the discipline of history itself to recover the changing ways in which historians have articulated their relationship to other forms of remembering; and also on studies of the shifting debates about the necessity and function of memory in democratic states (Kammen 1991: esp. 17–39; Hutton 2016). At the same time, we can supplement that top-down approach by going beyond intellectual and political elites to unearth what Alon Confino calls the "everyday history of memory" (1997a: 1402).

Building on these disparate efforts, this chapter will investigate how the spatio-temporal frameworks through which people remembered the past underwent dramatic transformations during the long nineteenth century. It will also examine the obverse: how the expansion of memory sites and practices transformed the ways in which people imagined themselves in time and space. In opposition to the tendency to explore these two dimensions in isolation, with "the new temporal studies" typically positioning itself against the prior dominance of "spatial theory," this chapter will consider them in conjunction with one another, time and space ultimately being inextricable. For reasons of academic specialization, the focus will be on the United States.

If historians of American memory agree about anything, it is that the long nineteenth century witnessed a belated yet extraordinary proliferation of mnemonic sites, institutions, and practices. Echoing developments in Europe, Americans founded public museums, beginning arguably with Charles Willson Peale's Philadelphia Museum (1786), in part to house collections of portraits and busts memorializing national-historical figures (Orosz 1990). They also founded other institutions for preserving the past, such as state historical societies (beginning with Massachusetts in 1791), libraries, and manuscript collections—although not yet public (government or state) archives (Blouin, Jr, and Rosenberg 2011: 32–49). By the 1820s, the national elite had overcome any lingering Puritan or republican misgivings about monuments and finally embarked on major projects, most notably soaring obelisks to honor the Battle of Bunker Hill and George Washington (Harris 1966/1982: 190–8). That decade also marked the official embrace of history painting as a means to memorialize episodes from the revolution and subsequent war, with John Trumbull's canvases installed in the Capitol Rotunda and subsequently reproduced in popular magazines and school textbooks (Fryd 1992: 42–61). Forms of calendrical memory also proliferated, with the growing celebration of Independence Day in the early republic and the establishment of further national holidays—in effect, special days for remembering—such as Decoration Day (1868, renamed Memorial Day in 1882), Thanksgiving (1870), and George Washington's Birthday (1880) (Travers 1999). New rituals of public commemoration, such as historical pageants and time capsule deposits (Figure 2.1), were forged to mark the anniversaries of the founding of the nation, a state, or a city—or to designate certain historic sites or structures (battlefields, birthplaces, etc.) as sacred (Glassberg 1990; Yablon 2019).

Mnemonic rites flourished in the private sphere, too, with the spread of a Victorian culture of remembrance that involved collecting souvenirs, keeping post-mortem photographs, tracing family trees, and visiting cemeteries. One might even count the emergence of history as an academic profession—and the hiring in 1881 of the first professor of *American* history, Moses Coit Tyler of Cornell University—as a further symptom of this larger memory boom (Kammen 1983). If, as Michael Kammen shows, Americans had been largely indifferent to memory at the outset of the century, neglecting their historic sites and records and denouncing the retrospective orientation of aristocratic European nations, by century's end the nation had acquired an impressive "arsenal of memory devices"—a "stockpile" that was "astonishing" in its "diversity" (1991: 53–62, 76–7, 94).

Mnemonic activity underwent not only a process of intensification and diversification but also one of spatial expansion. While the content of memories tended to remain local, their domain of circulation broadened from the local to the national. Through coordinated campaigns, for instance, holidays that had once been limited to certain regions were enshrined as national, as Thanksgiving was in 1863 (Baker 2009). Geographic mobility further expanded local memories, most visibly through associations such as the New England Society that sprang up beyond that region in an effort to preserve emigrants' roots (Kammen 1991: 74; Glassberg 1990: 18). Black migration after Emancipation

FIGURE 2.1: Unknown designer, Mosher's Memorial Offering to Chicago (detail from backmark of one of Charles D. Mosher's "memorial photographs," Chicago, n.d. One of the earliest examples of what would later be termed a time capsule, this "memorial offering" consisted of almost ten thousand photographic portraits of prominent and middle-class Americans, accompanied by their signatures and (in some cases) biographical sketches. The Chicago photographer, Charles D. Mosher, conceived the collection in 1876 and eventually sealed it in 1889 in a vault in Chicago's City Hall, for opening in 1976. Courtesy: Chicago History Museum.

similarly helped to expand "Freedom Day" celebrations (a tradition dating back to antebellum observance of the anniversary of the British abolition of the slave trade) from South to North, although Juneteenth still awaits its canonization as a national holiday (Kachun 2003: 11). This nationalization of memory infrastructure, however, was facilitated above all by new media technologies. By the 1840s, innovations in printing (such as the steam-powered rotary printing press) and techniques of mass marketing permitted the emergence of a new genre of popular history (and its offshoot, historical biography), which, unlike the deluxe, multi-volume works of patrician historians, was accessible and affordable to a broad, middle-class national audience (Pfitzer 2008; Casper 1999). Depictions of past events and individuals—and of surviving remnants of the past, such as commemorative trees, monuments, and other historic landmarks—were also increasingly transmitted, sometimes in chromolithographic color, through an array of new visual media, such as engravings, stereographs, postage stamps, and illustrated postcards. Artifacts, too, served as visual media for the spatial dissemination of memory, with the development of techniques for applying historical imagery to mass-manufactured beer trays or clock faces (Allen 2008: 59–114).[1]

The conscription of memory in the service of national identity—an endeavor, we should emphasize, that could never fully erase the prior, transnational memories of sub-groups such as blacks and immigrants—was accompanied by a *temporal* expansion of its content. At the dawn of the nineteenth century, American historical consciousness had remained somewhat shallow; with the exception of a few earlier episodes of discovery and exploration, it tended to reach only as far back as the 1760s (Kammen 1991: 161–2). The subsequent quest to implant a deeper sense of nationhood entailed a lengthening of that timeframe, which helped also to circumvent the divisive and controversial nature of events since the Revolution. Paralleling the nationalist invocation of ancient sites and legends in Europe, such as the preservation of Cologne Cathedral, the collecting of Gaelic bardic poems or German folk tales, or the development of a cult of Joan of Arc (Pohlsander 2008: 34–48; Trumpener 1997; Crane 2000a: 65–80; McMillan 1993: 359–70), American antiquarians, writers, and artists wove sites such as Plymouth Rock, indigenous mounds, or even the "natural antiquities" of ancient trees and forests into the national narrative (Seelye 1998; Yablon 2009: 45–59). This reaching backward was, of course, highly selective. It did not yet extend, for instance, to the ancient reminders of Spanish or Mexican sovereignty over the Southwest (Kammen 1991: 50).[2]

Yet, while European historians have viewed the ascendant nation-state as the agent behind this explosion of new forms of memory during the nineteenth century (Confino 1997b), the thesis does not fully apply to the United States. As Kurt Piehler and others have reminded us, the American state remained largely inactive in cultural affairs until late in the century. Belief in limited government and scarce federal resources (especially prior to the Civil War) contributed to an almost unquestioned assumption that such things as monuments, museums, archives, or historic preservation should be funded by private donations and administered by voluntary associations (Piehler 1995: 23, 27, 29). Only when the abandoned stump of the Washington Monument (Figure 2.2), still unfinished forty-three years after the donation of the first dollar, was described as a disgrace to a nation celebrating its centennial, did Congress finally relent and pass an appropriations bill to complete it, which still took a further nine years. Other half-built monuments were abandoned altogether through lack of private donations or mismanagement (Yablon 2012: 153–97). Moreover, public memory projects often worked to instill regional or racial/ethnic affiliations rather than a sense of common nationhood. Memorial associations of white Southern women, for instance, constructed monuments to Confederate generals and beautified Confederate cemeteries in an attempt to shore up a race-based sectional identity, while black leaders deployed freedom celebrations and orations to bolster their own community's sense of pride and hope during and after Reconstruction (Brundage 2005: 12–104; Kachun 2003: 97–206).[3]

Instead of attributing the proliferation of memory (either in the United States or elsewhere) to the rise of the nation-state, we might consider it a product of a deeper rending of the fabric of temporality during the long nineteenth century. Recent scholarship on temporality—in accordance with an older scholarship on modernity—has drawn attention to a pervasive sense during this period of being disconnected from the past (and future), of inhabiting a present that was empty, or unmoored from that which preceded it. Time itself appeared a problem, a mystery, an "abyss." It was in order to suture this split between present and past, scholars have suggested, that new forms of memory were crafted (Lowenthal 1985: 185–262; Mason 2009: xxiv–xxv).

What remains unresolved or unclear, though, is what exactly *caused* this temporal rupture. One explanation, borrowing from scholars such as cultural critic Walter Benjamin and historian Eugen Weber, focuses on the breakdown of traditional forms of cultural

FIGURE 2.2: "Beef Depot Monument," in *Leslie's Illustrated Newspaper*, 13, no. 323 (1862), 173. Surrounded by livestock for the Union Army, the unfinished stump of the Washington Monument came to be viewed as a symbol of Americans' failure to remember the founder's principles. Courtesy: Iowa State Historical Society, Iowa City.

transmission as communal life gave way to mass society. In earlier periods, the argument goes, a sense of embeddedness in time was achieved through the collective, communal perpetuation of tradition from one generation to the next, via oral traditions such as the *veillées* of rural France, winter-evening vigils in which the village gathered to work and to exchange stories (Weber 1976: 413–8). In modern, urbanized societies, such storytelling traditions were eroded by print-cultural forms such as the newspaper that transmitted "information" but not "experience," reporting events but not integrating them into a deeper, shared temporal narrative (Benjamin 1968: 87–9, 158–9). As the pioneering communications scholar Harold Innis argued in the 1950s, that temporal blindness was exacerbated by the media through which such information was transmitted. Whereas "heavy," durable media of inscription such as stone, clay tablets, and parchment had been "biased" towards the dissemination of knowledge over time (thus "binding" times together), lighter media such as printed paper (and, subsequently, telegraphy, radio, cinema, and television) prioritize command over space, thereby contributing to the "destruction of time" and the rise of "present-mindedness" in the modern West, especially the United States (Innis 1951: 33–60, 82–3). One might add to this the legal developments that further undermined contemporaries' sense of trans-generational continuity. The late-eighteenth-century abolition (in both the United States and France) of primogeniture, entail, and other instruments for controlling property for long periods beyond one's own lifetime, was perceived by commentators such as Alexis de Tocqueville as having weakened the family as an agent of historical continuity, thereby causing a forgetting of both past and future ([1835/40] 1988: 50–7).[4]

This line of argument, however, implies an opposition between "organic," traditional forms of memory and artificial, constructed, modern ones, and a nostalgia for the former, reminding us that even memory scholars are prone to memory fixations (Nora 1989: 7–24; Terdiman 1993: 30; Mason 2009: xxiv). The assumption that remembrance was once purely oral and unmediated—an intellectual legacy of nineteenth-century thinkers such as Ferdinand Tönnies (1887/2001)—is belied by the fact that humans have been displacing their memories onto things since the very invention of tools, as the philosopher Bernard Stiegler has reminded us (2010: 66–68). It also leads to the intellectual cul-de-sac of viewing new forms of memory as shallow, spurious substitutes for the real thing. Even the argument about primogeniture and entail has limits. According to one legal scholar, these doctrines of inheritance had little "practical significance" in the United States by the mid-eighteenth century, even though they persisted as a "powerful symbol" (Alexander 1997: 56).

A second explanation for the sense of temporal rupture focuses on the impact of seismic political and military events of the period. Peter Fritzsche has explored how the upheaval wrought upon an entire continent (and beyond) by the French Revolution and the Napoleonic Wars, with their mobilization of mass armies and their unprecedented disruption of civilian lives, confounded assumptions of historical continuity and predictability. Rather than a guide to those living in the present, the past came to appear obscure and remote, thus generating the widespread condition—and Romantic *topos*—of nostalgia (Fritzsche 2004). Similar arguments have been made for the impact of revolution and war on American temporal experience, most notably in Susan Matt's history of the emotion of homesickness, a sentiment that has as much to do with time as with space (2011: 30–5, 75–100).

Yet, it is not clear how socially pervasive this temporal impact was; Fritzsche's sources consist mainly of diaries and letters by the wealthy and literate. Did all groups experience such events as marking a breach in their lives? The Civil War may have been felt by Southern whites to have "broken the ribbon of time, severing the present from preceding eras," as Fitzhugh Brundage observes, but blacks "recognized no comparable discontinuity" (2005: 100). Questions are also raised about whether earlier military and political upheavals did not generate similar temporal crises. Reinhart Koselleck, whose explorations of the rhetorics of historical time strongly inform Fritzsche's book, in fact described the reconfiguration of the present's relationship to the past and future as a slower, more gradual process, dating as far back as the Thirty Years War (1985/2004: 9–25).

We therefore need to supplement our emphasis on singular events (or series of events) with an account of how broader populations were estranged from their pasts by deeper social and economic upheavals, from the industrial and market revolutions, which propelled vast migration flows, to revolutions in transportation and communication. We might also foreground the rapidity of such changes, which gave rise to an oft-mentioned perception that time itself was accelerating or, put differently, that the present was slipping ever more rapidly into the past. The acceleration of the capitalist production process by mid-century would have contributed to this impression of the present's premature obsolescence, as would the rapidity of urban growth especially in the United States, where towns could appear (and then, in some cases, disappear) within a generation (Harvey 1990: 260–83; Yablon 2009: 49–61).[5]

Such complex, ongoing changes, however, defied contemporaries' capacity to apprehend them in the abstract. Instead, they grappled with the relationship between material forces, temporal experience, and the problem of memory through certain physical and spatial objects. In nineteenth-century New York (among other cities), one such object that foregrounded the past's failure to cohere within the present was the holdout. As capitalist development moved up the island, and as the specialization of land use gave rise to distinct zones defined by class, ethnicity or function (business, residential, etc.), numerous older sites and structures—from churches, cemeteries, and mansions downtown to shanty settlements and farmhouses uptown—were left stranded in time and space. The latter could find themselves in the path of a street when surveyors implemented the grid plan, or else left literally high and dry, clinging to rocky outcrops, when those new streets were graded (Figure 2.3).

These various holdouts were described by commentators as abject, uncanny persistences—destined not to grow old gracefully or acquire age-value as ruins, but to be overshadowed by newer structures, defiled by re-use (as boardinghouses etc.), and ultimately demolished. Processes of capitalist urbanization prevented these holdouts from maturing as archaic elements within the cityscape, gathering stable associations and providing material links to the past—both the city's collective past and individuals' own pasts (their childhoods). Caught hopelessly between the past and present, holdouts appeared "untimely" (Yablon 2009: 131–45). If the city had served since antiquity, as Lewis Mumford argued, to bind "times past, times present, and times to come," both through storage of texts and through its "durable buildings and institutional structures," its capacity to do so came into doubt in nineteenth-century United States (1961: 99).

Temporal discontinuity was not always a by-product or symptom of deeper material forces; it could also involve *willful* disavowals of the past. The repudiation of what Hayden White called "the burden of history," associated in Europe with the late nineteenth and early twentieth century—from Nietzsche's critique of antiquarianism to the Futurists' urge to "demolish museums and libraries"—arguably has a longer history in the United States and is central to its myth of exceptionalism (Marinetti 2009: 95). It became especially prominent during the 1830s and 1840s, with the Young America movement: a faction of New York Democrats who proclaimed their political—and, in the case of literary and artistic affiliates such as Nathaniel Hawthorne, cultural—independence from the orthodoxies of the past and the influence of Europe, pronouncing America "the Great Nation of Futurity" (O'Sullivan 1839).[6] Ironically, in rejecting memory, the Young Americans may have contributed to the sensation of temporal rupture that fomented its very resurgence.

If the proliferation of new forms of memory was a cultural response—conscious or unconscious—to some, or all, of these perceived temporal rifts in the long nineteenth century, the question remains whether (and to what degree) these new forms appeared actually to repair those rifts. Certainly, faith in individual memory became increasingly

FIGURE 2.3: Brennan Farm House, 84th Street [and Broadway], 1879. Half-tone reproduction of a photograph, from the Geographic File (PR020), box 35, folder: 84th Street. This humble frame dwelling, constructed on a rocky outcrop in a rural setting in the eighteenth century, was notable for its associations with George Washington (who was said to have used it as a headquarters) and Edgar Allan Poe (who rented a room in the mid-1840s in which he allegedly wrote "The Raven"). Yet, rather than serving as a stable reminder of the region's and nation's storied past, it became a fragile holdout that suffered the indignities of being taken over by tradesmen, shaken by the dynamite that was used to level the streets around it, and stripped by relic hunters—before finally being demolished and carted off as scrap wood. (Collection of The New-York Historical Society, ID: #84696d).

shaky during that century. Its capriciousness and degradability, a concern of philosophers since antiquity, was now an object of full-blown cultural anxiety (Terdiman 1993). Scientific studies revealed a host of psychological "disturbances" or abnormalities to which memory was prone, from forgetting (the neologism amnesia was coined in France in 1804) to its opposite, the overwhelming condition of remembering *too* much, which Theodule Ribot christened "hypermnesia" in 1881 (Roth 2012: 3–22). Even nostalgia was diagnosed as a physiological disease, one that was believed potentially to be fatal (Roth 2012: 23–38). The extent to which individual memory itself appeared to be in crisis can also be gleaned from the number of new tricks and systems for "memorization" (or, to use another nineteenth-century neologism, mnemotechnics) that were now proposed (Matsuda 1996: 61–78; Miles 1848). Memory thus seemed an unreliable tool for bridging the growing chasm between present and past.

Yet, despite such doubts, there was a renewed belief in the nineteenth century that memory, mediated through material artifacts, could in fact span that temporal chasm. As Teresa Barnett has shown, middle-class Americans became fascinated by the apparent power of relics (or "association items") to transport them back in time and foster a visceral, affective contact with historic figures. Such association items were certainly present in earlier centuries, dating back to the curiosity cabinets of the early modern era, but were subordinated within those antiquarian collections to other categories of objects, such as ethnographic exotica, natural history specimens (shells, fossils, etc.), or rarities (unusual animals, ancient coins and medals, etc.). During the course of the nineteenth century, however, association items became the *dominant* object in the private collections of figures like John Fanning Watson and in the public collections and displays of state and local historical societies and museums (including the Smithsonian's "Section of Historical Relics," established in 1883). They embraced not just the possessions of famous figures such as Miles Standish's sword or Benjamin Franklin's knee breeches, but also objects that a famous figure merely touched *en passant*, such as a glass from which George Washington supposedly once sipped. The metonymic logic of "homomateriality"—whereby objects from the past stand in for, or embody, past episodes—also allowed them to include part-objects, such as fragments of the wooden step from which Colonel John Nixon gave the Declaration of Independence its first public reading. Fragments appeared in fact to exceed wholes in their associational value, insofar as they materially evoked memory's poignant tendency to erode. Later in the century, the association item expanded still further to encompass relics that had no connection to leading historical figures, but instead provided access to epic historical events, as in the bloodstained bible or bullet-torn uniform of an ordinary soldier killed in the Civil War. These various objects were widely believed—at least until the rise of museum professionals and positivist approaches in the early twentieth century—to allow the beholder to vicariously overcome the pastness of the past (Barnett 2013: 18–25).

The cult of the historical relic, however, was part of a larger faith in the capacity of the physical world to constitute a material linkage to that which was no longer present. While this conception of matter as memory is evident in the scientific study (by the 1830s) of geological and fossil records, it is most often associated with private practices of mourning family members or friends through the preservation—and periodic revisiting—of material traces of the deceased: locks of hair, scraps of clothing, or other personal items (Lutz 2015a; Pike 1980). Souvenirs were kept—typically by women—not just to preserve the dead, but also to preserve their own (or their family's) ongoing memories of births, friendships, courtships, vacations, and other transitory rites of passage—or, in the case of flower-pressing, the passing seasons. Commonplace books, and later scrapbooks, were filled with such items and sometimes ritually exchanged within social circles (Stabile 2004; Garvey 2012). The rise of the photographic portrait studio in the latter half of the century also stemmed in part from this widespread belief that a material—in this case, silver crystals—could preserve a memory or physical imprint, of the sitter's body (or even soul), enabling him or her to live on in the memory of future viewers. Photography thus built upon preexisting practices of perpetuating a direct or "indexical" trace, such as that of taking a wax or plaster cast of a person's face (or hands), a procedure applied to numerous military, political, and cultural figures in the nineteenth century, from Napoleon Bonaparte to Ludwig van Beethoven. One did not have to wait for death; molds were taken from living faces, a process endured by John Adams, James Madison, and Abraham Lincoln, the latter describing it as "anything but agreeable" (Figure 2.4) (Warner 2006: 21–58; Sherwood 2008).

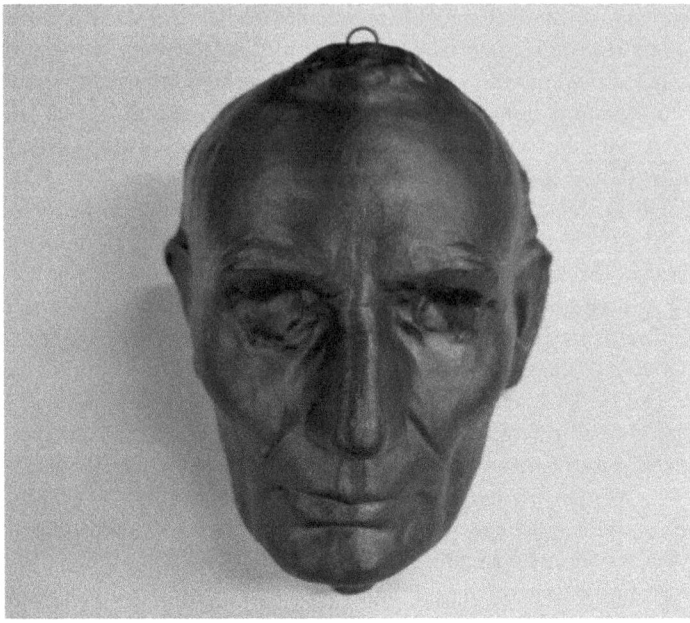

FIGURE 2.4: A copy of a life mask of Abraham Lincoln, taken by Chicagoan sculptor Leonard Wells Volk in Spring 1860 just days before Lincoln's nomination as Republican candidate for president. This copy was one of a limited set of bronzes cast in 1886. Courtesy: Special Collections, University of Iowa Libraries, MSC0036.

Even ink inscribed on paper in the form of a signature was believed to preserve a kind of imprint left behind by the body. Collectors often cut the autographs of historic figures out of larger documents and treasured them—especially those that had been scribbled spontaneously—for their capacity to allow an "almost mystical encounter" with the illustrious (Thornton 1996: 87). These various relics, moreover, functioned not in isolation but in conjunction. As Geoffrey Batchen has shown, a ringlet of hair inserted into a photographic locket served to call attention to, and thus supplemented, the indexicality of the portrait—and *vice versa* (2004). A similar doubling of indexicality is evident in a card that bears both the photograph and autograph of its subject.

If material objects harbored memories according to nineteenth-century Americans, so too did physical places. The de-territorializing effect on memory engendered by the circulation of historical imagery across the nation via print and visual media (discussed above) was countered by an increasing emphasis on the mnemonic power of place. First-landing spots (such as Plymouth Rock), battlefields, birthplaces of religious and political leaders, former abodes of writers, and Revolutionary meeting-places, among other sites, emerged as meccas for secular pilgrimages (Linenthal 1993; Bruggeman 2011; Bruggeman 2012; Mires 2002: 114–46). A preservationist movement, led by elite women, finally succeeded in purchasing historic houses, most notably George Washington's Mount Vernon estate in 1858, so as to restore them and transform them into museums. Advocates described such historic structures as portals to the past, offering a physical, sensory experience that could transport visitors back in time (West 1999: 1–37).

Sites of historic episodes did not require intact buildings to afford such trans-temporal experiences. Ruins came into vogue among middle-class tourists by the 1830s, as picturesque travel-writers and artists promoted decaying colonial forts such as Ticonderoga as attractions on the "American" or "Northern Tour" (Yablon 2009: 47). In the absence of any architectural remnant, ancient trees served as gateways to former times. Elms, in particular, were valued—in the words of contemporaries—as "living witnesses" to the past or as "connecting link[s]" across time, even if it was their worthlessness as lumber that had spared them from the axe. Some were given memorial names—typically that of a famous individual who (allegedly) once passed through, such as the Marquis de Lafayette. These elms came to inspire not only visitors but also poets, orators, artists— and, when they finally fell, relic hunters armed with pocket-knives (Campanella 2013: 162, 169–76). Finally, where nothing at all remained of the past, a historic site could be marked by commissioning a commemorative plaque or planting a fresh tree, both practices that became popular later in the century (Campanella 2013: 173; Mason 2009: 47–9, 54). The emphasis on visiting such places in person—that is to say, unmediated—was underscored by the patriotic rhetoric surrounding such sites, such as Daniel Webster's Plymouth Oration of 1820, which interpellated the American people as though they were all there, standing on the sacred rock (Webster 1825).

The commemoration of specific historic places was an expression of a larger, growing belief in the importance of constructing memory not merely in the abstract realm of the media, but also in physical space. There was, for instance, an increased attention to the spatial contexts in which monuments were sited. After decades of remaining a swampy landscape defiled by slave pens, Washington's National Mall or "monumental core" was re-envisioned, first as a picturesque, naturalistic landscape by Alexander Jackson Downing in 1851 and then along rectilinear, neoclassical lines in the McMillan Plan of 1901 (Savage 2009: 46, 66–74, 147–94). Other cities, such as Richmond, Virginia, laid out imposing "monument avenues," in large part to boost residential values for their white, propertied elite (Wilson 2003: 100–15). The naming (or renaming) of streets and parks in honor of American historical events and figures also served as a means to embed memory in physical space, as "critical toponymists" have begun to explore (Berg and Vuolteenaho, 2017). Public, urban space was essential to the historic pageant, too, a performative enactment of memory that flourished during the Progressive era. Hierarchical notions regarding the role of past groups were symbolically expressed through the order in which the ranks of costumed representatives appeared in the streets—just as the spatial layout of museums projected a stratified memory to the viewers who moved through them (Glassberg 1990: 43–67; Bennett 1995: 95–8). Such hierarchies could also be *challenged* through spatial practices of memory. A critical aspect of the Emancipation Day parades in segregated Southern towns and cities at the turn of the twentieth century was the way in which hundreds of black marchers reclaimed prominent public spaces, often in the face of contemptuous or hostile white onlookers, "thereby linking the ritual of procession with their own contemporary struggle for rights" (Brundage 2005: 55–88; quotation on 65).

Private domestic space, despite Tocqueville's assertions above, also played a heightened mnemonic role for Americans seeking trans-temporal attachments. In enshrining the home as a refuge and retreat, spatially distinct from the public worlds of work and commerce, Benjamin wrote, the bourgeoisie transformed it into a theater of phantasmagorical images, a place in which to conjure up "the far away and the long ago" (Benjamin 1999: 9). With its radical differentiation and demarcation of internal spaces, moreover, the middle-class home could serve as a literalized "memory palace." Like that ancient memory stratagem, it could preserve memories by distributing them across its various rooms, from the formal, quasi-public space of the front parlor to the more private rear parlor or sitting room (if a family could afford one), and from the dream-spaces of the bedrooms to the dusty archives of the attic or basement—the latter becoming communal with the advent of the apartment building in the 1870s (Grier 1992: 57–9; Tebbe 2008).

The most crucial of these memory spaces was the front parlor itself, a feature widely promoted in America from the 1850s to the 1890s (Grier 1992: 51, 62). Not just for receiving visitors or for signaling the family's cosmopolitan or genteel status, the parlor was also a museum, writ small, for the artful and self-conscious preservation and display of memory objects. Such objects included: the family bible (often inscribed with the family tree and other genealogical information), scrapbooks, photograph albums, and photographic portraits (encompassing both private and public figures and events); mementos from visits to world's fairs; and handiwork such as framed hair wreaths or hand-stitched samplers (often commemorating a wedding or birth); along with inherited items of furniture and other heirlooms. These were typically curated by the mother and prominently arrayed across the room on the center- or corner-tables, shelves, and mantelpieces, or on the walls (Weil 2013; Siegel 2010). Domestic space thus came to play a crucial role in structuring memory, just as memory did in structuring domestic space. Amid the spatiotemporal flux of real estate speculation and geographical mobility, the home was touted as a means to anchor the family in time. Even after leaving one's childhood home, one could reanimate those memories by mentally moving through its rooms, as Benjamin did in his 1930s recollections, *Berlin Childhood around 1900* (2006: 125–9, et passim).

If the Victorian family home was a spatial container of memories, it was itself filled with smaller containers. The transatlantic bourgeoisie was gripped by an apparent fixation with boxes of all shapes and sizes, from snuffboxes to jewelry boxes. "What didn't the nineteenth century invent some sort of casing for!" exclaimed Benjamin, who also noted their obsessive recurrence in nineteenth-century literature (1999: 220–1). Besides keeping the dust or the servants out, the encasement of things could serve diverse purposes: the cultivation of fantasy or intimacy (the box standing here for the body or heart, one that contains fragments of other bodies); the production of consumer desire or scientific knowledge; or the construction of the privatized bourgeois self within his/her domestic shell. But the key function of such vessels was arguably mnemonic. Cabinets or secretary desks served as the family's archives, for the filing away of letters or calling cards (Tebbe 2008: 206; Showalter and Driesbach 1983; Fig. 2.5). Further containers were devised *specifically* for the purpose of storing or displaying individual memories, such as keepsake boxes, children's treasure boxes, étagères, or lockets (Batchen 2004b 39, 65–76)—although Victorian women also used utilitarian boxes (sewing workboxes, lap desks, etc.) to secrete a lock of hair or a cherished letter, often in a hidden compartment or false bottom (Lutz 2015b: 47–51, 159–66) (Figure 2.6).

Public memories, too, were constructed through boxes, as we see with reliquaries containing collections of historical artifacts, a particularly interesting one being that of the antebellum Philadelphian antiquarian, John Fanning Watson (Piggush 2009; Stabile 2013). With their often-elaborate honeycomb of inner compartments, Victorian boxes were miniature memory palaces. Objects could be located in specific cubby holes, thus encoding meaning through spatial juxtaposition (Stabile 2013: 206), while in cases lined with velour or plush, they could leave behind their indexical trace (Benjamin 1999: 20). By closing the lid, they could be isolated in space—set apart from the everyday world around them, even if still visible through a glass window—yet also frozen in time. In the

TIME AND SPACE 51

FIGURE 2.5: Mahogany and veneered chest of drawers with secretary drawer, made by Michael Allison circa 1800–20. 134 x 115.6 x 54.6 cm. Its original owner, Clement Clarke Moore (1779–1863), is alleged to have composed the Christmas poem, "A Visit from St. Nicholas" (better known as "'Twas the Night Before Christmas") at this desk in his Manhattan home in 1822. New-York Historical Society, Gift of Blanche Austin Rockhill, object number 1956.169.

casket, wrote the phenomenologist Gaston Bachelard, "the past, the present and a future are condensed" (1958/1994: 84). And finally, by locking the container—and even photograph albums and diaries were designed with hasps for mini-padlocks—those memory-objects acquired the power and sanctity of holy relics.

Given this cult of the lockable box, it is not surprising that the time capsule—perhaps the ultimate spatial solution to the temporal problem of memory—emerged in the nineteenth century. Although cornerstone deposits (the leaving of objects in the first stone of a new building) date back to medieval Europe, and foundation and tomb deposits to ancient Mesopotamia, with similar rites originating in Chinese, African, American Indian, and other cultures, none have been found that specified an opening date. As a deposit with such a preconceived target, the time capsule appears to have born only in 1876, when such timed devices were conceived in Philadelphia and elsewhere as gifts from celebrants of the centennial to those of the bicentennial (Yablon 2019).[7] Over the subsequent half century, as many as thirty were launched across the country, in various metal and wooden chests and vessels. Albeit still lacking the mass publicity Westinghouse

FIGURE 2.6: Rosewood-veneer writing desk, made by Ball, Black & Co., *c*. 1830–1860. 14.9 × 33 × 25.4 cm. These portable desks (also known as lap desks) were designed to store stationery and writing implements and to provide (when opened) a sloped, leather-lined surface, enabling one to write in different locations. But their owners often also used their hidden compartments (of which this one had three) to store private relics, correspondence, diaries, and other memory objects. The lock and key allowed these to be kept from prying eyes. New-York Historical Society, Gift of Mrs. James McCosh Magie, object number 1970.6.1.

Electric Corporation would bestow in 1939 when it coined the term "time capsule," the practice became a thriving civic tradition by the Progressive era, attracting the interest of mayors, presidents, and even Harvard professors. Its proliferation reveals a heightened cultural concern not just with how the past was being forgotten—most visibly, in the destruction of historic buildings or the dispersal of important collections—but also with how their own present would be forgotten *in the future*, thus requiring attention to what might be called prospective memory (Assmann 2011: 45–7, 53–4, 149–50; Yablon 2019).

Time capsules' attention to the memory of the present was not their only appeal. Compared with prestigious mnemonic projects such as monuments, they could be compiled and completed quickly and easily, and by those whose ethnic, gender, or religious identity placed them outside the elite. They also proved (at least in the early decades) unusually collaborative, as the compilers were obliged to enlist contributions from the broader community. They thus generated a heterogeneous assemblage of often-conflicting memories—public and private, official and vernacular—with some including voices from the labor, suffrage, and black civil rights movements. At the same time, they exceeded libraries, historical societies, and archives in their receptiveness to new media (photographs, phonographs, and cinema) and to material artifacts. Yet, the sealing of such items in impregnable containers bespeaks a desire, above all, to repair the temporal breach wrought by modernity—in this case, that between present and *future*. Contributors typically addressed their messages not to some abstract future but to actual, putative individuals:

the coming members of a congregation, students of a college, inhabitants of a city, or citizens of the nation. They expressed a desire to connect with those others through tropes of emotional intimacy and physical, embodied touch (see, for example, Figure 2.1). The sealing of some time vessels similarly inspired participants and witnesses (of diverging political persuasion) to reflect on the present's ethical duty to posterity (Yablon 2019).

The disparate memory practices and institutions considered here all possessed a certain doubleness. On the one hand, they betrayed a melancholic sense of disconnectedness from the past, stemming not merely from the rise of print culture and the impact of political and military events, but also from the deeper social and economic forces of the long nineteenth century. Yet, on the other, they expressed an invigorated belief in the possibility (both now and in future times) of reconnecting with the past, of bringing it to life through various spatial means, from the assembling of relic collections and the visiting of historic sites and structures, to the inscription and enactment of memories in public and private spaces. Although nineteenth-century Americans, like their European contemporaries, did not yet group these activities under the unifying rubric of "memory"—that term still referred to individual rather than social remembering—they clearly exhibited a heightened self-consciousness about how the recovery of the past was crucial to cultural identity, and how it was dependent on the cultivation of certain shared practices and institutions. In other words, social groups who constructed and disseminated memories of historical episodes were not just legitimating their own political claims (oppressive or liberatory) in the present, but were also drawn to the deeper social function of remembering: the way in which it allowed them to re-orient themselves in time and space.

CHAPTER THREE

Media and Technology[1]

ELIZABETH EDWARDS

The nineteenth century was the period when memory became truly and expansively mechanized. If the colonial and imperial agenda depended on the increasingly technical management of the time and space—a "communication imperialism" through which power was exercised (Kaul 2014: 2), so expanded memory and memorializing potential were integrally and systemically connected to related processes of technological delivery. It was an era when European interactions and relations with the rest of the world were intensified and the values and memorializing capacities so exposed became increasingly fluid and porous. In this chapter I am going to consider specifically the role of media technologies, especially photography and its multiple formats, in fostering the consolidation and memorializing strategies of Empire.

Maurice Halbwachs (1992) formulated collective memory as a memory form that emerged from, and received its form, through social action and social contexts, and was thus dependent on socialization and communication. Whilst this position resonates here, my account draws especially on Jan Assmann's notion of "communicative memory" which is concerned with the constitutive "transmissions and transferences" of cultural memory (Assmann 2010). Media, and especially photography and its derivatives, was at the center of this process. Photography was the major form of mediated communicative memory in the age of high empire. Photography accelerated the "primacy of the visual" and constituted one of the "new connectors in temporal perspectives" which has marked memory construction from antiquity on (Ricoeur 2004: 116; see also Ruchatz 2010). These new externalized forms brought new forms of communication and longevity into memory practices, to the extent that the "tools, traces, and the expansion of technical means are a defining characteristic of late-nineteenth century European memory" (Matsuda 1996: 13).

A large proportion of the literature on colonial memory makes some references to the role of the press, photographs, engravings, and so forth, as viewing and consuming sites of memory became multiply experienced. Yet they are often an assumed quality and an assumed presence. Dominik Geppert and Frank Lorenz Müller (2015: 7) have argued, following Pierre Nora, that the idea of *sites* of memory works particularly well in the imperial and colonial context in that there is a concentration on the representation of specific sites, as communicative technologies cohere, consolidate, and concretize those sites and their specificity in the collective and memorializing imagination.

Memorializing practices by the latter part of the nineteenth century comprised a meshwork of topographies and technologies of communication which were both constitutive of, and constituted by, the hyper-visuality of the period. The nineteenth century saw the second great communication revolution, one more extensive and various than anything previously experienced. Indeed the phrase "networked publics," which is used of one-to-many communicative media of twenty-first century sets of social, cultural, and technical developments of the digital age (Ito 2008: 2), can be used productively of the nineteenth century, for communities of memory were "mobilized with and through media" as "reactors, (re)makers and (re)distributors" (Ito 2008:2–3).[2] These concepts from the twenty-first century are not as anachronistic as they might appear at first glance, for communicative media of the period offered accessibility to, and aggregation of, information, and thus multiple practices and communities of memory, on a scale hitherto unprecedented.

There is an extensive debate on the extent and nature of photography's and photographs' impact upon memory and how they confirm, shape, manipulate, or even replace memory. Yet all concur that the advent of photography constituted a sea-change in humankind's relationship with the past and thus with memory practices (see for instance Ricoeur 2004; Le Goff 1992). This rapid development of media technologies, especially visual ones, ensured a much wider consumption than we might assume: not only through the emerging illustrated press, but in displays in shop windows, in exhibitions from the great international exhibition set pieces to local mission displays, through lantern-slide shows in village halls and mission rooms, and at the very end of the period the picture postcard which became a dominant form of image circulation in the early twentieth century (Hoffenberg 2001: 162; MacKenzie 2011: 8; Flint 2000: 3–5). Collectively, these media forms both played on the imagination and created a language of connected public memory within the colonial domain (Hoffenberg 2001: 164).

Given the huge range of possibilities, there is inevitably much that is left out of my account, and that would warrant essays in their own right: sound recording, in the shape of the phonograph that inscribed sound on wax and made them portable (Matsuda 1996: 13); telegraphic technologies, which are profoundly entangled with those of photography, developed the first global information superhighways from the 1850s onwards (Standage 1998; Headrick 1991), and like photographs intervened in the natural rhythms of time and space.[3] Film is also absent from my account, for it only started to make an impact at the very end of our period here. Nor am I addressing museums, although their desire for permanence was represented by a variety of visual communicative forms. The photographs, paintings, and engravings that became part of museum collections and exhibitions, all represent strategies which can be said to have memorializing propensities (Crane 2000b). Indeed, natural history and anthropology museums of the period in particular, with their presentation within the frames of evolutionary theory, might be said to represent the deep history and memory of the human species. However, despite their absence here, the presence of these media forms resonates throughout my account. For as recent scholarship has increasingly stressed, photography was integrally connected, technically, conceptually, and culturally, with other forms of communication and media to form a fluid, intermedial matrix (see for instance, Natale 2012; Belknap 2016, Leonardi and Natale 2018 and more broadly Zierold 2010, Huhtamo and Parikka 2011). Indeed, one can contend that the thirst for, and acceptance of, photographically transmitted information was, at least in part, because of its symbiotic relationship with other technologies of transmission.[4]

I am focusing on communicative public memory in Britain in relation to its growing Empire. Similarly shaped but differently nuanced arguments could be made of other colonial powers, for arguably there is a collective colonial mind-set that translates into memory. There are marked visual and circulation similarities in the shape and articulation of European memory in relation to Empire (MacKenzie 2011; Sinnema 1998;

Marchandiau 1987). In France, *L'Illustration* (1843–1944) and in Germany publications such as *Berliner Illustrite Zeitung* (1891–1945), fulfilled similar roles with similar use of images to those in imperial Britain. In Britain, as elsewhere, collective colonial memory practices are far-reaching and complex, and the boundaries between personal and public memory are blurred as "public" photographs were absorbed into private memory practices (Flint 2000: 5). Private photographs in albums, for instance, become read through the photographic grids of public memory (see for example Blunt 2003). Further, if British, and more broadly by implication European, memory practices in relation to the colonial are constrained by the limits of a single essay, how much more so are those of the colonialized. Nonetheless, it should be marked that this latter aspect has attracted a robust and increasing analysis and literature in recent years and forms a counternarrative here (for instance, Lydon 2005; Chaudray 2012, Bijl 2015).

A word should also be said about archival practices. A detailed discussion of archives as memory forms is beyond the scope of this essay, however their function is at the core of Nora's concern with the "death" of "authentic" memory, which has been taken up by a plethora of commentators. At one level, the dynamics of media indeed constitute the transfer from mind to archival artifact, from recollection to storage, and from individual to collective, in the way that Jacques Le Goff (1992), Nora (1989), and Assmann (2011) have argued; this has been a central plank in memory studies. Many photographs were archived in the formal structures of record-keeping and history-making by governments and learned societies in precisely the structures described by Nora (Pelazzari 2003; Guha-Thakutra 2004; Edwards 2012; Joschke 2013) and in the service of colonial governance (Bennet et al. 2017; Edwards 2014). As Assmann has commented, "as a potential memory or a material precondition for future cultural memories, the archive takes on enormous significance" (2011: 330). However, while they have perhaps assumed a memory function in the intervening years, colonial archiving practices were often concerned with holding or recording knowledge in the contexts of governance in the nineteenth-century present rather than as an anticipated future "memory." Thus while many of the images and objects I discuss are now to be found in archives, this is part of a later structured institutionalization, historiographical engagement, and shifting critical assessment within a specific functional memory of which the archive is part, namely cultural heritage, and of both memory and the colonial itself (Assmann 2011: 330; Stoler 2009).

Thus, while in Britain photography and the public institutions of memory, notably museums and archives, came together to create stable spaces of externalized memory in the contexts I am discussing here, institutional archival power should not be over-weighted. Thus, Nora's implication that communicative technologies disturb traditional practices and spaces of memory do not necessarily appear to hold in this context (1989: 7). Rather, the role of communicative technologies in disseminating the values, practices, and objects of memory reached in many directions, allowing their absorption and even domestication within a huge range of memorializing environments. If the externalization of media accords with Nora's argument, the closing of distance represented by the immediacy of the photographic trace does precisely the reverse (Ruchatz 2010: 387). This is especially marked as networks of communication developed, "breaking down traditional knowledge and hierarchies" in modernity and "their replacement with virtual communities linked by media" (Kaul 2014: 3) in a complex media system (Zierold 2010: 402).

To consider the relationship between this communicative explosion and memory practices in the age of high empire, I focus on two expansive clusters of photographic images and their derivatives through which memory practices were mediated. First, I am going to look at the use of photography and circulation of photographs of the material remains of the past as self-conscious acts of preservation, monumentalizing, and more broadly the search for origins and the moral values which this entails. Second, I examine the circulation of photographs of memorializing acts and practices as they created commemorative landscapes of the colonial: namely flag-raisings and memorials to colonial experience, predominantly in India and in Oceania. Again, these events attracted an imagery that was intended to record and to imprint itself on the collective memory, both celebratory and reflective.

My concern here is less with the iconographical and even symbolic meanings and functions of these images, though this is a field that has received much attention. Nor, although they resonate here, am I concerned here with more abstract questions of power, gaze, spectatorship, and the politics of representation characterized through a largely Foucaultian grain, although it is of course integral to the wider analysis of the consumption of media, including those of memorializing propensity and intention. Rather, I am concerned with a patterning of photographic visualization as the imperial and colonial was increasingly "seen" rather than simply read about (Kaul 2014: 3). This patterning addressed, or becomes absorbed into, memorializing practice of the colonial experience, direct or vicarious. Further within this, the colonial itself was invested with a history and thus the potential for memorializing (Sen 2013: 2). How did images circulate, in what forms, and to what effect, within the memory practices of Empire? Spectatorship, while outwards looking in making things available to the eye (Flint 2000: 8), also facilitated a visual rhetoric and economy internalized within communities of memory. Guégan has called photographs "transmissible sites" of colonial and imperial memory which contribute to an institutionalization and coherence of practices of memorialization (2015: 22). Photographs and their derivatives become essentially portable monuments and memorials (Guégan 2015; Bijl 2015: 40) to the extent that they at least "partially [displace] the public monument" (Goldberg quoted in Ruchartz 2010: 375). At the same time, perhaps we need a note of caution here. As Jennifer Green-Lewis has pointed out, although practices of memorialization expanded and accelerated in the nineteenth century, it would be a mistake necessarily to ascribe memorializing function to all media or with equal intensity. For it "blurs the distinction not only between individual memory and public discourses, but also the specific processes of production, distribution, and reception" (2016: 7). Consequently, I am focusing on images and networks that have a clearly intentional link with the practice of memory and which constituted its tools and traces.

Weaving through my account is a publication entitled *The Queen's Empire* (1897–99), a substantial gathering of photographs for a popular and mass-audience, reproduced in poor-quality half-tone, which appeared in twenty-four fortnightly parts with twenty-four images each. Significantly its subtitle was "a pictorial description and *record* illustrated by photographs" (added emphasis). As MacKenzie has noted, dramatic changes in communications emerged in the last two decades of the nineteenth century, at the heart of which lay technical developments—photography, mass-production, printing, image reproduction, and mass-dissemination, which constitute a matrix of facilitation (1984: 16–23). *The Queen's Empire* draws heavily on such networks of photographic memory objects in ways that become almost emblematic of my account. It gathers together and reproduces, at the very end of the century, all the strands of memory practice that concern me here.

PHOTOGRAPHY AND COMMUNICATIVE TECHNOLOGIES OF EMPIRE

The nineteenth century produced what Erkki Huhtamo has described as modern media culture: "a cultural condition where large number of people live under the constant influence of media . . . a shared state of mind: (2013: 364). Media "reshaped the public sphere" (Hill and Schwartz 2015: 2). Its impact on memory practice has been described as "photomnemonics," that is "the impact of the camera cannot be limited to filling gaps in historical content. On the contrary, the profound technological mutation of the archive necessitates questioning the very concept of history, and exposing the collusion between representation and the time it has long presupposed" (McQuire 1998: 108). Such a culture and society produced "picture-minded people" exposed to images and their technologies on an unprecedented scale (Finnegan 2015: 131–2). There was a "bundling" of media forms (Huhtamo 2013: 364–5)—photograph, print, engraving, press, and, later, film which enabled the past and its commemorative potential to be multiply-experienced. Thus, linking memory practices to communicative media is not only singularly appropriate for the age of empire, but aligns with the call of theorist of history, Wulf Kansteiner, to treat memory studies as an exercise in production, consumption, and reproduction in that "collective memory studies should adopt the methods of communication and media studies" (2002: 179, see also Zierold 2010: 3403).

Communicative technologies were central to the operation and indeed very existence of empire and imperial and colonial endeavor (Headrick 1991: 50). The communicative infrastructures of Empire were both extensive and formative. The enabling technologies of imperial endeavor—railways, post and telegraph offices, shipping, and banking are, in part, technologies and structures of communication that enabled the permeation of an internalized imperialism, having an impact in all sectors of society. Significantly, these technologies were, in themselves, a major focus in the illustrated press (Sinnema 1998: 5). As Jonathan Boyarin puts it "new technologies of transportation and communication . . . have profoundly altered our sense of time and space, the 'reach' of power, and the possibilities of reifying and hence 'preserving' images of the past" (1994: 3).[5] This was related to a burgeoning and expansive print culture, especially in visual material, which increasingly circulated images of imperial actions and far-flung places. Publishing of all sorts was part of the network of influences and communication which "adopted imperial content within their cultural frameworks" (MacKenzie 2011: 2, 4). There was, in effect, a colonization of consciousness as Empire was consumed factually, imaginatively, for serious study, and for entertainment.

Of all communicative technologies the rise of the illustrated press was of particular significance. The printed press produced engravings first from watercolors and drawings and later from photographs. With the advance of electrostatic engraving and then half-tone printing technologies in the last third of the century, photographs themselves were reproduced. The invention of photographic relief block that could be inserted into a page and printed on an ordinary press was a major development. These "electros" were also much harder wearing than earlier woodcuts, contributing to the longevity of images. As a commentator put it in 1852 "a sunbeam paints a picture, and a galvanic current engraves it" (Weedon 2003: 80). These developments in mass-dissemination images, and the effective "domestication" of image technology (Gretton 2015:141), are of incalculable importance as conduits of colonial memory. However, it is important to understand that, until the 1880s when half-tone photographic reproduction become the dominant visual form in circulation, photography complemented and extended, rather than replaced, other media forms.

This expansion of photographic potential stimulated production of the illustrated press in the period to 1890 (MacKenzie 1984: 20). As Geppert and Müller have pointed out, commodities (such as photographs and other representations) acquire "symbolic sway within collective memories and thus as sites of memory" (2015: 4). Translation into engraving or half-tone seared events visually onto the collective imagination, constituting major actants in the formation of communities of memory. Circulating images provided both a focus and stimulus to recall and the reproduction and performance of values which cohered around concepts and actualities of empire.

Simultaneously social changes, notably the expansion of education and, over time, the adult franchise, resulted in an exponential increase in the market for reading material, and especially its visual forms (Weedon 2003: 31). By the third quarter of the nineteenth century that "to read an illustrated paper was also to be exposed to photography" (Belknap 2016: 32.0/659). In Britain, the pages of magazines such as *The Illustrated London News* and *The Graphic*[6] presented a visual narrative of colonial endeavor, and increasingly so through the period as they carried detailed visualizations of colonial wars. Indeed, they provided some of the "most striking imperial and militarist icons of the age" (MacKenzie 1984: 21). The truth claims of images were increasingly vested in the indexical and witnessing truth claims of photography and the visual style of its translations. The designation "from a photograph," found across the nineteenth-century communicative media, indicated an authoritative statement predicated on authentic practices of translation (Belknap 2016; Sinnema 1998: 21–2). *The Graphic* in particular drew its illustrations from photographs, and they were "utilized both within a discursive and visual framework that situates it as a representative example of the epistemological assertion of photographic trust" (Belknap 2016: 72). Photography and the idea of photography thus stood for a truthfulness to the physical world. This is not to argue that nineteenth-century readers had a naïvely realist view of photography; nonetheless photography and its derivative forms were embedded in discourses of translation that lent images a sense of authenticity and legitimacy.

Importantly these illustrated journals were seen, and saw themselves, as forms of memory objects, magazines of record (Gretton 2015: 142). An editorial in *The Graphic* in 1871 stated: "Our aim has been to produce a weekly paper which should not be merely of temporal interest, but should be worthy of being preserved as a constant source not only of entertainment, as a faithful literary of and pictorial representation of the times" (cited in Belknap 2016: 74.2) while the preface to the first issue stated: "it does not merely look forward, it also looks back, it treats alike the past and the future" indeed the journal itself was to be "worthy of preservation as an artistic record of the times in which we live."[7] Thus, the journal saw itself as fulfilling its readers' need for a tool of preservation and a sense of permanency. That is, its weekly record and visual narrative were perceived as having, and anticipating, a memory function.

These magazines had massive circulations, especially when one considers the readership multipliers in free public libraries for instance, which often subscribed to such journals.[8] For example, it is recorded that at Birmingham City Library, boys "of the poorer class" filled the library, sitting on the floor, devouring the images in *The Graphic* while old copies of the journal were sent to hospitals for the entertainment of patients.[9] The combined actions of representation, preservation, and circulation extended the potential of collective memories and extended their saturating propensities.

The intended readership of *The Graphic*, in particular, was very similar to that of *The Queen's Empire* (also a stalwart of public libraries). The latter publication, produced by the popular publisher Cassell to mark the Golden Jubilee of Queen Victoria in 1897, constitutes both a memory of Empire and a memorial of, and to, Queen Victoria herself. Much of its focus was on the current state of Empire and connections to "home" within a discourse of sameness and difference which was framed by paternalistic applications of racial and cultural hierarchy. As noted, it had clearly articulated memorializing functions. In the introduction to the series, which appeared in the first issue in 1897, MP and educator H.O. Arnold-Forster noted the publication's place in both "the common bonds of Empire" and an equal sense of "the Old Country," linking colonial and domestic memory. The work of photographic reproduction and communication, and its technological proficiency in relation to modernity, is made central to its *raison d'être*: "The pictures in this work are all authentic representations of the realities of life and scenery, of men and manners, of the works of man and the wonders of Nature throughout the Empire. Every picture is photographic reproduction, executed with a perfection which has only become possible in very recent years" (Arnold-Forster 1897: x). The work was structured around different experiences, and thus potential memory, of Empire, and it is this that "endow[s] these pictures with their fullest value and their highest use . . . every one has a lesson and meaning which could be impressed upon it by no other means" (Arnold-Forster 1897: xi). The series also functions as an anticipated memory of the glories and munificence of Queen Victoria herself "where ever the book may go within the Empire, by whatever eyes it might be scanned" (Arnold-Forster 1897: xii). Further, in a juxtaposition which cannot be ironic, each issue contained extensive visualized advertising for Mellin's infant foods, which claimed to produce sturdy generations, and presumably the future viewers of the series' anticipated memories and carriers of Empire.

The photographs themselves followed the major patterns of colonial circulation, similar to those constituting the memorializing clusters considered here. The photographers in the publication, such as Bourne and Shepherd in India, G.R. Lambert and Company of Singapore, W. Notman and Company of Canada, and B.W. Caney of Durban, represent the commercial sources of photographs which flowed through the colonial world and constituted the anticipated memory of the Victorian age that this Jubilee-focused publication implied. Indeed, *The Queen's Empire*, especially the first part, illustrating "The Government of Empire" is full of flag-raisings, unveilings, and statues, stressing the significance of these markers of remembrance across the popular domain and the shape of popular colonial memory. Significantly, in our contexts here, a whole part was devoted to technologies of communication "Her Majesty's Mails and Telegraphs." This is the only section of the series to include a fold-out map, and it shows the commercial routes of the world and ocean currents that formed the connective tissue and thus memorializing networks of Empire. It included half-tone photographs of the submarine cable despatching room of the Central Telegraph Office and the "whisperings of the electric transmitter" are spread across the globe. What is stressed, photographically and textually, is speed, technological wonder, connectivity and scale: "the slender single wire which dips down into the little window of the hut will in a few minutes . . . put the busy city of London into close and confidential communication with this tiny Indian hamlet."[10]

Colonial endeavor and thus colonial remembrance were integrated into these systems of knowledge and its dissemination, as images were transmitted through the massive, colonial postal network of communication: tucked into letters, packaged up and sent by photographers and their agents, and later as postcards. These processes and practices of narrative had both effect and affect: they established topographies of colonial memory which were focused through expansively mechanized forms through which memorializing potential saturated everyday consciousness.

FIGURE 3.1: "A Post Office in an Indian Tea District." *The Queen's Empire*, Vol. 2 (pt. 13), 3. 1897–9. © Bodleian Library, Oxford.

MONUMENTS AND ORIGINS

Nineteenth-century memory practices were embedded in material forms which were reproduced and disseminated in the ways that I have just outlined for photographic technologies. These were both explicit and implicit, spread across both the descriptive and signifying potential of images. One of the most explicit sites of memory work was in the growing discourse of the preservation of ancient material remains, linked to both the romantic imagination and the rise of scientific archaeology and history. Preservation of these antiquities as "monuments" of national memory gathered pace through the nineteenth century, and colonial authorities and British and European preservationists eyed the international field of historical decay with both paternalistic and appropriative zeal (Swenson 2013: 5; Hall 2011). Significantly, this pattern is not only British, it can be found with the Dutch in Indonesia, the French empire in Southeast Asia or the Russians and Germans in Central Asian empire where cultural and political cultures of memory converged.

While the extant literature on monuments seldom addresses questions of memory practice directly, nor the role of media technologies beyond their facility for mimetic recording, a sense of the past and an engagement and collective internalization runs beneath the surface of their account.[11] The material manifestations of collective memory, constructed as "the 'monument' became a central point of reference in the process of constructing a history by inventing a collective past around it" (Sen 2013: 14). Monumental "heritage" became a marker of benevolent governance both at home and abroad. It was also embedded in the production of national and nationalist memory and, conversely, contributed to a sense of a universal and evolutionary history of humanity (Swenson 2013; Sen 2013). However, the material remains of past civilizations and empires (such as the Mughal Empire in India) also served as reminder for the memory of past epochs and the fragility of political formations and the need for effective and strong rule. Thus, the growing, and increasingly institutionalized, discourses of preservation addressed not only the material preservation of the material remains of the past but invested them as temporal metaphors of memory.

The circulation of images of colonial monuments performed the memory potential of these monuments. Photography was not only central to the preservationist agenda, as a recording tool facilitating an increasingly *in situ* preservation, but also as a circulatory tool. It reproduced the moral values and cultural memory for which monuments were made to stand. Shifting visual practices, focused on photography, shifted the aesthetic and picturesque to the sense of scientific monument in which "the 'colony' needed to be assigned a history which would service the Empire. It is in this light that one can map the shift from exotic 'ruin' to knowable 'monument'" (Sen 2013: 11). Increasingly systematized photography marked colonial material and it was integrated into the record and thus preservation practices of colonial governments. For instance, the work of the Archaeological Survey of India absorbed the photographs of Bourne and Shepherd and many others, and increasingly produced its own (see Guha-Takhurta 2004; Guha 2010). Thus "the 'monument' became a central point of reference in the process of constructing a history by inventing a collective past around it" (Sen 2013: 14) and the visual became the major communicative form.

Within this, photographs and their derivatives formed the transmissible link between fixed, cultural sites of monuments and their memorializing potential (Guégan 2015: 27). If preservationist discourses privileged certain bodies of expertise (the emergent scientific archaeologist) to extract history and memorializing potential from these monuments (Guha-Thakurta 2004: 4), so these values were transmitted to the larger population (of both colonized and colonizer) through the circulation of media. A huge volume of photographs, official through government auspices and quasi-official as commercially transmissible objects, translated "fixed" monuments into spaces of a dispersed and memorializing imagination. The illustrated press increasingly carried accounts of archaeological discoveries; for instance *The Graphic* of January 10, 1884, offered a full-page montage of finds and views from excavations of classical antiquity in colonial Cyprus.

The massive output of commercial photographers such as Bourne and Shepherd in India circulated the intersection of a pre-colonial past, a colonial past and individual memory through the wide range of images available. Their catalogues are instructive on this point, offering a huge range of Indian monuments for public consumption. Their photographs were available not only in India but also through their agents Marion & Co. in London, and this was the pattern for many major colonial photographers. At the same time, general media circulation in journals and newspapers, shop windows and photography dealers, opened photographs to wider discourses of consumption and memory.

While less explicit and tangible, such monuments also became markers of racial and cultural memory within a colonial context. Read in conjunction with photographs of colonialized peoples themselves, they assumed a defining position in the idea of European civilization and "most ostensibly formed imperialist ideas about peoples with and without history" (Swenson 2013: 8). Photographs of "monuments" represented assumed evolutionary stages of culture and "civilization" and thus the hierarchies on which colonial

FIGURE 3.2: Ruins at Pollonanaru, Ceylon (Sri Lanka). Photographer: James Lawton. © Victoria and Albert Museum, London.

domination was premised. The past of peoples and places suggested the deep origin narratives of the human race and thus memory. Within the dominant patterns of evolutionary thinking that informed the colonial, recapitulation theory, formulated in the emergent biological sciences, posited that an organism passed through its successive historical developmental stages on the way to maturity, that is, it held biological memory within its own development. Applied to cultures within an evolutionary context it postulated that "lower types" represented past forms of "higher types" (Lightman and Zon 2014: 3). It implied the biological memory of human development as the former became the "race memory" of the latter. The past of the colonialized came to stand for the memory of humankind and intensified Europe's own memory of itself. This spawned a mass of visual representations in the press, from graphs and photographs to cartoons, but it also positioned the material remains of the past in a similar trajectory. Likewise it cohered assumed race memory within settler colonialisms: "The feelings thus kindled help to keep alive throughout the Empire the sense of the unity of stock" (Baldwin Brown 1905: 4), indeed heritage at home was seen as an imperial issue, "imperial assets" in the coherence of the mother-country. This had many manifestations as photographs and their derivatives mediated between material remains and imagined pasts. For instance, and particularly pertinent given the centrality of Christian belief in nineteenth-century Euro-America, was the use of photographs to reconstruct and reimagine a biblical past. Widely circulated and reproduced, such images constituted what Nassar (2006) has called a "biblification of the Near East" enabled through its colonial entanglements. In illustrated travel books, religious texts, and even Bibles, nineteenth-century Palestine was presented visually as a space of biblical and thus cultural memory of the Christian West.

Above all, however problematic, photographs and their derivatives gave solidity and the possibility of empirical belief to both abstract theories of human development, and the possibility that they might show part of that process through their capturing of the random inclusiveness out of which development might emerge. The flow of images across porous boundaries can be understood as the search for photographic confirmation and efficacy across a wide range of addresses to the question of origin, history, and memory. In this, photographs offered credible visual engagement with a complex and shifting world made up of complex and overlapping audiences. Thus *The Illustrated London News* for instance, juxtaposed on one page engravings of the ancient town hall at Leominster, Herefordshire, a "ducking stool" and "ancient chalice" preserved in the church there, a memorial cross at Kanpur, India and a memorial to the Crimean War, while *The Graphic* in 1884 juxtaposed extensive coverage of the "Soudan Rebellion" with an illustrated history of the City of London.[12]

All these strands, which coalesce around the multiple manifestations of material remains of the past, can be read as forming a matrix of memory possibilities within wider communities of memory. As I have suggested, memory emerges from a more generalized sense of the past that is not merely contained in official accumulations, but in the vast circulation and historical work of media operating at multiple levels within the broader practices of memory work.

COLONIAL MEMORIALS AND THE TOPOGRAPHIES OF COLONIAL ACTION

I now turn to the role of photography and its derivatives in tracing the political topography of colonial action and forging memorializing engagements across global networks. Nora has argued that history attaches itself to events while memory attaches itself to places (1989: 22). However, the representation of events actively interrupts transitional moments and turns them, materially, into memorializing sites. Thus photographs, integrally entangled with other communicative forms, notably the press, translate events into sites of memory and of the colonization of consciousness I noted earlier. While these images were collected and archived in state libraries and the like, their more powerful engagement was at a dispersed popular level in multiple photographic formats such as stereo-cards, album scraps or postcards, pages of illustrated press, guidebooks, travel and adventure writing, and international exhibition halls, as "news" became integral to popular culture as it moved through the communication networks of the colonial world (Hill and Schwartz 2015: 3).

Images of colonial annexation and settlement had both topicality and longevity, fixing places and actions in the public imagination. If material monuments, curios, and peoples themselves functioned, as outlined above, as markers of colonial memory, so too did the flag-raisings, statues, and commemorative landscapes which marked out colonial expansion and laid out the spaces in which memory was active. They provided a series of tropes through which commemorative and memorializing attention could be focused.

Flag-raising played a multi-faceted part in establishing topographies of colonial memory. They marked sites of action to be commemorated. An example is the dissemination of the iconography of the annexation of New Guinea by the British in 1883–4.[13] *The Illustrated London News* ran a triumphalist cover engraving of the initial event in 1883.[14]

FIGURE 3.3: Raising the Flag. New Guinea. Front cover of *Illustrated London News*. July 7, 1884. © Getty Images.

FIGURE 3.4: "Hoisting the Flag at Port Moresby." *Narrative of the expedition of the Australian squadron to New Guinea.* 1885. Plate 10. © Bodleian Library, Oxford.

This was followed by "official photographs" of 1884 events. These were published a year later as a sumptuous volume of thirty-five large prints plus two panoramas, the latter providing an inclusive visualization of colonial action.[15]

These luxurious albums were sent as gifts to Queen Victoria, government departments and state libraries, and thus entered state memory. However, the photographs, and others taken at the same time, circulated as engravings and photo-mechanical reproductions, and were displayed at international exhibitions such as Melbourne in 1888 (Holden 1988: 24). While the annexation itself was protracted and spawned a number of overlapping visualizations, what is significant is the way in which it connected events to the visual rhetoric of flag-raising, whether as moments of colonial swagger, such as *The Illustrated London News* cover, or through the pomp of ceremony such as the image of the flag-raising engraved "from a photograph" and published on the cover of *The Graphic* in January 1885.[16]

These images had widespread circulation both as specific reports of an event but also as a generic discourse of sites of colonial memory. Articulated over space and time, these images accumulated long histories of use and consumption as memory objects. Their projections and performances solidified that status. For example, the "annexation" photographs were used as the basis of engravings illustrating a popular missionary tales over several editions, such as *Pioneering in New Guinea* (1887), by the celebrated Reverend Chalmers of the London Missionary Society. Similarly, Charles Lyne's *New*

FIGURE 3.5: Raising the Flag. New Guinea. Front cover, *The Graphic*, January 24, 1885. © Bodleian Library, Oxford.

Guinea: an account of the establishment of the British Protectorate over the Southern Shores of New Guinea (1885) uses both the half-tone photographic frontispiece and illustrations. Both volumes, like the illustrated press, remediated the official photographs. Lyne's book is interesting, not only because of the flag-raising and related scenes are reproduced in half-tone, but, as "special commissioner" for the *Sydney Morning Herald*, he connects ideas of record and evidence within the beneficial narratives of the mission and the *Pax Britannica*, to future memorialization and to the work of the press. The tentacles of this memorializing imagery of colonial expansion move through multiple spaces of consumption as a form of communicative memory.

Significantly, and again demonstrating the longevity of these photographs, three "annexation" of New Guinea images were reproduced in half-tone in *The Queen's Empire*, nearly fifteen years after the event: two in relation to the colonial service of the Royal Navy, the third in the issue "Homes of the Empire," absorbed into that "record" that I noted earlier.

Importantly, the circulation of photographs and engravings of colonial topographies were not intended merely as retrospective but anticipated memory as "an opportunity to illustrate their achievements" to their successors within a landscape of future memorializing requirements (MacKenzie 1984: 19). They created memory by stamping their own mark on that anticipated future. This is not necessarily in any overt or self-conscious way, but a sense of the history that is culturally imbedded and a sense of what it might become.

FIGURE 3.6: Raising the Flag, Port Moresby, New Guinea. *The Queen's Empire*, Vol. 1 (pt. 1), 20. 1897–9. © Bodleian Library, Oxford.

While the extended iconography of flag-raising is complex, my concern here is the way in which flag-raisings and then monuments to mark the colonial become important memorializing strategies, absorbed into the everyday imaginings of colonial presents fast becoming colonial pasts—and as we saw in the previous section, integrated into broader translations of the past. Readers and viewers perhaps did not recollect the specifics of an

FIGURE 3.7: Statue of Captain Cook, Hyde Park, Sydney, Australia. *Illustrated London News*, August 10, 1878, 133. © Bodleian Library, Oxford.

event, but the repeated iconography—the flag is raised, amidst cheering, whilst the local population look on passively—linked to triumphalist narratives and shaped the consciousness of empire. Similar forms and patterns of transmissible commemoration can be found elsewhere, as communicative media marked colonial acquisition and settlement by creating a topography of colonial historical consciousness and memory. For instance, Kerry's studio in Sydney circulated photographs of Captain Cook's statue in Sydney, a monument that had been engraved for the *Illustrated London News* in 1878.[17]

They had also published wood engravings of the site of Cook's death, in the Hawaiian islands, in 1779.[18] More generally, photographs of places of first contact, settlement and their memorial markers became stalwarts of commercial photographic production in a global dissemination. Such images were, again, also displayed at exhibitions. Technical and industrial displays of the colonies were saturated with photographs showing raw material, engineering, and so forth; these same photos promulgated a narrative which legitimated colonial exploitation in the name of industrial modernity. As these topographies of colonial memory simultaneously wove through exhibitions, official presentations, tales of adventure, missionary accounts, and travel books, the patterns of photographic production and consumption represented an internalized imperialism and its community of memory (Hoffenberg 2001).

India was at the center of British colonial communications development, extending through cartography, tabulated and visualized information, photography, and telegraph. Thus it is no coincidence that one of the most active and archetypal sites of photography and colonial-memory making and multiple circulation formed around sites of the 1857 "Indian Mutiny."[19] Within this plethora of communicative media was the photographic circulation of the marble angel monument to the massacre of women and children at Kanpur (Cawnpore) in 1857, the most iconic site of colonial remembrance and memorialization through the latter part of the nineteenth century (Heathorn 2007: 1; Chaudhary 2012: 12–15, 68–9). This monument, erected to remember those who died in

FIGURE 3.8: Stereocard by James Ricalton, for Underwood and Underwood, of the memorial at the Cawnpore [Kanpur] massacre site, India. *c.* 1900. © Pitt Rivers Museum, PRM 1998.472.61.

what was perceived as the major atrocity of the "Mutiny,"[20] was circulated as a memory object well into the twentieth century, through multiple "transmissible" forms—engravings, stereo-cards, and photographic prints. Media forms constructed and sustained its collective power to the extent that many albums of British families with Raj connections contained photographs of this site and its memorial.

The media circulation of explicit memorialization was enormous and wide-reaching. The designs for the memorial were published in industry-specific magazines such as *The Builder*,[21] and by the late 1860s Bourne and Shepherd were offering eight photographs of the site in five different formats sized to suit all pocketbooks and uses, and which could be purchased in London as well as across India.[22] It is also the basis of an engraving in *Illustrated London News,* spread across the full page, with two supplementary images.[23] If it is one of Bourne's most widely disseminated photographs, it was also one widely emulated by other photographers, for instance James Ricalton's stereo view of 1889 published in the mass-market stereo-set by Underwood & Underwood in 1903,[24] while by the late nineteenth century voluminous numbers of postcards were in circulation. Indeed, six photographs of "mutiny" sites including Bourne photographs, were reproduced as half-tones in the *Illustrated London News* to mark the fiftieth anniversary as if, redolent with longevity, "just discovered in an old dispatch box."[25] One could continue to pile up examples for Kanpur and other sites of "Mutiny" memorialization, notably in Lucknow. What is clear is a density of visual images forming a matrix of circulating representations which both created and stabilized meaning within a community of memory. The topographies of violence which made up the British remembrance of the 1857 "Mutiny," became itineraries of memorializing pilgrimage experienced both in person, including visiting dignitaries, and through the visual narratives which were constructed and reconstructed over multiple but integrated media, to the extent that even "serious nineteenth-century general histories of India that did not dwell on the massacres at Cawnpore nevertheless contained illustrations or photos of the memorial well" (Heathorn 2007: 5).[26]

Sites of the "Mutiny" became the archetypical sites of colonial and imperial memory, imagined landscapes of memory as familiar to British audiences as those of Waterloo or Trafalgar (Gutpa 2003: 225). These photographic outputs and their derivatives in the press mark colonial action and recollection through images of statues, plaques, and sites of proclamations as markers of the past and its imperial glories. They also translated sites of colonial action into sites of colonial memorialization, framed by loss and nostalgia (Chaudhary 2012: 21). Whilst there was an unevenness in emotional and moral stakes, these topographies of colonial imagination were shaped through the same processes and mechanisms in their political performance and visual insistence. Not all colonial action or event had this longevity or commemorative impact, however; it appears that photographs of battles' aftermaths, and their related press dissemination, acted as "spot pictures" specific to the time/space relations of the event (Harris 1999: 36). Self-conscious practices of memorialization, clustered around structures of memorability (such as Kanpur), that accrue longevity and are absorbed into the practices of collective memory across generations through patterns of reproduction and consumption.

Again, their popular manifestations are found in the memorializing narratives of *The Queen's Empire*. In the second final part of the series "Places of Historical Interest in the Queen's Empire" (vol. 2. pt. 23), two Bourne and Shepherd photographs of sites of the "Mutiny" (the Residency at Lucknow and the Cashmere Gate, Delhi), and two

FIGURE 3.9: Engraving from a photograph of the memorial at the Cawnpore (Kanpur) massacre site, India. *Illustrated London News*, October 31, 1874, 421. © Bodleian Library, Oxford.

FIGURE 3.10: Embossed colored postcard of the memorial at the Cawnpore (Kanpur) massacre site. *c.* 1905. Author's collection.

photographs of the Massacre Ghat and the memorial at Kanpur both appear on p. 262 opposite an image of the ruins of the siege of Lucknow.

The memory of the "Indian Mutiny" becomes almost the closing act of the serial publication of *The Queen's Empire*. They are followed only by the Proclamation Tree, South Australia, which relates to the memorializing strategies around annexation and settlement as we have seen, and the final image of the series, the site of the Black Hole of Calcutta.[27] It coheres the colonial narratives of the series into one of collective remembrance: Bosworth Field, the tomb of Lord Nelson and the playing fields of Eton, metaphors for a specific form of patriotic Englishness, are juxtaposed with sites of colonial memories: the Battle of Rorke's Drift, a key engagement on the Anglo-Zulu war in 1879,[28] and the sites of Australian acquisition and the "Indian Mutiny."

CONCLUSION

The kinds of accumulations and circulations I have described, and they are the tip of the iceberg, constitute a nineteenth-century mass-media-cultural imaginary, "a state of being, where media have come to dominate minds to such an extent that they have replaced other reference points" (Huhtamo 2013: 365). The circulation of these memorializing images raises the question as to the nature and extent of that community of memory. While the circulation of media created a sense of common purpose and belonging, at the same time it was subject to shifting densities and foci of meaning over time. Memory is never static. While the consumption of photographs in albums and the like was restricted to those who could afford them and belonged to the realm of private, colonial albums of

FIGURE 3.11: Sites of colonial memory. The Proclamation Tree, South Australia and the site of the "Black Hole of Calcutta," India. 1899. *The Queen's Empire*, Vol. 2 (pt. 23), p. 264. © Bodleian Library, Oxford.

the period invariably contain these transmissible objects which connected to much wider communities of memory. The spatial range of empire and its demands on the practices of memory were well served by both the spatial reach and longevity of communicative technologies of the nineteenth century and their infrastructures.

Collectively, this massive circulation created a naturalized and indeed naturalizing "picture- mindedness," a habit of mind which impressed on the structures of memory and memorialization. The advent of visual mass-media and the reality claims of photographs and their derivatives, formed a Kuhnian moment in those memory practices from which there was, and remains, no return. As the historian Jacques Le Goff put it, photography "revolutionizes memory: it multiplies and democratizes it, gives it a precision and a truth never before attained in visual memory, and makes it possible to preserve the memory of time and of chronological evolution" (1992: 99). The force of this is felt in the "plenitude of metaphors, both contemporary and in later commentaries, which construe media and memory and vice versa" (Ruchatz 2010: 367). Collectively, these media forms both shaped the imagination and created a visual language of a connected public memory as they infiltrated and intersected the memorializing practices of the wider community. Its attendant notion of self-hood to be memorialized is profound, in both private and public spheres. The importance of communicative mass-media, photography, and photographic derivatives in the construction of colonial memory cannot be over-estimated. And it is for this reason that the media of memory "provide the most important metaphors and models for memory" (Assmann 2011: 137).

CODA: POST-COLONIAL MEMORY AND NINETEENTH CENTURY PHOTOGRAPHY

Writing of twenty-first century memory, Assmann and Conrad state: "the most obvious and basic paths along which memories move, cross-boundaries and extending to a global level, are the satellites of telecommunication, the channels of mass-media, and the internet." (2010: 3–4). To some extent it has ever been thus, at least in the nineteenth century with the domination of technologies of communication. What has shifted is scale, speed, location, facility and new forms of longevity.

Significantly, colonial memory technologies have been brought back into political play in contemporary cultures of memory with very different meanings for very different communities of memory. As Geppert and Müller argue there is a "lasting emotive capacity of memory sites created under imperial conditions" (2015: 4). Colonial memory is still active, and the traces of nineteenth-century memory practices are reinvigorated in new contexts, as nineteenth-century mechanical memory is translated into twenty-first-century digital memory. Again, the circulation of photographic and quasi-photographic images is at its center. Images that circulated to make colonial memory in the age of high empire are being absorbed in current imaging practices of identity and modernity which constitute simultaneously a "complex translational zone" which forms "a critique of colonial paradigms" and by implication their memorializing practices (Pinney 2003: 266). The memory functions of these images are not restricted to the structured time of their archiving but to the unstructured, everyday lived experience, addressing a colonial past. Memories and memory forms change as they transcend their original forms and habitats, moving into the growing interconnectedness of "memory worlds" and their "intervisuality" (Assmann and Conrad 2010: 6). It is no coincidence that memory practices related to colonial imagery and memory are the focus of the work of many contemporary artists of Indigenous heritage from, for instance, Australia, South Africa or Canada.[29] The potency of colonial memorializing practices is seen increasingly in the contestation of that topography of colonial memory that photographs contributed to so forcefully (Stanard 2011). While the social and cultural contexts might have shifted, the longevity of memory function remains, reformulated in the digital archive and the flows of social media. As Nora has famously argued sites of memory, "only exist because of their capacity for metamorphosis, an endless recycling of their meaning and an unpredictable proliferation of their ramifications" (1989: 19). The flow of photographs and their derivatives remain active in precisely this way.

CHAPTER FOUR

Knowledge: Science and Education

THOMAS DODMAN

In December 1903, Henri Bergson began his fourth cycle of lectures at the Collège de France on the topic of the "History of theories of memory." The French philosopher was already drawing capacity crowds the previous year for his course on notions of time. His *magnum opus*, *Matter and Memory*, had been published only seven years earlier, prompting the American psychologist William James to herald a Copernican revolution comparable to those initiated by Berkeley's *Principles of Human Knowledge* and Kant's *Critique of Pure Reason*. Clearly, memory was in the air and Bergson the person to talk about it. Yet when he broached the topic from his prestigious Chair of Ancient Philosophy at the Collège it was neither Antiquity nor philosophy that he first turned to, but rather psychology. "What is the analysis of memory?" he asked, but the "sum of findings provided by psychology." Bergson readily conceded that psychologists were still in the dark about much of the brain's functioning and that they continued to rely on time-tested metaphors like their predecessors. He himself tellingly compared the workings of memory to a string light web of flickering Edison bulbs (recently commercialized and a technological wonder of his day). Still, he felt that psychologists had at least identified four key moments central to the "scientific study" of memory: the formation of a cerebral mechanism; a "short circuit" causing a reminiscence; the association of memories; and their localization in the past. It was only once these empirical findings were fully accepted, Bergson continued, that one might also identify a role for "intuition," and thus philosophy, in the understanding of memory (his personal contribution to the field). As for ancient ideas about the topic—the very subject of the course, after all—they would have to wait fourteen lectures until mid-April before receiving a cursory historical overview (Bergson 2018: 29). By Bergson's own admission, then, it seemed as if at the dawn of the twentieth century the professional study of memory had—in Europe at least—been handed over to psychologists, entering a new and ostensibly "scientific" age.

While this may seem unsurprising to us today, there was something quite radical about it at the time. Until a few decades earlier, memory had by and large been thought of as an "art" rather than a "science." Ever since antiquity, European rhetoricians and religious scholars had devised increasingly ingenious mnemonic techniques and devices designed to improve people's recall capacities. By the Middle Ages and Renaissance, these had blossomed into elaborate memory theaters and systems for an architectural mnemonic (or spatialized ordering of experiences). The classical *ars memorativa* didn't lay claim to any new knowledge about memory and instead continued to draw from Platonic and

Aristotelian ideas about inscribed mnemonic traces and images. As Frances Yates (1966) has shown in her classic study of the topic, it eventually morphed from a disciplined exercise of memorization into an occult art open to the workings of the imagination and compatible with the rational outlook of the scientific revolution. To Enlightenment *philosophes*, memory came to be a relatively straightforward, dependable mental faculty central to the formation of the rational subject. Per Paul Ricoeur (2004: 79), the modern "equating of identity, self, and memory" was the work of John Locke. The British philosopher took static Renaissance metaphors of mnemonic storehouses and made them dynamic by accounting for processes of memorializing and forgetting. Memories, according to Locke, were emotional, at once associative and entropic, and as such played a critical role in our very sense of self. For his Scottish colleague David Hume, this was a rather fragmented self, due to the mind's tendency to blur memory and the more fanciful mental operations of imagination, resulting in dangerous flights of fancy. Disentangling these two faculties became the goal of the Abbé de Condillac and of the sensationalist psychology that came to dominate the late Enlightenment, spurring French revolutionaries into ambitious social and pedagogical programs to tame wayward imaginations (Goldstein 2005: 21–100). By the turn of the century, then, memory was both viewed as a precious bulwark of psychic and social stability, and believed to be in "crisis" as the disruptions of the revolutionary epoch tore past and present apart, causing a widespread sense of loss (Terdiman 1993). One outcome of this was the romantic turn to introspection and a broader "autobiographical impulse"; another was the development of self-professedly "scientific" explorations of memory. With the appearance of the first experimental studies in the 1880s, it became possible to think of preceding millennia as one long "dark age" in the history of memory (Tulving 1983; Berrios 1996: 211).

But the nineteenth-century science of memory was in fact *many sciences*, a fluid field of competing and overlapping claims to deep knowledge entangled with logics of power. Ian Hacking (1995) has influentially spoken of a "memoro-politics" to describe how nineteenth-century sciences of memory mobilized expert knowledge to wield a new form of power over the subject (replacing what had previously been moral discourses about the soul). This article surveys these competing truth claims and political practices that made "memory" into what Mieke Bal has aptly called a "travelling concept," that is one that takes on different meanings in different contexts.[1] My focus over the following pages is very much on the European and North American scientific community, particularly in its late nineteenth-century flourishing. However, I situate this North Atlantic focus within a global—and specifically imperial—setting, and treat these scientists' findings not in isolation, but rather in relation to broader historical phenomena. The sciences of memory came into being as they did in response to a set of pressing concerns characteristic of their time and that included, among other things, a new relation of individual to group and to historical time; new dynamics of mass politics and education; and new and intertwined logics of nation-building and empire-grabbing. It is within this context that scientists "discovered" new things about the workings of memory, whether they focused on "locating" memory or on "measuring" it, and whether they sought ways to deflect "involuntary" memories or coax very deliberate ones into pedagogical projects.

LOCATING MEMORY

Largely forgotten today, it is hard to imagine just how popular theories of bodily and organic memory were for much of the nineteenth century. There was, for a start, something radical about them and about their brazen materialism in particular. In the early 1800s, learned discussions about memory were generally framed either by associationist or eclectic mixes of philosophical psychology. In Britain, sense perceptions and the association of ideas continued to dominate the intellectual scene. Elsewhere in Europe, speculative philosophy was on the ascendancy, postulating a more active model of the mind, including memory, for an *à priori* notion of the self (as in Victor Cousin's influential formulation in France) (Goldstein 2005). Both held onto a fundamentally psychological understanding of memory that rejected materialism as crude (and, furthermore, dangerous due to its perceived revolutionary political implications). Nonetheless, heretical views also emerged at the time, buoyed by a revival of interest for physiognomy and the heated debates over slavery and racial differences that went hand in hand with renewed imperial expansion in the early 1800s (Staum 2003). These opened up a conceptual space, as it were, for attempts to locate memory in the body; by the end of the century, they would have themselves become the new common sense.

When the Austrian physician Franz Joseph Gall introduced his "organology," or cerebral localization of mental faculties, to Parisian audiences in 1807, he caused a sensation. Gall and his associate Johann Gaspar Spurzheim brushed aside professional scorn and took their method for "reading" skulls—rebaptized "phrenology"—around Europe, soon building a considerable following and a slew of phrenological societies in the 1830s and 1840s. Phrenologists disagreed about where exactly to locate memory on the skull and whether it didn't actually implicate multiple cranial zones. Gall, for one, leaned towards parsing out six distinct faculties of memory: for facts, places, numbers, words, names, and people. Phrenology's great promoter in the anglophone world, George Combe, suggested that memory be viewed as a "mode of activity" of all mental faculties (rather than one itself)—in other words, the ability that each faculty had to recall examples and actions for whatever it was tasked with (Combe 1830: 515–22). Mid-century popularizations tended to identify one organ of memory, prominently located at the center of the forehead (although they continued to also identify an organ of "inhabitiveness," or attachment to one's home, at the back of the skull).

Phrenology never achieved the institutionalization it sought and remained tainted with quackery in spite (or perhaps because) of its popular following. Nonetheless, the push to localize mental functions such as memory outlived Gall's followers and found unexpected allies elsewhere. In 1824, the French physician Jean-Baptiste Bouillard advanced the radical idea that human brains were lateralized into two, unequal hemispheres. He drew from earlier speculative research on aphasia (or language impairment due to brain damage) that was in turn spectacularly confirmed in the 1860s when the French physician and anthropologist Paul Broca presented the results of a dozen autopsies performed on the brains of patients suffering from speech impairments (including the famous "Monsieur Tan," who had lost the ability to speak but not to reason or produce sounds). From his pulpit at the *Société d'Anthropologie de Paris*, Broca marshalled evidence to prove the existence of a neurological site responsible for expressive aphasia and situated it in the frontal lobe of the left cerebral hemisphere (known, since then, as "Broca's area"). His findings spurred a wave of further research into brain localization, leading the German physician Karl Wernicke to associate receptive aphasia (or impairment in language comprehension) to damage in the posterior regions of the left temporal lobe.[2] But the quest to track discrete "engrams" (or neural memory traces) in the brain proved largely elusive and was shelved in the early twentieth century by the American psychologist Karl Laschley. Instead, Laschley pointed to the kind of diffuse model of memory circuits

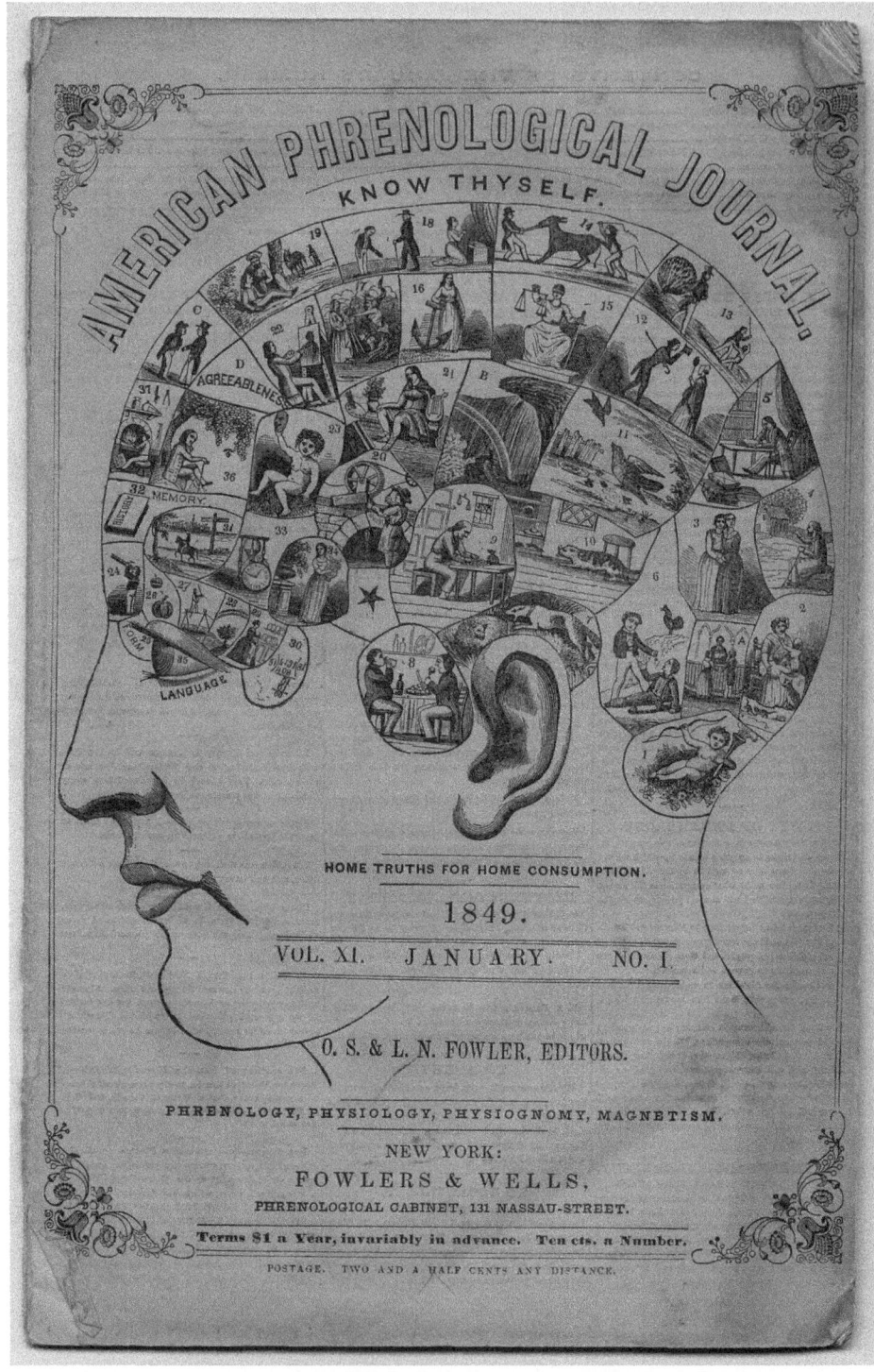

FIGURE 4.1: *American Phrenological Journal* 11:1 (January 1849), front cover. Note the location of "memory" as a discrete mental faculty in the forehead (#32). Faculty #4 at the back is "inhibitivness", or attachment to home and memories of childhood. Courtesy of the Amherst College Libraries and Special Collections.

implicating multiple parts of the brain that neurologists and neuroscientists continue to operate with today (without having entirely given up on the quest to "capture" images of memory traces).[3]

For many others at the time, it was not the brain that harbored the elusive seat of memory, but the body itself. In 1870, the German physiologist Ewald Hering (best known for his work on optical illusions) delivered a paper on memory as a fundamental reproductive property of all living matter that took the international scientific community—and wider public—by storm.[4] Hering argued that memory had to be viewed as both a conscious (psychological) and unconscious (physiological) process that had its origins in the nervous systems of living organisms. Memory was a "material trace" that became habit over time and, in the long run, furnished a species' instinct. Just like a muscle, it was acquired, trained, and maintained, ultimately passing from one generation to another. The theory of "organic memory" rested on two scientific pillars: Lamarck's theory of the inheritance of acquired characters (which postulated organic changes over one generation in reaction to environmental constraints); and Ernst Haeckel's biogenetic law that "ontogeny recapitulates phylogeny" (which tied individual development to that of the race). Hering could not prove his ideas at a molecular level and left it to his follower Richard Semon (1921) to try to reconcile his hypothesis with experimental biology and mendelian genetics (following the rediscovery of Mendel's Law of inheritance in 1900).

Regardless of what it could actually find in the body, the theory of organic memory benefited from the prestige that experimental physiology and evolutionary biology held at the time. It also tapped into a propitious political context. The late nineteenth-century obsession with identity and origins—whether national or racial—helped elevate the notion of a hereditary bodily memory to the status of scientific truth, especially among those worried about racial mixing and social Darwinism in the high age of empire. For the English novelist Samuel Butler, who helped promote Hering's ideas in the Anglophone world, the notion of "unconscious memory" (as he preferred to call it), added a psychological dimension to theories of evolution, wielding Lamarck to "temper" Darwin's unpalatable materialism (Butler 1878 and 1890). These views influenced the great popularizer of physiological psychology of the *fin de siècle*, Théodule Ribot, who famously put it that memory was "essentially a biological phenomenon (*fait biologique*) [and only] by accident a psychological one" (Ribot 1881: 1). According to the French psychologist, it accumulated in the body over a generational continuum, proof being that amnesiacs tended to forget the most recent memories first, not those that had had time to sediment and become habitual (the basis for Ribot's famous law of retrograde amnesia).

The idea of an organic, species-specific form of memory proved attractive beyond the limited circle of researchers to acquire a far broader cultural resonance. Unsurprisingly, it was enthusiastically embraced by champions of degeneration theory from Bénédict Morel to Max Nordau, and countless advocates of anti-miscegenation laws in European colonies and the American South. To the Italian criminologist Cesare Lombroso, and the many police forces he influenced, these findings made it possible to identify "born criminals" among biological "throwbacks" to a savage age. For the wider public, it was through novels such as those of Emile Zola and Thomas Mann that the idea of intergenerational "hereditary taints" became second nature. As Gilles Deleuze (1977) has famously suggested, this *"fêlure"* (hereditary "crack") *is* the real protagonist of Zola's novels, the agent of degeneration running through the Rougon and Macquart family lines.[5] In the long run, the theory of organic memory fared far better in its pseudo-scientific and often overtly racist political forms—Nazi Aryanism most infamously—than in experimental science. Nonetheless, it is possible to see shades of its original materialist intent in current research on the epigenetic transmission of trauma from one generation to another (or, more troublingly perhaps, in the growing use of neuroscientific findings in the criminal justice system). Of course, not everyone was swayed by attempts to locate memory in the body already in the late nineteenth century. The theory of organic memory was roundly criticized by Bergson, who rejected its materialist reductionism, and by William James, who shared the concern to ground psychology in physiological processes, but insisted that memory was by definition conscious (and as such non-reducible to a form of bodily habit). In fact, contemporaneously to the study of organic memory, there emerged in the late nineteenth century a very different approach to memory that placed it firmly in the hands of the psychologist, following the lead of Hermann Ebbinghaus.

MEASURING MEMORY

If Broca was the pioneer of an anatomical science of memory, Ebbinghaus was unquestionably the founding father of a statistical one. The German psychologist sought to wrestle the study of memory from both metaphysical speculation and materialist reductionism, to instead make it available to experimental research and what he viewed as a properly scientific psychology. His doctoral dissertation (defended in 1873) criticized the notion of unconscious processes in organic nature and he spent much of his career working out empirical ways of quantifying the manifest workings of memory. Over the course of several years, Ebbinghaus devised and performed upon himself a series of experiments designed to measure his capacity for retention. He wrote series of three nonsensical syllables on cards (always a consonant followed by a vowel followed by a consonant) and memorized random lists of these series by reading them repeatedly. He then proceeded to learn the lists over again at varying intervals of time—from half an hour to thirty-one days—and compared how many repetitions he required each time. By tinkering with the parameters and reproducing similar experiments over and over, Ebbinghaus was able to establish that retention was a function of time since original learning, but that it operated counter-intuitively: forgetting was rapid at first and then gradually tapered off, so that one would forget little more over the course of a month than over the space of eight hours. Ebbinghaus published his preliminary findings in 1885 in his landmark *Über das Gedächtnis*.[6] The elaborate graphs and plentiful statistical data gave the study of memory an air of positivism, obtaining a generally positive reception within the psychological profession. James (1890: 676) hailed Ebbinghaus' undertaking as "heroic," and Wilhelm Wundt's pupil, Edward Titchener (1915: 152), dubbed it the most important work on memory since Aristotle. The basic research protocol inspired many others to further experimentation, ever refined with new measuring instruments and laboratory paraphernalia designed to make psychology look like a natural science.[7] Not everyone was impressed, though: Ebbinghaus' colleague in Berlin, Wilhelm Dilthey, accused him of remaining confined to surface sense experiences, without getting at the deeper logics of *Erlebnis* (life experience). The problem, for Dilthey, was methodological, and fundamentally opposed natural and human sciences: Ebbinghaus may well have sought to *explain* memory, he could not properly *understand* it within the confines of his epistemological framework.[8]

For all his groundbreaking accomplishments, Ebbinghaus' "mathematisation of memory" (Draaisma 2000: 93) did not appear in a vacuum. Others had already conducted ad hoc experiments on the duration of after images and sensitivity of nerves to repeated touch. More significantly perhaps, technological innovations had already laid claim to capturing and accessing "memories" of sorts. Right around the time that Ebbinghaus was conducting his experiments, the first phonographs began to appear on either side of the Atlantic. By 1887, Thomas Edison was able to use a wax cylinder to faithfully reproduce recorded sound multiple times. Before the phonograph promised to overcome the transience of sound, the photographic camera had already done so for images. In 1839, Louis Daguerre had rolled out a revolutionary photographic process made of silver-coated copper plates, mercury vapor, and kitchen salt. The daguerreotype was soon replaced by cheaper and more versatile photographic processes with seemingly limitless applications. In 1872, Charles Darwin famously based his study of emotions on photographic stills of facial expressions, paving the way to Lombroso's criminal anthropology (both quests continue to mobilize considerable scientific efforts and financial resources today). As Douwe Draaisma (1995) has shown, these inventions inspired new, ostensibly scientific metaphors of memory as recordings of sound and sight. In the early 1890s, the French psychologist Alfred Binet published findings of his research on young mathematical prodigies and chess players to advance claims on what would subsequently come to be known as "photographic memory" (Binet 1894). But the question that seemed to most interest memory researchers at the time, was not so much that of mnemonic wonders, but of memory disorders.

Starting in the early nineteenth century, and in concomitance with the emergence of psychopathology, memory came under the purview and gaze of medical practitioners as well.[9] The first psychiatrists frequently observed a "derangement of memory" (as Benjamin Rush called it) among the mentally ill, especially in cases of delirium and dementia. Military physicians were particularly concerned at the time with what they called "nostalgia," or a morbid form of homesickness endemic among soldiers (especially young conscripts), sailors, and African slaves in the Americas (Dodman 2018). Although not thought of explicitly in mnemonic terms (as it is today), this "nostalgia" belied general anxiety about temporality and loss in an age of revolution and momentous social transformations. Early attempts at drawing taxonomies of these disorders—such as those by the Austrian philosopher Ernst von Feuchtersleven and German psychiatrist Wilhem Greisinger—typically distinguished between various forms of "abnormal" memory: unusually heightened (hypermnesia); dangerously weakened (dysmnesia and amnesia); and altered or distorted in various ways (paramnesias). The adoption of a clinical perspective—based on detailed observations of case studies—did not fundamentally alter this broad division, but it did reinforce the normative claims physicians increasingly felt entitled to make between "normal" and "pathological" forms of memory. In an 1865 article on "amnesia" for a standard French medical encyclopedia, the prominent psychiatrist Jean-Pierre Falret described amnesia as "symptomatic" of other morbid conditions, rather than a disease in itself. Some forgetting and confusion was perfectly normal; what wasn't was repeated partial or temporary, and eventually complete and permanent amnesia. Falret (1865: 725–42) marshalled clinical observations to parse a typology of morbid amnesic states and of their many causes, both organic and psychological (ranging from heredity and commotion to insanity and strong emotions).

As Michael S. Roth (1989) has argued, this normative stance was common to a wider obsession with *maladies de mémoires* at the end of the nineteenth century. In France in particular, it betrayed continued efforts to define normality in terms of a "healthy" balance between past and present. Ribot's classic 1882 study on the topic was only the tip of the iceberg and, in his case, the salvo for a much more ambitious psychological enterprise. According to Ribot, the study of partial amnesias in particular was not merely of relevance to the workings of memory, but to the understanding of personality disorders.[10] His famous "law of regression" didn't simply elucidate the psychological and physiological mechanisms behind pathological amnesia; it also reasserted what a "healthy" connection to the past looked like. In other words, memory stood in for, and allowed scientific access to, the self itself—and particularly troubled selves. Many others followed in Ribot's wake, focusing especially on the paramnesias, a term introduced in 1886 by the great German psychiatrist Emil Kraepelin to describe all forms of memory errors and distortions. Earlier in the century psychiatrists had already sought to explain double perceptions and memories in terms of temporal disjuncture between the two cerebral hemispheres. Others focused on the delusional psychic and sensory mechanisms that produced hallucinations of past events and other mnemonic illusions. The consummate nosologist, Kraepelin sought to parse all these "qualitative" memory disturbances onto two broad categories: partial distortions of true memories, and complete falsifications of autobiographical facts, which he termed "pseudoreminiscences." Kraepelin examined and reported of others examining paramnesiac patients who were both psychotic and perfectly sane; who were lucid, asleep, or visibly confused; and whose distorted recollections were either durable or fleeting. He was particularly interested in the pseudoreminiscences that often accompanied severe psychosis: patients who insisted they had seen Jesus on the cross, or who could recount in minute detail the fifty bullet wounds they had survived in battle and details of life on Mars.[11] Intense debates on the nature and etiology of paramnesias played out in leading European scientific journals and societies throughout the 1890s. In 1896, the neurologist François-Léon Arnaud published a detailed study of an extraordinary case of chronic "*déjà vu*," a phenomenon familiar to nineteenth-century novelists and poets, but which he was the first to bring up in a scientific publication. The patient, a soldier with a history of amnesia named Léon, suffered from systematic instances of *déjà vu* (including his brother's wedding, which he claimed to have attended twice). Arnaud concluded that what Léon perceived as a memory was in fact a retrospective perception, and that the disturbance lay not in the past, but in the present. Léon's sense of uncanny repetition was in fact an instance of false recognition; but that did not stop other clinicians from continuing to explore similar experiences as memory disturbances of one form or another.

INVOLUNTARY MEMORIES

Fin-de-siècle fretting about amnesia and paramnesias was symptomatic of an age riddled with anxieties of all sorts. It is hardly surprising that, faced with dramatic social transformations and a palpable sense of accelerating time, people should have worried about loss and forgetting. More unexpected, perhaps, is the fact they would ultimately come to anguish far more over the opposite problem: a surfeit of memory, typically in the form of involuntary and intrusive reminiscences. Already in the 1870s, Friedrich Nietzsche (1997: 61; 1989: 57–8) suggested that animals were happier than men because of their ability to forget. He urged his contemporaries to also live "unhistorically" in the present, unburdened by the "great and ever greater pressure of what is past." Soon thereafter, the French psychologist Pierre Janet would make forgetting a central plank of any cure for dissociative personalities paralyzed by what he called a "phobia of memory" (Janet 1914–15). But why the fuss? By the turn of the century, the long "memory crisis" had coiled around a new, controversial but equally paradigmatic concept that promised to anchor a third major science of memory—a psychodynamic one: trauma.

Trauma was not a new word in the last decades of the nineteenth century; what was new was its psychological acceptance (Leys 2000). Until then, it had been used by physicians solely to denote a physical wound (a battle wound, for example). It is only in the 1860s that people started entertaining the idea of psychic trauma, in the wake of a series of high-profile train crashes, reparation claims, and a first attempt at defining a fright syndrome (dubbed "railway spine") by the British physician John Erichsen. The controversy that ensued pitted against one another proponents of an organic explanation based on microlesions of the nerves (headed by the German neurologist Herman Oppenheimer) and of a psychological one indebted to Jean-Martin Charcot's efforts to legitimate conversion hysteria as a functional disorder (that is, one with no visible physical causes). It was Pierre Janet who, in the 1880s, first sought to tie together a psychological understanding of trauma—as a blow to the psyche—with memory disturbances (both amnesias and hypermnesias), in developing a comprehensive theory of dissociation. Janet argued that sudden, powerful emotions could prove overwhelming to the mind and leave traumatic memories that proved impossible to digest and integrate within existing cognitive schemas. In turn, these would cause a split in consciousness—the process of dissociation—and lead to a fragmentary reliving of the trauma in emotions, behavior, and memory. To treat such cases of split personality, Janet turned to hypnosis, initially with the intent of removing the traumatic memories, but eventually with the goal of folding them into a reconstruction of the self through narrative (Janet 1889).[12]

Janet was hardly alone in trying to bring together disparate research on double consciousness, hysteria, hypnosis, emotions, and memory at the time. These were all very much *dans l'air du temps*, especially in France. In Bordeaux, the physician Eugène Azam spent much of the 1870s developing a theory of "*doublement de la personalité*" and experimenting with a "scientific" form of hypnotism as therapy. His protégé Philippe Tissié would go on to acquire a certain notoriety for his research on cases of serial fugue accompanied by amnesia (Hacking 2002). Over in Paris, Ribot would by the late 1880s turn his attention from *maladies de mémoire* to identifying a specifically affective form of memory, tied to the senses and typically manifested as involuntary reminiscence. The idea proved seductive and Ribot's follower Frédéric Paulhan defined "affective memory" as "the spontaneous or willed reawakening of affective facts as affective facts" (by which he meant traces left in the mind by past emotions or feelings) (Paulhan 1904: 5 and 12; and Ribot 1894). He found examples in the works of illustrious predecessors such as Jean-Jacques Rousseau and Restif de la Bretonne, but it was a contemporary novelist of his who made the most of the idea. With his notion of "involuntary" (as opposed to "voluntary") memory, Marcel Proust sought to grasp the overwhelming affective experience of accidental memory traces, particularly those that surfaced unexpectedly when triggered by the body's senses. He gave an iconic example of this enchanting form of bodily memory with the famous tasting of the madeleine in *Swann's Way* (originally published in 1913); he also explored darker undertones to the flood of involuntary reminiscences the narrator experiences once confined to a mental institution at the end of *Time Regained* (orig. pub. 1927). Often cited as an influence on Proust, Bergson had famously elaborated a similar understanding of "pure memory" as a spontaneous and timeless preservation of personal memories in the unconscious in *Matter and Memory*. But unlike his second cousin, Bergson radically separated this form of reminiscence from the body, which on the contrary he saw as the repository for the more mechanical acquisition and functioning of "habit memory" (Bergson 1990).[13] For someone like William James, the very idea of an affective memory was nonsensical, as the actual feeling of an emotion was always a physiological phenomenon first and foremost, and as such could only exist in the present. Ultimately, it was not in Paris, but in Vienna, that emerged a radically new attempt to explain how memory and emotions operate behind our backs, beneath the threshold of our consciousness, and in response to traumatic situations (whether real or imagined).

For all of its subsequent departure into uncharted terrains and metaphysical speculations, Freudian psychoanalysis arose very much from within a matrix of late nineteenth-century European science, specifically pathological anatomy and neuropsychiatry. As Katja Guenther (2015) has recently shown, the young Sigmund Freud first found his way in debates that pitted phrenologists and proponents of discrete localization of mental functions against advocates of a connectivist model intent on identifying complex circuits of brain cells with the findings of reflex physiology (a dispute that still resonates today in different approaches to neuroscientific findings). In his first book *On Aphasia* (1891), Freud pushed the associative and connectivist tenets of his professor, Theodor Meynert, into a radical critique of localizationist explanations for aphasia (which had been dominant since Broca's day). This was the basis for his own turn from a physical to a psychological understanding of trauma and to the development of psychoanalysis proper—itself a whole new kind of science of memory. "Hysterics suffer mainly from reminiscences," famously wrote Freud and Breuer in their classic *Studies on Hysteria* (1895). They argued that the hysterical symptom was a manifestation of a buried memory that lay dormant in the unconscious and that typically harked back to childhood, in particular to childhood sexual abuse. For Freud, memory was constitutive of the unconscious, a timeless and non-localizable region of the mind that stored repressed wishes and experiences. These periodically erupted through the threshold of consciousness in distorted forms in dreams, slips of the tongue, and neurotic symptoms. If memory and its repression was thus central to the etiology of mental disorders, so was it critical to the therapeutic protocols that Freud recommended in clinical analysis. Like Charcot and Janet, he initially championed hypnosis as a way of uncovering and removing the problematic memory trace. He soon abandoned hypnosis, however, having established that repressed memories were not static but subject to ongoing revision, distorted manifestations (what he called "screen memories"), and deferred effects (*Nachträglichkeit*) that only occurred after a subsequent event (a phenomenon associated to trauma and which Freud fully integrated into his model of the psyche in the wake of the first world war and the epidemic of war neuroses it caused). These findings pushed Freud towards a more dialogic clinical setting focused on narrative reconstruction and "working through" of the repressed past. He readily conceded that this was a lengthy and potentially interminable process, one that disowned Nietzsche's injunction to forget in favor of an ongoing constitution of the subject.[14]

Freud maintained until the end that psychoanalysis was a science and "no illusion" (as religion was), despite the barrage of criticism that accompanied his clinical work and the increasingly speculative realms that he broached later in his career (Freud 1927/1961: 55). In his twentieth-century works on culture and religion he increasingly sought ways to connect individual memories to collective ones and to a phylogenetic "archaic heritage" that he continued to speak of in Lamarckian terms, as inheritance of acquired characteristics across generations, until the end of his life (Freud 1939/1964: 97). Few of his hypotheses have stood the test of time, yet it ought to be noted that in this respect as well Freud was very much articulating a science of memory for his day. Much like researchers of epigenetic inheritance and transgenerational trauma today, he sought ways to connect his focus on individual memories to wider environmental determinants. He found these in social forms of remembrance, as well as in anthropology and archaeology (a discipline from which he drew insights and metaphors aplenty)—in other words, in new forms of knowledge characteristic of his time of mass politics, nationalism, and imperialism.

LEARNING MEMORY

"Collective memory" only really became an object of scholarly attention in the twentieth century (and as such is beyond the scope of this article). It is associated in particular with the pioneering sociological work of the French sociologist Maurice Halbwachs, who rejected the highly individualistic psychology of his lycée professor Bergson in favor of the sociological approach promoted by Emile Durkheim. In his landmark study *The Social Frameworks of Memory* (1925), Halbwachs argued that memories were only deceptively personal things; instead they relied upon and were woven into collective "frameworks" of remembrance. For Halbwachs, an individual only remembered as part of a sociological group—families, associations, classes etc.—bound together by common experiences, concerns, and memories that were passed on from one generation to another (and that provided the slowly changing frames onto which personal memories could be "nailed" and made sense of at any given moment in time). Halbwachs' program for a social and cultural study of memory would go on to dominate much of so-called "memory studies" up to this day, particularly with late twentieth-century programs to map out "realms" and "sites" of memory.[15] Yet it is important to note that collective forms of remembrance were already a concrete concern of the nineteenth century, and that they informed political practices indissolubly tied with legitimating scientific discourses. With the aid of new disciplines such as history, archaeology and anthropology, and widely accepted "truths" such as climatology and scientific racism, nineteenth-century states and educational institutions enrolled memory into pedagogical enterprises aimed at forging "imagined communities" (Anderson 1983) be they local, national or imperial in scope.

The professionalization of the historical discipline during the nineteenth century went hand in hand with the construction of national master narratives that could, in turn, be relayed to the masses in the classroom. As Stefan Berger has noted (2017), romantic historians of the early 1800s wrestled history writing away from Enlightenment universalism and aligned it closely with nation-building instead. This nationalist bent was not called into question by their positivist successors, who, by the latter half of the century, were busy promoting national history education as the expansion of compulsory schooling offered European states new ways of tapping into people's sense of belonging. Probably the most successful example of this was the French historian Ernest Lavisse, who wrote hugely successful textbooks and supervised curricular reforms to provide the French Third Republic with a new "republican gospel" (his "*Petit Lavisse*" elementary school manual was reprinted yearly from 1884 up to the Second World War). Such historiographical nationalism was of course closely intertwined with the creation of invented traditions such as those at play in Albert Bettannier's *La Tâche noire* (1887), where French pupils dressed in military uniform and within easy reach of a gun rack stare attentively at the "black stain" of Alsace and Lorraine, recently annexed by the German Empire following the Franco-Prussian war (1870). Under the paternal gaze of their instructor—a secular,

FIGURE 4.2: Albert Brettannier, *La Tâche noire* (1887). Oil on canvas. 110 × 150 cm. © Deutsches Historisches Museum/S. Ahlers.

but rather priestly state employee—they learn about these "lost provinces" and partake in a collective experience of national humiliation and *revanchisme* (revenge). In the background the map of Paris marks the capital of the nation and modernity (as underscored by the gas chandelier), pegging the young men's sense of belonging to a symbolic center.

These national narratives were typically hammered into pupils' heads through monotonous memorization exercises. Despite the criticism of pioneering educational reformers such as Rousseau, Johann Pestalozzi, and Johann Herbart, rote learning, or memorization through repetition, remained very much the norm in classrooms such as this one, where it went hand in hand with barrack-like discipline (Brubacher 1966: 204–11). It is only at the turn of the century that its wisdom was seriously challenged by proponents of "experimental pedagogy." These borrowed from the findings of experimental psychologists such as Ebbinghaus and James, who openly questioned the value of rote memorizing. For the Swiss psychologist and pedagogue Edouard Claparède (1911: 57), the role of memory in education had to be thought of holistically, as part of a "gymnastics of the mind" (and body) in which "overloading" and fatigue (both physical and intellectual) were the number one impediment to effective learning.

Ultimately, it is not so much in the classroom, however, but in other public institutions that memory was most effectively pressed into political service. These arose in large part in response to a new historical consciousness ushered in by the upheavals of the American, French, and Haitian revolutions, further prolonged by the Napoleonic Wars and the Latin American Wars of Independence. Across Europe, a nostalgic cult of ruins permeated the romantic sensibility of the early 1800s, turning the romantic collector into the archetypal figure of an introspective and aestheticized relation to the lost past. This highly personal attitude to memory in turn gave way to collective efforts of memorializing driven by state and local actors, in particular learned societies. By mid-century, countries such as Germany and France teemed with historical associations geared towards the valorization of local heritage (Crane 2000a; Gerson 2003; Fritzsche 2004). These fought for the conservation of monuments, organized historical pageants, and funded archaeological digs and historical publications. Most often, they worked in tandem with state organisms, who recognized their worth in helping to foster a sense of national belonging across the country. These partnerships came to fruition in the formation of public museums, prime sites for the "fixing" of memory (as Susan Crane has called it) in a rational and pedagogical way. Whether art galleries or new natural history and ethnological museums, these institutions projected to the masses narratives of identity and progress designed to naturalize nation-building and imperial hierarchies among other things (Crane 2000b; and Bennett 1995).

But the place where political pedagogies of memory and science were most tightly interwoven in the nineteenth century was in the colonies themselves. When Napoleon Bonaparte set off to conquer Egypt in 1798, he famously took with him an army of artists and scientists as well as soldiers. These included geologists, mathematicians, doctors, engineers, archaeologists etc., intent on "(re)-discovering" Ancient Egypt in the modern age. The scientific expedition produced famous paintings and a multi-volume encyclopedic description comparable, at least in ambition, to Diderot and D'Alembert's *Encyclopédie*.[16] It also led to the plundering of innumerable archaeological relics that wound up in the Louvre or, in the case of the Rosetta Stone, the British Museum—emblems of imperial strength knitted into the fabric of national consciousness. The Egyptian campaign thus gave birth to two related discourses central to the justification of nineteenth-century imperialism: "orientalism," or a distorted representation of the "Orient" that establishes the positional superiority of the "West"; and a "civilizing mission" (or "burden") with which white Europeans justified colonial expansion and the subjection of "primitive" peoples (Said 1978; Conklin 1997). Practices of collective memory were central to both of these discourses, as the case of French Algeria makes abundantly clear. As in Egypt, military conquest (and violent repression of indigenous populations) went hand in hand with lofty scientific ambitions and an official commission of *savants* tasked with exploring the colony. Among its many offshoots, were archaeological societies which, after the inevitable plundering of the early conquest, developed a conservationist approach to Algeria's ancient Roman vestiges in the second half of the nineteenth century. The memorialization of the colony's *patrimoine* (cultural heritage) was in turn associated to a valorization of its natural environment, with ambitious projects of land drainage, reforestation, and protected natural reserves. It also dovetailed nicely with the work of philologists and self-professed racial cataloguing experts intent on tracing the genealogical roots of local populations (in this case, of "orientalized" Arabs and "Westernized" Berbers). Common to each of these discourses and practices, was a desire to legitimate the French presence in North Africa by rediscovering the region's Roman roots, resurrecting a mythical trans-Mediterranean "Latin race," and restoring what had once been known as the "granary of Rome" (against the presence of "nomad" Muslims blamed for the destruction of the natural environment).[17] In colonies such as Algeria, memory became a highly fungible thing, "molded" by science (as opposed to "discovered," ready-made, by science) according to instrumental logics of power.

But what these imperial practices of memory *occluded* from the stories they told was often as important as what they *included* in them. In the colonies, the past was more easily silenced than elsewhere, not least when it came to erasing the violence of colonial conquest and its victims.[18] In French classrooms such as Bettanier's, nobody read about the expropriations and exterminatory practices—"unfortunate necessities" as the liberal Alexis de Tocqueville (2001: 70) infamously dismissed them—that halved the indigenous population of Algeria by the turn of the century (no school pupil in France would until the very end of the twentieth century!). The history of European imperialism in Africa is littered with similar genocidal massacres—of the Mau Mau in Kenya (by the British) or Herero in contemporary Namibia (by the Germans)—kept safely under seals by governments and complicit custodians of untarnished national memory (Hull 2004; Elkins 2005). Instead, late nineteenth-century historians offered whiggish tales of progress that omitted (or at best caricatured) indigenous people, presenting colonial conquest as a discovery and utilitarian repurposing of virgin land. This was especially important to young nations born out of European expansion overseas such as the United States and Australia. In his 1893 presidential address to the American Historical Association, Frederick Jackson Turner famously expounded his "frontier thesis" about the origins of American society, claiming that it was in expanding westwards—"an area of free land," as he put it—that Americans developed their rugged individualism and unique democratic culture. Native Americans did not fit in the picture—or on these lands—except as a foil for a tale of manifest destiny endlessly rehashed in novels, films, textbooks, and political speeches ever since (Turner 1983). Until recently, Australian historians peddled a similar narrative of nation-building, perpetuating myths of a "terra nullius" (nobody's land) and "doomed (aboriginal) race." In its very first lines, a best-selling 1916 history textbook made it clear what did and did not belong in the collective memory of the then nascent nation: "This *Short History of Australia* begins with a blank space on the map, and ends with the record of a new name on the map, that of Anzac. It endeavors to elucidate the way in which the country was discovered, why and how it was settled, the development of civilized society within it, its political and social progress, mode of government, and relations, historical and actual, with the Empire of which it forms a part" (Scott 1916: v).[19] This "Great Australian Silence," as the anthropologist W.E.H. Stanner called it in 1968, systematically erased Aborigines from history books, perpetuating a collective amnesia about the spoliations, massacres, and child abductions they endured from the colonial era though independence.[20] Although this only became apparent following the second world war and decolonization, the relation between memory and genocide—whether at the level of individual traumas or collective remembrance—was very much a product of the late 1800s.

Our twenty-first century "science of memory" is both very different and strangely similar to its nineteenth-century forerunner. On the one hand, a quick perusal of trending topics in the field could well give the impression that it has narrowed considerably and been handed over exclusively to neuroscientists. In May 2018, the new frontier seems be the successful transfer of a memory from one marine snail to another via RNA, or ribonucleic acid (the polymeric molecule that acts as a messenger for DNA within cells). The injection of RNA from sensitization trained Aplysia (who have been habituated to electrical shocks) in untrained ones induces the same behavioral change, suggesting that the transfer of memory happens within the nucleus of neurons, as epigenetic change, rather than in the synaptic connections between neurons (as most memory researchers tend to believe). And this, the authors of the study claim, brings us closer than ever to identifying a discrete engram (Bédécarrats et al. 2018). At the same time, an important compendium to the field also reminds us that "pluralism is the ambrosia of science." A "new science of memory" may well be emerging on the horizon, but it "rises on the shoulders of giants" and must find ways to bring into dialogue disciplines that don't all speak the same language. Here the starting point is not so much some new lab discovery, as good old-fashioned hermeneutic work on translating concepts across fields of knowledge (Roediger et al. 2007: 1, 10).

There is a certain uncanniness to this flashforward to our time. The questions, terms, and debates that animated the long nineteenth-century science of memory remain relevant today, repackaged and reframed in new ways where necessary. We are still looking for and trying to quantify concrete memory traces in the body without necessarily agreeing on where these traces hide, what they actually are or might even mean to one living being as opposed to another. Like Bergson's psychologists of old, today's neuroscientists have been handed the keys to the field—but the field itself remains fractured and polyphonic, for better and for worse. In 2018, like in 1918 or even 1818, the science of memory remains very much *many sciences* of memory.

This article has sought to trace and map out the coming into being of memory as an object of scientific knowledge in the North Atlantic during the long nineteenth century (Daston 2000). This was, unquestionably, something quite new. But the novelty lay not so much in the attainment of some putative certainty about what memory is. Quite the contrary, in fact: nineteenth-century scientists of different stripes disagreed vehemently about where to find it, how to quantify it, what it was good for and in what amounts. By the end of the century, the Enlightenment notion that memory was somehow central to our sense of self had both been reinforced and shattered by the realization that reminiscences could be intrusive and traumatic. Many experimental researchers of memory would forge on unperturbed, but for others the modern self would never quite recover from this splintering. Be that as it may, the true novelty of the time ultimately lay elsewhere: in the way in which memory became a technology of power, a pedagogical tool legitimated by scientific discourse and eagerly tested on citizens and colonial subjects. As a form of knowledge and a collective practice, memory thus became a central plank in the forging of national communities and imperial phantasies. And in this respect, the nineteenth-century sciences of memory paved the way to the many "memory wars"—clinical, geo-political, and historiographical—of the twentieth century.

CHAPTER FIVE

Ideas: Philosophy, Religion, and History

STAN M. LANDRY

As the disciplines of philosophy, religion, and history were increasingly professionalized and institutionalized in settings such as academies, universities, and museums, the presence of memory persisted in both elite and popular forms of expression. This dialectical process was not entirely recognized by two principal scholars of memory studies. Indeed, in their magisterial works on the topic, both Maurice Halbwachs and Pierre Nora famously contrasted memory and history. According to Halbwachs, "General history starts only when tradition ends and the social memory is fading or breaking up. So long as remembrance continues to exist, it is useless to set it down in writing or otherwise fix it in memory" (1992: 78).

Thus, for Halbwachs, history was superfluous anywhere memory was still strong. And whereas history was merely a record of events, memory was the depository of social tradition. According to Halbwachs, when these traditions disappeared, history stepped in to speak for the "deceased" memories (1992: 84), Likewise in *The Realms of Memory*, Pierre Nora drew on Halbwachs' claim that history was destructive of memory. Nora famously argued sites exist that are vestiges of living memories, sites of memories nearly forgotten. The existence of these sites is a symptom of forgetting, for "if we still dwelled among our memories, there would be no need to consecrate sites to them" (Nora 1996: 2). *The Realms of Memory* dissects these sites—these sites which commemorate; whose purpose is to stop time and to stop forgetting (Nora 1996: 15). But the very existence of these *lieux de mémoire* is predicated on the essential opposition between history and memory. For Nora, history reminds us of the memories we have forgotten, but it can only reconstruct memory, never revivify it or make it present.

But during the nineteenth century, as the discipline of history was professionalized, and as philosophy, religion, and theology were historicized, the presence of memory persisted in new forms and among multiple collectives. According to Halbwachs, as history rose, memory died. But if we look carefully, we will discover that memory's death was only an apparent death, as it survived and was expressed in a myriad of ways. Indeed, during the nineteenth century memory found popular expression in spaces amid the professionalization of philosophy, religion, and history but also through popular consumption of historical novels, patronage of museums, and participation in historical commemorations and anniversary festivals. The rehabilitation and rebirth of memory became manifest for the very same reason the century witnessed the rise of history and historical consciousness—the traumas and upheavals of the nineteenth century, which represented a break in time, and in the desire to find a usable past in an accelerated present. This chapter recounts how memory manifested itself—and was legitimized and delegitimized—in philosophy, history, and in religion both in the elite and popular realms, but also how those disciplines functioned as forms of memory, or ways of remembering.

THE EMERGENCE OF HISTORICAL CONSCIOUSNESS

The rise of historical consciousness during the late eighteenth and nineteenth centuries contributed to the emerging presence and accessibility of memory. Historians have variously located the emergence of this historical consciousness in the upheavals of the Industrial Revolution, the French Revolution, and in Romantic philosophy. For example, the historian Modris Eksteins argued that the Industrial Revolution instilled an acute awareness of change and transitoriness in the European masses and engendered an increasingly universal historical consciousness. Moreover, writers and artists began to include historical themes into their works, lawyers studied the law as a historical phenomenon, and Jesus and the Bible became objects of historical interest. Indeed, Eksteins noted that "[t]he growth of historical awareness was such a prominent feature that one can readily speak of the nineteenth century as a *saeculum historicum*" (1985: 5).

This awareness of change and distance from the past had a corollary: a melancholy over the "loss" of the past and a nostalgia for an often-idealized former state of affairs. This is what the historian Peter Fritzsche has called the "melancholy of history." Fritzsche located the emergence of mass historical consciousness in the lived trauma and social upheaval caused by the French Revolution and the Revolutionary Wars (2004: 5–13).

The art historian Stephen Bann also recognized the emergence of mass historical consciousness in Europe but located its origins in Romanticism. Bann was especially concerned with history as a new language or trope, using visual images to map a break between an era when history was merely alluded to in images as a setting or prop, and the Romantic period, when images could be "coded" historically and presumably their historicity recognized by all observers (Bann 1995: 5, 53). That is, during the Romantic period history had become a mass medium of representation.

The Scottish writer Walter Scott (1771–1832) perhaps best represents the use of history and historical memory as a mass medium of representation. In his best-selling historical novels, such as *Waverley* (1814) and *Ivanhoe* (1819) along with his work as museum curator and patron of a neo-Gothic estate, Abbotsford, Scott demonstrated how the past might function as a genre of literature and a source of identity. Not only was Scott instrumental in helping to historicize the consciousness of the reading public by locating the setting of his novels in the past, he also contributed to the growing popularity of historical societies and antiquarian clubs. Scott's novels and scholarship also inspired artists, authors, painters, craftsmen, and consumers to immerse themselves in the history and memory of the medieval world, and helped to inspire public commemoration of the past through memorials, monuments, and anniversaries and the use of period-specific décor and home furnishings (Rigney 2014: 65). Indeed, Scott's own life would be commemorated with a massive Gothic memorial in Edinburgh, pointing to how Scott's own memory, the memory of his literary output, and the memory of the medieval past were inextricably embodied in material culture – in this case, memorial architecture (Quinault 1998: 322).

While Scott perfected the historical novel and introduced the medieval past as a mnemonic tableaux, the French artist Madame Tussaud's (1761–1850) wax museum

FIGURE 5.1: The Walter Scott Monument, Edinburgh (designer: George Meikle Kemp, 1838–46).

embodied the histories and memories of the French Revolution in her sculptures of historical figures. After fleeing the Terror, Tussaud opened her famous wax museum in London in 1802. Among the most popular exhibits in the museum were the "Chamber of Horrors" that depicted graphically-violent scenes from the French Revolution, including sculptures of Marat in his tub, a "working" guillotine and gallows, and five heads on pikes—among them Louis XVI and Marie Antoinette, whose heads were modeled on the severed heads of those figures cast by Tussaud herself. This museum provided spaces for English visitors of every social class, including women and children, to experience or imagine the Revolution, as it was the first institution to commemorate the Revolution and one in which history was represented, neigh, literally embodied (in wax), as horror, as spectacle, and trauma (Melman 2006: 29–30).

SECULARIZATION, HISTORICISM, AND MEMORY

Part and parcel of the rise of historical consciousness and the professionalization of history was the setting of religious figures and traditions—including Jesus, the Gospels, and Martin Luther and the Reformation—within a historical context. This was a process that began with the German theologian W.M.L. de Wette (1780–1849) and represents a challenge to the historian Leopold von Ranke's (1795–1886) claim to the status of "Father of Modern History" and originator of historicism. Against the rationalist criticism of the Bible practiced by the French philosophes, de Wette advocated a historical (rather than purely rational) critique of biblical texts (Howard 2000: 8). Biblical texts were to be evaluated historically in terms of the time, culture, and place in which they were composed rather than for internal contradictions. Historicism was able to transcend its origins in early nineteenth-century biblical criticism and theology and was adopted by professional historians because the paramount historians (and historicists) of nineteenth-century Germany and Switzerland—von Ranke, Jacob Burckhardt (1818–97), J.G. Droysen (1808–84), and Theodor Mommsen (1817–1903)—were the sons of pastors and/or had studied theology. Indeed, Burckhardt actually studied with de Wette, whose biblical criticism caused Burckhardt's loss of faith before pursuing a career in history (Howard 2000: 5). These figures "imported" their historicist training in biblical criticism and theology into their historical scholarship. But treating Christianity as an object of historical analysis led to an infamous "crisis" of historicism that contemporaries worried would lead to moral relativism and doubt. In the 1835 *Life of Jesus*, the German theologian David Friedrich Strauss (1808–74) conceived of the New Testament gospels as the embodiment of cultural myths, ideas, or traditions. He did not regard the New Testament gospels as fictions or subjectively authored frauds, but instead as literary manifestations of the messianic expectations of ancient Jewish traditions. Strauss was quick to note that his historical criticism of the New Testament did not entail a rejection of the essential message of the gospels, but merely rejected the historical veracity of the New Testament, which he considered unessential. Strauss recognized these ideas and expectations as historical myths, neither fictions nor frauds, but cultural traditions which reflected "the notions of the age and . . . Old Testament predictions" espoused by Jews (Strauss 1972: 63).

Another Young Hegelian theologian, Bruno Bauer (1809–82), would later claim that the Gospels were in fact products of the self-consciousness of their authors, thus underscoring the subjective, rather than communally generated character of the Gospels. In the *Critique of the Synoptic Gospels* (1841–2), Bauer argued that the Jewish and Gentile Christian communities of the first centuries A.D. had no messianic expectations at all. Instead, he argued that these alleged expectations were retrospective—projected onto Jewish and early Christian communities by the later church. As the Gospels were reflective works and products of their individual authors' self-consciousnesses written after Jesus' death, they naturally reflected the interests and objectives of the early Christian sects to which the authors belonged. Contemporaries immediately recognized the implications of Bauer's critique: the evangelists had invented the Christ legend and the historical existence of Jesus was unsustainable. For this insight Bauer was formally discharged from the theological faculty at the University of Bonn on orders of King Friedrich Wilhelm IV himself (Landry 2011: 11–14).

The historicization of Martin Luther follows this trend. Just as Strauss would famously historicize Jesus Christ and Bauer the Gospels, other writers would historicize Martin Luther with similar results: a historical Christ could be rendered as a socialist, liberal, or sacred figure just as Luther's memory would be deployed by orthodox, atheists, liberals, nationalists, Christians, Jews, and a myriad of diverse groups. Strauss's Jesus was a figure whom the evangelists and authors of the Gospels could project their hopes and beliefs. The commemoration of Luther as a site of memory rather than an historical figure, also emerged during this period beginning with the 1817 anniversaries and reaching a zenith during the 1883 anniversaries of Luther's birth.

Memories of Martin Luther and the Protestant Reformation were invoked both by intellectual elites and in popular memory through history, hagiography, pamphlets, plays, sermons, and material culture. The historians Lutz Winckler, Rainer Fuhrman, Max L. Baeumer, and Johannes Burkhardt have recognized this memory culture as an enlightened expression of nascent German liberalism, of bourgeois class formation, as susceptible to cynical political manipulation and early forms of German civil society and secular sociability. But religious adherents, Catholic, Protestant, and Jewish, still had deep and profound memories of Luther and the Reformation. To be sure, a secular memory of Luther and the Reformation was becoming more accessible to non-Lutherans, but it did not imply that the reformer's memory had been thoroughly secularized. Indeed, religious figures continued to resist the image of Martin Luther as a secular figure. But due to the ascendance of historicism and mass historical consciousness, the "presence" of memories of Luther and the Reformation became increasingly available to Europeans of every faith.

The effusion of new historical works produced on Luther and the Reformation, including but not limited to Leopold von Ranke's *German History in the Age of the Reformation* (1839–47), contributed to this tendency to render Luther and the Reformation increasingly accessible. This elite memory or commemoration of Luther reflected the nineteenth-century tendency of memory to take the form of history writing. But this form of memory did not always necessarily reflect a concern with objective history and instead expressed itself in hagiography and hero worship. These memories, along with active acts of forgetting, were invoked in a popular fashion at anniversaries, celebrations, and jubilees that were accompanied with "elite" commentary. But elites also referred to Luther throughout the century in response to any number of intellectual developments. Luther and the Reformation were "go to" memories, authoritative frames of mnemonic reference, or foils against which one could agree, disagree, and ultimately position themselves in academic and popular debates about confessional and national identities.

Memories of Luther and the Reformation thus served as touchstones or bellwethers around which elites and ordinary people could orient themselves to any number of issues or topics. This increased with the rise of historical sociability (or popular and elite historical societies), the development of history as a discipline, popular commemorations and anniversaries, and the establishment of societies dedicated to preservation and collecting, heritage industries and museums for preserving memory and history. This proliferation of the cultural memory of Luther and the Reformation during the nineteenth century served as a prelude to their contemporary invocation. Indeed, this view, which posits Luther as "the first modern," was first cultivated during the nineteenth century at the 1817 anniversaries of the Reformation.

While the process of secularization played a role in this, with the de-emphasis of liturgy and declining church attendance replaced by participation in secular celebrations of religious memories, religion, religious history, and religious figures still provided nineteenth-century Europeans with a palette from which to craft their own narratives. Apart from these reasons, Martin Luther's own theology made his memory an accessible one for invocation. Luther's theology recognized every man as a priest, every reader capable of understanding Scripture without the benefit of clergy, and every believer worthy of salvation. Just as Luther's thought rendered Scripture and salvation more accessible, memories of the reformer were rendered increasingly accessible. Just as everyman could speak with some authority on Scripture and achieve salvation, everyman could invoke memories of Luther and the Reformation. Any academic prerequisites for opining on Luther or the Reformation increasingly vanished.

But the result of the divergence of academic history and popular history led to an explosion of conflicting, and even contradictory histories and memories of religious figures such as Martin Luther as a mnemonic tool or touchstone. In subversion of the professionalization of history and memory—or at least, memory as history-writing—popular memories of Luther and the Reformation helped to maintain the reformer's presence and his memory's instrumental and didactic quality. The presence of Luther's memory, as opposed to the academic study of Luther as a historical figure, made the memory not only accessible, but usable. A "present" Luther could be used, abused, and deployed against any argument or position. The Luther of history, distant from the present and an object of scholarly analysis, was restricted by facts, fidelity to sources, and historiographical conventions. Popular memories, especially "accessible" memories of Luther and the Reformation, subverted the professionalization of history in which state institutions like universities and museums and academic societies claimed "ownership" of history and memory.

PROFESSIONAL AND POPULAR HISTORIES AND MEMORIES

Academic history writing represented one form of how elites remembered the past. Indeed, the historian Patrick H. Hutton has identified professional history as memory's "official" form. Hutton argues that history might be seen "as a kind of official memory, a representation of the past that happens to enjoy the sanction of scholarly history," in which collective memory is manufactured by official memory. This manufacture of collective memory, for which certain sites of memory trigger specific recollections of the past, is called commemoration (Hutton 1993: 77–80). But acts of popular commemoration might conceivably escape or even bear influence on the "sanction" of professional history. Non-elites also remembered the past, but through commemorations, anniversaries, and participation in jubilees and holidays. To be sure, both of these tendencies came out of a proliferation of memory and history that was part and parcel of the nineteenth century rise of mass historical consciousness and has been recounted by historians such as Hayden White, Stephen Bann, and Peter Fritzsche.

Historicism signified the de-instrumentalization of history and memory—both the sacred histories and hagiographies of the Middle Ages and the didactic or moral histories of the Enlightenment. In other words, historicism represented the domestication of historical consciousness for elite purposes even though, as Bann and Fritzsche have suggested, popular awareness of history is what led to the professionalization of the discipline. Bann argued that the increase in historically-coded visual images during the Romantic period pointed to the emergence of mass historical consciousness. If the masses were not historically conscious, observers of visual images would not recognize or understand the historical references contained in Romantic images. To be sure, this is a moot point for paintings confined to royal palaces or aristocratic parlors in which the masses had no access. Visual images in newspapers, pamphlets, and editorial cartoons, however, would have reached a popular audience. To be sure, Bann argued that these historically-coded images were not necessarily symptoms of growing historical consciousness, but that they did contain "a generative force" which could also produce historical consciousness in their viewers (Bann 1995: 165). According to Bann (1995: 5) the extent that historical consciousness was growing among the European masses, it was from the "top down," a result of intellectuals' and elites' interest in the past.

Alongside the rise of "scientific" historians such as Leopold von Ranke, during the nineteenth century for Bann, history "became meaningful not only to a small band of passionately committed 'antiquarians' but to a mass reading public." History was not only given a "scientific" foundation and hermetically institutionalized against antiquarianism and dilettantism, but also constituted a "paradigmatic form of knowledge" and "a substratum to almost every type of cultural activity" (Bann 1995: 4–6). Indeed, history itself could function as a medium of representation, a new language or trope. Thus, the Romantic period witnessed the emergence of a widespread historical consciousness which permeated the cultural topology of the period—Romantic literature, visual art, theater, and photography were all heavily imbued with historical referents. Thus, historical consciousness was not simply institutionalized and restricted to professional historians, but pervaded nineteenth-century culture. While Bann looked to visual images to find evidence of mass historical consciousness, Peter Fritzsche looked to ruins and autobiographies as media of historical representation.

The professionalization of history insulated or inoculated the discipline from being conflated with these instrumentalist uses of history and memory, and protected professional historians from charges of being amateurs or dilettantes for whom history was a mere pastime or hobby. Alongside his contemporary Ranke, G.W.F. Hegel applied historical thinking to the discipline of philosophy and penned a poetic defense of historicist philosophy in his *Philosophy of Right*: "When philosophy paints it gray on gray, then has a form of life grown old, and with gray on gray it cannot be rejuvenated but only known; the Owl of Minerva takes flight only at dusk," implying that we cannot understand history *in media res*, but only after some distance has separated the present from the past. Philosophy and philosophical writing in the historicist tradition would thus function as a new form of recollection. To understand philosophy and philosophical systems and traditions one would have to contextualize them in terms of their historical origins and development. Historicism rendered the understanding not only of the history of philosophy, but of the past itself historically and cultural contingent. And this historicist impulse manifested itself within philosophy, history, and the studies of religion and theology.

But while Hegel proposed that contemporaries must understand the past within its appropriate historical context(s), Friedrich Nietzsche (1844–1900)—who identified man as "the animal that remembers"—suggested a "strategic forgetting" of burdensome memories as a form of philosophical and cultural practice, and as a means of self-transcendence. Indeed, Nietzsche believed that the nineteenth century suffered from a surfeit—a "consuming fever"—of historical consciousness (1997: 59–60). In the essay "On the Uses and Disadvantages of History for Life" he complained that his contemporaries could not live authentically in the present because they were too enamored with, and resolutely determined to revive, the past in order to animate the present. According to Nietzsche, his contemporaries worshipped the past at the expense of the present and were content to "let the dead bury the living" (1997: 72). Nietzsche's essay was directed at practicing historians who Nietzsche claims were unimaginative and lacked creativity, and to cultural critics (i.e., those who critique rather than create culture), and to German university students in training to become state bureaucrats.

The very practice of history was professionalized by Ranke and institutionalized in the German university. As a result of its professionalization, history was institutionalized in the university. State institutions such as the university history department, the new historical museum, and publicly-sponsored historical societies now held a monopoly over how history could be represented. Antiquarians and amateurs were typically collectors of historical objects. The antiquarian desire to preserve their collections and to preserve the material experience of history by sharing them with others through institutions of historical sociability raised nineteenth-century historical awareness (Crane 2000a: 92). Additionally, the antiquarian preservation of historical objects and texts would in turn be used by professional historians as primary sources—antiquarians preserved history while historians interpreted it. But as a result of its professionalization, history was institutionalized in the university. State institutions such as the university history department, the new historical museum, and publicly-sponsored historical societies now sought to monopolize how history could be represented. Amateur historians were marginalized as dilettantes and women were precluded from historical training. Both of these groups' contributions to professional history were written out of the historical record (Smith 2000: 2–3).

A group of nineteenth-century French intellectuals (which included Charles Augustin Sainte-Beuve, Gustave Flaubert, Theophile Gautier, Hippolyte Taine, Ernst Renan, and the Goncourt brothers) who met at Magny, a Parisian restaurant, suggests another challenge to the Rankean narrative of the origins of modern historical scholarship. The *dîners Chez Magny* were predecessors to the French *Annalistes*; the Magny group studied the history of societies against the Rankean emphasis on the political history of the nation-state, which they claimed could only provide an incomplete representation of the past, claimed scientific status for their historical methods, and enjoyed an international appeal during the nineteenth century (Dewald 2003: 1011, 1019–23).

Despite their popularity, the members of the Magny group were derided as amateurs, unworthy of the respect of professional historians "who devoted themselves to scientific method and the establishment of verified facts" (Dewald 2003: 1030). None of the *dîners Chez Magny* were trained as professional historians, and the inter-disciplinary character of their histories (which considered social, biographical, and psychological questions) were evaluated against institutionalized forms of history (i.e., history written from inside university history departments) and von Ranke's conception of history as a singular subject, a discipline with its own distinct methods and conventions. The Magny group, whose interests and methods found resonance with the *Annalistes* and so closely resemble contemporary historiography, present another challenge to the Rankean narrative of the origins of modern history. Historians have tended to overlook the *dîners Chez Magny* because they practiced an early form of social history rather than political history and because their histories were conceived outside of university history departments. That is, they are unacknowledged because they have traditionally been evaluated in terms of a Rankean paradigm of historical scholarship.

HISTORY, MEMORY, PRESENCE, AND ABSENCE

The Industrial and French Revolutions, along with their associated upheavals, contributed to the rise of mass historical consciousness in Europe. In *Stranded in the Present*, Peter Fritzsche argued that modern mass historical consciousness resulted from the upheavals, speed of change, and transitory nature of the French and Industrial Revolutions. As a result, contemporaries thought of the past as gone, lost, and distinctly separate from themselves and the present. Fritzsche noted that upheaval created historical consciousness by implying distance between the present and the past.

Indeed, the French philosopher Henri Bergson (1859–1941) theorized about the relationships among memory and presence. Most notably in his 1896 volume *Matter and Memory*, Bergson posited that memories never simply recall the past; in addition to recounting the past they shape the present and define its future possibilities. Memory has elements of the past, the present, and yet unrealized potentials or possibilities. Indeed, according to Bergson, memory is always embodied, material, and present. Recollection manifested the past into presence or called the past into being. Memories also represented the conditions of possibility for an individual, presaging what the evolutionary biologist Richard Dawkins would later call "memes," or units of cultural transmission. Other forms of commemoration, including festivals and anniversaries, also manifested the presence of the past through their performance. As the intellectual historian Matt K. Matsuda noted, paraphrasing Bergson, "memory was not recollection of the past, but choices made of the past applied in the present" (1996: 98).

Romantic historians were also attuned to the idea of history, or at least memory, as presence. On the one hand, Enlightenment historians such as Jean Francois-Champollion (1790–1832) believed that the practice of history consisted of simply presenting the past to the historical observer. The past was intelligible with no mediation—it could speak for itself. The historian was not required to interpret the past, but only to unearth, dust off, and present the past to his contemporaries (Gossman 1986: 38). Romantic historians like the Frenchman Jules Michelet (1798–1874), on the other hand, conceived of history as decipherment. The role of the historian was that of the prophet: he was to decipher the unintelligible past and represent it in such a way that contemporaries could understand it. The past, according to Romantic historians, could not speak the language of the present and was unintelligible without that historian's translation. The past was wholly Other to the present (Gossman 1986: 38–40, 48–9).

But even the Romantic conception of historian as "translator" of a departed or absent past still suggested distance between the subject and historical object, that the object of analysis was somehow absent and that only the historian's objective, "detached" approach to the past could confer meaning. In this conception of the past as Other and unintelligible we may recognize the unacknowledged ideological premises of Romantic historiography. Like the past, which could not speak for itself but required the historian to speak for it, the Other—colonized peoples, women, proletarians—had to be taught to speak or be spoken for. Accordingly, Romantic historians were complicit in and perhaps even reinforced the "white man's burden" of civilizing the uncivilized world and condescendingly speaking for the Other (Gossman 1986: 51). But the requirement that the historian be the figure to "present" the past to his reading public still implied that rather than speaking for itself, the past required someone to speak for it. This insight was codified in the professional history of Ranke, but professional historians were not the only figures presenting, or speaking for the past and reminding contemporaries of its presence.

THE "CULT OF THE CENTENARY"

The historian Roland Quinault has noted the proliferation of centennial anniversaries and celebrations during the nineteenth century, which he dubbed the "cult of the centenary". Those commemorated at cult of the centenary anniversaries and celebrations increasingly included "secular saints": cultural figures such as writers and philosophers in addition to political and military figures and notable events from a nation's past. Indeed, in his 1840 essay "On Heroes, Hero Worship and the Heroic in History" the Scottish historian

Thomas Carlyle (1795–1881) argued that history was nothing more than the achievements of great men. The cult of the centenary crystallized around these figures. Centenary celebrations included anniversaries, festivals, popular assemblies and processions, parades, lectures, museum exhibits, the creation of historical societies, publications, and sermons and speeches. Centenary celebrations also entailed the creation and construction of monuments and memorials, which the literary historian Ann Rigney has dubbed a nineteenth-century "epidemic statue mania" (Rigney and Leerssen 2014: 4). Memory was performed at these celebrations, and the acts of commemoration represented an invocation of the presence of the objects of memory.

Anniversaries and anniversary festivals were a paramount organizing frame of nineteenth-century memory. Anniversaries are moments at which memories are recollected, contested, and remade. Anniversaries focus the mind on the objects of their commemoration. But memory is historically conditioned. Memories of the past evoked by anniversaries are remembered in relation to contemporary concerns. The meaning of the memories and the anniversaries that commemorate them are remade in the process. These centenaries also provided popular consumers of history and participants in anniversary celebrations to engage the past outside of an academic setting and they allowed for multiple collectives to contest a singular meaning of the past.

In France, the centennial anniversaries of the death of the Enlightenment-era philosophes Voltaire (1694–1778) and Jean-Jacques Rousseau (1712–78) gave the nascent Third Republic a mnemonic rudder by which to steer the nation through the tumult of republicanism, reaction, and demands for a restoration of the monarchy. In the German lands, the Reformation anniversaries of 1817 and the 1883 anniversaries of Luther's birth are perhaps the paramount expressions of this cult of the centenary, and also demonstrated how the memory of religion worked through multiple collectives: religious, national, and political.

THE APOTHEOSIS OF THE PHILOSOPHES: VOLTAIRE AND ROUSSEAU IN NINETEENTH-CENTURY FRENCH MEMORY

Even before his death, a cult of his personality surrounding Voltaire was in full production. In 1770, the salonière Madame Necker (1737–94) commissioned a monument to the philosophe, which found realization in the sculptor Jean-Baptiste Pigalle's classically-inspired *Voltaire Nude* in 1776 (Boudrot 2014: 158). And in 1778, after a performance of the comedy *Irene*, Voltaire was feted at the conclusion as a French national treasure in a fashion typically reserved for monarchs and Catholic saints. Indeed, Denis Diderot observed that France "has paid you the homage that they have usually withheld from their sovereigns"—Voltaire was more popular than Louis XVI (Bonnet 1998: 238).

Immediately after his death, thousands of Frenchmen flocked to see the French sculptor Jean-Antoine Houdon's famous smirking bust of Voltaire. Contributing to the material culture of Voltaire's memory, Madame Tussaud had memorialized both Voltaire and Rousseau in wax in France before her move to Britain in 1802 and the opening of her eponymous wax museum. The tendency to honor these intellectual figures—Pigalle's sculpture had been the first to depict a living author—had begun during the mid-eighteenth century in the Académie française, where eulogies were delivered to men of letters. Indeed, the historian Jean-Claude Bonnet has recognized in this process the creation of a Pantheon "on paper" even before its construction in 1758 and secularization in 1791 as a burial site and memorial to the great men of France.

FIGURE 5.2: Jean-Baptiste Pigalle, *Voltaire Nude* (1776). Marble, height 150 cm. Musée du Louvre, Paris.

Upon his death in 1788, the Church refused to allow Voltaire a religious burial. He was quietly laid to rest at an abbey in northeast France, but in 1791 his remains were moved to the Pantheon. Voltaire's burial in there in 1791 included a procession of millions of Frenchman, and popular festivals and celebrations. Begun in 1758 under the direction of architect Jacques-Germain Soufflout (1713–80), the edifice now known as the Pantheon was originally constructed as a church dedicated to the patron saint of Paris, Saint Genevieve. But during the Revolution itself the church was rechristened the Pantheon and the relics associated with Saint Genevieve were removed from the building. At this point, the Pantheon was repurposed as a mausoleum for the interment of the nation's famous men and a new pediment constructed with the slogan "from a grateful fatherland, dedicated to great men." The first Frenchman to be buried in the Pantheon was not Voltaire, but the revolutionary hero Mirabeau and then Voltaire, and later Rousseau. The building reverted back to a church during the Bourbon Restoration, and then during the Second Republic, back to a secular mausoleum. The Pantheon thus functioned as the

FIGURE 5.3: Jean Antoine Houdon, Bust of Voltaire (1778). Marble, height 18 ⅞in. Metropolitan Museum of Art, New York.

French nation's memorial to itself, a site of memory at which contemporaries could construct an identity and a national narrative vis-à-vis the Revolution.

The commemoration of Jean-Jacques Rousseau, like Voltaire's, did not require a lengthy passage of time. During the early Revolution, Rousseau was remembered fondly; the 1789 Académie française eulogy was dedicated to his memory—and copies of his Social Contract were widely read and circulated by the revolutionaries. Revolutionaries also made pilgrimages to Rousseau's tomb in Ermenonville before his remains were moved to the Pantheon in 1794. And a "Society of the Friends of Jean-Jacques Rousseau" was established and enjoyed a popular reputation throughout the decade. The sculptor Houdon also cast a bust of Rousseau, which enjoyed a placement in the Hall of the Consuls. Indeed, by 1794—a mere fifteen years after his death and during the reign of Napoleon as First Consul—Rousseau was seamlessly commemorated as a precursor to the Revolution and a revolutionary hero and memorials were constructed in his honor and his remains moved to the Pantheon.

The one-hundredth anniversary of Rousseau and Voltaire's deaths in 1878 occurred within the context of the Third Republic, and the new government wasted no time or energy in claiming the philosophers for their own cause. With Republican candidates winning recent elections despite the persistence of Catholic and royalist sympathies, the republican government celebrated both men as enlightened figures, recalling Rousseau as the Frenchman par excellence, and remembering Voltaire for his irreverence, polemicism, and anti-clericalism. The Third Republic, still less than a decade old at this point, sought to legitimize itself by appealing to the memory of the Revolution and further back to the Enlightenment, sponsoring commemorations of Voltaire and Rousseau to do so (Boudrot 2014: 152). Catholics and royalists objected mightily to this commemoration of Voltaire and noted his coziness with Friedrich the Great as evidence of his friendship with Prussia, his disdain for France, and his blasphemy, which was compounded by the fact that the 1878 centenary of Voltaire fell on the feast day of Joan of Arc (Boudrot 2014: 154). In their polemics, Republicans linked contemporary opposition to this commemoration of Voltaire as an outdated nostalgia for the Old Regime and antithetical to the progress of the French nation.

Indeed, the immensely popular French writer Victor Hugo (1802–85) helped to commemorate the memory of Voltaire at one of the centenary celebrations by giving a speech at the Museum of Arts and Trades in which he praised the philosophe for singularly helping to initiate progress in France. These commemorations typically included thousands of spectators, were attended by republican political figures, and, apparently forgetting Voltaire's reverence for the absolute monarchy of Louis XIV, included thousands waving the tricolor (Boudrot 2014: 153–4). Indeed, the Third Republic's effort to "claim" Voltaire as a brilliant Enlightenment figure and revolutionary hero rather than a monarchist with fondness for the *gloire* of Louis XIV was quite intentional—it was designed to counteract increasing calls for restoration in the early Third Republic.

COMMEMORATING RELIGIOUS CONFLICT AND RENEWAL: THE ANNIVERSARIES OF 1817 AND 1883

The German historian E.W. Zeeden's magisterial *The Legacy of Luther* recounted how Luther was remembered by clergy and educated laymen from the Reformation through the early nineteenth century. Zeeden explored the varied and often conflicting interpretations and representations of Luther and the Reformation by German Lutheran theologians, philosophers, and historians from 1546 to 1800, noting the tendency of these figures to see in Luther "the archetype of the religious aspirations dominant at the time" (1954: xiii). This was a decidedly top-down intellectual history of Luther and the Reformation, which declined to account for popular representations and commemoration of Luther and the Reformation. To be sure, the historian Robert Scribner has provided extraordinary accounts of popular representations of Luther, the Reformation-era Pope Leo X (r. 1513–21), and other early modern church figures (1986: 38–68). But the seventeenth- and eighteenth-century anniversaries of the Reformation and the Augsburg Confession were administered by Lutheran church and civic authorities and celebrated more like holy days of obligation or feast days than the festive atmospheres of the nineteenth-century anniversaries (Zeeden 1954: 36).

The nineteenth century marked a change in how memories of Luther and the Reformation were commemorated and signifies the emergence of new representation of Martin Luther as a thoroughly "modern" figure whose Reformation helped to initiate modernity. The Reformation anniversaries of 1817 provided the setting for this turning point in Luther and Reformation memory. Celebrated in the wake of German liberation from Napoleonic France, in the midst of the Awakening Movement, and increasing sectarianism within

German Protestantism, the tercentennial anniversaries of the Reformation allowed celebrants to invoke Luther as a touchstone to craft a usable present. As the historian Deborah L. Fleetham has noted: "In their use of Luther to fortify their arguments against one another, nineteenth-century Protestants, in a sense, *invented* the myth of Luther. This Luther was a figure, not of his own time, but of the nineteenth century" (Fleetham 2001: 210–11).

THE REFORMATION ANNIVERSARIES IN HISTORY AND HISTORIOGRAPHY

Surveying the elite response to Luther and the Reformation, Gérald Chaix identified the Enlightenment as the turning point in the understanding of the Reformation, noting that figures from Gotthold E. Lessing (1729–81) to Johann Salamo Semler (1725–91) to Prussian King Freidrich II (r. 1740–86) celebrated Luther's translation of the Bible, his struggle on behalf of rationality against papal authority, and the Reformation's place in the development of freedom of conscience and thought (2001: 13). For the Romantics, on the other hand, Luther represented the pinnacle of genius. According to Johann Gottfried von Herder (1744–1803) he was a hero of the German nation, founder of a German national religion, and embodied the genius of the folk and the German language. And of course, G.W.F. Hegel (1770–1831) famously proclaimed that the Reformation represented a new dawn that marked the end of the Middle Ages and a new, (early) modern phase of human history. But popular forms of commemoration of the memory of Luther and the Reformation suggest that the turning point came not with the Enlightenment or Romantic thinkers, but with the 1817 anniversaries of the Reformation in Germany (Chaix 2001: 17).

Anniversaries to commemorate the Protestant Reformation have been celebrated inside Germany since 1617 and outside of that country since the nineteenth century. Often accompanied with worship services, academic lectures, historical re-enactments and popular festivals, these anniversaries have variously commemorated the Reformation, usually reflecting contemporary concerns, as a seminal religious event that nevertheless split Western Christianity, a social revolution that helped to usher in the bourgeois class, a celebration of proto-German nationalism, and an important historical-cultural process that gave birth to the modern worldview.

The historian Johannes Burkhardt identified the 1817 Reformation anniversaries and the 1830 Anniversary of the Augsburg Confession as the first sites at which the memories of Martin Luther and Reformation were celebrated in a secular and communal manner. That is to say, that while elites participated in these ceremonies and produced sermons, speeches, pamphlets, histories and hagiographies, this output was mainly for public rather than academic consumption. And indeed, while political and religious traditions were manifest in these anniversaries, each was celebrated with what Burkhardt calls a "bourgeois feel" and represented the embourgeoisement (*Verbürgerlichung*) of memories of Luther and the Reformation. Luther's memory was celebrated and commemorated in public spaces such as churches, schools, universities, city halls, lecture halls, and marketplaces with no official direction or oversight. These spaces of memory suggest the public character of Luther's memory and the communal character of the festivals. So popular memories of Luther and the Reformation expressed at the anniversaries were neither exclusively confessional, nor exclusively elite (Burkhardt 1988: 220, 227). Burkhardt concluded his analysis of the 1817 jubilees by noting that these Reformation festivals celebrated not merely events of historical significance, but the significance of history itself (1988: 231). In other words, these celebrations were where Germans learned how to become conscious of history and aware of the presence of the object(s) of historical representation. Contemporaries' memories of Luther and the Reformation were at the center of this celebration of the significance of history. Nineteenth-century memories of Martin Luther and the Reformation allowed individuals to appreciate or recognize the importance, impact, or influence of history on their everyday lives.

THE WARTBURG FESTIVAL

The 1817 Wartburg festival may be recognized as a prelude to the public and secular celebrations of Luther and Reformation memory that Burkhardt identified with the 1817 anniversaries. On October 18, 1817 a group of German university students with liberal and nationalist tendencies, many of whom were veterans of the Wars of Liberation, assembled at the Wartburg Castle in Eisenach. United under the mantra of "Honor, Freedom, Fatherland" the students agitated for a reform of German colleges, demanded a liberal constitution for Prussia and envisaged a unification of the German states. The occasion for the Wartburg Festival itself was heavy with nationalist sentiments. October 18 was in fact the fourth anniversary of the Battle of Leipzig, a decisive Prussian victory over Napoleon. The year 1817 was also the tercentennial of the Protestant Reformation, and the students' political demands and the Wartburg Castle itself were steeped in memories of Martin Luther and the Reformation. Indeed, the Wartburg Castle was the place where Saxon duke Friedrich the Wise (1463–1525) had given refuge to Martin Luther after the latter's excommunication from the Roman Church and where Luther translated the New Testament into German.

Luther's memory was manifest among the students, who celebrated the reformer as a German citizen and patriot who had embodied the liberal characteristics of reason, virtue, and freedom. The celebrants of the festival sang the Lutheran hymn "A Mighty Fortress is our God" along with other patriotic songs, and in a ritual that recalled Luther's burning of the papal bull that excommunicated him, burned books written by conservative, and anti-democratic authors. As such, the celebrants of the Wartburg festival identified the Reformation as the first salvo of a long process of German national liberation and unification. Indeed, claimed the students, just as Luther had freed the German people from the spiritual bondage of the Roman Catholic Church, the Wartburger would advocate for the political liberation of the German states from the conservative princes.

The students' invocation of Luther's memory and re-creation of acts from his life were notable, as it was not until the 1817 Reformation anniversaries that the iconic image of Luther nailing or posting the Ninety-five Theses to the Wittenberg Church door was widely known or circulated. The image or memory of this singular act of defiance, commonly identified as the "start" of the Protestant Reformation, was constructed and cultivated at the 1817 anniversaries. The 1817 Reformation anniversaries precipitated, according to Max L. Baeumer, an "epidemic" of Luther and Reformation commemoration throughout the nineteenth century (Howard and Knoll 2014).

A LUTHER FOR EVERYONE

This epidemic of Luther and Reformation memory afflicted both elites and ordinary individuals. Indeed, Martin Luther and the Reformation functioned not merely as sites of memory, but also battle grounds in the struggle between professionalization of history and popular memory. Memories of Luther and the Reformation could function as sites of mnemonic "struggle" because of the diverse participation in festivals, ceremonies, and rituals designed to commemorate those memories, which included elites, ordinary people, and everyone in between. As the historian Karin Friedrich noted:

> [M]ultiple performers of diverse ranks appear [at German festivals]: the elite at court whose lives—in peacetime—were defined by ritual and ceremony, and who—at times of war—displayed their prowess in splendour on the battlefield; the burghers and citizens who forked out the money required to welcome their prince with due honours and spectacle; the urban populace who watched and cheered the cortege; and the rural poor (together with their urban fellows) whose relaxation was to stare in awe at the sight of the Body of Christ as it was carried through the streets and who danced and got drunk on feast days. Festivals involved the whole of society.
>
> —Friedrich 2000: ix

Popular participation in anniversary celebrations and jubilee parades and processions revealed "everyday" memories of Luther and the Reformation. But intellectuals and clergy also maintained and invoked Luther memories during the "off season" periods when no anniversary or centenary of Luther or the Reformation was on the calendar (Howard 2016: 3). As such, memories of Luther and the Reformation remained present, accessible, and malleable for every occasion. The 1817 Reformation Anniversaries led to a myriad of Luthers that variously painted the reformer as a secular figure, an orthodox churchman, a political revolutionary, and a German nationalist.

The 1817 anniversaries represented a turning point in the festive culture associated with the memory of Luther and the Reformation. But earlier in the century, stone and bronze statues, along with other monumental art was produced to commemorate Luther's memory. Beginning in 1802 statues were commissioned and built in Mansfeld, Eisleben, and a ten-meter statue built in the Wittenberg marketplace. By 1841, a new railway connection allowed visitors to travel directly to the "Luther city" (Chaix 2001: 15). And at later anniversaries, sites such as Luther's home in Wittenberg and his monastery in Erfurt opened as museums opened to the public (Howard 2016: 75).

Luther was not only accessible to Protestants in memories, memorials, and anniversary celebrations. He was also present in in the memories of Roman Catholics as the embodiment of the confessional divide. German Catholics remembered Luther as a figure who had disrupted the cultural vitality of the late middle ages and as a schismatic who splintered the unity of the Church—a confessional antagonist but a national hero all at once. Indeed, both Catholics and Jews, who were conspicuous attendees of the 1817 anniversary festivals throughout the German lands, appropriated the memory of Luther and the Reformation to support their own agendas. The proliferation of competing memories of Luther—a veritable "Luther for everyone"—marked the most significant development of the historiography of the Reformation in early nineteenth-century Germany. To be sure, memories of Luther and the Reformation commemorated at the German anniversaries were decidedly Protestant sites of memory that provided a usable past to Protestants during an era in which nostalgia for the past, and especially medieval ruins, had a confessional connotation that was mnemonically coded "Catholic." These Protestant anniversaries were part of a wider trend of the occlusion of Catholic memories of Luther and the Reformation and increasingly used as catalysts of confessional strife and religious conflict. But this did not preclude Catholics and in some instances German Jews from using and abusing memories of Luther and the Reformation.

While German Protestant princes and pastors celebrated the memories of Luther and the Reformation, German Catholic historians such as Johann Adam Möhler (1796–1838) acknowledged the need to reform the medieval church, but decried Luther's Reformation as "unnecessarily revolutionary and destructive" (Dickens and Tonkin 1985: 180). Moreover, exclaimed the Catholic theologian Ignaz von Döllinger (1799–1890), the "faults and schisms" that Luther and the Reformation had created within the church emboldened contemporary atheists, who need only to point at the disunity of the Christian churches to demonstrate their case (1872: 12–14). The German Catholic essayist Joseph Görres (1776–1848) went still further and identified Luther's Reformation as mankind's "second original sin" (1821: 76).

Contemporary enlightened and Reform Jews regarded Luther as a reformer who had embodied religious toleration and emancipation (Wiese 2003: 169–71). The Berlin librarian Saul Ascher (1767–1822), a proponent of Reform Judaism, used the occasion of the 1817 anniversaries to call for a Jewish Reformation. But Orthodox Jews also used and abused memories of Luther and the Reformation. The Breslau historian Heinrich Graetz (1817–91) lauded Luther not for his spiritual emancipation of the German people, but for his piety, humility, and faith, and used the reformer as a foil against Reform Jews that had enlisted Luther for their cause (Wendebourg 2012: 250, 255–6). In fact, Luther's anti-Jewish writings were completely unknown in early-nineteenth century Germany (Wallman 1987: 86–7). This fact made memories of Luther and the Reformation usable to contemporary German Jews of both Reform and Orthodox congregations.

THE 1883 ANNIVERSARIES OF MARTIN LUTHER'S BIRTH

While memories of Luther and the Reformation took a new shape at the 1817 Reformation anniversaries, and remained present during the "Reformation of the Nineteenth Century," it was the 1883 anniversary of the reformer's birth that represented the apotheosis of the idea of a Luther-memory accessible to everyone and every interest group, however contradictory. Here, memories of Martin Luther were invoked by German liberals against conservatives, German conservatives against liberals, and by both against socialists, the French, and Roman Catholics at home and aboard. Luther was considered a proto-nationalist and compared favorably to German Chancellor Otto von Bismarck (r. 1871–90) and the Reformation was seen as a precursor to German nationalism. The nationalist historian Heinrich von Treitschke (1834–96) regarded the Franco-Prussian war as a final victory for German Protestantism over German Catholicism. This rhetoric imagined German unification as the fulfillment of a process begun during the Reformation. Indeed, these anniversaries, which the historian Thomas A. Brady recognized as a "belated birthday party for the new German Reich," were sites of memory at which the Protestant celebrants explicitly conflated Protestantism with German national identity (1998: 15). The anniversaries were accompanied by highly-politicized commemorations of Luther and the Reformation and represented the culmination of the Protestant confessionalization of the German national idea and the symbolic marginalization of German Catholics in Wilhelmine Germany.

Responses to the Protestant-cum-nationalist inflection of the 1883 anniversaries predictably broke along confessional lines. Protestant Germany—including orthodox Lutherans and Cultural Protestants—triumphantly celebrated the memory of Luther as a Protestant-German national hero. German Catholics abstained from the festivities and mourned the anniversary as a day of sorrows that recalled the German confessional divide. Orthodox Lutherans and Cultural Protestants who participated in the 1883 anniversaries celebrated Luther as both a Protestant confessional and German national hero. Orthodox remembered a Luther who was father of the Evangelical Church, herald of a pure Lutheran confession, the new patron saint of Germany, and as a thirteenth apostle (Herntrich 1982: 275). But Luther was more often remembered as a German national hero than a religious figure at the 1883 anniversaries.

German nationalists and Cultural Protestants celebrated Luther as the quintessential German man, liberator of the German conscience, author of every significant German intellectual and social achievement, and no less than the creator of a new ideal of humanity and as the initiator of modernity. German liberals invoked a Luther who was a hero of freedom, an idol of progress, an intellectual hero, and a fierce opponent of clerical tutelage (Herntrich 1982: 275). Luther was held in the same esteem as German national heroes, past and present—from the barbarian Arminius to Otto von Bismarck—and recognized as the embodiment of Germanness and a foil against foreign (read: French and Catholic) influence.

Perhaps the most belligerent anti-Catholic expression of a political-national memory of Martin Luther came from the Prussian nationalist historian Heinrich von Treitschke. In his 1883 essay "Luther and the German Nation," Treitschke maintained that the Luther anniversaries were for German Protestants only, and that German Catholics had no place there (1883: 470). Treitschke derided Catholics as foreign to German society and claimed to pity them for being unable to comprehend Luther's significance for and contributions to the German nation (1883: 470). Because German Catholics could not share the sense of German-Protestant national consciousness that Luther had originally inspired, Treitschke identified Catholics as decidedly non-German. Like the Jews, who Treitschke would later infamously regard as Germany's "misfortune," German Catholics remained fundamentally alien to Germany.

Treitschke also remembered Luther as the first champion of a German national identity and solidarity. It was Luther who had initially stirred the feelings of German national pride and had liberated Germany from the yoke of an oppressive foreign influence. The "kleindeutsch" unification of the German nation in 1871 had been the ultimate realization of this act. Indeed, Treitschke claimed that Luther's "political" liberation of German Christianity from Roman authority represented a more powerful and enduring act than his Reformation of the church (1883: 475). For Treitschke, the origins of German nationalism and the contemporary German nation lie with the Protestant Reformation and with Luther. German history began with Luther, and the establishment of a Protestant-kleindeutsch empire represented the culmination of this history. This confessionally-exclusive narrative of German unification—one that began in 1517 and concluded in 1871—explicitly conflated Protestantism with German national identity, perpetuated the confessional divide, and further marginalized Catholics from German political culture.

On the other hand, German Catholics invoked a Luther who had destroyed the cultural vitality of the late middle ages and the Reformation as destructive of Christian unity, electing to forget or ignore the memories that their contemporaries recalled. As the historian and cultural theorist Jan Assmann has noted, "For a functioning communicative memory, forgetting is just as vital as remembering. [. . .] Remembering means pushing other things into the background, making distinctions, obliterating many things in order to shed light on others" (2006: 3). Unlike their Protestant counterparts who recalled Luther as a German national hero and cultural benefactor, contemporary German Catholics remembered Luther as a tragic figure who had disrupted the cultural vitality of the late middle ages and as a schismatic who had violated German confessional and national unity (Lehmann 1983: 110). The ultramontane faction within the Catholic Church recognized the 1883 Luther anniversaries as a continuation of the policies of the Kulturkampf and as a "call to arms" against German Catholicism. This sentiment was widely shared among German Catholics, who regarded the conflation of Protestantism and German national identity at the 1883 anniversaries as an occasion for sorrow and mourning (Düfel 1984: 77–8).

LUTHER IN AMERICA

In contrast to Europe, Luther's mnemonic presence in nineteenth-century North America manifested itself almost exclusively as opposition to Roman Catholicism. If Luther himself was not yet present in North America, the perceived threat of papalism was, and Luther's memory was deployed as a foil to Roman Catholicism, immigrants from southern European countries, and the 1870 Vatican Council. The 1817 Reformation anniversaries in North America were limited in scope and celebrated primarily by Lutheran immigrants (Howard 2016: 77–8). But the 1883 anniversaries of Luther's birth represented the high point of Luther's presence in American historical consciousness, at which the reformer was recognized as a figure who had helped to initiate freedom and democracy, and thus a figure increasingly accessible to modern Americans. On the occasion of the 1883 anniversaries of Luther's birth, the United States Congress even commissioned a monument to Luther—a replica of the Luther statue of Worms and a gift of Kaiser Wilhelm I—that was unveiled in 1884 in a ceremony accompanied with great pomp and circumstance (Howard 2016: 85). During the First World War, the American celebration of Luther's memory was more muted, especially during the 1917 Reformation anniversaries, as Luther and the Reformation were suspected of contributing to German militarism and imperialism (Granquist 2016). Nevertheless, Luther's memory had crossed the Atlantic and provided a present, usable past for Americans as well.

CHAPTER SIX

High Culture and Popular Culture

KATHRIN MAURER

In 1847, chemist Justus Liebig invented a procedure for extracting meat into a highly-concentrated bouillon paste. The sales of this industrially mass-produced condiment skyrocketed due to Liebig's innovative marketing strategy: the attachment of a small colorful *Liebig Sammelbild* (Liebig trading card) to each packet. These trading cards circulated between 1875 to 1940 among meat extract consumers, presenting a wide array of motifs: animals, technology, food, traditional costumes, literature, art, and music. Many of these cards also depicted historical themes, such as battles of the European Wars, the feats of high-powered military generals, or the rise of the Roman Empire. Figure 6.1 displays the German Wars against Napoleon and the image clearly conveys an effort to educate a larger audience in national history. Often, these images were highly politically charged, as when they represented ethnic groups from the (German) colonies during the Wilhelmine era, German mythological figures (Widukind), or the German Emperor Wilhelm II. Historian Bernhard Jussen has argued that this collection was probably more powerful in shaping collective memory than historical painting (Jussen 2002: 2–15). Anybody who could afford to buy bouillon could learn a snippet of history.

The Liebig trading cards exemplify two general trends characteristic of nineteenth-century memory culture in Germany and in Europe in general. Firstly, the cards display the visual configuration of memory culture. As will be discussed in this chapter, many storage media were visual in nature, such as museums, panoramas, illustrated books, photography, and magazines. The rather unknown nineteenth-century German author Friedrich Oldenberg characterized his time as a "seeing age" due to its relentless production of images. This age of the *Bilderflut* (flood of images), to use another of Oldenberg's expressions, created in turn collective visual memory (Oldenberg 1859: 27).[1] Secondly, the trading cards show how this visual memory intertwines popular and high cultural forms of historical knowledge. On the one hand, Liebig commercialized and popularized the past on these mass-produced trading cards, making it into an object of consumption. The cards suggest that history is for sale; a commodity to be traded and sold for the sake of entertainment. On the other hand, Liebig's business strategy reiterates the historicist educational program's traditional guidelines, such as, that society has to be understood in a historical context, that we need to learn from national history, and that the past plays a significant role in understanding the present. Although they were not aesthetically complex, the Liebig trading cards were thoroughly researched by their creators, based on knowledge found in scholarly historiographies as well as in popular history books.

FIGURE 6.1: In an effective marketing strategy, Liebig's Meat Extract Company attached a trading card to each jar of bouillon paste. Above, the Prussian military in action during the so-called Wars of Liberation in 1813–15. Deutsches Historisches Museum.

Moreover, the trading cards yield important theoretical questions. During the nineteenth century, how are the distinctions between high and popular culture in the realm of memory constructed? What political purposes does historical memory serve? How, precisely, does the visual configuration of memory make sense of the past? To answer these questions, the discussions below will identify, investigate, and interpret examples of visual memory culture, demonstrating their close entangling of, and the discursive interaction between, elements of high and popular cultural forms.[2] Having set out some theoretical considerations on history and memory, this chapter will use the example of German academic historicism to illuminate this intertwinement between popular and scholarly history in the age of empire. Illustrating academic historicism's aspirations to high culture, the chapter then gives special attention to popular forms of visual memory culture, including, in particular, historical panorama paintings, illustrated history books, historical novels, sculptures, and museums. These marked combinations of high and popular culture in single memory objects and contexts exemplify many of the key and general characteristics of memory culture during the nineteenth century. Naturally, this chapter cannot present an exhaustive narrative about the development of cultural memory in its various aspects. Rather, the goal is to investigate individual examples and genres of memory culture that can shed light on the reception, political ramifications, and power dynamics of remembering the past during this time. Germany is a particularly interesting case, since it was the cradle of academic historicism as well as a showcase of popular memory culture. However, although Germany is in focus, it is crucial for this chapter to open up for some comparative views and discuss nineteenth-century memory culture in a European context. Such comparative perspective will help us to understand that memory culture during this time is not an isolated phenomenon, but rather a multi-national and multi-medial phenomenon, whose individual *Wirkungsgeschichten* (histories of effectiveness) are closely entangled with each other.

STORING THE PAST: HISTOIRE AND MÉMOIRE

Mapping memory culture in nineteenth-century Germany and Europe is no small task. Memory seems to be everywhere.[3] The era was marked by the French Revolution, the Napoleonic Wars, the liberal revolutions, and imperialism. The many historical and political changes that came with these revolutions are documented in a vast array of storages, such as archives, history books, images, libraries, and museums. Jürgen Osterhammel, emphasizing the sheer mass of data that became available in the nineteenth-century, characterized these as *Erinnerungshorte* (memory hoards) rather than *Erinnerungsorte* (memory spaces) (Osterhammel 2009: 31). A common sorting principle was the organization of stores of data according to high and popular historical culture. Thus, academic elite historians' investigations were carried out as high culture, while the historical pop culture of the time spectacularized the past into a sensational commodity.

The dichotomies between high and low, elite and popular, professional and mainstream forms of historical culture can be also found in the theoretical discussions about memory and history. In the introduction to his three volumes set on French memory and culture, historian Pierre Nora suggested the following distinction: "*Mémoire* is rooted in the concrete: in space, gesture, image, and object. *Histoire* dwells exclusively on temporal continuities, on changes in things and in the relations among things. *Mémoire* is absolute, while *histoire* is always relative" (Nora 1996: 3). In this passage, Nora offers *mémoire* as a form of historical imagination that differs from an *histoire*, which is taken to be the intellectual, critical analysis of history. Deeply rooted in personal experience and affection, *mémoire* embodies a mode of dealing with the past based on visual and spatial configurations. Visual forms of historical memory are present in paintings, sculptures, museums, and in poetic works (i.e. illustrated literary texts as well as novels and poems that make use of visual poetic strategies). Thus, this definition of objects and texts as exemplifying *mémoire* also provides a way of integrating aesthetics as a historical experience, since *mémoire* can be based on subjective and affective forms of reception. Furthermore, the spatial dimension (topographies, geographical settings of history, spatial orders of time in the museums) is crucial to *mémoire*, and stands at odds with the focus on temporality and development in the realm of *histoire*. Both the visual quality and the spatial dimensions of memory will also be central to this analysis of historical memory culture in the nineteenth century.

Whereas *histoire*, which demands intellectual endeavor on the part of its producers (writers, historians, and artists), seeks the status of universal authority, and calls for rational analysis, *mémoire* reconstructs the past by means of iconic, spatial, and aesthetic strategies, and can even go against the backdrop of narrative and temporal organization. Although Nora considers cases of memory culture in which *histoire* and *mémoire* are combined, the two categories describe an opposition to each other. In many ways, Nora based these distinctions on Maurice Halbwachs' theories about collective and historical memory, which he established in his works *The Social Frameworks of Memory* (1925) and *The Collective Memory* (posthumously published in 1950). Like Nora, Halbwachs also pointed to the idea that historical memory (*histoire*) lacks the living, spontaneous, and heterogeneous nature of collective memory. Historical memory is unitary, abstract, and disconnected from the individual experience. In the German context, Étienne François and Hagen Schulze likewise examined various places that figure prominently German memory activity, an endeavor that associates specific concepts (identity, freedom, revolution) with historical themes, figures, and places (Weimar, Volkswagen, and Nietzsche) while deliberately eschewing a linear and chronological narrative (François and Schulze 2008).

In the disciplines of cultural studies, history and the social sciences, this sharp distinction between *mémoire* and *histoire* has been intensely debated, and has been seen as outdated for a long time. Scholars discussed the importance of individual experience to the formation of collective memory, and thus its crucial role in the investigation of history.[4] Visual memory, which Nora and Halbwachs exclusively connected to the field of the non-scholarly modes of remembering (*mémoire*), has been integrated in the academic discipline of history as well. Today, images are no longer seen as mere illustrations to a historiographical narrative, but rather, in the context of the so-called iconic turn, they have gained their own epistemological function and hermeneutic power (Paul 2011). For many contemporary historians, images deploy their own specific iconic language to make sense of the past, and image theories by Aby Warburg and W.J.T. Mitchell have become crucial (Böhm and Bredekamp 2008).

Many scholars of academic nineteenth-century historicism in Germany, however, considered *mémoire* as a kind of counter-weight against *histoire*.[5] This view is overstated. The boundaries between the academy and popular memory culture were always in flux. The popularization of the past shaped collective perceptions of history that can be found in scholarly historicism, and vice versa, scholarly methods were also often used in the production of historical pop culture. The division between high-culture and elitist forms of historical representation, on the one hand, and popular forms of memory on the other, thus does not hold. More usefully, already in the 1980s the historian Otto Gerhard Oexle defined German historicism as an interdisciplinary phenomenon that is constitutive of modernity, and vital to the formation of different discourses of knowledge (1986: 119).

Other scholars have also noted this entwinement between *mémoire* and *histoire* in reference to German historical culture. As Susan Crane aptly pointed out, the collection activities of amateur historians with reference to the Napoleonic Wars are directly connected to academic historiography (Crane 2000a). In fact, it was these efforts by auto-didactic antiquarians and private collectors that led to the development of a more professionalized study of history as a scholarly discipline. At the same time, this turn toward historicizing culture did not remain behind the walls of the academy. In the course of the nineteenth century, historians opened up their knowledge to the "public," and, with the help of new visual media, tailored it to the expectations of the mass bourgeois audience, and popularized it. It is important to insist that this popularization did not always entail a simplification or a loss of academic quality.[6] Rather, popularization typically meant the usage of a different set of rhetorical tools and media technologies to convey historical knowledge. Rather than necessarily "dumbing down" history, the medial translation of knowledge to the general public created reciprocal interactions between scholarly and non-scholarly discourses. Thus, academic historicism's influence on historical culture in the nineteenth century was therefore linked to both high and popular conceptions of the past. Before taking up specific cases of this interaction between popular and scholarly modes of staging the past in nineteenth-century Germany and Europe, some thoughts about the concept of historicism and its origins are in order.

GERMAN ACADEMIC HISTORICISM AND HIGH CULTURE

Historian Reinhart Koselleck has suggested that, around the end of the eighteenth century in Europe, the meaning of the term "history" began to change: history was no longer only about telling *Geschichten* (stories); it became a symbolic concept with scholarly and philosophical ramifications, namely *Geschichte* (history) (Maurer 2013: 8). History acquired the potential of being a "collective singular" by which it gained an epistemic authority to make sense of the past, as well as to shape a reflexive discourse about itself (Koselleck 1972: 647–52). The events of the French Revolution were crucial to history's career shift. Its bloody and terror-filled finale, the collapse of the Republic and the rise of Emperor Napoleon, shattered the Enlightenment ideals of reason, humanity, freedom, and tolerance.

Many European intellectuals posited a fundamental crisis of history, politics, and civilization. In France, the conservative and royalist politician and historian François-René de Chateaubriand not only rallied against Napoleon in 1814, but also his essays, such as *The Genius of Christianity* (1801), were highly influential for the development of literary Romanticism. In Germany, Friedrich Schiller's famous letters of 1801, *Über die ästhetische Erziehung des Menschen in einer Reihe von Briefen* (*Letters on the Aesthetic Education of Man*) record what Schiller considered the deep crisis in the processes of modern European civilization. Johann Gottfried Herder's scepticism about universal and rational categories gained a specific historical dimension, which was typical for Romantic thinkers, writers, and artists of the time. According to Herder's *Ideen zur Philosophie der Geschichte der Menschheit* (*Philosophical Ideas about the History of Humankind*, 1784–91), historical processes no longer embodied a progressive linear development towards the universal idea of history as it is found in Hegel's systematic philosophy of history. Rather, historical processes are constituted by the individuality and uniqueness of historical events, subjects, and nations.

This re-evaluation of history as a "collective singular" was also crucial to the formation of academic historicism. Leopold von Ranke (1795–1886) aimed to professionalize history and intended to install—in however naive a way—a paradigm of objectivity. He wanted to show only "the naked truth without any ornaments, thorough analysis of the details; the rest under God's command; no fiction, not even in details, no fantasizing" (Ranke 1884: 24). The archive thus embodied the ideal workplace for this kind of historian, along with new techniques essential to history writing, ushering in the apparatus of footnotes, references, and bibliographies (Grafton 1997). As these techniques emphasized distance, objectification, and the thorough elaboration of source material as essential, Ranke's efforts to professionalize the academic discipline come close to what Nora has called *histoire*.

However, it is important to note that Ranke was from the beginning closely affiliated to the study of aesthetics.[7] He was well-educated in philology, translation, and classical and romantic literature. Here, he considers history writing to be an essentially aesthetic practice: "History differs from other scholarly disciplines, because it is at the same time art. History is science, since it collects, finds, and thoroughly examines; history is art in the way how it represents the findings and discoveries. Other sciences only describe the findings: to history belongs the faculty of reproduction (*Vermögen*)" (Ranke 1975: 72). Accordingly, Ranke's conception of historicism merged academic discourse with aesthetics, and it was precisely the realm of art that enabled the interpretation of scholarly discoveries. This aesthetic configuration invites forms of *mémoire*, since it allows for the power of imagination, the subjects' individual experience, and a certain artistic autonomy or freedom concerning representation.

For many nineteenth-century historians, this aesthetic configuration of investigating the past was rather common. Not only in Germany, also in France one can find similar developments. The works by the historian and author Hippolyte Adolphe Taine show the strong influence of literature and style in his writing about the history of the French ancient regime (*The Origins of Contemporary France*, 1875). While focusing on history, this work coalesces literary aesthetics, nationalist essentialism, historicist methodology and sociological positivism. In fact, the aesthetic frame was often seen as the necessary precondition for history's emergence as a modern academic discipline. In Germany, the so-called Prussian School, which was composed of Gustav Droysen, Heinrich von Treitschke, and Heinrich von Sybel, and demanding a political radicalization and nationalization of the Rankean version of historicism, entrenched their efforts to represent history within aesthetics (Jaeger and Rüsen 1992: 86–92). Droysen highlighted the historical narrative as an autonomous poetic form of historical representation and emphasized the study of philological-hermeneutic sources as essential to modern history writing. Beyond this group there was the historian Gottfried Gervinius and his history of German literature (*Geschichte der poetischen National-Literatur der Deutschen*, 1835–1842), a work which applied not only a historicist method, but also articulated patriotic and political opinion by writing a national history of German literature. And the famous Swiss art historian Jacob Burckhardt simply claimed all history as poetry. Seen in this light, it is less surprising that the 1902 Nobel Prize for literature was awarded to the historian Theodor Mommsen for his book on Roman history.

In today's research on German historicism, this connection between scholarly history and aesthetics is still prominent. Historian Jörn Rüsen has emphasized the instrumentalization of aesthetics as a necessary step in formulating history as a modern "disciplinary matrix" (Jaeger and Rüsen 1992: 88). In addition, researchers have demonstrated the presence of eighteenth-century aesthetic and literary traditions in Ranke's and Droysen's historiography (Hinrichs 1954; Fulda 1996). Symptomatic of this scholarship is the fact that history's aesthetic design is debated exclusively within the context of so-called "high culture," such as the intellectual and literary works of German Romanticism, Goethe's novels, and Schiller's plays.[8] It is imperative to note, however, that Ranke's and other scholarly historians' integration of the aesthetic set of practices was not only restricted to the high-culture aesthetics of Romanticism and Weimar classicism. Several studies show that, for example, Ranke's writings reiterate popular modes of perception of the past as practiced in the optical medium of the panorama: Ranke's historiography is often set in all-encompassing, picturesque, landscape and mountain panoramas (Maurer 2013: 17–72; Hebekus 2003: 43–69; Hess 1975: 555–91). This picturesque and touristic aesthetic locates Ranke's representation of history as closely indebted to modern mass media practices of spectacularizing the past, such as the panorama. Viewed in this way, academic historicism's influence across the Anglo-Euro cultural sphere, was deeply entwined with historical popular culture, and was clearly shaped by its collective perception modes.

SPECTACULARIZNG THE PAST IN THE PANORAMA

In the course of the nineteenth century, the production of panorama paintings became a flourishing industry. Panoramic representations of tourist attractions, such as the mountain vistas, cityscapes, and views on monuments were fashionable. Audiences could enjoy these breathtaking sights without ever leaving home. Aside from picturesque tourist motifs, panoramas also displayed historical events, such as military battles, war scenes, and the deeds of "war heroes." Important examples of early historical panoramas include: the grand 1822 panorama of *The Battle of Waterloo* by Henry Aston Barker, son of Robert Barker, the medium's inventor; the 1811 historical panorama *Gibraltar* by painter William Barton; and the work of military painter Colonel Jean-Charles Langlois. In the early decades, many of these historical panoramas toured in Germany and, by the last third of the century—the beginning of the *Gründerzeit* (Founding Epoch)—more and more professional painters in Germany began to craft historical panoramas themselves.

One exemplary, highly-popular historical panorama was Anton von Werner's *The Battle of Sedan*, which opened in Berlin on the battle's anniversary, September 1, 1883. Since 1871, the date had been designated a national holiday, marked by festivals, marches, theater plays, and parades. This decisive Franco-Prussian battle, which resulted in the capture of Napoleon III, and France's capitulation to the German Empire, was a key moment in the collective memory about Prussia's national glory. The Sedan Panorama was one of the costliest paintings of its kind. Its gigantic screen was exhibited in a monumental rotunda in Berlin. Visitors could see not only the painting of the battle, but additional dioramas of historical scenes. They could also enjoy the restaurant hall in the basement and music by a live military orchestra. Figure 6.2 shows the brochure that accompanied a visit to the Sedan Panorama. Besides the reproduction of a part of the panoramic image to the right, the picture also, on the left side, invites the visitor to the restaurant located in the rotunda. In addition to the culinary delights, the visitor could also enjoy twelve historical paintings and electric lighting in the evenings. To view the main picture, the audience had to pass through a hallway in the basement, climb up a staircase, and then step onto a circular balcony. Standing in the dark, the audience was

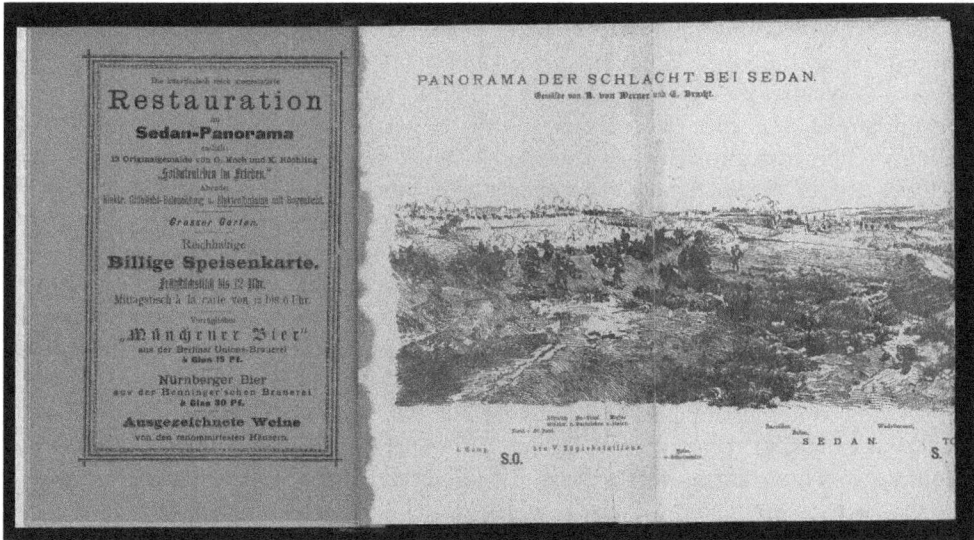

FIGURE 6.2: Anton Werner, Eugen Bracht, Ludwig Pietsch. The Sedan Panorama. Berlin: Photographische Gesellschaft, 1885.

immersed in the middle of the Floing plateau in the Ardennes of Northern France, where the battles between Prussian infantry and the French cavalry had taken place. Different eye-catching scenes of combat between the enemy armies were on display, each geographically, temporally, and historically reconstructed with utmost precision.

The Sedan Panorama exemplifies, on the one hand, the spectacularization of the past within the context of Prussian imperialism and its geopolitical ambitions. Visitors were eager to see this sensation; it became a site for a national cult and a moneymaking machine. Although there was no elevated sovereign in the picture (the emperor was not visible in the Sedan Panorama), the state's power is still exerted by the all-encompassing nature of the painting itself. The omnipresence of the event of the "grandiose" battle overwhelms the visitors visually, turning them into "virtual" participants in it—as soldiers, patriotic fighters, and individual makers of history.[9] The panorama was an important instrument in the maintenance of an ostentatious fantasy of national super-power. According to Benedict Anderson, nations are built through the act of imagination and in a national community the images of enemy and ally constitute its framings (Anderson 1983). The panorama as a medium spectacularizing collective memory was key to shaping this imaginary national community.

However, on the other hand, this nationalistic popularization of the past never gave up its scholarly historicist traditions. Exemplifying the entanglement of *mémoire* and *histoire* and the imprecision of distinctions between these in practice, as well as the vitality of aesthetically rendered history, Werner also spent a fortune on historical research and source study. He had employed a whole team of photographers, historians, and landscape painters who studied not only panoramic painting technique, but closely investigated historical documents, eyewitness accounts of the battle of Sedan, as well as historical uniforms, horses, and weapon types (Grau 2003: 116).

Many panoramas exhibited this simultaneity of spectacularizing politics and scholarly rigidity; also, in the context of German and European colonialism. This was notably the case in so-called "travel" panoramas that invited the viewer to journey to exotic and distant countries. Dolf Sternberger's 1938 essay *Panorama oder Ansichten vom 19. Jahrhundert* (Panorama or Views of the Nineteenth Century) reveals the panoramic perspective on the Middle East to be a vehicle for imperialist ideology. Behind the medium's picturesque surface lies a powerful colonialist perspective—one that appropriates another culture's "otherness" into the aesthetics of picturesque. Art historian Linda Nochlin critically discussed so-called oriental painting of the nineteenth century, such as works by the French painter Jean-Léon Gérôme (2004: 289–398). He was known for his ability to paint vast panoramic scenes, and his paintings about the culture of the Middle East often display a monumental and an all-encompassing perspective. Together with other representative painters of this "Orientalist School" he exoticized the Middle East by presenting it as a spectacular and picturesque travel attraction.

In Germany, panoramas often exhibited a colonialist fantasy, most prominently in the Deutsches Kolonialmuseum (Colonial Museum, 1899–1925), which was not only constructed in a panorama-shaped rotunda, but also exhibited panorama paintings (as well as dioramas) of the German colonies. Carl Hagenbeck's *Völkerschaus* (shows of the people; live performances in the Berlin Zoological Garden of representative foreign people, such as Mongolians, Somali, or Laplanders) serve as another example of this kind of German orientalism (Ames 2004: 313–27). All these spectacularizing venues exhibiting other ethnic groups were seen as a scholarly ethnographic and anthropological endeavors. The promotion of a "scientifically" proven colonial perspective was essential to building the ideological frames that justified overseas ventures and military interventions during the Wilhelminic era in Germany as well as in the European Empire. Emperor Wilhelm II's speech to the German Marine Corps in 1901, the so-called *Hunnenrede* (Hun speech) delivered before going off to suppress the Chinese Boxer Rebellion provides a clear example. Here, Wilhelm II made use of an abundance of racist stereotypes, that appeared in the travel and colonial panoramas for decades. The horrible scenes of the Chinese Boxer Rebellion were re-enacted on meadows and in parks in Europe and reproduced in popular culture. In 1901, the Boxer Revolution was even made into the topic of one of the first documentary films as well as becoming a theme of post cards (Osterhammel 2009: 81). The postcard in Figure 6.3 reflects the Chinese as a threat and danger to the Western imperium and portrays the Chinese soldier in stereotypical and racist ways. Post cards in general became an important aspect of visual historical culture, and were—in ways similar to the Liebig trading cards—often instrumentalized for nationalist and political agendas (Holzheid: 2011).

A similar intertwinement of popularized and politized collective memory through reliance on scholarly traditions can be found in the genre of history painting. With its debut in the Renaissance, this genre aims to represent historical themes, myths, and historical figures. During the beginning of the nineteenth century, the genre was used by many French artists (such as Jacques-Louis David and Carle Vernet) to depict Napoleon as the hero of the epoch. Their artworks stand in stark contrast to for example Spanish artist Francisco Goya's historical paintings. Goya's oil *The Third of May 1808* (1814) about the Spanish resistance against Napoleon's armies displays the brutality and atrocities of war in an unprecedented graphic fashion. In Germany during the nineteenth century, history paintings were often very closely related to academic historicism. They were

FIGURE 6.3: Postcard from the Boxer Rebellion. Deutsches Historisches Museum, 1900–1.

thought to be conveying historical knowledge, and to accompany scholarly historiographies produced in the academy. And many painters, for example Friedrich Gunkel, instrumentalized historical painting as political propaganda (Hager 1989). Gunkel's monumental painting, *Hermannsschlacht* (depicting the Battle of Hermann, a contest between Germanic tribes and Romans in the Teutoborg Forest) promotes the myth of German military strength and courage.

The invention and popularization of photography during the mid-nineteenth century certainly created a competition to the genre of historical painting. The birth of "authenticity" and the recordings of "real" history threatened the era of great and grandiose historical paintings. Pioneering battle site photography from the American Civil War or the Crimean War offered different kinds of insights into the battles than painting and could be distributed to many people. War heroes, emperors, and kings could be photographically reproduced in portraits and hung onto the walls in private living rooms (Osterhammel 2009: 77). On the one hand, photography could undermine the colonial memory politics of the panorama and counteract the exoticizing of the Orient. Photographic images could thus "disenchant" conceptions of a "magic" Orient, such as the early photographs of the Chinese opium dens or from scenes from the Indian Rebellion in 1857 (Osterhammel 2009: 79). On the other hand, photography was also quickly discovered as an instrument to propagate colonialism within an ethnographic and archaeological scholarly frame and was often implemented as a technology to construct the cultural "Other," as Elizabeth Edwards has shown in her work on nineteenth-century colonial culture photography (2008: 239–46). The work by the nineteenth-century anthropologist Albert Frisch, who was one of the first to photograph the indigenous people from the Amazon and whose pictures were shown at exhibitions in the 1860s in Paris, serve as another example of this type of colonialist photography.

In sum, this development of mass media, such as illustrated newspapers and magazines, not only increased the circulation of images during this time, but also created mass audiences that consumed them on a daily and weekly basis.[10] A phenomenon that was by no means restricted to Germany, but can easily be found in other European countries and the US (Britain was the cradle for panoramas, Paris a show case for the World Fair, and illustrated newspapers and magazines with colonial and imperial themes were widespread around the globe). The representation of the past—in a colonial or a national context—was clearly popularized by new printing techniques, technologies of image reproduction, and distribution logistics. In this context, also the genre of illustrated history books emerged and became a crucial shaper of collective memory.

ILLUSTRATED HISTORY BOOKS

During the second half of the nineteenth century, developments in the printing and reproduction of images led to their proliferation on a massive scale in Europe and around the globe. Academic historians began to work with images and, in so doing, mediated their research as national education to the public. The illustrated history book was ideally suited to their purpose. France was the most advanced in technologies of historical image reproduction. Napoleon's media and propaganda machine certainly propelled the development of visual culture. Napoleon was eager to stage his military feats on all kinds of media channels: sculptures, paintings, panoramas, festivals, parades, novels, magazines, and illustrated history books. Around the beginning of the nineteenth century the genre of the illustrated history book boomed displaying the war feats of the French general to

HIGH CULTURE AND POPULAR CULTURE 125

the masses and, in doing so, a whole collective imaginary of the Napoleonic Wars was created (Mieszkowski 2012).

Paul Mathieu Laurent de L'Ardèche's *Histoire de L'Empereur Napoléon* (*History of the Emperor Napoleon*, 1827/1839) is an example of a French illustrated history book, which became a historical bestseller and was read by a mass audience (Samuels 2004). The artist Horace Vernet used the new technique of wood engraving for cheap and fast image reproduction in L'Ardèche's book; a method that was invented by Thomas Bewick in Britain around the end of the eighteenth century.

Figure 6.4 displays a scene from L'Ardèche's illustrated history book showing Napoleon's invasion of Egypt in 1798. The image provides a close-up of Napoleon riding

FIGURE 6.4: Image of Napoleon at the Battle of Embabeh in 1798 in Egypt in Paul Mathieu Laurent de L'Ardèche's *Histoire de L'Empereur Napoléon* (*History of the Emperor Napoleon*, 1827/1839). Illustration by Horace Vernet, p. 124. Kongelige Bibliotek, Copenhagen.

his horse towards the pyramids. He is surrounded by his troop; one can see the excitement on the faces of the soldiers. As the image shows a dynamic, dramatic scene of conquest, the text that embeds this image likewise uses exclamation marks and a vivid language to picture this decisive historical moment. The image seems to draw the reader into the historical scene. Thus, he or she can easily lose distance from the historical event and experience the situation as an engaged eyewitness (Burke 2007). In his study on French illustrated history books, Maurice Samuels described the innovation offered by wood engraving like this: "Unlike traditional woodcuts, in which an image was carved on a plank with the grain running horizontal to the surface (*bois de fil*), the new technique, pioneered in England in the eighteenth century, used harder wood (boxwood), cut the engraving into the end of the wood (*bois du bout*), with the grain perpendicular to the surface, and used a burin instead of a knife" (2004: 68). According to Samuels, wood engraving allows for high-quality images to appear on the same page as the text. This was also possible with other printing techniques, but wood engraving was much cheaper and became the reproduction technology for popular magazines all over Europe.

In many ways, Germany's visual culture during the first half of the nineteenth-century was in comparison to France's rather undeveloped, in terms of the media hype and its image circulation around Napoleon.[11] Nevertheless, when nationalist movements took another turn around the 1840s, German artists and historians were not only eager to work with new printing techniques, they were also looking for a German national hero comparable to Napoleon's stature. In this context, the cult around the Prussian King Frederick the Great was revived in 1840 (which was precisely one hundred years after his inauguration). During this time, literary works about the king, monuments, and visual art surged in the realm of collective memory (Peterson 2005: 97–145). Christian Daniel Rauch's monumental equestrian statue of Frederick II in Berlin, inaugurated in 1851 and on view on Unter den Linden today, was also a product of this Frederick cult. As these textual, visual, and aural forms of remembering proliferated, many illustrated history books about the king were written.

The painter Adolph Menzel, who became one of the Empire's most famous artists, is crucial in this context. Known for his historical oil paintings of the Prussian regime, Menzel's patriotic works often satisfied the public's taste and supported the continual expansion of Prussia's power throughout the nineteenth century.[12] Menzel's art also takes pride of place in the context of illustrated history books, which, similar to historical (panorama) painting, also popularized history and made it available for the masses. Together with the art historian Franz Kugler they published the *History of Frederick the Great (Geschichte Friedrichs des Großen)* in 1842.[13]

Kugler and Menzel suggested that Frederick II's era should be portrayed as exemplary for the national power of Germany, and it propagates a pro-Prussian attitude, backing the militaristic and aggressive power politics of the regime. Key for them was to make the reader an active participant in this national educational endeavor. It is interesting that Menzel also used the technique of wood engraving. In fact, he knew about the French illustrated history books and was in contact with wood engravers in Paris (Düwert 127–88). Comparing Menzel's illustrations with the ones in L'Ardèche's history book, one can find many similarities, such as the merging of text and image, the close focus on individuals and their emotions, as well as the ornamental initials of each chapter.

How does the printing technique of wood engraving shape the historical memory of Frederick II as displayed in Figure 6.5? The wood engraving shows Frederick II riding through an intense and dangerous battle. The text and the image do not portray this war

FIGURE 6.5: Adolph Menzel and Franz Kugler, *Geschichte Friedrichs des Grossen*. Leipzig: Hermann Mendelsohn, 1876, 251. Adolph Menzel portrays Frederick the Great in the *History of Frederick the Great* (1842) as a mounted military leader in the Seven Years War. The image seems to emerge out of the text and draws the spectator right into the historical event.

situation separately, as it was done in older illustrated history books in which the image a war hero was put on separate sheet and often covered with a silk paper. Rather the image in the text fuses the textual and the visual, which in turn seems to suggest that the image reaches out and draws the reader almost bodily into the action as an active participant. Thus, the era of Fredrick II should no longer be understood as the distancing period of anti-bourgeois absolutism; the visual-textual composition identifies and celebrates Frederick II as the founder of the national era in Germany, and it is the reader's weighty task to continue this history.

This eye catching, engaging style of imaging is in many ways reminiscent of the panorama and its immersion of the viewer into a type of historical presence. This popularization of the past is again defined by the entwinement of *histoire* and *mémoire*. In his foreword, Menzel emphasized that he conducted many in-depth scholarly studies to prepare himself for the book illustrations: he sought out collections of images to learn about fashion, military uniforms, and architecture, and additionally that he used oil paintings and copper engravings as historical sources. Kugler was also well versed in analyzing Prussian historical sources, and he studied works about Frederick II by contemporary historians. In other words, although the authors were both eager to spectacularize the past, their illustrated history book clearly served a scholarly purpose. Such books were supposed to be well-researched, based on solid historical scholarship, and were to be understood as an academic venture. In contrast to the products of early traditional academic historicism (Ranke, Droysen, Sybel), these history books were made available to the general bourgeois audience, and the power of their narratives resulted in great part from the use of text interspersed with and inseparable from images.

As with the panoramas, colonial exhibitions, and historical paintings, so the French and German (and other European) illustrated history books represent a form of collective memory that is shaped according to the political ideologies of the respective regime promoting nationalism and imperialism. However, not all illustrated history books were necessarily nationalistic. Adolf Bär and Paul Quensel's 1890 *Bildersaal Deutscher Geschichte: Zwei Jahrtausende deutschen Lebens in Bild und Wort*) (Gallery of German History: Two Millennia of German Life in Image and Text), represents "antiquarian" coffee table book that musealizes German history.[14] Another example of this trend are British coffee table books that circulated in Victorian England and had a clear decorative function (Price 2012). The texts and narratives play only a marginal role in these kinds of books; the book does not convey action, stories, plots and events. Rather its main purpose is to bring into being an art historical storage place, a museum of history, which in turn conserves rather than retells history. These rare and often unique editions embody memory culture against the mass popularization of memory as well as the instrumentalization of the past in service of national ideology.

Critical voices against official discourses of memory can also be found in the realm of poetic historical fiction. Historical novels can display forms of counter-memory, which is often used to capture traumatic memory occluded by official versions of historical narratives and their suggestions of continuity.[15] Counter memory can thus refer to a different angle of the memory; a perspective beyond the grand narratives enforced by state governance. This kind of memory culture whose effect and purpose is to articulate resistance and opposition to a government's instrumentalization of the past and reflects on its representability, its ownership, and its different voices are pertinent in historical literary texts of the nineteenth century. In the following section, historical fiction is the focus, and examples of critical counter-memory (as well as more affirmative types) will be discussed. Since novels, poetry, or drama can give voice to different perspectives and understandings of the past, literature constitutes an integral part of memory culture. Often, literature enables a certain degree of freedom and autonomy on the part of the reader to remember the past, since, as a poetic discourse, it is at greater liberty than scholarly historiography to expand into the world of the imaginary.

COUNTER-MEMORY IN HISTORICAL FICTION

The genre of fictional historical prose, although by definition closely affiliated with historical reality, works with the power of imagination. During the genre's boom in the nineteenth century, historical novels and novellas often reached bestseller status, fostered by a mass reading culture developed with the advance of public libraries, reading circles, and innovative mass-printing technologies. This genre had its offspring in Scottish Romanticism with the novels by Sir Walter Scott. His *Waverley* (1814) is often seen as the first historical novel, and the stories about the young British soldier and Romantic, Edward Waverley, were an instant success. Scott's works influenced many European authors and their way of writing historical fiction. However, not only the so-called great men of historical novels, such as Tolstoy, Balzac, and Cooper were inspired. Female authors, in fact, had even preceded Scott and developed their own approaches to writing about the past. The Scottish historical novelist Jane Porter, for example, was deeply entrenched in the Romantic tradition of representing history. Her 1810 work, *The Scottish Chiefs* on the life of the Scottish knight William Wallace, who fought during the Scottish wars of independence in the late thirteenth and fourteenth century was a great success. On the one hand, this novel has clearly nationalist aspirations simply by focusing on Wallace's struggles for freedom and independence. War heroism, patriotism, and self-sacrifice are central themes; and the novel was even forbidden in France during Napoleon's regime. On the other hand, the construction of collective memory in this novel is somewhat different and more complex (Price 2006). Porter's novel does not propagate historical change, but rather conveys a type of melancholic awareness about the repetitive character of history, emphasizing a cyclical model of the past. Although, the novel's concept of stability does not make Porter's works radically subversive of national expansionism, it nevertheless raises some "counter-memory" questions about the aspects of change, progress, and revolution commonly associated with nationalist novels.

In Germany, one of the first female writers of historical novels was Christiana Benedikte Naubert, who published anonymously over fifty historical novels between 1779 and 1827. Her writing often consists of sentimental plots against a historical back drop highlighting the view of the individual as well as their emotions. Naubert is also often seen as a writer inspired by Scott, but there is a debate whether it was in fact she who was the pioneer of the sentimental romantic historical novel (Blackwell and Zantop 1990: 198–205).

Whereas the historical novel in the Anglo-Saxon and French tradition of the historical novel was closely associated with the literary movement of Romanticism, in Germany the genre was often much more interwoven with the academy. The unprecedented rise of historical fiction in Germany during the early nineteenth century should be viewed in the context of the rise of academic historicism. Whereas academic historians made their work accessible to the public (e.g. in magazines, museums, and illustrated history books), many literary authors became "academic" by writing realist historical novels. Literary authors of historical prose challenged the academic monopoly on truthful and beautiful historical representation.

The poetic genre of the so-called *Professorenroman* (academic novel) is symptomatic of this competition to more powerfully capture and represent the past. For example, in the preface to his historical novel *Ekkehard: Eine Geschichte aus dem zehnten Jahrhundert* (Ekkehard: A Story from the Tenth Century, 1855), Viktor Scheffel declares that the historical novel should become the "brother of history" and "enter into a deep friendship" with the academy (Scheffel 1876: 7).[16] While Scheffel aimed to write more vividly than his academic colleagues, he nevertheless inserted 285 footnotes into the literary text. These footnotes reference the original Latin sources, elaborate on specific notions, and comment on the background of historical persons and places. Aside from these scholarly congruencies, Scheffel also reinforced the nationalist agenda of writing history, which had been prominent among historians of the "Prussian School." Similar to the early Romantic poetic writers, such as Novalis and Friedrich Schlegel, Scheffel's idyllic pre-Reformation Catholic medieval age provides the basis for the novel's phantasm of a united German nation state.

In the rich literary landscape of nineteenth-century historical fiction, however, one can also find numerous examples that do not repeat the political positions of academic historiography. During and around the *Vormärz* (Pre-March) era, literary authors Heinrich Heine and Georg Büchner had close ties to the revolutionary precepts of Karl Marx and Ludwig Anselm Feuerbach, and their works were clearly critical of national history writing. However, Büchner and Heine worked primarily in poetry and drama. The genre of a critical ("other") historical novel first emerged during the second half of the nineteenth century, and it aimed to counter-act the ideology of nationalism, criticize the political instrumentalization of the past, and write against nationalist myth making (Geppert 1976). Literary author Wilhelm Raabe, for example, always had a strong interest in history and a sure tendency to subvert official narratives. He experimented with archaeological themes in his 1864 work *Keltische Knochen* (Celtic Bones), an early novella conceived and written during a journey to the Hallstädter See, where a large prehistoric gravesite was discovered in 1846. In this novella, two quirky archeology professors quarrel endlessly over the correct classification of these ancient bones. Through the use of irony, Raabe not only makes fun of the academic discipline and its rather disheveled representatives; his text clearly takes a stance against writing official histories of events, with a national agenda. In their frantic efforts to dig up and reconstruct the past, the archaeologists have clearly lost their bearings and Raabe's representation of history is a rather obscure, multi-layered, and incomprehensible affair, determined by its geographical location and its deep geological past.

Similar counter-fictions and efforts to write a type of counter-memory can also be found in the works of Theodore Fontane. Although Fontane's ambivalent position on Prussian politics has been subject to many scholarly debates, his novels often take a stance against Prussia's military codes, bourgeois concepts of honor, as well as national expansionism. Notable is Fontane's obsession with historical monuments. He was an active member of numerous monument associations, and close friends with both Prussia's leading conservator, Ferdinand von Quast, and art historian Franz Kugler. Monuments became a source and an inspiration for his literary writing (Thielking 2000). For his preliminary work for the multi-volumed travelogue *Wanderungen durch die Mark Brandenburg* (Wanderings through the Mark Brandenburg, 1862–89), for example, he often visited up to ten villages a day and all the monuments he could find, frequently

FIGURE 6.6: The Hermann Monument in the Teutoborg Forest was established in 1875, commemorating Arminius, whose Germanic Cherusci tribe fought against the Roman Armies during the ninth century. Wikimedia Commons.

pushing himself to the limits of physical exhaustion. During the "monumental" Bismarck-era, Fontane could indeed indulge his passion. Medieval German emperor Frederick Barbarossa and Hermann the Cherusci were the subject of sculpture cults. Figure 6.6 displays the Hermann monument in the Teutoborg Forest, commemorating Arminius, whose Germanic Cherusci tribe fought against the Roman Armies during the ninth century. In 1875, the monument of Hermann became a place of national worship, remaining so until the end of National Socialism.

The preservation of monuments became a leading task in Prussian cultural politics, and state officials were eager to administer the committees involved in building monuments and in hiring conservators. This trend to build national monuments to commemorate and store cultural memory was not limited to the European continent. For example, the Washington Monument was completed in 1888, and during the same time many national parks (Yellow Stone National Park in 1872) were established in the United States.

The narrator of Fontane's *Wanderings* indeed describes numerous national monuments, such as obelisks, churches, statues, and architectural sights. However, his depictions are typically not synthesized into one grand narrative about the rise of the German nation; rather, they remain dispersed and fragmented. Fontane's text focuses on the monument's location, its materiality, singularity, and its interpretive complexity. For Fontane, monuments represent more transitory spaces of subjective memory, rather than elements of Prussia's glory. In this context, Fontane's travelogue can also be seen as a type of counter-memorial project. Although there is no irony or satire, Fontane's relentless collecting, preserving, and compiling suggest a type of restorative utopia, rather than an effort to propel the reader into the future of German world power and national hegemony. In some ways, Fontane's literary counter-memory is reminiscent of the antiquarian spirit of private collectors, which defined the first two decades of the nineteenth century, before historical objects became systematized in museums, where professional historians were eager to construct national history.

THE AGE OF THE MUSEUM

The museum of the nineteenth century is frequently associated with the sphere of high memory culture. It is often understood as an institution of elitist conservationism, in which privileged culture was intended to be presented for national identification. A view of the museum had already been put forward by turn-of-the-century avant-garde artists who rejected the museum as a reactionary space as Louis Althusser would do in the 1980s (Althusser 1984: 1–60). Nevertheless, the sharp division between high and popular culture in nineteenth century museums, particularly in the context of historical museums, does not quite hold. In the beginning of the nineteenth century, the word "museum" could refer to a variety of things, such as, a place to study, a private collection, or a preservation society. The word could even refer to a publication, for example Friedrich Schlegel's literary journal, *Deutsches Museum* (German Museum), which flourished during the early years of German Romanticism. During the Napoleonic Wars, antiquarians, so-called *Liebhaber* (dilettante), began to gather objects for their own private collections. Often motivated by the fear that Napoleon's troops could take cultural treasures away, these collectors accumulated objects of patriotic value in order to prevent their endangerment (Crane 2000a: 143–77). Already these early museum-like collections, though un-systematic, local, and geographically dispersed, functioned as sites for public discourse, communication, and exchange of knowledge. In contrast to Renaissance curiosity cabinets, such as the Museum Wormianum (1654) in Copenhagen, the purpose of these collections was to convey the experience of historicity (Crane 2000a: 111). It was no longer enough that the object was old; it had attained an educational purpose and a symbolic value.

However, within the course of the nineteenth century this antiquarianism and its universalist scope became increasingly systematized and nationalized (Hartung 2010). The new academic discipline of museology emerged, as well as many of the museum types that we know today, including art museums, ethnographic collections, historical museums, and technique museums. The museums' differentiation also corresponded with the delineation of new scholarly disciplines in the universities (Vieregg 2008: 6). Although the museums were of different types, they often shared the goal of becoming a forum for national education and identification, such as the National Germanic Museum (Germanisches National Museum) in Nuremberg, founded in 1852 by Hans von Aufsess (initially a private collector), or the first museum for national history, formed in Hungary in 1802.

A perhaps less-well known case of this shift from antiquarianism to the national institutionalization concerns memory culture about the pre-historic past in the German-Danish borderland Schleswig-Holstein. J. Laurence Hare's recent study (2015) investigates the era of nineteenth-century antiquarianism, in which Danish and German collectors, history enthusiasts, intellectuals, and Romantics began to discover Nordic pre-history as a historical field of knowledge and as a source of identity.[17] Although often guided by patriotic sentiment, during this time, antiquarian collectors worked within a close and non-rivalrous cross-border exchange of archaeological knowledge.

The work of archaeologist Johanna Mestorf (1828–1909) is crucial in this context. While still entrenched in the antiquarian tradition, her research on the Danevirke (a defense wall of the Viking age) as well on the Viking city Hedeby, highlights a transnational practice in her archeological method in the border region. She did not divide the academic community into national camps, but rather kept local, regional, provincial traditions viable in her research and museum politics. However, this more fluid antiquarian practice was soon to change radically with the emergence of modern professional archeology during the second half of the nineteenth century.

Due to the political contests during the Danish-German Wars in 1848–51 and 1852–64, pre-historic archaeology in the borderlands developed into a political activity claiming origin, ownership, and copyrights of Nordic pre-history. This politicization, however, was executed through the rhetoric of academic scholarship. Precisely this academic professionalization of archaeology, its organization by the government, and reliance on state funding that were the stepping stones to its nationalist and political agenda. The Danish archaeologist Jens Jacob Asmussen Worsaae, director of the Danish National Museum from 1864 to 1875, played a decisive role in this process. He not only nationalized Danish history in the context of his museum administration, but he also stirred and polarized the debate about how to utilize Nordic mythology. The tendency to nationalize pre-historical archeology became even more marked during the First and Second World Wars, when it became a key element in geopolitical conflicts between Denmark and Germany.

These instances of museum culture illustrate the museum's development from a heterogenous concept defined by the practices of individual collectors to a national and professional institution, a trend that is equally present in other parts of Europe and not restricted to Germany or Scandinavia. Within this shift, not only did the symbolic value of the exhibited objects change, but the representation of the past became more state-controlled, and could be used as a repository of official ideology and its politics of exclusion. As state-centered institutions, however, museums nevertheless maintained a key interest in popularizing historical knowledge and in continuing to attract visitors, with the aim of educating the bourgeois audiences.

HISTORICAL MEMORY AS A MULTI-MEDIA PHENOMENON

This chapter's preceding discussions of German examples of broader trends in European and imperial memory culture demonstrate that *mémoire* and *histoire* are deeply intertwined. Popular visual memory culture utilizes scholarly techniques, whereas academic historicism made use of popular modes of representing and interpreting the past. Thus, nineteenth-century memory culture must be understood as a heterogenous phenomenon, which embraces different media types, audiences, functions, and models of history. Despite the long-held views of scholars of *histoire,* given the multi-mediality of this memory culture, text-based narrative no longer exercises an ultimate monopoly on representing the past. Rather, during the nineteenth century, Clio, the muse of history, gained sharper eyesight. Images of history were mass-produced and thus reached an extensive range of recipients in an unprecedented manner. This visual configuration of historical memory also gives rise to modes of interpreting the past beyond the exclusive paradigm of temporality. The temporal paradigm, with its dimensions of development, teleology, events, and progress, has often been significant to academic historicism's interpretation of the past. However, by focusing on visual culture, we see models of spatiality come to the foreground. Be it the panorama, the historical atlas or the museum, topographical, geographical, and geo-historical imaginations of the past are vital to highlight the importance of spatiality in representing and understanding the past.

Historian Karl Schlögel has pointed to the spatial paradigm in history, criticizing the scholars of German historicism for shaping a historical discourse that "silences" the spatiality of history (Schlögel 2007: 44). Historicism has long promoted a model of history monopolized by the notion of temporality and neglecting the factor of "space." Intertwining *mémoire* and *histoire* opens up pathway to discovering this spatial dimension of the past and of understanding historical memory culture in all of its categorical and medial complexity.

It should be noted that the presence of visual and spatial configurations of memory culture does automatically imply a kind of counter-movement against the official political and ideological narratives of history. As shown, the panorama, historical sculptures, and museums were often in sync with the political agenda of the Prussian Regime. But there were some exceptions. This chapter provided examples of literary writers of historical fiction, whose prose suggested a critical stance on nationalism. Raabe and Fontane questioned the past's instrumentalization for national propaganda. Taking the early decades of the nineteenth century into account, one can find strong liberal and anti-authoritarian movements for democratic ideals, the search for the constitution, and parliamentary self-regulation.[18] Efforts, as it is well known, that came to a halt after the failed 1848 revolution and upon the rise of the "iron chancellor" Bismarck and his authoritarian *Realpolitik*. But whether one investigates the works of the pro-Prussian memory aficionados or their critics, high or popular culture, textual or visual representations of the past, representing the past during the nineteenth century has one consistently significant trait: That is the centrality of the individual and his or her experiences. This perspective towards the individual represents the pivotal turn to understand memory culture of the nineteenth century in Germany and Europe; an aspect that also defines our grasps of memory culture today.

CHAPTER SEVEN

The Social: Ritual, Faith, Practices and the Everyday

CECILIA MORGAN

INTRODUCTION

"I wish," Ellen Currer Langton confided to her journal in 1837, "now that we are once more on *terra*, to banish what is past from my thoughts, and, if I could, the feelings of my last sight and touch of my first-born, but the stunning sensation can never be forgotten, and my feeling when the ship cleared the pier-head must ever remain as long as memory lasts."[1] On August 25, 1858, Amelia Ryerse Harris's thoughts were taken back to a different kind of memory, as she wrote in her diary that "This morning eight years I was watching over a dying husband. The weather looks the same and I can scarcely realize that eight years have passed since then. What a day of anguish. It makes me tremble to look back upon it. When I think of all his sufferings and all that we suffered. The time is near at hand when we shall again meet." (Harris 1994: 83). Memories also were the subject, this time expressed in a letter of Nahneebahweequa's (Catherine Sutton), thoughts, as she told her aunt Eliza Field Jones "Dear Sister—It is a long time since I first thought I would write to you but owing to my bad spelling I thought it best not to write then I would again think perhaps you would think I would have forgotten you all or I did not care of writing to you. But believe me dear sister that my love to you is as great as ever."[2]

Residents of the British colony of Upper Canada, these women differed in their living conditions, age, marital status, and ethnocultural locations. Langton lived on a frontier farm recently carved out of Indigenous territory, a dwelling very different from the large Regency-style home, set on eleven acres in the city of London, occupied by Harris and her large family. Nahneebahweequa, a member of the Indigenous Mississauga band near Toronto, wrote to her "dear sister," her English aunt Eliza Field Jones, from her new home on the Newash band's territory near the village of Owen Sound, 204 kilometers north-west of London. Langton was an elderly widow, recently arrived in the colony, while Amelia Ryerse Harris, born in Upper Canada and of Loyalist descent, was, at the age of sixty, remembering the death of her husband, John. At the age of twenty-three, Nahneebahweequa and her husband, Methodist lay minister and English immigrant William Sutton, were recent arrivals to their new home: Nahneebahweequa's letter testified to the many happy memories she bore of her childhood days under Eliza's Christian tutelage. Yet they all shared one important characteristic, that of living within a British settler colony. As such, like many of their counterparts, settler and Indigenous, in other such societies—Aoteroa/New Zealand, the Australian colonies, and the Cape

Colony—these women's memories of social life were shaped by the expansion of the British Empire, the mobility and movement that its growth entailed.

Though settler colonies—and then settler nations—built their share of monuments and staged historical pageants, memories which dealt with the daily rounds of life and the domain of the social in which ties to kin, friends, faith, and home were maintained, were no less significant. Coming to us in either fragments or in more fleshed-out narratives, evocations of the social dimensions of nineteenth-century life also deal with the realms of affect and emotion. Shaped by the processes of mobility, migration, and displacement, memories of daily life and social rituals were an important way of maintaining ties to home, of providing stability and security in new environments, ones peopled with strangers and unfamiliar practices. As historian Geoffrey Cubitt has argued, attachments to places, often manifested in objects such as family heirlooms, have allowed individuals to reiterate their emotional connections to a more far-reaching, collective past (Cubitt 2007: 140). For settler women in particular, who bore much of the responsibility for creating domestic life and intimate spaces, social memories were a means of shaping one's world to accord with previously-forged values, customs, and assumptions. Furthermore, just as they created either new institutions and practices or adapted older structures to new settings, over time these women fashioned memories of the new society. In both cases, social memories might inflect practices such as cooking, household routines, manners and deportment, childbirth and childrearing, and religious practices that ranged from marriage to funerary rites. Reminders of "home" also were implicated in the choices settlers made regarding material culture: items such as stoves and china, dresses and furniture, musical instruments and mirrors, and, in particular, photography and portraits might have particular mnemonic significance (or, alternatively, might represent decisions to ally oneself with the new world).

Much of this sounds somewhat benign, perhaps unremarkable. And to some extent that was the case: the memories that shaped daily lives did not ostensibly bear the weight of those that dealt with contentious political events or people. Yet like other daily practices, the memories that settlers both brought to their new homes and those that they forged in those places can provide a "lens onto [their] intimate, everyday engagements with a settler colonial place in the making" (Ishiguro 2018: 262). Moreover, theirs were far from being the sole forms of social memory in these societies. Although they did not always realize it, settlers also entered into places and practices that already bore significant meanings for Indigenous nations and societies, ones that had been imbued with multiple forms of remembrance. While not all Indigenous memories of place, spirituality, and the routines of daily life were destroyed because of the presence of settlers, colonial governments, and settler nation-states, there is no denying that such memories were at best interrupted or disrupted, reworked, and, in some instances, all but shattered. Indigenous knowledge and understandings of land, hunting and fishing practices, language, family and childrearing, and ceremony were grounded in local, daily practices, ones conveyed through oral tradition and mnemonic devices, and, by the early nineteenth century, written texts.

CREATING THE SETTLER EVERYDAY

As Frances Porter and Charlotte Macdonald have pointed out, in moving to the new colony of New Zealand and remaking their lives and communities, "people tore up their old connections," none more so than *Pakeha* (white) women (Porter and Macdonald

1996: 3). The rupture of upheaval might be felt most acutely by British women who emigrated to the Antipodes in the early nineteenth century. Like their counterparts at the Cape Colony, they travelled further than those who went to British America, had fewer prospects of returning to Britain, and entered into landscapes that were completely unlike those of home. To be sure, some were sanguine, telling those they had left behind of their shipboard experiences—often in great detail about their experiences of seasickness—but also writing of their anticipation of their new surroundings (Colman 2006: 4). Even for those who traveled across the Atlantic, though, the departure could be particularly heart-wrenching, as the memories of those places and, in particular, people they were leaving became particularly acute. Such was the case for Frances Ramsay Simpson, about to leave her childhood home in London to accompany her husband George Simpson, governor of the Hudson Bay Company, first to the fur-trading post of York Factory and then to the settlement of Red River (present-day Winnipeg). Arising on the morning of their voyage, her heart ached and her mind was "agitated by the various emotions of grief, fear and hope. "Grief, at parting from my beloved parents, and a large and united family of brothers and sisters, from whom I had never been separated; fear, for the changes which might take place among them during my absence; and hope, which in the midst of my distress, diffused its soothing influence, and acting as a panacea, seemed to point to the home of my infancy, as the goal at which, at some future period, (however distant) I should at length arrive" (Devereux and Venema 2006: 133).

It was not just the initial rupture from home represented by the sea voyage that distressed Simpson. She returned to England in 1833 until the Simpsons settled permanently at the Quebec village of Lachine (near Montreal) in 1845; however, once back in British America she continued to remember her family with great longing, particularly her parents. "How my heart sinks," she confessed to her sister Louisa Barkly Simpson, when thinking of their father giving his children his blessing every morning, "while I am far away, and may perhaps *never more* hear that blessing pronounced by those loved and honored lips. But you will not have forgotten the absent one, I know full well, and in the affectionate greetings, and warm congratulations of the day, the names of those across the ocean will mingle, and in spirit we shall all meet and be together" (Devereux and Venema 2006: 149). The fear of forgetting the faces, voices, and touch of loved ones could be matched by the dread of being forgotten oneself.

Food—the item itself, its preparation, and its serving—could serve as an important site of memory for settler families, a means of providing security, stability, and comfort in places that no matter how beautiful, also were alien (and at times alienating). The evidence suggests a complex mixture of practices, ones that over the course of the nineteenth century combined elements of "diffusion and tradition": diffusion in their engagement with Indigenous food ways and tradition in that they suggested long-standing links to recipes (and their creators) encountered in childhood (Rangan, Alpers, Denham, Kull, and Carney 2015: 135). The extent to which they did so differed from place to place, though, as well as varying within a range of items. Settlers in Australia, for example, were mostly receptive to indigenous seafood, animals, and birds provided they bore a resemblance to British game: new arrivals harvested and hunted crabs, oysters, fish, brush turkey, and wild duck (Santich 2011: 68). As well, Australian cookbooks offered a number of recipes featuring local wildlife, most notably kangaroo, wild birds, and plants (Singley 2012: 38). Yet despite the use of local fare (a choice prompted, food historians suggest, by the difficulty of importing perishable British food), settlers tended to balk at adopting Indigenous forms of food preparation, either refusing to accept gifts of food cooked by their neighbors or shunning their cooking practices (Norman 2012: 44–5; Santich 2011: 76). Moreover, even using local plants to make tea was not a rejection of British practices: rather, it "allowed the colonists to reproduce a comforting and familiar ritual" (Singley 2012: 40). In the Australian context "colonial experimentation required indigenous ingredients to be culturally appropriated, plucked from one culture and incorporated into another so that the foreign became familiar" (Santich 2011: 76). Settlers also did not forget the food that they—or their ancestors—had enjoyed, since over the course of the nineteenth century new fauna and flora, such as pheasant, sheep, and vegetables, were imported, with the result that over the course of the nineteenth and early twentieth century Australian settlers' diets began to resemble those in Britain (Santich 2011: 76; Singley 2012: 41). Events in one's new home also might shape memories in which food played a prominent role. For Upper Canada's Loyalists, the year 1789 became enshrined in individuals' memories as the "hungry year," a time when families were forced to bleed pigs, eat roots and berries, and, in one case, the family dog.[3]

If acquiring and preparing food involved a complex negotiation in which local circumstances were paired with memories of food from Britain, for those who wished to preserve their genteel status in their new home its presentation could be an even more fraught process. The rituals of colonial dining were laden with significance. To family members, they represented "nurturing continuity and a controlled and stable environment." To European peers, they were a "display of both goods and knowledge" that demonstrated "rank and status and hence power," a statement that European practices had not been forgotten and that they could—and for some, must—be reiterated and repeatedly performed in order to reassure all involved to maintain imperial prestige and power (Lawrence 2012: 193). That such rituals and the material culture that enabled their performance—the formal dining room with polished dining tables and matching chairs, along with table arrangements, silverware, fine linen, and good china—could not always be realized, particularly outside of urban centers, did not make them any less significant. When living conditions made such rituals impossible, though, settler women helped create other forms of hospitality, ones more spontaneous, less formal, and less dependent on the material trappings of genteel culture (Lawrence 2012: 198–200). Often known as part of "bush culture," in some colonies, particularly in Australia, such rituals also might become part of both domestic and national memory, marks of a more egalitarian society than Britain.

Nor did British women forget the gardens they, or their ancestors, had left behind. Gardening itself had a particular significance in colonial contexts. In Britain, the "genteel" female gardener held a special status; she was a paragon of purity who brought beauty to the domestic landscape and enhanced her household's morality by doing so. This image carried over to settler colonies in which taming alien topography was central to European expansion: settler women's ability to impose particular forms of visual order was—at least partly—an extension of their male counterparts' work of surveying and fencing. Women's gardening "endeavors were therefore entirely in keeping with the ideological values of gentility and colonialism alike" (Lawrence 2012: 140). To be sure, like the food they cooked, the evidence suggests a range of attitudes and practices. There is ample evidence that settler women actively sought out native fruits and vegetables and took great pride in being able to cultivate them for their tables; at times they also enjoyed growing native flowers or appreciated the presence of indigenous trees and bushes (Lawrence 2012: 147, 152–3). Yet as the images of Anne Langton's family home in Toronto and of the home of a New South Wales family demonstrate, these women's front

FIGURE 7.1: Anne Langton's home, Toronto. Archives of Ontario.

gardens greatly resembled those in British middle-class homes. Neatly set out, they featured a geometrical design with circular drives and a central bed, in which had been placed an urn, statue, or singular plant. While different colonial contexts and degrees of change over time led to some variations, as these images suggest such designs could be found in a number of British colonies (Lawrence 2012: 145, 156).

Moreover, despite their incorporation of indigenous flora, British women also continued to value that of their homes, longing for smooth green lawns, for example, in climates that were not at all conducive to them, or using their gardens as a means of expressing nostalgic longings for familiar places and faces. When imported plants fared better in the colonies than they had at home, settler women reveled in the memories they evoked (Lawrence 2012: 145–6).

Looking at genteel domesticity as a set of rituals that needed to be performed continually in order to keep not just a status but a memory alive also sheds new light on relationships with servants. Much has been written about settler women's ongoing struggle to find "suitable" servants, ones who could perform their duties to their mistresses' standards and would not answer back, demand higher wages or more time off, entertain male visitors, or simply decamp if they were not happy with their employer (Porter and Macdonald 1996: 146–8; McKenzie 1997: 10–11). Historians have examined these conflicts as symptomatic of colonial contexts in which labor shortages and more egalitarian attitudes on the part of working people ran up against middle-class anxieties over status (Porter and Macdonald 1996: 146–8). Prior to the abolition of slavery in the British Empire, the problem ostensibly could be resolved with unfree labor, although colonial women's diaries and letters demonstrate that slaves might also exert their own forms of agency, including flight (McKenna 1990: 190–2). (And in early nineteenth-century Tasmania, convict women were able to parley knowledge and skills gained in middle-class British homes into better working conditions and more respectful treatment (Reid 2003:

FIGURE 7.2: Australian Garden in New South Wales, c. 1872. National Library of Australia.

11)). However, other aspects of this situation deserve further reflection. Clashes with servants over the correct way of preparing vegetables, setting the table, doing the laundry, or behaving properly spoke to the important role they might play in those daily rituals of domesticity that reminded colonial women of their homes. Moreover, colonial mistresses also encountered their servants with memories—however exaggerated or distorted they might have been—of the deference and respect they had been given in Britain.

At times the dissonance between their remembered lives and colonial realities was a source of significant frustration and unhappiness. Writing in 1839 from Cape Town to her friend in England, Mary Ann Smith, Eliza Fairbairn complained, "I have not one female friend in south Africa not one to whom I can talk politics, or poetry, or nonsense as suits the whim of the moment—not one to whom I can could talk of my own affairs, my children my husband and without a fear of being treasonous" (McKenzie, 1997, 18). Fairbairn was not alone in her depression. From Kaipora, New Zealand, Lizzie Heath told her sister Anne, back home in England, that "I feel very fainthearted at times and often meditate and wish you were at a come-at-able distance that I might open my heart to you for you must not think I have found a piece of the world where there is no trouble. I can issue you I have my troubles and no one to relieve my heart to" (Porter and Macdonald 1996: 172).

Surrounding oneself with the material culture they had left in Britain might have provided some consolation. As historians of nineteenth-century networks within the British Empire have pointed out, domestic goods—decorative tiles and floor coverings, sheet music and the instruments on which it was played, and British textiles and fashions—played an important role in the economic traffic between Britain and the colonies (Magee and Thompson 2010: 151–61). Those who arrived in Sydney in the mid-1790s were astonished to find not a backwoods outpost but, rather, a "flourishing colony of decidedly English character," one that by 1840 imported so much furniture from Britain and India that it was the former's second largest market, bigger than that of North America (Young 2004: 205). Notably, as well as dining room tables, pianos, bookcases, and writing desks featured prominently in the catalogues of such goods; piano-playing became one of the hallmarks of genteel nineteenth-century womanhood, along with the pastimes of novel reading and letter-writing (Young 2004: 209). Such pursuits also, though, could be yet another vehicle to maintain memory: in the case of the piano, it might evoke both those moments of domestic sociability when family and close friends gathered for entertainment and for the cultural origins of the music itself. For European settlers in New Zealand, "the piano, as artifact, as instrument, as symbol, helped to invest the new cultural space with familiarity and meaning … [it] brought with it powerful associations of "home"; something known, reassuring, comforting" (Moffatt 2009: 722–3). The young woman standing to read her sheet music beside her family's piano in an Ontario parlor may not have thought of herself in those terms: she was, though, performing a very common ritual of colonial domesticity.

FIGURE 7.3: Young Woman at the Piano, Ontario, *c.* 1880s–90s. Archives of Ontario, 10013524.

Furthermore, family memories might be preserved in everyday items, such as clothing, samplers, quilts, and toys, that were brought by women from Britain for both practical and affective reasons, preserved over the generations as a reminder of one's roots. As well as those items that accompanied families, domestic activities that were continued in the colonial context, such as quilting and sewing, had practical significance; they also marked a "process of remembering and history-making in the fabric of time," often being preserved alongside written family histories (Evans 2012: 214; Higgs and Radosh 2013: 53). Such family histories might have been more complicated than an artifact might suggest. Elizabeth Johnson Clench, who in 1839 left the sampler depicted below unfinished, was descended from both Upper Canada's Loyalist elite and, through her grandmother, the well-known Kanien'kehá:ka (Mohawk) Brant family. Working on the sampler helped her perform European gender roles. Simultaneously, though, she was aware of her interracial family history: her father's name was Brant Johnson and her eldest son, Joseph Brant Clench, became an interpreter with the colony's Indian Department and would go on to hold various positions within it.[4]

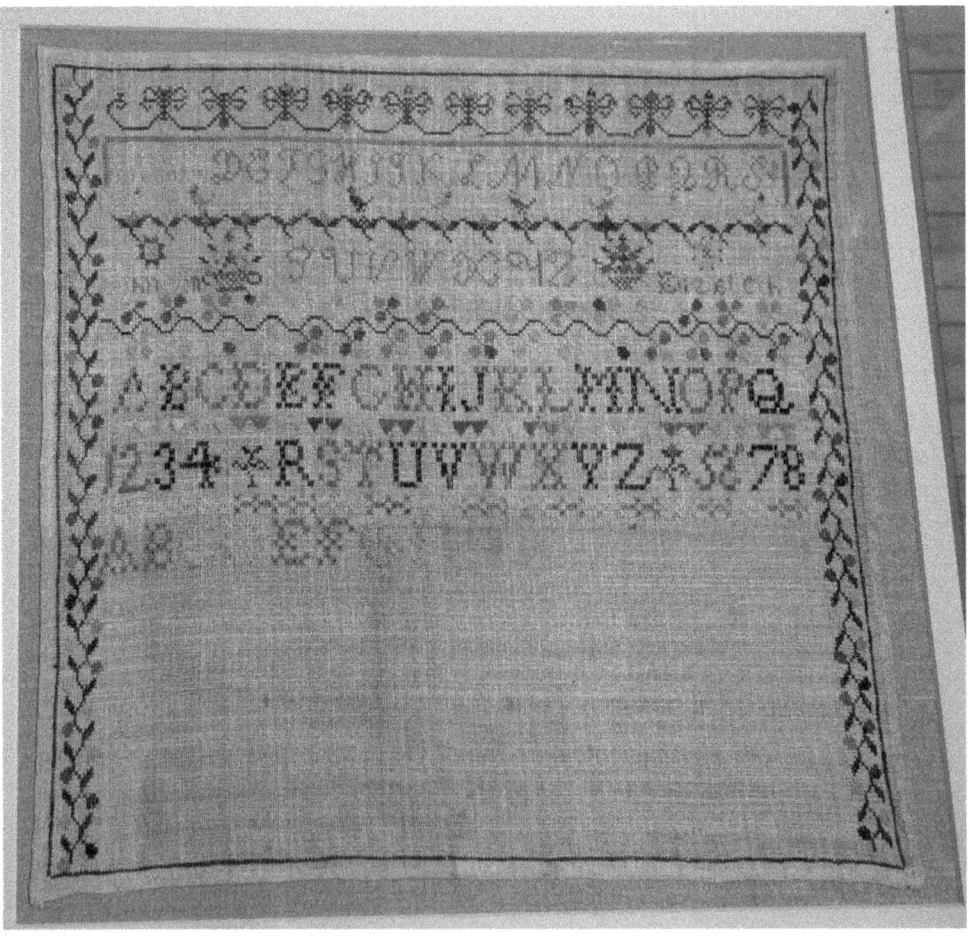

FIGURE 7.4: Sampler, Elizabeth Johnson Clench. Niagara Historical Museum.

Other practices helped settler women enact polite, middle-class social status. The ritual of paying social calls, for example, was transferred to colonial settings, one meant to remind its participants of their status "back home" and to affirm it in the new context. Although in the late eighteenth and early nineteenth centuries the spaces in which calling took place might be rudimentary, by the 1850s (if not earlier), social calls generally took place in the living room. "No woman who held herself to be genteel, or had ambitions in that direction, would dream of making a life in the colonies without a living room," one which reflected a legacy of "aesthetic traditions" inherited from Britain (Lawrence 2012: 78–9). Ideally, colonial living rooms were to be furnished and decorated with the accoutrements of rugs, curtains, potted plants, armchairs, sofas, pictures, floral arrangements, and ornaments, items that demonstrated genteel status, no matter how difficult to obtain in certain colonies (Lawrence 2012: 76–128). As well as being filled with items that served mnemonic purposes, settler women's living rooms remind us "how intimately connected spatial relations are to social relations, as well as of how constitutive architectural idioms can be of the practice of remembering" (Burton 2003: 18). Yet given the uncertainty of colonial society and the need to establish hierarchies of not just class and gender but also of race, determining who would call on whom could become a very contentious question. Life in a settler colony might present both challenges and opportunities to establish a claim to a more elevated status than its residents had previously enjoyed.

Such was the case for Loyalist refugee Hannah Peters Jarvis, whose husband held an appointment in the new Upper Canadian colonial government. Observing the rituals of social calling (to which she would have been exposed in both New England and England), was a way of transcending her family's considerable financial problems. Others who were part of the same social circle might find that the memory of their intimate and domestic past, circulated in the form of rumors and gossip, might pose insurmountable obstacles to achieving the status of white, genteel womanhood (McKenna 1990: 179–80; McKenzie 2004). Such incidents remind us that rumor and gossip, often seen as both informal means of social regulation and as exchanges that colonial societies might seek to control (Marks 2000: 388–93), also might become forms of memory that could haunt members of colonial society, even (or especially) when their relationship to the truth was ambiguous or partial.

Rituals that marked settlers' lifecycles, such as weddings, christenings, and funerals, were marked by both continuity and change, their forms dependent on the colony in question. Little has been written explicitly about settlers' weddings and christening ceremonies as a way of reinforcing—or reshaping—imperial ties and the memories in which they were encased. Both types of ceremonies, of course, marked the creation of something new. Weddings celebrated the formation of new relationships, both that of the newlyweds and of the extended family that their marriage might create, while christenings marked the arrival of a new member of communities both sacred and secular. Yet as religious rituals, both ceremonies affirmed ties of intimacy and of those bonds linking families to a wider, global set of sacred traditions, the latter suggested in the words and performances of the ceremonies in question but also through the material culture used in them. The 1890s christening gown owned by British immigrant Mae Hagen suggest that the child-focused ceremonies of the mid-nineteenth century Victorian middle class (Gillis 1996: 170–1) were transferred to settler societies.

We do not know if Hagen made the gown herself, purchased it in Britain, or had inherited it from a family member. However, such objects may have been ubiquitous: for example, Hagen's gown is only one of over thirty christening gowns in the Niagara Historical Museum. Such items had the potential to evoke memory in multiple ways. If

FIGURE 7.5: Mae Hagen's Christening Gown, *c*. 1890s. Niagara Historical Museum'.

inherited, they might remind families of the particular place in which they had been previously worn and the people who attended the ceremony; even gowns purchased or made for newborn settler infants could fulfill similar functions. As well as material culture, the date chosen for the christening could have a certain meaning, such as a saint's feast day or secular anniversary. To be sure, even well-planned ceremonies might go awry. A broken saddle girth prevented New Zealand's George Selwyn from arriving on time for his second son's christening on June 23, 1844; he and wife Sarah then realized that they were better off holding it the next day, "St. John [the] Baptist's Day and the second anniversary of <u>our</u> coming to New Zealand." Moreover, choosing a name could be a way of maintaining ties of both affection and remembrance. The Selwyns were torn between naming their son George, after his father, or John, after Sarah's: the latter being her husband's choice, Sarah felt she "could not gainsay [it]" while also trusting and praying that their child would be worthy of his name. At the ceremony Sarah was taken "back to the day of his baptism in Windsor Church—the outward circumstances were somewhat different in this case; but we had a good and loving group around us on this occasion, and I doubt not many hearty prayers for the dear little babe also." Afterwards the family gathered with their friends and "the course of our evening talk naturally took us back to Windsor and Eton" (Macdonald 2006: 47–8, 51).

Letters and diary entries also hint at the competing emotions that an upcoming nuptial might provoke. Perhaps not surprisingly for those attempting to create a ceremony that mirrored those of their British relatives, details of their struggles to organize the food and drink, wedding license, minister or priest, and, of course, the appropriate clothing dominate much of their correspondence (Porter and Macdonald 1996: 219, 239, 247–8; Harris 1994: 280–1). While not everyone had the resources to invest in a white wedding dress, photographs such as that of Mrs. Harris, posing for a studio portrait in New South Wales, suggest that this newly invented tradition (Gillis 1996: 146–7) circulated throughout the British imperial world. Wedding photographs, such as that of the group celebrating the nuptials of the couple married in Tasmania, also demonstrate both the transfer of the white wedding and the practice of inviting family and friends.

The wedding day also, though, was a moment to reflect on those who could not be there. "How I miss my beloved parents," wrote Maria Wilson of Opotiki, New Zealand, as she anticipated her imminent marriage in 1842 to Henry Tracy Kemp, a government

FIGURE 7.6: Mrs. Harris's Wedding Portrait. National Library of Australia.

FIGURE 7.7: Wedding in Tasmania, 1875. National Library of Australia.

interpreter (Porter and Macdonald 1996: 237–8). Even when surrounded by family members, the day's happiness might be overshadowed by recent losses. Although Amelia Ryerse Harris was very pleased that her son Edward was marrying Sophia Ryerson, she predicted (accurately) that the day would be "sad and gloomy," given the death of Edward's sister Helen four months prior to the wedding (discussed below). Despite the bride looking "very pretty" and the wedding decorations being attractive, there was a "feeling of sadness about it all. We had all anticipated such a happy merry wedding which there would have been had dear Helen been there" (Harris 1994: 165–6). Although the wedding day was not always made poignant by the memories of absent friends and relatives, settler women's correspondence suggests that capturing its memory for others was important (writing down the details also might have helped the author remember the day as well). New brides and their female relatives provided faraway family members and friends with detailed descriptions of the day (Porter and Macdonald 1996: 237–9, 241–2, 247–51). For Maria Atkinson, it was laden with multiple veins of memory. "The day is already becoming dreamy to me," she confessed to her close friend Margaret Taylor, as she described her wedding to Arthur Taylor at New Plymouth, New Zealand on January 20, 1855. As she walked to the church with her brother William, Maria "tried to follow back the stream of circumstances that had assembled such a party in that spot. I couldn't feel the present to be a reality, but looking back only made it more strange and wonderful" (Porter and Macdonald 1996: 239–40).

Wedding anniversaries, too, were occasions for reminiscing. Sophia Ryerson Harris marked her one-year anniversary with the thought that "the time seems far longer to both George and I . . . I have been so happy," living with a "kind and good husband" who had never uttered a cross word or found fault with any of her words or actions (Harris 1994: 428). They also, though, might be anticlimactic. After six years of marriage, Mary Gapper O'Brien wrote that "our wedding day has often before been one of my disappointed holidays, this particularly so" (her husband had attempted to plant a tree for her but because of illness he was unable to complete his task).[5] If O'Brien felt let down on her anniversary, for a widow the day might evoke even more acutely-felt sentiments. "This is the 43rd anniversary of my wedding day," Amelia Ryerse Harris confided to her journal on June 27, 1858. "How fresh and bright and beautiful was that morning. And I, how young I was and full of life and hope. How little I know of the world or its cares." Yet Harris, whose husband John had by then been dead eight years, did not despair, since all her children were "good and doing well. My labors and cares are nearly ended" (Harris 1994: 75).

Although Harris's "labors and cares" would continue for another twenty years, death in settler societies was marked in ways that represented both continuity and change. Certain aspects of these rituals transcended geography. The centrality of "codified religious beliefs and ceremonies," the careful managing of loss and grief, and the hope for a "good death" in which the loved one either went peacefully (for those who were staunchly evangelical in their beliefs) or loudly affirmed their faith in Christ and abjuration of Satan: all can be found, to varying degrees, in settler women's writings (Porter and Macdonald 1996: 452–3). Sarah Greenwood's Christian faith and "naturally cheerful and buoyant temperament" appears to have sustained her at the death of her thirteen-year-old daughter, Agnes, who died in Motueka, New Zealand, of fever on July 23, 1854. Agnes expired "without the least struggle" and was buried with the help of the neighbors, who arrived "unasked" to bear her coffin and follow it: "during their absence we read the beautiful service at home." When Sarah herself died in 1889, her daughter Annie felt her loss deeply but told her sister Ellen (living in Switzerland), that their mother's wish to pass "from quiet sleep without one pang to the rest of God" had been granted (Porter and Macdonald 1996: 476–7). Not all were able to bear their losses so calmly, though. Eliza Maundrell's husband Frederick died of dropsy shortly after arriving in New Zealand; although his end was calm and Frederick was resigned to his death, Eliza "felt in an agony of despair" and wished that she could be buried with him. The fact that she was in a strange country, had no close female friends, and was pregnant exacerbated her misery (Porter and Macdonald 1996: 462–3). To be sure, for every peaceful or triumphant departure, there were those whose deathbeds were remembered as full of agony and despair, as in the case of Harris's daughter Helen Portman. Nine days after giving birth, Helen died from puerperal fever. Although Amelia had been at her daughter's bedside, feeding her, changing her nightdress, and praying over her, near the end her family had banished Amelia from the sickroom "for fear my grief would injure" Helen. Allowed back into the bedroom for one last embrace just before Helen died, Amelia had to be dragged away from her daughter, whose body was "laid out in white" by female friends and family members. Placed in her "lined and cushioned" walnut coffin, and visited first by her mother and then by her husband, who "went many times to take a last look of his loved and loving wife," Helen looked "perfectly beautiful" (Harris 1994: 143–7).

Amelia Harris does not mention whether Helen was photographed in her coffin. However, this image from late nineteenth-century Ontario of a dead infant suggests that

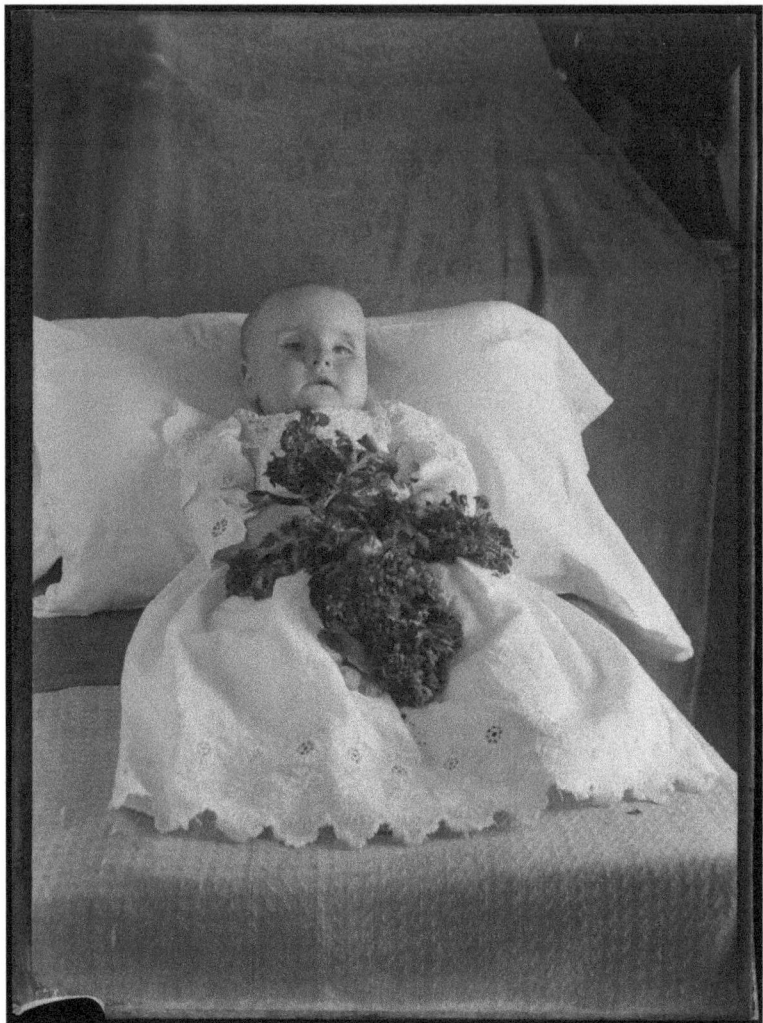

FIGURE 7.8: Post-mortem photograph of an infant, *c.* 1890s. Archives of Ontario.

such postmortem photography could help the living remember the good death their loved one had experienced; such photographs also might serve as a form of material remembrance that could be sent to far-off family members (Gillis 1996: 207–8; Fraser 2012: 120–1).

Other images created during the deceased's life also might help grieving families. After Agnes Greenwood's death her mother Sarah wrote to her mother asking her for a favor, "namely to send me back <u>by the first post</u> . . . my likeness of my dear child. My heart yearns to see it and it will be a delightful task to me to copy it. You shall be sure to have it restored to you" (Porter and Macdonald 1996: 461). Georgiana Molloy, living near the Blackwood River in Western Australia, might have been comforted by such an image. Instead, she told her friend Helen Story in 1833, the grave of her "little angel," daughter Mary, "though sodded over with British clover looks so singular and solitary in this wilderness of which I can scarcely give you an idea" (Coleman 2006: 153).

In New Zealand, English ways of marking death persisted and were deeply rooted in Christian religious traditions, even when individuals adapted them to particular circumstances (Fraser 2012: 120). Maintaining those practices might be a struggle, though. Not only was Frederick Maundrell unable to survive long enough to fulfill his wish of dying at home in England, his widow Sarah found his grave "a dismal looking place" and asked her sister Charlotte and brother-in-law Robert to obtain a "handsome looking tombstone and iron railings" that she could not buy in Lyttleton. Once those familiar markers were in place, Sarah planned to plant flowers over the grave "that will flower summer and winter" (Porter and Macdonald 1996: 463). Communities also worked to provide continuity for the dying and bereaved. New Zealand's missionaries, for example, retained their spiritual and theological beliefs around death; the geographic distribution of missionary settlements, though, meant that missionaries were forced to change their own burial practices of separating the dead from the living. Instead, the graves of family, European workers, and Indigenous Christians were to be found in places close to missionaries' homes (Ballantyne 2014: 185–9). Funerary practices and mourning diverged most clearly from those of Britain in Australia where "traditional Christian way[s] of death declined more rapidly," particularly among the poor and rural communities. Fewer clergy and religious institutions to provide such services in the colony's earlier years, combined with a working-class population that had given up regular church attendance and a scattered European population in the colony's rural areas led to an "Australian" way of death, one shaped by life in the bush and, too, by gender (Jalland 2002: 4–5). Although the dominant cultural representations of death in nineteenth-century Australian society were both violent and masculine, focusing on the heroic—or notorious—fates of outlaw bushrangers, women performed the vast majority of intimate rituals and roles for the dying (Jalland 2002: 6–7). Nursing, cleaning and laying out the corpse, grieving within the privacy of the home (a process that included wearing the appropriate mourning clothes, following prescribed rituals, and confiding one's feelings to a diary or letters to far-flung family members) were the province of women, although class and ethnicity might shape the specific details. Poor or convict women, for example, lacked the financial resources to purchase mourning wear or seclude themselves within the home (Jalland 2002: 7).

INDIGENOUS MEMORIES AND DAILY LIFE IN SETTLER COLONIES

If settlers needed both resourcefulness and creativity either to maintain their affective ties of memory or to forge new ones, Indigenous people were confronted with circumstances even more pressing. Across nineteenth-century British settler colonies, Indigenous communities encountered the growing encroachment of settlers on their traditional territories and the intrusions of colonial governments and, then, settler nation-states, all of which affected their daily lives and social relations. To be sure, this process could be protracted and occur in uneven ways. At times, Indigenous communities were able to negotiate changes to their daily lives, depending on demography (whether they outnumbered Europeans) or in their histories of contact with Europeans (Morgan 2017a: Chapter 1). Furthermore, both continuity and change existed simultaneously within communities, depending on where one looks and the kinds of issues that might be at stake.

In treaty negotiations in Upper Canada and New Zealand, Indigenous representatives stressed that residing on traditional territories had shaped their societies' daily lives and, moreover, that the memory of those patterns of living were integral to their sense of community (Miller 2009: 101–2; Orange 2011: 19–31, 193–4). While fish, game, vegetation, and the places from which they were harvested sustained Indigenous peoples' abilities to feed themselves, they also were intertwined with their spiritual practices and ceremonies and, in the case of certain plants, were crucial to Indigenous medicine. Such points were reiterated in Anishinabeg writers Peter Jones and George Copway's nineteenth-century histories of the Ojibwa people of the Great Lakes area.[6] While Indigenous societies of north-eastern North America had a lengthy history of trade and military alliances with Europeans that had brought new food into their communities, in the nineteenth century they saw a number of changes wrought by the land surrenders of treaties, the pressure larger numbers of settlers exerted on their territories, and the actions of the state and missionaries. For Indigenous people in many settler colonies, food became scarce as settlers cut down forests that had protected game and plants, depleted fishing stocks, and allowed their livestock to pollute sources of water, so that people were forced to turn to mission stations for provisions (Norman 2012: 33; Reynolds 1987: 9). At other times a scarcity of game might push Indigenous communities into trade with settlers, making, as Jones remarked, baskets, brooms, wooden bowls, and other utensils that they exchanged for European foodstuffs.[7] Intense hunger or even famine was created by either increased competition for resources or because of the actions of settler governments, who withheld promised rations in order to force Indigenous people, often already weakened by infectious diseases, to obey state policies such as moving onto reserves or sending their children to residential schools (Daschuk 2013: 125–6, 176; Worden 1994: 134; Wanhalla 2015: 145–52). This is not to argue that Indigenous people forgot their own practices or did not pass them down to their descendants. Oral histories and ethnographic studies provide evidence of the transmission of such knowledge, particularly by women who often had primary responsibility for growing and/or gathering food (and, in some cases, supervising its distribution), dressing and cooking game and fish, or gathering plants for medicines (Ballantyne 2014: 61–2; Burnett 2010: Chapters 2–4). Even the laments of government agents, missionaries, and (by the mid-twentieth century), social workers about Indigenous peoples' diets and other bodily practices suggest their persistence (Rutherdale 2005: 238–9; Walters 2012: 437, 442–3).

Material goods also had symbolic and practical meanings for Indigenous communities, no less so than for settler communities. Trade—particularly the seventeenth- and eighteenth-century fur trade in northern North America—had brought a number of new commodities into peoples' lives, from cooking utensils to textiles, livestock, and guns. By the early to mid-nineteenth century, a growing missionary presence in Indigenous communities meant an even greater exposure to European-style clothing and domestic goods. Believing their use signified the adoption of Christianity and Indigenous peoples' assimilation to "civilization," missionaries devoted considerable time and resources attempting to persuade Indigenous people to incorporate certain forms of European technology and dress (Morgan 2004: 33–6; Brock, Etherington, Griffiths, Van Gent 2015: 168). Yet like foodstuffs, the incorporation of new goods into communities, and their potential to replace older practices and forms of social memory, varied in its significance, being dependent on the timing and conditions of adaptation. Some decisions might have been made pragmatically, as communities decided that some goods were more efficient and longer-lasting (the case with cast-iron cooking pots) or could be incorporated into Indigenous ceremonies, such as the Pacific Northwest Coast potlatch, where community members gathered to witness important ceremonies, record significant changes (birth, marriage, death), and redistribute

FIGURE 7.9: Tsimshian Tea Party, c. 1890s. Library and Archives Canada.

wealth within the community (Muckle 2004: 497). In the case of the Tsimshian people from the Pacific Northwest who are holding a tea party, what is notable is the mixture of European-style dishes and clothing with Tsimshian dress, such as the large, woven hats and blankets worn by women on the left. What we do not know is whether the tea that they drank was a European import or was made from native plants.

Although European forms of clothing—the dresses worn by the women in the photo's foreground or their male companion's black jacket—were often heralded as indicative of a person's assimilation, like the Tsimshian's tea party matters could be more complex. As art historian Ruth Phillips reminds us, for Indigenous people, "dress has traditionally been one of the most important sites for the aestheticized expression of group and individual identities," with tattoos, body paint, and ornaments conveying "personal histories of achievement," along with the gifts given to the person by spirit guardians in dreams and visions (Phillips 2004: 599). For those living in the Great Lakes area of North America, contact with Europeans led to them incorporating certain trade goods but in ways that reflected Indigenous beliefs and histories (Phillips 2004: 600). In particular, Indigenous and Métis women in British America had a long history of combining European materials into the clothing they created, both for personal use and for sale, while simultaneously using those materials in motifs from their cultures that held messages about their histories and traditions (Racette 2005: 22–3, 27–8; Phillips 2004: 606–10). By the mid-nineteenth century, the daily clothing worn by people of the Great Lakes area was similar to that of their settler neighbors; however, for formal gatherings, especially when political issues were at stake, "dress remained an important medium for the expression of distinctive identity and adherence to past traditions" (Phillips 2004: 600).

We also should keep in mind that choosing to wear Western-style dress was a decision made within the context of pressure from colonial governments and the exigencies of settler societies. Methodist missionaries in British Columbia were quick to herald the appearance of Tsimshian convert Elizabeth Diex, who was photographed just prior to her 1872 conversion wearing late-Victorian dress. Yet although Diex became the "poster child" for the missionaries, she had her own reasons for conversion. Her alliance with them and her image as a respectable Indigenous woman who eschewed Tsimshian dress and other forms of body modification that conveyed messages about her community's history allowed her to gain status and respect within her own community of Indigenous converts (Williams 2003: 101–6). In the case of Nahneebahweequa, European dress did not automatically mean renouncing one's identity as an Indigenous person. Presented to Queen Victoria in 1860 to ask for the return of her land taken from her family by the colonial government, she deliberately chose to wear European clothing: as she put it, to display herself as a Christian woman. Yet Nahneebahweequa also very proudly and openly declared herself to be an "Indian woman" who had suffered injustice at the hands of a colonial government and who was determined to resist their treatment (Morgan 2017b: 92).

Nahneebahweequa's image and speech invite further reflection. Great Lakes peoples' clothing from this period should be understood as a "materialization of negotiations and inventions" (Phillips 2004: 606). In Nahneebahweequa's case, her European dress can be read as a materialization that spoke to her own and her community's history of negotiations with Europeans, specifically Methodist missionaries, a group which included her uncle, Mississauga chief Peter Jones. Her speech, though, staked out a history of Indigenous belonging and identity. Given the primary of oral communication and hearing that, Phillips reminds us, was common to many Indigenous communities in North America, as opposed to visual messages and seeing (Phillips 2004: 593–4), it is possible that the history presented in Nahneebahweequa's words meant just as much to her and her Indigenous listeners than her Western-style gown and hat.

Nahneebahweequa was also photographed holding a book, another form of European technology, that of the "paper world" of pens, paper, and published works (Ballantyne 2014). By the middle of the nineteenth century, that world was no stranger to those who had been exposed to European missionary education, had engaged with colonial governments, or were tied to Europeans through marriage and intimacy. While European literacy had the potential to do much damage to oral transmissions of Indigenous knowledge, oral histories continued to convey important memories, as did those conveyed in media such as pictographs, birchbark, wampum, and ceremonies (Van Toorn 2006: 10–15, 211–12; Cruikshank 1996: 442–9; Miller 2009: 40, 82, 107). In Māori communities, women often wrote and performed *waiata*, songs that dealt with love, grief, and significant events, thus creating a historical record. Once Māori men and women began using written forms of communication, their letters document their concerns about land; it was an important source of concern and contention and was central to Māori relationships (Porter and Macdonald 1996: 24–6). Letter-writing, then, may have been a new form of technology for Indigenous people but it was also one that allowed them to express their cultures' traditions and their desire to maintain their histories.

Other rituals of daily life, though, came under either direct threat from colonial governments or were altered through more subtle and circuitous means. Missionaries had long been concerned about Indigenous marriage practices, such as the payment of bride wealth to a woman's family, polygamy, divorce, and matrilocality. However, they usually lacked the legal authority to change them and had to rely either on moral suasion or prohibiting those who practiced such rituals from living within mission villages (Ballantyne

FIGURE 7.10: Naneebahweequa/Catherine Sutton, *c.* 1860. Grey Roots Archival Collection, Owen Sound, Ontario.

2014: 141–2, 171). Governments, whether Dominion, state, or provincial, attempted to exert more control over Indigenous marriages and forms of intimate relations, seeing them as a threat to colonial stability and the offspring that came of them as a potential drain on the state's resources. In the new Dominion of Canada, for example, the 1876 Indian Act stripped Indigenous women of their "Indian" status if they married non-Indigenous men, thereby cutting them off from their communities and from the state's treaty obligations to them. The legislation also disenfranchised their children from their communities, potentially severing links with the latter's histories and memories. The government also worked to suppress polygamy and divorce, practices that had particular historical meanings in Indigenous communities. Although these initiatives were not entirely successful—bands might marry off girls to older, already-married men in order to keep them out of residential schools, while Indigenous couples practiced informal divorce as a way of fulfilling individual desires and preserving community harmony—nevertheless over time pressure from Indian agents and missionaries were important factors that eroded the ceremonies that surrounded Indigenous marriage (Carter 2008: Chapter 6).

An equally important means of conveying Indigenous beliefs, histories, and traditions was childrearing. Children in Indigenous communities learned from their elders in multiple ways: through the emulation of daily routines, being taught particular skills (hunting, preparing food, constructing homes, or making clothing), and in spiritual ceremonies. Story-telling was a particularly important form of education, one that conveyed morals and memories. However, missionary and government intervention in childrearing—while varied in its impact—could have disastrous results on a community's ability to pass on its collective memory. In the Canadian context, taking children from their families at a young age and placing them in residential schools, where they were forbidden to speak their mother tongue, stripped of their clothing (and, for boys, their hair), dressed in Western-style uniforms, and denied regular contact with their families and extended kin, were practices aimed at eradicating Indigenous culture and the memories that were integral to its continuation (Milloy 1999: 64, 131–2). Moreover, the high mortality rates in many late-nineteenth- and early-twentieth-century residential schools in Canada (often because of disease and malnutrition) also meant that Indigenous communities had to struggle with the shock of children's deaths in unfamiliar places, surrounded by missionary and lay staff who often had no knowledge of Indigenous communities' funeral rites and practices. While missionaries might memorialize the deathbed scenes of children in sentimental terms, depicting them on their sickbeds as embracing Jesus and looking forward to their heavenly "home" just before they breathed their last (Cassidy 2002: 211–13), it is doubtful that parents and other kin were left with such consolation (Miller 1997: 147, 150, 177; Milloy 1999, Chapters 5 and 6).

It is beyond the scope of this chapter to provide detailed descriptions of the many different funerary rituals in the myriad Indigenous communities in these colonies. Moreover, in the case of the societies studied here death has been examined primarily through the lens of causality, as a consequence of the depredations of settler colonialism (disease, abuse and violence, and neglect), less so as an event to be examined in its own right (Fraser 2017: 3). Mass deaths, though, had the potential to seriously weaken collective memory. As Joseph Masco has argued, for the Pacific Northwest Coast Kwakwaka'wakw people, losing seventy per cent of their population in an 1862 epidemic must have "seriously complicated the ritual logistics for managing the travel of souls between domains," a travel that involved dispersing the deceased's possessions in a potlatch. Furthermore, the relocation of their villages had serious consequences for the Kwakwaka'wakw belief in reincarnation: souls returning to their people would become lost and the community would wither away (Masco 1995: 60). To be sure, Indigenous death rites captivated many European missionaries and anthropologists, who viewed them as a way of passing judgements on the level of "civilization" attained by a community. Such was the case with the cremation and lengthy periods of mourning for widows practiced by British Columbia's Carrier band (MacLaren 2006: 6–7). In New Zealand's Bay of Islands during the early nineteenth century, missionaries also became avid ethnographers of Māori funerary rites, believing that the most effective way to challenge and change Māori spirituality was to understand their cosmologies surrounding death (Ballantyne 2014:189–202). They did not always do so, as the case of the last days of the Māori *rangatira* (chief) Ruatara in New Zealand's Bay of Islands suggests. Local missionaries, horrified by his kin's prohibition on Ruatara's eating and drinking, insisted on bringing him sustenance, which was seen by his family not as a means of keeping him alive but as food for his death journey. And while the missionaries saw Ruatara's last breath as signifying his final departure from the earth, for the Māori a spirit did not leave the body until three days after death and during that time could hear all that was said around it (Salmond 1999: 51). Yet by the 1820s those Māori with connections to missions began to change their ways of marking death, asking for missionary rites if they feared death was imminent and directing their families that they be buried in mission cemeteries (Ballantyne 2014: 206–7).

Indigenous death ways—as in other aspects of social memory—might incorporate European customs with older traditions. In late nineteenth-century British Columbia, for example, historian Carol J. Williams has found that Indigenous people were quick to adapt a range of photographic practices for their own spiritual and social purposes, practices that included a small number of Indigenous photographs meant to memorialize both adults and children, the latter taken after the child's death. The photographs of dead children suggest that an Indigenous mother could use the medium of photography to display "status and honor of the kin," as she dressed her child in fine clothing for his burial (Williams 2003" 152–63). In that sense they were not unlike settler postmortem photography, which could be used to reassure distant kin and friends that the bereaved parents had the wherewithal to provide a proper funeral and memorialization for a child. They also, though, testify to the devastation wrought by diseases such as smallpox. While settler children also might succumb to infectious illness, the deaths of Indigenous children were frequently the result of germs brought by European settlers, thus making the posthumous photograph a testament to catastrophes both individual and collective. Overall, though, as historian Lyndon Fraser has argued, "we know far less about the ways in which ordinary men and women shaped their mortuary beliefs and practices, including their relations with the dead, in response to momentous changes wrought by contact and colonialism" (Fraser 2017: 3).

CONCLUSION

For both settler colonists and Indigenous people, then, rituals and artifacts were important expressions of social memory, ones that in turn were tied to particular places. In some ways, both communities relied on social memory to forge individual and collective subjectivities, particularly in the case of rituals that marked significant events such as marriage and death. Yet the process of claiming these forms of memory, and the stakes involved in doing so, was not the same for each group. Ellen Currer Langton, her arrival in Upper Canada marked by sadness from the memory of a child she left in England, closed her "little journal" on arriving at her son Thomas's home in the bush with the observation that if "God in his mercy grants us health we may be happy, free from many cares in this quiet retreat."[8] Judging by her daughter Anne Langton's observations of her mother's activities, Ellen seems to have indeed found happiness, even though the many tasks she took on—upholstering furniture, cooking (including "rolled pig's head"), baking, helping Anne with the school she ran in their home—were not likely to have been part of her domestic routine in the well-off suburban home she had left in Liverpool.[9] Although generally cheery, Ellen was not, though, above comparing her new home to England, an assessment in which the colony was found wanting: "her ground of complaint being the slovenly nature of its inhabitants, instanced by the scattering of lime and water over her flower-beds."[10] Like many of her counterparts, Ellen also found Upper Canadian servants wanting, telling one of the family's maids not to iron the best table cloth, as "'I always do.'"[11] While Ellen's counterpart, Amelia Harris, enjoyed a life shaped by the markers of successful middle-class status, her household role removed from the kinds of labor Ellen undertook, as we have seen her memories of loss and grief were ones shared with white, middle-class women in other settler colonies.

We should not, then, overlook the difficulties settlers faced, forging new forms of daily ritual and memories while simultaneously maintaining that which had been brought to their new homes: these processes could be fraught and emotionally painful. At the same time, though, settlers had a range of choices they could make: to keep, to discard, and to create anew. Indigenous communities did not have that luxury: the "choices" they might make in their daily lives and beyond were ones shaped by contexts that, as the nineteenth century wore on, were not of their own making. In many ways Nahneebahweequa's story exemplifies the situation faced by her people who might have little option but to take on new ways of being: converting to Christianity, wearing European clothing, and deploying Western forms of literacy. It should be noted, too, that these practices had their own complicated histories for Indigenous people; they were by no means new or novel. Yet the activism Nahneebahweequa performed in defense of her land—forging connections with sympathetically-minded humanitarians (which might include welcoming them into one's intimate circles), making speeches in English, appearing in front of the Crown, and, above all, reminding her audiences that her sense of selfhood was grounded in her Indigenous community's history—also had their own particular histories for Indigenous communities around the British Empire. That Indigenous men and women such as she were able to maintain a sense of self through practices such as negotiation, adaptation, and (most importantly) persistence is a testament to their creativity and resolution.

CHAPTER EIGHT

Remembering and Forgetting

STÉPHANE GERSON

In 1858, François Guizot issued a warning about the perils of collective forgetting. "Forgetting, disdaining one's past is a source of disorder and weakness for nations," declared the French historian and minister. Though nations had the right to break with antiquated or repressive institutions, neglecting their past "would fan revolutionary sentiments" (Guizot 1858–67: Vol. 1, 336–7). Regardless of their political leanings, others shared this conviction. Guizot's commitment to national history and memory, as a historian and as Minister of Education in the 1830s, earned him the respect of opponents precisely because it broke with patterns of collective forgetfulness. What a brilliant idea it was, exclaimed Republican politician Eugène Pelletan, to "resuscitate a forgotten France, buried under the powder of archival documents and the brambles of crumbling abbeys" (Pelletan 1840: 160). Spurred on by Guizot, residents of the French provinces undertook archaeological digs, penned histories of their locality, and staged this history in pageants that inspired one conservative journalist to rejoice that "an entire century springs from the tomb of forgetfulness . . . to remind the people . . . of its history, which it was forgetting."[1] Such forgetting of the local past left the working class vulnerable before the siren songs of ambition and radicalism.

There were more personal reasons to eschew collective forgetting. Was the latter not part of the crisis of memory that, according to Richard Terdiman (1993), Peter Fritzsche (2004), and others, made contemporaries fear that the past was vanishing before their eyes in the wake of the French Revolution and then the rapid social and economic changes that accompanied Western modernity? Disconnected from the present, the pre-revolutionary past acquired a new sheen as a domain to explore, preserve, and interpret. But the unending stream of new experiences and memories that displaced older ones seemed to keep this past just outside one's grasp. A "profound forgetfulness pursues us," bemoaned Chateaubriand, who committed himself to recollection with desperation and resolution (Fritzsche 2004: 61).

The century's cult of memory takes on added urgency when considered alongside this battle against forgetting. The contemporary affection for mementoes (locks of hair, inscriptions, photographs) and predilection for journal-writing sought to conjure the threats of losing memory and thus oneself, of forgetting others, of being forgotten in life and death. Consider the poem that one Catherine Christ slipped in a daguerreotype case in Letherolfsville in 1859: "When I am dead and in my grave / As when my bones are rotten / Remember me / When this you see / or shall I be forgotten" (Batchen 2004: 47).

The century's new funerary practices—individual and familial tombs replacing communal graves—served the same purpose. As one contemporary put it in 1844 about Paris's new Père Lachaise cemetery. "Man regains at last his dignity, and his remains are no longer condemned to oblivion [*l'oubli*]" (Marty 1844: 1).

Forgetting clearly acquired a specific valence in the nineteenth century, and yet we know less about it than we do about memory. Architectural historian Adrian Forty complained in 1999 that "questions of how societies *forget* remain uninvestigated," both empirically and theoretically (1999: 2). A decade later, scholars were still regretting that forgetting was seen as mere slippage or absence of memory rather than as a phenomenon whose workings in specific historical conditions warrant analysis (Varley 2008: 77, Lavabre 2013: 12–17).

Regarding the nineteenth century, we can explain this neglect in several ways, beginning with the visibility—to historians as to contemporaries—of memorial ventures. With the exception of amnesia and other "morbid psychic states" (Ribot 1881/1906: 164), most contemporary philosophers and psychologists devoted relatively little attention to the matter. One contemporary reported in 1917 that he had identified many recent treatises on memory, but only one on forgetting, *L'oblio: saggio sull'attività selettiva della coscienza* (Degas 1917: 37). Works on memory tended to mention forgetting as an aside or a function of a healthy mind. For William James, "selective ability" made remembrance possible (1890); for philosopher Frédéric Paulhan, the mind's formal organization excluded memories that did not agree with its dominant ideas or desires, producing a "great law of systematic inhibition" (1904: 47) Such language evokes of course Freud's analysis of the forgetting of names, of displacement that excluded troublesome thoughts from consciousness. "I wanted to forget something, I *repressed* something." Still, Freudian repression, as articulated in *On the Physical Mechanism of Forgetfulness* (1898) and other essays, properly belongs to a twentieth-century history of memory and forgetting.[2]

The study of forgetting also runs into practical and methodological difficulties. Scholars have found it easier to investigate what we know than what, how, or why we do *not* know. Forgetting is decreed less often than commemoration; as a political undertaking, it tends to conceal its own operations; and, when it is successful, traces can prove elusive. In some cases, the process has proven so deep-rooted that it shapes the very questions that surface in our historical imagination (Lok 2014: 43; Proctor and Schiebinger 2008: vii). No wonder that scholars have paid more attention to collective *remembrance* as a mode of social cohesion and nation-building.

To be fair, a few scholars began to study forgetting in the 1980s. Benedict Anderson argued that the century's new historical consciousness involved "characteristic amnesias" that made possible the emergence of national narratives (2016: 204). Anderson quoted Ernest Renan's famous proposition, made at the Sorbonne in 1882, that citizens come together by forgetting the brutal means by which their country has been constituted. "The essence of a nation is that all individuals have many things in common; and also that they have forgotten many things" (2016: 6). This conception of forgetting as a natural, even necessary component of collective remembrance and a means of social integration surfaces in Maurice Halbwachs' classic essay on collective memory. "Society can live only if there is a sufficient unity of outlooks among the individuals and groups comprising it," Halbwachs wrote. "This is why society tends to erase from its memory all that might separate individuals, or that might distance groups from each other" (1992: 182–3). Only by forgetting social constraints and divisive questions will individuals embrace collective frameworks. This notion of "collective amnesia" (a more totalizing concept than forgetting) thus appears, for instance, in Robert Gildea's study of the past in modern French history, in which countries forget traumatic events in order to preserve grandeur (1994: 119). Other scholars have approached the question from more critical perspectives. Michel-Rolph Trouillot's classic book on the "silencing of French colonialism" in post-revolutionary Haiti suggests that historical forgetting constitutes a defining mark of nineteenth-century modernity (1995: 60, 100). New procedures—making and classifying sources, writing narratives—"obliterated" certain events and individuals from the historical record and collective memory.

In recent years, scholars have turned their attention to forgetting as "a defining characteristic of the modern period."[3] Beyond their differences in terminology, these historians suggest that the nineteenth century did not only resist forgetting, but also made it its own. One thinks of Nietzsche's pronouncements on forgetting as liberation from a "historical malady" that saps vital strength. "Without forgetting," Nietzsche wrote, "it is quite impossible to live at all" (1980: 23, 10). But Nietzsche's perspective remains singular in the nineteenth century, restricted to what Luisa Passerini calls oblivion, a personal state of mind she contrasts with the social process of forgetting (2003: 238). Recent scholarship on the latter is drawing the contours of a *political* history of nineteenth-century forgetting that was aimed at others beyond oneself. Politics here is understood in a broad sense to encompass power in all its forms, including doctrine, law, bureaucratic techniques, spatial inscriptions, new forms of knowledge and expertise, as well as literary and iconographic representations. Some of these scholarly works make forgetting itself their object of analysis; others address the matter while investigating questions about war, social strife, empire-building, slavery and emancipation, man-made disasters, or nature tourism. Because these explorations take place in separate silos, the full contours of this phenomenon remain hazy.

A single essay cannot remedy this situation. I make no claims to exhaustivity (France and the US will constitute my main case-studies). My hope is that, by placing some of these works in conversation, the reader might, first, discern the actors at play, their motivations, and their historically-situated modes of operation; second, grasp the factors that made the process less totalizing than it might appear at first glance; and, third, begin to imagine a history of forgetting that, by integrating the collective and the intimate, endows this political history with deeper texture.

I.

The Great Forgetting: the expression Adam Hochschild coined to describe the aftermath of colonial violence in the Belgian Congo points to something larger in the historiography (1999). A first narrative holds that, responding to the deep-seated political, technological, and social changes that marked nineteenth-century modernity, collective forgetting acquired a specific urgency, a practical utility, and widespread cultural resonance. It did so via newfangled procedures that sometimes originated at the highest reaches of government or media institutions and sometimes took form at ground level. To grasp this politics of forgetting, we must first describe what was forgotten (or what certain actors sought to forget) in the public realm. This will enable us, in the following section, to address analytical questions about who forgot, how contemporaries went about it, and why they deemed it indispensable.

Disasters have pride of place in this history, beginning with military defeats. Following the debacle of the French expeditionary corps in the former colony of Saint-Domingue (coupled with the emergence of the sovereign state of Haiti in 1804), "the mechanisms of forgetting set at once into motion," argues Marcel Dorigny (2005: 47). References to the victory of insurrectional slaves over a European army remained few and far between in French media. Silence likewise surrounded the Haitian Resistance and the French officers who suffered humiliation on the battlefield. General Charles Leclerc, the expeditionary corps commander, thus obtained but a modest funerary procession despite his exploits in Egypt and capture of slave leader Toussaint-L'Ouverture.

In 1815, Napoleon's defeat at Waterloo and the occupation of significant portions of northeastern France by coalition forces defied memorialization as well. Experienced in France as a shock, a humiliation, and a foreign abuse of power, this occupation entered what Christine Haynes calls "collective amnesia" (2016: 536). In 1870, another cataclysmic French defeat against the Prussians suffered a similar fate. This debacle was, it is true, the first French conflict commemorated on a mass scale, with hundreds of memorials to fallen soldiers, a law stipulating the size and shape of military tombs, and annual gatherings by veterans' organizations. Still, there were no state-sponsored museums, no official commemorations of the battle of Sedan (during which Emperor Napoleon III was captured), and few realistic depictions of battle scenes. As Gustave Doré's *Black Eagle of Prussia* (1871) makes clear, the defeated power could retain its honor and purity— free from cowardly or unpatriotic defilement—and the promise of rebirth vis-à-vis an evil enemy (Figure 8.1). Such responses are part of what Wolfgang Schivelbusch calls a *culture of defeat* that, in the West, now erased the political and military causes of defeat while insisting that the vanquished nation had ceased fighting of its own free will, due to an internal crisis from which it would now emerge with renewed vigor (2003: 14, 30). Forgetting, selective remembrance, and the production of myth made defeats glorious and even necessary (Clark 1989: 68–9; Boime 1995: 105–6).

Besides military failures, the nineteenth century was rife with natural and industrial catastrophes: floods, earthquakes, hurricanes, mine inundations, steamboat explosions, massive fires, and railroad accidents. A few disasters have left traces (however scant) in national memories—in general, due to their unique circumstances, high number of

FIGURE 8.1: Gustave Doré, *The Black Eagle of Prussia* (Paris, 1871). Courtesy of the Dahesh Museum of Art, New York, USA/Bridgeman Images.

victims, or resonance with contemporary anxieties or political struggles. In France, one thinks of the Bazar de la Charité department store, which went up in flames in 1897, taking the lives of 126 Parisians, most of them women; in the United States, there is the sinking of the *General Slocum* in New York's East River in 1904, with 1,021 victims. The vast majority of disasters, however, have vanished from memory. "Most of us prefer to back away from the scene of torment, with its inconsolable survivors and its insoluble problems," historian Christine Stansell explained in 2009.[4] Commemorations were rare and formulaic; monuments and plaques remained scarce; investigation commissions produced heartening reports; authorities retained little information about the said event (Clavandier 2004: 154–5; Ford 2016: 75). A sudden, unforeseen fracture in everyday life, the disaster made it clear that human beings could not control the nature they claimed to master or the technologies they had set into motion in this self-consciously modern century. Though one could not avert all dangers, it was possible to devise mechanisms that would efface guilt and reassure the populace.

Domestic conflicts have long elicited calls for collective forgetting as means of reconciliation (Loraux 2002). In the long nineteenth century, we observe this first in the aftermath of the French Terror, when the new regime, the Directory, sought to forget the violent opposition between Jacobins and their opponents. During the trial of a revolutionary who had drowned political opponents in Nantes, an unnamed contemporary counseled leniency. We must, he said "replace the bloody waters of the Loire with the salutary flows of forgetful currents."[5] In 1814, such forgetting took on legal form in the charter that opened the Restoration's constitution. "We have erased from our memory, just as we would like to erase them from History, all the evils that have afflicted the fatherland during our absence," declared Louis XVIII. To live together after years of infighting—and, in the case of deputies, to govern the country—it was essential to forget one's neighbors' past political choices, even if they included regicide. "Forgetting alone can cauterize the wounds," declared the baron de Bignon, a deputy.[6] One heard similar language in the post-Napoleonic Netherlands, where, in 1813, the provisional government proclaimed that "all internal strife has ended. All suffering is forgotten and forgiven." In France, this language resurfaced after the fall of the Bourbon monarchy in 1830, when the new regime (the July Monarchy) forbade commemorations of Louis XVI's execution on the grounds that they disrupted "thoughts of union and forgetting."[7]

In the United States, David Blight (2001) and other scholars have argued that a *reconciliationist* memory of the Civil War supplanted an *emancipationist* one from the 1870s on. Whereas the latter saw the war as a struggle over freedom, race, and slavery, with deep differences between North and South, reconciliationist memory romanticized a noble conflict between two armies that had made equally heroic sacrifices to defend equally legitimate causes (federalism and states' rights). Northerners and Southerners now marched side by side in Decoration or Memorial Day rituals. In a public address at Vicksburg in 1908, the Governor of Mississippi praised veterans for coming together to "blot out and forget all that might excite or perpetuate bitterness on account of the late unpleasantness" (Madison 2003: 215).

Around the same time, official memories of Paris's left-wing, insurrectionary Commune proved contentious for the regime that emerged in 1870, the Third Republic. Officials sought to forget, not only military defeat against Prussia, but also an insurrection that broke with law, state authority, and unified sovereignty, yielding a brutal civil war. They recalled instead heroic National Guardsmen and resilient Parisians who, overcoming cold and hunger, had withstood four months of Prussian siege. Louis-Ernest Barrias's 1878 *Defense of Paris* depicted an allegory of Paris protecting a wounded guardsman and a vulnerable girl. No armed Communards or internecine killings, no working-class demands or divisions between factions of the Left: nothing but a moral victory for a united country (Clayson 2002: 347–8) (Figure 8.2).

Here as elsewhere, historians have unveiled efforts to occlude the emergence of an industrialized society in which new forms of ambition, resentment, and strife threatened social and public order. In the United States as in France, urban elites staged pageants and celebrations that effaced conflict and social inequalities, and invited working-class

FIGURE 8.2: Ernest Barrias, "Puteaux—Monument de la défense (1870–1871)" (*c.* 1900). Courtesy of the Archives départementales des Hauts-de-Seine.

residents to substitute consensual urban identities to class-based identifications. In Buffalo, for instance, a local soap manufacturer sponsored an allegorical ballet about the city that left out all references to class. In northern France, notables went further by recruiting laborers to build floats and parade alongside them in historical pageants that depicted harmonious, pre-revolutionary, pre-capitalist, and hence pre-modern towns in which all knew their place (Gerson 2003). In the city of Douai, local elites selected a scene from the city's glorious medieval past and invited residents from all social backgrounds to become knights, burghers, or pages for a day (Figure 8.3). In one respect, this recovery of the local past was a symbolic defense of a glorious provincial heritage that present-day Parisians, certain of their superiority in a centralized country, "would prefer to forget." In another respect, such spectacles and the images that accompanied them were expected to thwart more acrimonious forms of historical consciousness among workers. By dressing as medieval folk, men and women "from the class of the *peuple*" would make theirs the values of their moral ancestors and forget troublesome social identities.[8]

Landscape artists, guidebook authors, and tourists similarly gravitated toward pastoral paintings that, escaping contemporary history, depicted wholesome rural life, quaint villages, and savage wilderness. In Fontainebleau, just beyond the suburbs of Paris, the local forest became a primeval, fantastic preserve whose trees and rock structures now bore legendary names (*Pharamond, Nestor*) that had nothing to do with industrial modernity. Fontainebleau was, in the words of a journalist in 1839, "a sacred, necessary oasis in the midst of the impious invasion of a destructive and improvised civilization"

FIGURE 8.3: "Quatrième fête historique de la Société de bienfaisance de Douai, représentant la gloire de Philippe-le-Bon, Comte de Flandre, (XVe siècle)" (Douai, 1849). Courtesy of the Bibliothèque Municipale de Douai.

FIGURE 8.4: Claude-François Denecourt, *Promenades dans la Forêt de Fontainebleau* (Paris, 1844). Courtesy of the Bibliothèque nationale de France.

(Jones 2008: 20) (Figure 8.4). In Nantucket, the Catskills, and the White Mountains, tanneries and sawmills, quarries and fishermen, struggling towns, social and racial diversity were forgotten as well, obscured behind Thomas Cole's luxurious forests and Washington Irving's imaginary creatures. The same was true of the considerable labor (ordinances, forest management, home renovations) required to "sacralize" nature and invent picturesque, old-world regions, impervious to change (Stradling 2007: 19, 49–67, 120–2; Brown 1995; Sears 1989: 53).

Violence and the threat of violence lay at the heart of the Great Forgetting. Much of the scholarship links the latter to the erasure of political unrest and the naturalization of new conquests. In France, this included the popular uprisings of the 1790s, the Parisian left-wing uprisings of the early 1830s (seldom commemorated, even on the Left), the insurrections that in June 1848 targeted a Republic that neglected workers' rights, and even the popular resistance to Louis-Napoleon's coup in December 1851. The Third Republic forgot all of this along with its own insurrectional roots. On September 4, 1870, Léon Gambetta had proclaimed the destitution of Napoleon III in Paris's City Hall. A regime that sought to ground itself in law had to forget the symbolic and physical violence that accompanied its political birth. Moderate Republicans accordingly forbade commemorations of the event, selected July 14 rather than September 4 as the nation's new national holiday, and occluded mobs from official memory (Hazareesingh 2009; Bouchet 2000: 113; Gribaudi 2014: 324; Le Trocquer 2006; Taithe 2003).

Violence was equally troublesome when it originated in imperial possessions, as we have begun to see in Haiti. French officials responded to the abolition of slavery in 1848 by, in the words of the provisional governor of Martinique, "recommending that all forget the past"; this encompassed slavery as a social, economic, and political organization.[9] As Myriam Cottias has argued (2006: 154–61), past grievances could generate violence and thus imperil public order and private property. Blending forgiveness and memorial erasure, forgetting became an instrument of social control (Chivallon 2009: 87–8).

Seeking their own emancipation in 1871, 200,000 Kabyle subjects took arms in Algeria against a regime that had curtailed their political rights and seized their lands. To maintain the myth of a benevolent civilizing occupation, France had to forget this uprising and instead memorialize loyal subjects. It also had to forget its own bloody repression (Varley 2008: 97–102). As in other colonial empires, most violence was perpetrated by the colonizers, and this is precisely what was omitted in universal exhibitions, schoolbooks, public commemorations, and pictorial representations. In the Danish West Indies in the 1830s, the watercolors of the naval officer Frederik von Scholten provided idyllic depictions of harmonious landscapes and calm plantations, devoid of violence and coerced labor (Danbol et al. 2018). In French New Caledonia, colonial prisons were closed in 1897 and then allowed to rot and disappear from local histories (Victorien 2016). In Belgium, King Leopold III made the Congo his personal fiefdom and then, in 1898, established a Museum of the Congo whose galleries would display colonial products, stuffed jungle animals, and a Hall of Memory dedicated to the country's colonial pioneers. Nothing was said about imperial plunder, the destruction of local traditions, and the brutal exactions that accompanied the production of rubber (van den Braembussche 2002; Vellut 2005: 13; Silverman 2015).

Violence and hence forgetting also took environmental forms in metropoles and empires. To create Central Park, Seneca Village, one of the earliest communities of black landholders in New York City, was destroyed in 1857, its homes undervalued and seized through eminent domain. The *New York Daily Tribune*'s claim that this raid "would not be forgotten" seems hollow given its absence from collective memory (Alexander 2008: 166–73). Likewise, the invention of wilderness required that Yosemite or Yellowstone become pure natural wonders. Native Americans were deemed part of this wilderness until the Civil War, but only as noble relics of a static past, impervious to social and technological change. In later decades, preservationists sought to protect necessarily *uninhabited* expanses. To recover this original, pre-human state, natives were moved to reservations, their ancient presence omitted from guidebooks. "The traveler in the park will see or hear no more of them [Native Americans] than if he was in the Adirondacks," declared one visitor to Yellowstone in 1886.[10]

By that time, American reconciliationist memory was forgetting slavery as a system of violence that had nourished the American economy before causing the Civil War. Already in 1867, politician Horace Greeley entreated the parishioners of Richmond's African Methodist Episcopal Church to "forget the years of slavery, and secession, and civil war . . . forget that some of you have been masters, others slaves" (Blight 2001: 62). The Lost Cause mythology remembered slaves, when it did, as faithful to their owners—not as escapees or Union soldiers who had fought for emancipation. The auction blocks in which "long cotton and rice negroes" were sold to the highest bidder left nary a trace—leading one historian to speak of "a massive breach in historical memory" (Bailey 2017: 9, 22). Black veterans likewise faded from view in memoirs of the war, magazine articles, and battlefield commemorations. The battle of Gettysburg's transformation into what Margaret Creighton (2005) calls a "whites-only event" occluded memories of Colored Troop regiments and of black civilians who had cooked in hospital kitchens, recovered remains, and rebuilt railroads. Neither victims nor agents of their own destiny, former slaves struggled to escape their continued incarceration in the plantation memorial complex.

II.

To explain the Great Forgetting, scholars have returned to the major ruptures and conflicts reconfiguring the nineteenth century. Building on the insights of Renan and Benedict Anderson, they have fleshed out the necessary forgetting that accompanied or made possible nation- and empire-building against a backdrop of domestic conflict. In 1818, the *Dictionnaire des gens du monde* defined forgetting as "means of ending revolutions" (Baudoin 1818: 157). Laws outlawed suits against former foes, required citizens to take on new names (in the French Caribbean), and promulgated individual and collective amnesties. Without necessarily forgiving, amnesty institutionalized forgetting by allowing condemned or guilty individuals to lead ordinary lives under the protection of law. "In political language, forgetting bears the name of amnesty," Victor Hugo declared in 1876. He was referring to the Communards (fully amnestied in 1880), but one finds similar references regarding former slaves, maroons, rebels, regicides, and rioters.[11]

Rituals would likewise extinguish the bellicose passions that still lurked within rational civilization. In Martinique, assembled men and women were told in 1848 to "vow to forget the past" by cleansing their hearts of hatred.[12] Such cleansing extended to public spaces. Streets and national parks were renamed; the houses in which Communards shot a French general were leveled; ruins that evoked defeat or conflict or collective disasters were replaced by new constructions and pristine parks. In the late nineteenth century, this mix of political reordering and urban renewal encompassed the ruins of Civil War battle sites, Parisian edifices lit ablaze by the Communards, and post-earthquake debris in San

Francisco (Fournier 2008). Material removal included bodies, both living and dead, with captured Communards shipped off to penal colonies in New Caledonia and their dead comrades thrown into common graves around which funeral ceremonies were outlawed (Nelson 2012; Solnit 2006).

What scholars such as Paul Connerton call *prescriptive* or *conciliatory forgetting*—intent on bringing former foes together—merges here into *repressive erasure* or *symbolic annihilation* of the histories, belief systems, and forms of resistance that threatened the cultural or racial hegemony of dominant states, institutions, and actors (Connerton 2008: 62; Eichstedt and Small 2002). Immigrants to the US were thus expected, in Theodore Roosevelt's words, to "lose all remembrance of Europe" in the new wild preserves of the West.[13] The relics, documents, and fossils of subjugated Native, Mexican, and African Americans were deemed too profane and un-national to warrant inclusion in archives, museums, natural history collections, and libraries (Mayor 2008: 164; Bodnar 1992: 30). In France, the Third Republic's creed of national assimilation and aversion toward internal difference spurred a myth of French abolitionism that found its icon in politician Victor Schoelcher (Taithe 2001: 143; Schmidt 2012: 107–8). The statue to Schoelcher (by Barrias again) that was erected in Guiana in 1896 depicted the Frenchman as a benevolent patrician who, having unshackled a barely-clothed slave, receives his eternal gratitude (Figure 8.5). The monument bore the following inscription: "The Republic no longer intends to make distinctions within the human family. It excludes no one from its immortal axiom Liberty-Equality-Fraternity." The regime could only articulate its civilizing ideology by concealing its denial of fraternity in imperial settings, the decisive interventions of former subjects in their own liberation, and the enduring economic and political oppression of former slaves. The contemporary photograph of the statue also draws our attention to its limitations as an instrument of remembrance. More than a century after its inauguration the statue stands forlorn in the middle of the roundabout, surrounded by empty space rather than onlookers who might derive civic inspiration; it blends into the background or even into oblivion.[14]

FIGURE 8.5: Statue of Victor Schoelcher, Place Schoelcher (Cayenne, Guiana, 1896). Wikipedia Commons.

The Great Forgetting was thus in one respect a top-down process, initiated by elected representatives, appointed officials, and military officers. The scholarship shows the growing role of bureaucratic states whose new "procedures of forgetting"—institutional modes of organizing knowledge, representing space, and disseminating information—could yield neglect, indifference, and partial or complete erasure (Artières 2014: 120). Because none of this required a deliberate plan of action, we may speak of accidental or mechanical forms of forgetting. Archives are a case in point. For much of the century, archivists were too poorly trained and funded to produce exhaustive inventories. In 1839, a French ministerial envoy decried the disorder he encountered in the departmental archives he had been asked to organize: "The few ancient documents one could find were stacked without the slightest design, bound to be forgotten." Few French colonial possessions had trained archivists until the twentieth century. If archives thus erased significant actors and questions, it was partly due to ignorance, neglect, piecemeal approaches toward disposal, rudimentary classifications, partial cross-references, and happenstance preservation.[15]

At the same time, such forgetting could constitute a strategic operation (Namer 1987). Building on Trouillot's work and Frantz Fanon's claim that colonial domination inherently "distorts, disfigures, and destroys" the past of oppressed subjects (1963: 210), scholars have documented, for instance, the purging of Belgian documents about violence in the Congo. On King Leopold III's orders, these exactions were, as one royal aide put it, "systematically . . . condemned to silence" in the 1890s.[16] In this setting and others, state actors pushed for collective forgetting to maintain public order, burnish personal and collective reputations, and convince citizens and opponents of their capacity to govern expertly. States sought to govern public emotions that could weaken their authority during times of instability. Sociologist Gaëlle Clavandier has approached technological disasters—train crashes, bridge collapses, steamboat accidents, and other catastrophes linked to modern forms of technology—as political threats to the legitimacy of regimes that might be blamed for failing to anticipate or prevent accidents (2004: 99, 123, 128). The same can hold true of natural disasters that, while not directly connected to modern technologies, nonetheless reveal governmental insufficiencies. To maintain public trust and manage collective emotions—anger and resentment, mourning and shame—authorities disposed of maimed bodies, removed wreckage, flattened accident sites, and praised courageous saviors and expert officials (Clancey 2006; Foote 1990: 389–90). Their "curative logic of forgetfulness" hence kept few traces of collective death and suffering (Clavandier 2004: 128).

If the authorities played a key role in this story, so did a "local voluntarism" (Brundage 2005: 121–2) that extended its reach with the rise of memorial entrepreneurs—agents of remembrance and forgetting working in the midst of civil society. Men as well as women, progressives as well as conservatives, these entrepreneurs included members of local associations; new producers of knowledge (historians, ethnologists, archivists); urban journalists, writers, artists, and others tied to new media economies; as well as commercial leaders and owners of local businesses. Some embraced public forgetting because they had too little capital to resist dominant norms. Following the emancipation of slaves in the French Caribbean, mulatto candidates in local elections commonly promised to disregard the violence of slavery as well as charivaris and other local practices that, as one of them put it in 1848, "summoned a past that forgetting now devours."[17] They did so in order to seal political alliances with white plantation owners, establish their Frenchness, and win respectability within a social world in which such collective memories—their own—had little purchase.

Mostly, scholars have drawn attention to actors who sought to buttress their dominant position within an increasingly market-driven social order. In Fontainebleau, guides, painters, and writers reinvented and commodified nature as a virginal preserve in which metropolitan visitors could resource themselves. Here, the politics of emotion revolved around the inner lives of men and women who needed to forget and cleanse themselves from the moral dross of the competitive society they helped bring into existence (Green 1990: 130). Following the San Francisco earthquake, local business owners, journalists, and politicians chose to "forget as soon as possible" a disaster that, according to historian Ted Steinberg, made the inherent risks of late capitalist urban development all too obvious. This "seismic denial" depicted the event as freak, natural occurrence, erased human responsibility, promised residents they could return to their dwellings, and allowed developers to erect new structures (Steinberg 2001: 105).

Ultimately, collective forgetting was not only a means of shoring up authority, but also a response to events and forces that destabilized fragile cognitive frameworks. The insurrection, the industrial disaster, the former slave who aspired to full citizenship created fissures in prevailing narratives about immemorial political regimes, national sovereignty, social harmony, scientific progress, and ethnic or racial distinction. One sought to forget the social and political forces that modernity had ushered in—and in which one often participated—or else older forces that proved frighteningly resilient during this most modern of centuries. Here, what contemporaries called forgetting falls within the broader category of aphasia: knowledge that is disabled and inaccessible, language that fails to make sense of things, "political, scholarly, and cognitive domains" that redirect attention, generate disregard, and overlook certain pasts (Stoler 2011: 167).

Among many examples, we may consider the posterity of Michel de Nostradamus, the Renaissance astrologer whose predictions had survived his death. In the nineteenth

FIGURE 8.6: "Salon—Grand Hôtel et Fontaine Adam de Craponne," postcard (Salon-de-Provence, *c.* 1914). Author's collection.

century, contemporaries encountered the name in dailies and pamphlets, dime novels and magic shows, board games and dream books. As mass culture gravitated toward his dark, cryptic quatrains, defenders of legitimate culture distanced themselves from a name whose currency suggested that, even in modern times, progress and reason had failed to contain superstition. No learned academy or pantheon, no national commemorations or canon deemed Nostradamus or his predictions fit for inclusion. Even in his native Salon-de-Provence, local leaders sought to forget this stigmatized symbol of desolation and popular delusion, at odds with the values this town, now a major soap and olive oil producer, wanted to project to the world. Instead, they commemorated another eminent burgher, the Renaissance engineer Adam de Craponne, whose canal had irrigated the city (Figure 8.6). Unknown anywhere else, this civic-minded scientist reinforced the optimistic, rational image local residents held of themselves and their era (Gerson 2012). In this provincial town as elsewhere, collective forgetting and remembrance came together against a backdrop of shame and tenuous self-definition.

III.

Without rejecting the political valence of forgetting during the nineteenth century, some scholars have cast doubt, on conceptual and empirical grounds, about the notion of a Great Forgetting. Juggling between scales of analysis, investigating local and domestic settings alongside official and public ones, they depict forgetting as a fluid social and political process and an uncertain end-goal rather than a cohesive phenomenon that encompassed entire nations, societies, or eras (Varley 2008: 21 and 77–8; Cohen 2001: 132). "The prescription to forget," writes political scientist Silyane Larcher, "is the redundant sign of the difficulty, or even the impossibility of forgetting" (2006; 158). Burrowing into the interstices of memorial regimes, this scholarship refines our understanding of collective forgetting in three ways.

Internal frictions. The notion of a Great Forgetting risks minimizing the internal disagreements, uncertain paths of action, and unrealized projects that limited the reach of this phenomenon. It also makes it difficult to analyze the latter as a process that unfolded in multi-faceted historical situations. Caroline Janney's research on veterans' and women's organizations from both sides of the Civil War unveils an enduring "tension between the reconciliationist spirit and sectional memories of the war" (2013: 270). Many Americans redefined reconciliation, not as all-encompassing forgetting, but instead as a supple framework in which reunion allowed for memories of slavery and distinct regional visions of the war.

Detailed political histories also unearth processes that are anything but linear. One example will suffice: the French Restoration's apparent attempts to reconcile France's warring factions after 1815. For one, the scope of this royal forgetting was limited, Louis XVIII kept the memory of regicide alive by transferring the remains of Louis XVI and Marie-Antoinette to the Royal Basilica of Saint-Denis and prescribing on the dates of their execution annual masses that later became compulsory days of mourning (Frederking 2008: 449–52). Expiation was thus interlaced with a politics of forgetting that raised suspicion among opponents. In fact, even fellow royalists raised questions about this course of action. How does one forget when everywhere people speak of the past? asked a deputy. How does one forget when aristocratic property, seized during the Revolution, remains in the hands of one's enemies? asked one émigré in London. The baron de

Norvins tried to chart a path forward by recommending that one forget past slights while memorializing the causes that lay behind them. "To forget such calamities would be criminal" for future generations, he wrote, making clear the ambivalences and semantic distinctions that complicated the politics of forgetting.[18]

Memorial Counter-Politics. In 1900, the Parisian police tore down the inscriptions that, at the Père Lachaise cemetery, marked the thirtieth anniversary of the Commune. Among them: "To the Forgotten, victims of [General] Gallifet" (Artières 2017: 197). While the state's politics of forgetting responded to perceived political threats, it could also invigorate and sometimes give life to counter-forces. Again, slavery provides a telling example. In the US, attempts to forget these depths of suffering, the true causes of the Civil War, and the violence of reconstruction did not go uncontested. White critics such as Albion W. Tourgée denounced a vision of the past that hid the conflict's essence and the sacrifices of black Americans, whose ancestry was now erased. The most vocal opposition came, however, from black preachers, reformers, writers, and journalists (Blight 2001: 220–1; Leight-Alexander 2017: 61–2, 76–7). In the 1850s already, Frederick Douglass instructed white audiences to "remember the chain, the gag, the bloody whip" and "the tears of my brethren, . . . disregarded and forgotten." His crusade against forgetting gained intensity after the Civil War, when many resurgent southern Democrats and weakened northern Republicans seemed to accept intersectional reconciliation. Forgetting the subjugation of slaves and their contribution to the North's victory, Douglass intoned, would serve the continuing effort to silence blacks.[19]

In 1903, W.E.B. Du Bois likewise inveighed against what he called a conspiracy of silence. "Almost everyone seems to forget and ignore the darker half of the land," Du Bois wrote before providing a harrowing portrait of Georgia's "well-nigh forgotten" Black Belt. The dark soil, the cotton fields, the abandoned plantations were suffused with echoes of the slaves' pain and longings and also with physical traces of the economic system that, before the Civil War and afterward, subjugated entire peoples. Du Bois listened to slave songs and stood silently before ruins that spoke of abuse and desolation, as if to intuit the past and push back against collective forgetting (1986: 488, 442, 457). Later, he called upon historians to reject the idea that "evil must be forgotten, distorted, skimmed over" (1992: 722).

Alongside such words, material objects and practices undermined the politics of forgetting. Debora Silverman argues that, while the Belgian Museum of the Congo denied colonial violence (including its own plunder of artifacts), colonial objects tell a more complicated history once one traces their provenance and their circuits of circulation between Africa and Europe. The same is true of artworks in which Belgian Art Nouveau artists ostensibly celebrated Belgian colonization. In Philippe Wolfers' "Civilization and Barbarism," a document holder exhibited in the colonial section of the 1897 Universal Exhibition of Brussels, two silver creatures—white civilization and black barbarism—battle it out around a Congolese ivory tusk. The documents in the holder praise Belgium's civilizing mission, and yet, Silverman argues, the African raw material is bolted in place with a violence that evokes a painful past. Such "wounded objects" uncover memorial counter-politics within the material strictures of colonial forgetting (Silverman 2015: 648).[20]

Intimate and Local Dissonances. Anticipating or following Du Bois, some Americans did turn the memories of former slaves and Civil War veterans into historical narratives.

Elsewhere, they commemorated Lincoln's birthday and staged festivals about emancipation (Kammen 1993: 168–70; Brundage 2005: 57–93; Blight 2011). Still, white violence and segregation did not lend itself to facile memorialization. In fact, Alexander Crummell and Booker T. Washington urged blacks to leave this "servile past" behind them (Blight 2001: 316–27). More importantly, these memorial ventures faced considerable opposition within a Southern public culture that remained wedded to a vision of the true South as white (Hall 1998: 463–4). One might conclude, then, that by the end of the century, forgetting prevailed over remembrance even within black communities.

And yet, historians who have delved into the domestic realm and scrutinized vernacular documents, personal writings, correspondences, and familial dynamics, have uncovered a rich and still poorly understood memorial universe in which memories of oppression and lynchings, of defeat and humiliation could coexist with public forms of forgetting. In Martinique, former slaves retained memories of their experiences in Creole proverbs and tales, magical and religious beliefs, dances, and rural traditions (Larcher 2006: 158). Following the Civil War, this was also true of white veterans and civilians. Recalling and reworking what others wanted them to forget, all could "negotiate the experience of mass violence and trauma" by sharing tales and displaying photographs, documents, battlefield souvenirs, and other relics that gave tactile form to painful and sometimes shameful memories (Barnett 2013: 80–125).

In post-1870 France, too, efforts to cleanse public space failed to extinguish a subterranean world of remembrance in people's homes and libraries. Parisians recalled—and perhaps learned to live with their own memories of—the Prussian Siege and Commune

FIGURE 8.7: "Souvenir historique. Déclaration de la Guerre. 17 juillet 1870" (Paris, *c.* 1870s). Courtesy of Jean-François Lecaillon.

by displaying shell fragments and creating collages that included dried flowers, pieces of bread, commemorative medals, the dates of major battles, and the prices of key foodstuffs (Figure 8.7). Collectors and antiquarians likewise accumulated vestiges of destroyed buildings and produced catalogs of burned libraries whose memories, one of them explained, might eventually diminish "in our hearts, but without ever being erased, or forgotten" (Stammers 2014: 64). Far from ministerial offices and public celebrations, contemporaries retained affective ties to the past and recomposed personal memories that, shared as they were with kin and neighbors and sometimes strangers, were also familial and national.[21]

Shifting one's perspective from national institutions, discourses, and elites toward local situations similarly tempers all-encompassing statements about collective amnesia. Recent scholarship on the local politics of forgetting in provinces, towns, and villages points toward a disjuncture between, on the one hand, top-down calls for forgetting and, on the other, rich local memories anchored in emotional experiences. While local memorial practices were partially shaped by the capital or metropolitan centers, local actors retained considerable autonomy. Karine Varley's work on the Franco-Prussian War depicts a complex memorial landscape in which, during the postwar decades, moderate Republican politicians sought (as we have seen) to forget Sedan while town residents resisted the town's stigmatization and expulsion from national commemorations by pushing for a glorious monument to heroic soldiers. Here as elsewhere, local representatives and civilians sought to retain memories, not of the entire war, but of local experiences—notably of suffering—that continued to imprint their individual and collective lives (Varley 2008: 15 and 84–6). Along the same lines, survivors of technological disasters and local residents typically retained what Clavandier calls an intuitive, emotional, "event-centered memory" of the event in its full horror (2004: 174–80). Their relics, oral accounts, grassroots commemorations, and spontaneous homages bear memorial traces that rarely surface in the speeches, reports, and statistics of the central state. This local reckoning with human suffering was at once a form of mourning, an effort to create meaning, and a step toward the reconstruction of a multi-layered collective identity.[22] All of this was of course imbued with politics.

We are left to contemplate a future history of forgetting that broadens our understanding of politics by blending scales of analysis as well as the collective and the personal, the intimate and the emotional. Historians are beginning to explore the interfaces between top-down and bottom-up perspectives without resorting to binary frameworks that essentialize each one. They complicate, on the one hand, the black legend of state or capitalist frameworks that systematically repressed all local expressions and, on the other, romantic visions of local actors who connected with past suffering in a pure apolitical realm. In so doing, they also show the limitations of conceptual frameworks that deploy memory and forgetting as distinct, adversarial processes. Instead, they draw our attention toward flows, movements, interplays of social remembrance, forgetting, and disremembering, and what Guy Beiner calls "dynamics of generating, repressing, and regenerating social forgetting"—all of which shifted over time according to political and other factors that require elucidation (2018: 606).

There is still much we do not fully understand about the conflicting forces that pushed and tugged actors in multiple directions at the national, local, and personal levels. Did some political regimes (whether liberal or authoritarian) gravitate more than others toward collective forgetting? By 1900, did the politics of forgetting by and large regulate public spaces (and if so which ones), or did such efforts contribute to a privatization of memory? "African Americans seem to have preserved emblems of specifically African-American struggles," declares Teresa Barnett in her excellent book on relics, but without indicating how widespread this practice was and what memorial practices such preservation entailed (2013: 6).

Similarly, which class-based habitus made it permissible or on the contrary forbidden to retain certain memories in professional, associational, or private settings? What was audible, what could be heard, say, in working-class homes? Some social scientists suggest that there is a specific form of forgetting within certain working-class strata, whose labor is stigmatized and hence not deemed worthy of remembrance. Unlike the middle classes, workers are not always socialized to transmit traces of their own familial and professional histories as collective heritage (Verret 1984; Delon 2014; Ferrette 2006). We should test this notion in the nineteenth century—at the intersection of race as well as gender. "Women cannot contemplate the prospect of forgetting an intimate relationship," declared the (male) author of a French *Dictionary of Love* in 1846. "Though love does not kill [women], forgetting may do so" (Duflot 1846: 198). The notion that women served by choice or not as "natural" guardians of familial memory in the domestic space and thus resisted the pull of forgetting requires further exploration.

These gendered representations bring us back to the question that opened this essay: anxieties about excessive forgetting. At the close of the century, how-to books with titles like *The Instantaneous Art of Never Forgetting* provided practical guidance for middle-class professionals—lawyers, judges, and politicians whose success on both sides of the Atlantic was linked to public speaking. "What anxiety this man feels when he loses his train of thought" wrote the French psychologist Francisque Bouillier in 1887. To win this "battle . . . against forgetting," readers had better follow his strategy, "analogous to that employed by the general who seeks to conquer a besieged stronghold" (Bouillier 1887: 159 and 163–4).[23] This military comparison was not innocent. For much of the nineteenth-century, forgetting loomed as a stated political threat and an unsaid political necessity. On the one hand, forgetting the national past would lead toward radicalism (Guizot); on the other hand, forgetting proved indispensable to naturalize new conquests and forms of subjugation, bolster new social and racial hierarchies, or more generally soften the violence of nation-formation, empire-building, and capitalist modernization. By the end of the century, as Bouillier shows, male professionals who might have embraced forms of (collective) forgetting in other settings felt compelled to combat it in their personal lives in order to maintain their composure, reputation, and dominant status as male professionals. The struggle may have moved from public spaces to private selves but, for the psychologist and the *mind-trainer* as for the minister Guizot and countless others, forgetting remained an inherently political question.

NOTES

General Editors' Preface

1. https://www.memorystudiesassociation.org/ (accessed February 3, 2020).
2. Agenda-setting in this respect was Cesari and Rigney (2014). For a review, see Erll 2011: 4–18.

Introduction

1. The term "sites of memory" has become essential to memory studies. Coined by Pierre Nora and his collaborators in their foundational study of French memory, *Les Lieux De Mémoire* (1984–92), it can be a useful concept. It is important to note, however, that Nora invoked *lieux de mémoire* as a reaction to the disappearance of what he understood to be more authentic *milieux de mémoire*. As such, Nora's understanding was deeply nostalgic and rooted in his interpretation of modern French history.
2. On German memories of war see Hagemann 2015; Cramer 2007.
3. On these "historical appetites" see "Clio in Part: on antiquarianism and the historical fragment" in (Bann 1990), PP. 100–21, especially 114, 116–18; see also "The Historical Composition of Place: Byron and Scott" in (Bann 1984), 93–11, 102–3.
4. I would like to thank Elizabeth Edwards for generously sharing with me images from the album as well as her research. Her forthcoming book *Photographs Sites and Monuments* will discuss the album in greater detail.
5. Memories of "first contact" also emerged as a popular theme in nineteenth-century literature; see Lutz 2007.
6. Terdiman explores Proust's notions of memory in depth in two chapters (1991); see also the brief explication of Proust, Bergson and "the madeleine incident" in (Whitehead 2009: 101–14).

Chapter One

1. Louis Bougainville (1859), *Circumnavigation of the Globe*, London: T. Nelson and Sons, 222.
2. Tahiti Infos (2017), "Pina'ina'i: la littérature autochtone va résonner samedi sur le paepae a Hiro," http://www.tahiti-infos.com/Pina-ina-i-la-litterature-autochtone-va-resonner-samedi-sur-le-paepae-a-Hiro_a153929.html
3. J. Williams (1834), *A Narrative of Events, Since the First of August, 1834*, electronic edition, documenting the American South, University of North Carolina. http://docsouth.unc.edu/neh/williamsjames/williams.html, 9
4. N. Sarkozy (2010), "Statements made by Nicolas Sarkozy, President of the Republic, during his joint press conference with René Préval, President of the Republic of Haiti (excerpts)," released by the Embassy of France in London (February 17, 2010).
5. D. Elmer (December 29, 2009), "Execution of Akmal Shaikh: China defiant in the face of criticism," *The Telegraph*, 1.

6. J. Lovell (July 23, 2014), "The Opium War Comes to America (The Book, That Is); A Q &A with Julia Lovell," interviewed by Jeffrey Wasserstrom, *Los Angeles Review of Books*.
7. Remark made to Louis Antoine Fauvelet de Bourrienne, diplomat (1801), S. in Jaques (2018), *The Caesar of Paris*, Pegasus Books.
8. *The Times Dispatch* (December 2, 1904), "Great Fair Now But A Memory," 1, http://chroniclingamerica.loc.gov/lccn/sn85038615/1904-12-02/ed-1/seq-1/#words=fair+Purchase+Louisiana+Fair+Exposition
9. I. Makazaga (June 21, 2017), "En Colombia la verdad y la memoria deben estar al servicio de la paz," *El Pais*.
10. Joshua M. Rosenthal (2017), "Memory and Peace in Colombia," *AHA Today: Everything Has a History,* March 20, http://blog.historians.org/2017/03/memory-and-peace-in-colombia/
11. A. Lagresille (1881), *Du vagabondage et de la transportation*, Nancy.
12. P. Le Roy (1901), *Vagabonds nomads et gens sans aveu*, Chalon-sur-Salone, 207.
13. A. Lacassagne (1906), *Précis de medicine légale*, Paris: Masson et Cie., 92.

Chapter Two

1. See also Kate Elliot (Luther College), "Selling Horror: The Recirculation of Images of the Dakota 38 in Early Twentieth-Century Breweriana," unpublished paper presented at Organization of American Historians Annual Meeting, 2017.
2. Anglo-Americans (such as Charles Lummis) began to memorialize the Southwest's Spanish past more actively around 1900 (Smith 2000: 119–44). Note also how the archaeologists who came across Indian mounds in the Ohio valley and elsewhere earlier in the century celebrated them as the work of prior *European* settlers (Yablon 2009: 48–9).
3. National identity was not, of course, incompatible with these other identities.
4. Both entails and primogeniture were subsequently restored (and abolished again) in France.
5. This sense of time as accelerating, to be sure, was not unique to the nineteenth century; on Martin Luther's perception of temporal compression as a sign of the imminence of the Final Judgment, see Koselleck 2004: 12.
6. Widmer reminds us, however, that the Young Americans in fact "venerated their grandparents" even as they "repudiated their parents' generation for its flaccid conformity and bourgeois materialism" (1999: 23).
7. The time capsule did have precursors, such as manuscripts sealed in libraries for a fixed number of years (see Yablon 2019: 100, 122).

Chapter Three

1. I should like to thank the various colleagues who have made invaluable comments and suggestions: Josh Bell (with whom I started the work on photographs of annexation of New Guinea, work that is absorbed here), Susan Crane, Leigh Gleason, Gill Grant, Philip Grover, Liz Hallam, Clare Harris, David Harris, Chris Morton, and Laura Peers.
2. The invention of printing and movable type might be said to constitute the first communication and thus information revolution in the "global west"; the late twentieth and twenty-first centuries—the digital age—constitute the third.
3. Both telegraph and photography translate and transmit invisible forces—electronic currents, and light rays—channeled through material forms—cables and cameras—which are translated into material objects of dissemination—cables/telegrams and photographs.

NOTES 177

4. Eventually telegraphy and photography merge in the transmission of photographs telegraphically. This emerged in a recognizable form in the 1890s and became viable in the 1920s, becoming the "wire-photo," the staple of photo-journalistic communication until the digital age.
5. The engineering work for railways and telegraph often resulted in the exposure of archaeological layers of material history and prehistory, skulls, fossils, material fragments, which were themselves visualized and reported across communicative media.
6. For a detailed analysis of the broader work of images and text in the *ILN* and their effects see Sinnema 1998.
7. *The Graphic*, preface, Issue 1 December 1869 (p. v).
8. *The Graphic* and *Illustrated London News* had sales readerships of *c*. 10,000 each and occasionally sold 200,000 copies of a single issue on special occasions (Belknap 2016: 478.6). However, this is an underestimate in terms of reader multipliers. For instance, these titles were taken by public libraries and reached substantial working-class audiences.
9. Birmingham City Library, *39th Annual Report* (1900–1): 2.
10. *Queen's Empire*, Part 13 (first issue of Part 2).
11. As Swenson (2013: 5) points out British commitment to colonial preservation predates domestic commitment to such endeavors by about half a century.
12. *Illustrated London News (ILN)*, March 27, 1858. Issue 910: 310. *The Graphic*, May 3, 1884: 411–4.
13. The British flag was first raised at Port Moresby in 1883, and followed by formal annexation by Captain Erskine of the Royal Navy on November 6, 1884. Photographs were made, probably by two New South Wales Government Printing Office photographers, Augustine Dyer and John Paine, who were aboard Erskine's flag-ship HMS *Nelson*, and an unknown photographer(s) on board a supporting ship HMS *Espeigle*.
14. *Illustrated London News*, July 7, 1883, with accompanying report page 6.
15. The prints measured 21.2 x 28.4 cm. In addition, there were two panoramas, marking an inclusive vision.
16. *The Graphic*, January 24, 1885: 1.
17. *Illustrated London News*, August 10, 1878: 133.
18. *Illustrated London News*, March 3, 1877: 292.
19. I am using the contemporary phrase "Indian Mutiny" although this is both contested and inappropriate in some contexts. The events of 1857–8 have also been called in the nineteenth century the "Sepoy Rebellion," and in the twentieth, the "Great Mutiny," "Great Rebellion," "Indian Rebellion," and "First War of Independence."
20. For an excellent analysis of the responses to, and emergent memory practice around, the "Cawnpore massacre" sites see Heathorn (2008).
21. "The Cawnpore Memorial," *The Builder* XXI (1863): 267.
22. *Photographic Views in India, by Bourne and Shepherd*, Calcutta and Simla. 1878.
23. *Illustrated London News*, October 31, 1874: 421–2.
24. See photographs.prm.ox.ac.uk/pages/1998_472_61.html (last accessed 13.11.2017).
25. *Illustrated London News*, December 28, 1907: 957.
26. It was also photographed by Indian photographers for the British market, for example by Lala Deen Dayal.
27. In the 1900-1 reissue there is a final part "The Imperial Forces in South Africa" to mark the memory of Boer War. This replaced the Part 24 of the earlier edition Supplement on the Government of Empire.
28. A conflict garishly illustrated by *The Graphic*.
29. For instance, Zig Jackson (USA Mandan, Hidatsa, and Arikara heritage), Brook Andrew (Australia, Wiradjuri heritage) or Jeff Thomas (Canada First Nations, Iroquois heritage).

Chapter Four

1. Bal (2002: 1). I borrow this point, and many others throughout the following pages, from Whitehead's rich introduction to the topic (2009: 3–4).
2. On Broca, Wernicke, and research on aphasia, see Jacyna (2000).
3. Laschley's lifelong research is summarized in his landmark article "In Search of the Engram" (1950). Present days neuroscientist papers speak of a "renaissance" in the field, of "still searching for the engram," even of "finding the engram."
4. On Hering and the other proponents of "organic memory" discussed in this section, see the excellent study by Otis (1994).
5. For an extended discussion, see Otis (1994: 53–74).
6. The study was translated into English—and significantly enough, by Columbia University's Teachers College—as *Memory: A Contribution to Experimental Psychology* (Ebbinghaus 1913).
7. For a useful overview of Ebbinghaus' findings and the other researchers he inspired, see Murray (1976).
8. On this controversy, see Todd et al. (2004: 25–8).
9. The following two paragraphs rely on exhaustive overviews of nineteenth century memory psychopathology by Roth (1989); Berrios (1996: esp. 208–28); and Berrios and Hodges (2000).
10. Ribot (1881: 75). Other important French studies of memory disorders from the time include ones by Sollier (1892) and Guillon (1897).
11. On Kraepelin and pseudoreminiscences, see Berrios (1996); and Berrios and Hodges (2000).
12. For contrasting readings of Janet's theory, see van der Kolk et al. (1989) and Leys (2000: 105–19).
13. For a useful analysis of Bergson and Proust, see Whitehead (2009: 101–14).
14. Freud also gave a somewhat different explanation for war neuroses in his introduction to Ferenczi et al. (1921). For two good overviews, see Whitehead (2009: 88–101); and Zaretsky (2015: 275–79).
15. See in particular, the mammoth project directed by Nora (2001–10), as well as Winter (1995).
16. This was the famous *Description de l'Egypte*, initially published in twenty-three volumes between 1809 and 1818 (an expanded edition was published in the 1820s).
17. On these imperial practices in Algeria, see, among others, Lorcin (2002), Oulebsir (2004), Davis (2007), and Ford (2016). For both comparable and quite different examples in the case of German imperial expansionism, see Marchand (2009).
18. On this systematic silencing in historical narrative, see in particular Trouillot (1995).
19. Scott tellingly pinned the birth of the Australian national narrative to the ANZAC (Australian and New Zealand Army Corps), then heavily involved in the First World War in Europe, and object of the main national commemorations in Australia ever since.
20. For a good overview, see Moses (2004).

Chapter Six

1. This term *Bildgedächtnis* (visual collective memory) spans a large debate in cultural studies and history, see Assmann (1991) and Assmann (1997).
2. For more on the term of discursive interaction and interdiscursivity, see Maurer (2006).
3. For an expansive discussion on the term mapping, Harrow and Watts (2012).

4. The debate about making use of collective memory and individual experience within the scholarly frameworks of history has been discussed by many historians and scholars of cultural studies. For exemplary works see Crane (1997); Funkenstein (1989); Hutton (1993) and Wilson (2004). For a more general introduction into the term, see Olick, Vinitzky-Seroussi, Levy (2011).
5. Symptomatic for this division between popular forms of memory and academic historicism, see Jaeger and Rüsen (1993).
6. For a discussion about the popularization of scholarly knowledge in nineteenth-century Germany, see Schwarz (2003: 221–34). For more theories on popularization, see Burke (1990) and Freitag (1989).
7. For an extended discussion on aesthetics and historicism, see Maurer (2013: 12–13).
8. My discussion on historicism is based on my book *Visualizing the Past*. See Maurer (2013: 13).
9. For the immersive effects of the Sedan panorama, see Maurer (2018: 78–94).
10. Kirsten Belgum has explored the genre of illustrated newspapers and its impact on the discourse of nation in mid nineteenth-century Germany (1998).
11. The following discussion of Menzel and Kugler's history book is based on my analysis in *Visualizing the Past* (2013: 118–144).
12. Despite Menzel's reputation as "the Prussian painter," however, many of his paintings, particularly his later works, also often displayed ambivalence about the regime (Suckale 1999: 19–31).
13. See Maurer (2013: 115–24).
14. See Maurer (2013: 152–6).
15. For the early debate on counter memory, see Foucault (1977). The discourse about the counter monument is also important; see, for example Young (1992: 267–96).
16. For more on Scheffel, see Maurer (2006: 51–6).
17. For an interesting study on Norway's antiquarianism, see Eriksen (2014).
18. German liberalism is strongly connected to nationalism and many of the student protest movements against the restoration regime were infused with nationalism and at times anti-Semitism.

Chapter Seven

1. Ellen Currer Langton, journal excerpt, n.d., June 1837, in H.H. Langton, ed., *A Gentlewoman in Upper Canada: The Journals of Anne Langton* Toronto: Irwin Publishing, 1950, 10.
2. Nahneebahweequa (Catherine Sutton) to Eliza Field Jones, March 25, 1847, Peter Jones Fonds, Box 5, File 7, Victoria University Library, University of Toronto.
3. J.J. Talman, ed., *Loyalist Narratives from Upper Canada*, Toronto: The Champlain Society, 1946, 66–7, 156–7.
4. Bruce G. Wilson, "CLENCH, RALFE," in *Dictionary of Canadian Biography*, Vol. 6, University of Toronto/Université Laval, 2003–, http://www.biographi.ca/en/bio/clench_ralfe_6E.html (accessed February 19, 2019), Daniel J. Brock, "CLENCH, JOSEPH BRANT," in *Dictionary of Canadian Biography*, vol. 8, University of Toronto/Université Laval, 2003–, http://www.biographi.ca/en/bio/clench_joseph_brant_8E.html (accessed February 19, 2019).
5. Mary Gapper O'Brien, diary entry May 13, 1836, *The Journals of Mary O'Brien*, ed. Audrey Saunders Miller, *The Journals of Mary O'Brien 1828–1838* Toronto: Macmillan, 1968, 251.
6. Peter Jones, *History of the Ojibway Indians*, London: A.W. Bennett, 1861; George Copway or Kah-ge-ga-gah-bowh, *The Traditional History and Characteristic Sketches of the Ojibway Nation*, London: C. Gilpin, 1850.

7. Jones, *History of the Ojibway Indians*, 74.
8. Langton, *A Gentlewoman in Upper Canada*, 24.
9. Ibid, 73, 77, 83, 85, 88, 92 119, 145.
10. Ibid, 94.
11. Ibid, 157.

Chapter Eight

1. *L'Emancipateur de Cambrai*, n.d. [1839?], Bibliothèque municipale de Cambrai, Delloye 38/72.
2. See Sigmund Freud, *On the Psychopathology of Everyday Life*, http://psychclassics.yorku.ca/Freud/Psycho/chap1.htm; see also Roth 1989: 49–68.
3. Amsterdam School for Heritage, Memory, and Material Culture, research program "Absent Memories: Social and Political Forgetting" (September 6, 2016), http://ahm.uva.nl/content/research-groups/absent-memories/absent-memories.html (accessed July 25, 2017).
4. Stansell, Christine (2009), "The Aftermath and After," *The New Republic*, September 5.
5. *Mémoires de René Levasseur, ancien membre de la Convention nationale* (Paris: A. Levasseur, 1831), 4: 109.
6. Baron de Bignon, parliamentary session of January 17, 1818, *Archives parlementaires. Seconde Restauration. Règne de Louix XVIII* (Paris: Paul Dupont, 1870), 309. See also Kroen 2000 and Scholz 2010.
7. Minister of the Interior to prefects, circular of January 7, 1831, Municipal Archives of Douai, 5 D 30. See also Lok 2014: 49.
8. *Congrès archéologique de France. Séances générales tenues à Dunkerque, au Mans et à Cherbourg en 1860* (Paris: Derache, 1861),184. As David Glassberg points out (1990: 126–36), ethnic conflicts were erased as well in the US.
9. Provisional Governor of Martinique (Claude Rostoland), proclamation of May 23, 1848, repr. in Lara 2005: 71.
10. George Wingate, *Through the Yellowstone Park on Horseback* (New York: Judd, 1886), 36, quoted in Spence 1999: 55. The paragraph above draws from Spence's book.
11. Victor Hugo, speech in the French Senate, *Journal officiel*, May 23, 1876, http://www.gauchemip.org/spip.php?article7658 (accessed September 7, 2017) See also Gacon 2002.
12. *Courrier de la Martinique*, May 26, 1848, in Lara 2005: 514.
13. Theodore Roosevelt, *The Winning of the West* (New York: G. P. Putnam's Sons, 1889), quoted in Nash 2014: 149.
14. Thank you to Susan Crane for her bracing reflections on the interplay between monuments and forgetting.
15. I am grateful to Fabienne Chamelot (University of Portsmouth) for her reflections on this matter. We still know little about the constitution and management of nineteenth-century archives. See Eugene de Certain to Minister of Public Instruction, November 1839, Archives Nationales (Paris), F17 3291. On archival practices, see Stoler 2002, Phillips 2016, and Georghallides 1985.
16. Maximilien Strauch, quoted in Hochschild 1999: 294. See also van Grieken and van Grieken-Taverniers 1957: 6–11.
17. Pierre-Marie Pory-Pary, address of April 29, 1848, quoted in Cottias 1997: 302.
18. Parliamentary session of 29 December 1817, *Archives parlementaires*, 191; Jean-Gabriel Peltier, "L'Union et l'oubli," *L'Ambigu* 57 (April 1818, 10), 35; and Norvins 1819: 113.

19. Douglass, "To My Old Master," *The North Star* (September 8, 1848); idem, *My Bondage and My Freedom* (New York: Miller, Orton, and Mulligan, 1855); and idem, *The Reason Why the Colored American Is Not in the World's Columbian Exposition* (1892), in Stauffer and Gates 2016: 418, 124, and 524. See also Blight 2001: 50 and 337.
20. See also "Civilisation et barbarie," notice produced by the King Baudouin Foundation, http://www.heritage-kbf.be/collection/civilisation-et-barbarie (accessed January 21, 2018). Literary scholar Colette Wilson (2007) argues that, despite official efforts to forget the Commune, the event haunted French novels, magazines, and universal exhibitions. On the history of material objects, see Auslander and Zahra 2018.
21. Megan Nelson makes the same point about the US in her *Ruin*, 232. See Crane 2000a.
22. On the local ethnography of post-disaster communities, see also Oliver Smith 2011: 27–9.
23. See also Loisette 1896 and Larrowe 1886.

BIBLIOGRAPHY

Alexander, Gregory S. (1997), *Commodity and Propriety: Competing Visions of Property in American Legal Thought 1776–1970*, Chicago: University of Chicago Press.
Alexander, Leslie M. (2008), *African or American? Black Identity and Political Activism in New York City, 1784–1861*, Urbana, IL: University of Illinois Press.
Alexander, Shawn Leight (2017), "T. Thomas Fortune, Racial Violence of Reconstruction, and the Struggle for Historical Memory," in Carole Emberton and Bruce E. Baker, eds., *Remembering Reconstruction: Struggles Over the Meaning of America's Most Turbulent Era*, 59–83, Baton Rouge: Louisiana State University Press.
Aljoe, Nicole N. (2004), "Caribbean Slave Narratives: Creole in Form and Genre," *Anthurium: A Caribbean Studies Journal*, Vol. 2, No. 1.
Allen, Thomas M. (2008), *A Republic in Time: Temporality and Social Imagination in Nineteenth Century America*, Chapel Hill: University of North Carolina Press.
Alpers, Edward A., Tim Denham, Christian A. Jull, and Judith Carney (2015), "Food Traditions and Landscape Histories of the Indian Ocean: Theoretical and Methodological Reflections," *Environment and History* 21 (1): 135–57.
Althusser, Louis (1984), "Ideology of Ideological State Apparatuses" in Althusser, *Essays on Ideology*, London: Verso.
Ames, Eric (2004), "From the Exotic to the Everyday: The Ethnographic Exhibition in Germany," in Vanessa R. Schwartz and Jeannene Przybliski, eds., *The Nineteenth Century Visual Cultural Reader*, 313–27, New York: Routledge.
Anderson, Benedict [1983] (2016), *Imagined Communities: Reflections on the Origin and Spread of Nationalism*, London and New York: Verso.
Arnold-Forster, H.O. (1897–9), *The Queen's Empire: A Pictorial and Descriptive Record*, London: Cassell and Co.
Artières, Philippe (2014), *Rêves d'histoire: pour une histoire de l'ordinaire*, 2nd ed., Paris: Verticales.
Artières, Philippe (2017), "Policing Writing in the City, 1852–1945: The Invention of Scriptural Delinquency," in Martyn Lyons and Rita Marquilhas, eds., *Approaches to the History of Written Culture: A World Inscribed*, 183–201, New York: Palgrave Macmillan.
Assmann, Aleida (1991), *Erinnerungsräume, Formen und Wandlungen des kulturellen Gedächtnisses*, München: Beck.
Assmann, Aleida (2011), *Cultural Memory and Western Civilization*, Cambridge: Cambridge University Press.
Assmann, Aleida and Sebastian Conrad, eds. (2010), *Memory in a Global Age*, Basingstoke: Palgrave Macmillan.
Assmann, Jan (1992), *Das kulturelle Gedächtnis: Schrift, Erinnerung und politische Identität in frühen Hochkulturen*, Munich: Beck.
Assmann, Jan (1997), *Das kulturelle Gedächtnis*, München: Beck.
Assmann, Jan (2006), *Religion and Cultural Memory: Ten Studies*, Stanford: Stanford University Press.

Assmann, Jan (2010), "Communication and Cultural Memory," in Astrid Eril and Ansgar Nünning, eds., *Cultural Memory Studies: An International and Interdisciplinary Handbook*, 109–18, Berlin: de Gruyter.

Assmann, Jan (2011), *Cultural Memory and Early Civilization: Writing, Remembrance, and Political Imagination*, New York: Cambridge University Press.

Auslander, Leora and Tara Zahra, eds. (2018), *Objects of War: The Material Culture of Conflict and Displacement*, Ithaca, NY: Cornell University Press.

Bachelard, Gaston ([1958] 1994), *The Poetics of Space*, Boston: Beacon Press.

Bailey, Anne C. (2017), *The Weeping Time: Memory and the Largest Slave Auction in American History*, New York: Cambridge University Press.

Baker, James W. (2009), *Thanksgiving: The Biography of an American Holiday*, Lebanon: University of New Hampshire Press.

Bal, Meike (2002), *Travelling Concepts in the Humanities: A Rough Guide*, Toronto: University of Toronto Press.

Ballantyne, Tony (2014), "Contesting the Empire of Paper: Cultures of Print and Anti-Colonialism in the Modern British Empire," in Jane Carey and Jane Lyndon, eds., *Indigenous Networks: Mobility, Connections and Exchange*, 219–40, New York: Routledge.

Ballantyne, Tony (2014) *Entanglements of Empire*, Durham, NC: Duke University Press.

Bann, Stephen (1984), *The Clothing of Clio: A Study of the Representation of History in Nineteenth-Century Britain and France*, Cambridge: Cambridge University Press.

Bann, Stephen (1990), *The Inventions of History: Essays on the Representation of the Past*, Manchester: Manchester University Press.

Bann, Stephen (1995), *Romanticism and the Rise of History*, New York: Twayne Publishers.

Bar, Doron and Kobi Cohen-Hattab (2003), "A New Kind of Pilgrimage: The Modern Tourist Pilgrim of Nineteenth-Century and Early Twentieth-Century Palestine," *Middle Eastern Studies*, 39 (2): 131–48.

Barnett, Teresa (2013), *Sacred Relics: Pieces of the Past in Nineteenth-Century America*, Chicago: University of Chicago Press.

Batchen, Geoffrey (2004a), "Ere the Substance Fade: Photography and Hair Jewelry," in Elizabeth Edwards and Janice Hart, eds., *Photographs Objects Histories*, 32–47, New York: Routledge.

Batchen, Geoffrey (2004b), *Forget Me Not: Photography and Remembrance*, Princeton NJ: Princeton Architectural Press.

Baudoin, Alexandre (1818), *Dictionnaire des gens du monde, à l'usage de la cour et de la ville*, 2nd ed., Paris: Eymery.

Bédécarrats, Alexis, Shanping Chen, Kaycey Pearce, Diancai Cai, and David L. Glanzman (2018), "RNA from Trained Aplysia Can Induce an Epigenetic Engram for Long-Term Sensitization in Untrained Aplysia," *ENeuro*, May 14, 2018.

Beiner, Guy (2018), *Forgetful Remembrance: Social Forgetting and Vernacular Historiography of a Rebellion in Ulster*, Oxford: Oxford University Press.

Belgum, Kirsten (1998), *Popularizing the Nation: Audience, Representation, and the Production of Identity in Die Gartenlaube, 1853–1900*, Lincoln, NE: University of Nebraska Press.

Belknap, Geoffrey (2016), *"From a Photograph": Authenticity, Science and the Periodical Press, 1870–1890*, London: Bloomsbury Publishing.

Benjamin, Walter (1968), "On Some Motifs in Baudelaire," in *Illuminations*, trans. Harry Zohn, New York: Schocken.

Benjamin, Walter (1999), *The Arcades Project*, Cambridge, MA: Harvard University Press.

Benjamin, Walter (2006), *Berlin Childhood around 1900*, Cambridge: Belknap Press.
Bennett, Tony (1995), *The Birth of the Museum: History, Theory, Politics*, London & New York: Routledge.
Bennett, Tony, et al., eds. (2017), *Collecting Ordering Governing: Anthropology, Museums, and Liberal Government*, Durham, NC: Duke University Press.
Berg, Lawrence D. and Jani Vuolteenaho, eds. (2017), *Critical Toponymies: The Contested Politics of Place Naming*, London & New York: Routledge.
Berger, Stefan (2017), "History Writing and Constructions of National Space: The Long Dominance of the National in Modern European Historiographies," in Maria Carretero, Stefan Berger, and Maria Grever, eds., *Palgrave Handbook of Research in Historical Culture and Education*, London: Palgrave Macmillan.
Berger, Stefan, et al., eds. (2012), *Popularizing National Pasts: 1800 to the Present*, London: Routledge.
Berger, Stefan, et al, eds. (2017), *Palgrave Handbook of Research in Historical Culture and Education*, London: Palgrave Macmillan.
Berger, Stefan, Heiko Feldner, and Kevin Passmore, eds (2020), *Writing History: Theory and Practice*, London: Bloomsbury Publishing.
Bergson, Henri (2018), *Histoire des théories de la mémoire. Cours au Collège de France, 1903–1904*, Paris: Presses Universitaires de France.
Bergson, Henri [1896] (1990), *Matter and Memory*, Cambridge, MA: Zone Books.
Berrios, German E. (1996), *The History of Mental Symptoms: Descriptive Psychopathology since the Nineteenth Century*, Cambridge: Cambridge University Press.
Berrios, German E. and John R. Hodges, eds. (2000), *Memory Disorders in Psychiatric Practice*, Cambridge: Cambridge University Press.
Bewell, Alan (2008), "Traveling Natures," in Keith Hanley and Greg Kucich, eds., *Nineteenth Century Worlds: Global Formations Past and Present*, London and New York: Routledge Press.
Bijl, Paul (2015), *Emerging Memory: Photographs of Colonial Atrocity in Dutch Cultural Remembrance*, Amsterdam: Amsterdam University Press.
Binet, Alfred (1894), *La Psychologie Des Grands Calculateurs et Joueurs d'échecs*, Paris: Hachette.
Bird, William L., Jr. (2013) *Souvenir Nation: Relics, Keepsakes and Curios from the Smithsonian's National Museum of American History*, Washington, DC: The Smithsonian Institution and Princeton Architectural Press.
Blackwell, Jeannine and Susanne Zantop, eds. (1990), *Bitter Healing: German Women Writers from 1700 to 1830*, Lincoln NE: University of Nebraska Press.
Blight, David W. (2001), *Race and Reunion: The Civil War in American History*, Cambridge, MA: Harvard University Press.
Blight, David W. (2011), "Forgetting Why We Remember," *New York Times*, May 29.
Blouin, Francis X., Jr. and William G. Rosenberg (2011), *Processing the Past: Contesting Authority in History and the Archives*, New York: Oxford University Press.
Blunt, Alison, (2003), "The Lucknow Albums," in Joan M. Schwartz and James R. Ryan, eds., *Picturing Place: Photography and the Geographical Imagination*, 243–60, London: I.B Taurus.
Bodnar, John (1992), *Remaking America: Public Memory, Commemoration, and Patriotism in the Twentieth Century*, Princeton, NJ: Princeton University Press.
Boettcher, Susan R. (2004), "Luther Year 2003? Thoughts on an Off-Season Comeback," *Sixteenth Century Journal*, (35): 785–809.
Böhm, Gottfried, and Horst Bredekamp, eds. (2008), *Ikonologie der Gegenwart*, Paderborn: Wilhelm Fink.

Boime, Albert (1995), *Art and the French Commune: Imagining Paris After War and Revolution*, Princeton, NJ: Princeton University Press.

Bonnet, Jean-Claude (1998), *Naissance du panthéon: Essai sur le culte des grandes hommes*, Paris: Fayard.

Bouchet, Thomas (2000), "Le cloître Saint-Méry (5–6 juin 1832). Histoire d'un cheminement vers l'oubli, 1832–1862," *Revue d'histoire moderne et contemporaine*, 47 (1): 113–30.

Boudrot, Jean-Claude (2014), "Voltaire 1878: Commemoration and the Creation of Dissent," in Joep Leerssen and Ann Rigney, eds., *Commemorating Writers in Nineteenth-Century Europe: Nation Building and Centenary Fever*, London: Palgrave.

Bouillier, Francisque (1887), *Nouvelles études familières de psychologie et de morale*, Paris: Hachette.

Bouwers, Eveline G. (2012), *Public Pantheons in Revolutionary Europe: Comparing Cultures of Remembrance, c. 1790–1840*, New York: Palgrave Macmillan.

Boyarin, Johnathan (1994), "Space, Time and Politics of Memory," in Boyarin, ed., *Remapping Memory: The Politics of Timespace*, 1–38, Minneapolis: University of Minnesota Press.

Brady, Thomas A. (1998), "The Protestant Reformation in German History," Occasional Paper No. 22 of the German Historical Institute.

Brantlinger, Patrick (2003), *Dark Vanishings: Discourse on the Extinction of Primitive Races, 1800–1930*, Ithaca, NY: Cornell University Press.

Braw, J.D. (2007), "Vision as Revision: Ranke and the Beginning of Modern History," *History and Theory*, 46 (4): 45–60.

Brock, Peggy, Norman Etherington, Gareth Griffiths, and Jacqueline Van Gent, eds., *Indigenous Evangelists and Questions of Authority in the British Empire 1750–1940*, Boston: Brill, 2015.

Brown, Dona (1995), *Inventing New England: Regional Tourism in the Nineteenth Century*, Washington and London: Smithsonian Institution Press.

Brown, G. Baldwin (1905), *The Care of Ancient Monuments*, Cambridge: Cambridge University Press.

Brown, Matthew (2016), "Creating National Heroes: Simon Bolivar and the Memories of the Spanish American Wars of Independence," in Alan Forrest, Karen Hagemann and Michael Rowe, eds., *War, Demobilization and Memory*, London: Palgrave Macmillan.

Brubacher, John (1966), *A History of the Problems of Education*, New York: McGraw-Hill.

Bruggeman, Seth C. (2011), *Here, George Washington Was Born: Memory, Material Culture, and the Public History of a National Monument*, Athens: University of Georgia Press.

Bruggeman, Seth C., ed. (2012), *Born in the U.S.A.: Birth, Commemoration, and American Public Memory*, Amherst: University of Massachusetts Press.

Brundage, W. Fitzhugh, ed. (2000), *Where These Memories Grow: History, Memory, and Southern Identity*, Chapel Hill: University of North Carolina Press.

Brundage, W. Fitzhugh (2005), *The Southern Past: A Clash of Race and Memory*, Cambridge MA: Harvard University Press.

Burke, Peter (1990), "Popular Culture Reconsidered," *Storia del la Storiografia*, 17: 40–9.

Burke, Peter (2007), *Eyewitnessing: The Uses of Images as Historical Evidence*, London: Reaktion Books.

Burkhardt, Johannes (1988), "Reformations-und Lutherfeiern: Die Verbürgerlichung der reformatorischen Jubiläumskultur," in Dieter Düding, Peter Friedemann and Paul Münch, eds., *Öffentliche Festkultur: Politische Feste in Deutschland von der Aufklärung bis zum Ersten Weltkrieg*, Hamburg: Rowohl.

Burnett, Kristin (2010), *Taking Medicine: Women's Healing Work and Colonial Contact in Southern Alberta, 1880–1930*, Vancouver: University of British Columbia Press.

Burton, Antoinette (2003), *Dwelling in the Archives: Women Writing House, Home, and History in Late Colonial India*, Oxford: Oxford University Press.

Butler, Samuel (1878), *Life and Habit*, London: Trübner.

Butler, Samuel (1890), *Unconscious Memory*, London: Longmans.

Campanella, Thomas J. (2013), "As a Witness upon the Field of History: The American Elm as Commemorative Vessel in Nineteenth-Century New England," in David Gobel and Daves Rossell, eds., *Commemoration in America: Essays on Monuments, Memorialization, and Memory*, 159–76, Charlottesville: University of Virginia Press.

Caplan, Jane, ed. (2000), "Introduction," *Written on the Body: The Tattoo in European and American History*, London: Reaktion Books.

Carlson, Keith Thor (2010), *The Power of Place, the Power of Time: Aboriginal History and Historical Consciousness in the Cauldron of Colonialism*, Toronto: University of Toronto Press.

Carter, Sarah (2008), *The Importance of Being Monogamous: Marriage and Nation Building in Western Canada to 1915*, Edmonton: University of Alberta Press.

Casper, Scott E. (1999), *Constructing American Lives: Biography and Culture in Nineteenth Century America*, Chapel Hill: University of North Carolina Press.

Cassidy, Cheryl M. (2002), "Dying in the Light: The Rhetoric of Nineteenth-Century Female Evangelical Obituaries," *Victorian Periodicals Review* 35 (3): 206–13.

Chaix, Gérald, translated by Reinhard Tiffert (2001), "Die Reformation," in Etienne François and Hagen Schluze, eds., *Deutsche Erinnerungsorte*, Munich: C.H. Beck.

Chalmers, James (1887), *Pioneering in New Guinea*, London: Religious Tract Society.

Chartier, Roger (1982), "Intellectual History or Socio-Cultural History?" in Dominick LaCapra and Steven L. Kaplan, eds, *Modern European Intellectual History: Reappraisals and New Perspectives*, 30, Ithaca, NY: Cornell University Press.

Chartier, Roger (1998), "Introduction," in Roger Chartier, ed., *Cultural History. Between Practice and Representations*, 4, Cambridge: Cambridge University Press.

Chaudhary, Zahid R. (2012), *The Afterimage of Empire: Photography in Nineteenth Century India*, Minneapolis: University of Minnesota Press.

Chivallon, Christine (2009), "Resurgence of the Memory of Slavery in France: Issues and Significations of a Public and Academic Debate," in Ana Lucia Araujo, eds., *Living History: Encountering the Memory of the Heirs of Slavery*, 83–97, Newcastle: Cambridge Scholars.

Clancey, Gregory (2006), "The Meiji Earthquake: Nature, Nation, and the Ambiguities of Catastrophe," *Modern Asian Studies*, 40 (4): 909–51.

Claparède, Edouard (1911), *Experimental Pedagogy and the Psychology of the Child*, New York: Longmans, Green and Co.

Clark, T.J. (1989), *The Painting of Modern Life: Paris in the Art of Manet and His Followers*, Princeton, NJ: Princeton University Press.

Clavandier, Gaëlle (2004), *La Mort Collective: Pour Une Sociologie des Catastrophes*, Paris: CNRS.

Clayson, Hollis (2002), *Paris in Despair: Art and Everyday Life under Siege (1870–71)*, Chicago: University of Chicago Press.

Cohen, Stanley (2001), *States of Denial: Knowing about Atrocities and Suffering*, New York: Polity.

Coleman, Deirdre, ed. (2006), *Women Writing Home, 1700–1920: Vol. 2, Australia*, London: Pickering and Chatto.

Combe, George (1830) *A System of Phrenology*, 3rd ed., Edinburgh: John Anderson.
Confino, Alon (1997a), "Collective Memory and Cultural History: Problems of Method," *American Historical Review*, 102 (5): 1386–1403.
Confino, Alon (1997b), *The Nation as a Local Metaphor: Württemberg, Imperial Germany, and National Memory, 1871–1918*, Chapel Hill: University of Northern Carolina Press.
Conklin, Alice (1997), *A Mission to Civilize: The Republican Idea of Empire in France and West Africa*, Palo Alto: Stanford University Press.
Connerton, Paul (2008), "Seven Types of Forgetting," *Memory Studies*, 1: 59–71.
Cottias, Myriam (1997), "'L'oubli du passé' contre la 'citoyennete': troc et ressentiment à la Martinique (1848–1946)," in Fred Constant and Justin Daniel, eds., *194–1996: Cinquante Ans de Departementalisation Outre-mer*, 293–314, Paris: Harmattan.
Cottias, Myriam (2006), "Oubli, pardon et ressentiment: la citoyenneté à la Martinique (1848–1850)," in Alessandro Stella Cottias, and Bernard Vincent, eds., *Esclavage et dépendances serviles: histoirae comparée*, 153–68, Paris: Harmattan.
Crais, Clifton, *Poverty, War, and Violence in South Africa*, Cambridge: Cambridge University Press, 2011.
Cramer, Kevin (2007), *The Thirty Years' War and German Memory in the Nineteenth Century*, Lincoln, NE: University of Nebraska Press.
Crane, Susan A. (1997), "Writing the Individual Back into Collective Memory," *American Historical Review*, 102 (5): 1372–85.
Crane, Susan A. (2000a), *Collecting and Historical Consciousness in Early Nineteenth-Century Germany*, Ithaca, NY: Cornell University Press.
Crane, Susan A., ed. (2000b), *Museums and Memory*, Palo Alto: Stanford University Press.
Crane, Susan A. (2020), "Photographs at/of/and Museums" in Gil Pasternak, ed., *Handbook of Photography Studies*, London: Bloomsbury Publishing.
Creighton, Margaret S. (2005), *The Colors of Courage: Gettysburg's Forgotten History*, New York: Basic Books.
Cruikshank, Julie (1996), "Discovery of Gold on the Klondike: Perspectives from Oral Traditions," in Jennifer S.H. Brown and Elizabeth Vibert, eds., *Reading Beyond Words: Contexts for Native History*, 433–59, Peterborough, ON: Broadview Press.
Cubitt, Geoffrey (2007), *History and Memory*, Manchester: University of Manchester Press.
Danbol, Mathias, et al. (2018), *Blind Spots: Images of the Danish West Indies Colony, Exhibition Catalog*, Copenhagen: Royal Danish Library.
Daschuk, James (2013), *Clearing the Plains: Disease, Politics of Starvation, and the Loss of Aboriginal Life*, Regina, SK: University of Regina Press.
Daston, Lorraine, ed. (2000), *Biographies of Scientific Objects*, Chicago: University of Chicago Press.
Davis, Diana K. (2007), *Resurrecting the Granary of Rome: Environmental History and French Colonial Expansion in North Africa*, Athens: Ohio University Press.
De Deckker, Patrick, ed. (1980), *George Pritchard: The Aggressions of the French at Tahiti and Other Islands of the Pacific*, Auckland: University of Auckland Press.
Degas, Ludovic (1917), *La mémoire et l'oubli*, Paris: Flammarion.
Deleuze, Gilles (1977), "Zola et la fêlure," in *Logiques du Sens*, Paris: Éditions de Minuit.
Delon, Margot (2014), "Faire mémoire(s) de lieux disparus. Le cas des bidonvilles et cités de transit de Nanterre," *Ethnologie française*, 44 (1): 341–53.
Dening, Greg (1992), *Mr. Bligh's Bad Language: Passion, Power, and Theater on the Bounty*, Cambridge: Cambridge University Press.

Dessalines, Jean-Jacques (2006), "The Haitian Declaration of Independence," in Laurent Dubois and John D. Garrigus, eds., *Slave Revolution in the Caribbean, 1789–1804*, New York: Palgrave.

Devereux, Cecily and Kathleen Venema, eds. (2006), *Women Writing Home, 1700–1920: Vol. 3, Canada*, London: Pickering and Chatto.

Dewald, Jonathan (2003), "A la Table de Magny": Nineteenth-Century French Men of Letters and the Sources of Modern Historical Thought," *The American Historical Review*, 108, (4): 1009–33.

Dickens, A.G. and John M. Tonkin with Kenneth Powell (1985), *The Reformation in Historical Thought*, Cambridge MA: Harvard University Press.

Dodman, Thomas (2018), *What Nostalgia Was: War, Empire, and the Time of a Deadly Emotion*, Chicago: University of Chicago Press.

Döllinger, Johann Joseph Ignaz von, translated by Henry Nutcombe Oxenham (1872), *Lectures on the Reunion of the Churches*, New York: Dodd and Mead.

Dorigny, Marcel (2005), "Aux origines: l'indépendance d'Haïti et son occultation," in Nicolas Bancel, Pascal Blanchard, and Sandrine Lemaire, eds., *La fracture coloniale*, 45–55, Paris: La Découverte.

Douglass, Frederick (1893), *Lecture on Haiti*, https://www.loc.gov/resource/mfd.25020/?sp=4.

Douglass, Frederick (2016), *The Portable Frederick Douglass*, eds. John Stauffer and Henry Louis Gates , Jr., New York: Penguin.

Draaisma, Douwe (1995), *Metaphors of Memory: A History of Ideas about the Mind*, Cambridge: Cambridge University Press.

Du Bois, W.E.B. ([1903] 1986), *The Souls of Black Folk*, in *Du Bois, Writings*, New York: Library of America.

Du Bois, W.E.B. ([1935] 1992), *Black Reconstruction in America, 1860–1880*, ed. David Levering Lewis, New York: Free Press.

Düfel, Hans (1984), "Das Lutherjubiläum 1883: Ein Beitrag zum Luther-und Reformationsverständnis des 19. Jahrhunderts, seiner geistesgeschichtlichen, theologischen und politischen Voraussetzungen, unter besonder Berücksichtigung des Nationalismus," *Zeitschrift für Kirchengeschichte*, 95 (1):194.

Duflot, Joachim (1846), *Dictionnaire d'amour: études physiologiques*, Paris: Comon.

Düwert, Viola (1997), *Geschichte als Bildergeschichte: Napoleon und Friedrich der Große in der Buchillustration um 1840*. Weimar: Verlag und Datenbank für Geisteswissenschaften.

Ebbinghaus, Hermann [1885] (1913), *Memory: A Contribution to Experimental Psychology*, New York: Teachers College, Columbia University.

Edwards, Elizabeth (2008), "Photography and the Making of the Other," in Pascal Blanchard, et al., *Human Zoos: Science and Spectacle in the Age of Colonial Empires*, 239–46, Liverpool: Liverpool University Press.

Edwards, Elizabeth (2012), *The Camera as Historian: Amateur Photographers and HistoricalImagination 1885–1918*, Durham, NC: Duke University Press.

Edwards, Elizabeth (2014), "Photographic Uncertainties: Between Evidence and Reassurance," *History and Anthropology*, 25 (2): 171–88.

Eichstedt, Jennifer, and Stephen Small (2002), *Representations of Slavery: Race and Ideology in Southern Plantation Museums*, Washington, DC: Smithsonian Books.

Eksteins, Modris (1985), "History and Degeneration: Of Birds and Cages" in J. Edward Chamberlin and Sander L. Gilman, eds., *Degeneration: The Dark Side of Progress*, New York: Columbia University Press.

Elkins, Caroline (2005), *Imperial Reckoning: The Untold Story of Britain's Gulag in Kenya*, New York: Holt.

Eriksen, Anne (2014), *From Antiquities to Heritage: Transformations of Cultural Memory*, New York: Berghahn Books.

Erll, Astrid, ed. (2008), *Cultural Memory Studies: An International and Interdisciplinary Handbook*, Berlin: de Gruyter.

Evans, Richard (2016), *The Pursuit of Power: Europe, 1815–1914*, London: Penguin.

Evans, Tanya. "The use of memory and material culture in the history of the family in colonial Australia," *Journal of Australian Studies* 36, 2 (June 2012): 207–28.

Falret, Jean-Pierre (1865), "Amnésie," in *Dictionnaire encyclopédique des sciences médicales*, Vol. 3, Paris: Asselin et Masson, 725–42.

Fanon, Frantz (1963), *The Wretched of the Earth*, trans. Constance Farrington, New York: Grove.

Ferenczi, Sandor, Karl Abraham, Ernst Simmel, and Ernest Jones (1921), *Psychoanalysis and the War Neuroses*, London: International Psychoanalytical Press.

Ferrette, Jean (2006), "Des ouvriers sans héritage," *revue ¿ Interrogations?* 3, http://www.revueinterrogations.org/Des-ouvriers-sans-heritage.

Finnegan, C.A. (2015), *Making Photography Matter: A Viewer's History from the Civil War to the Great Depression*, Urbana: University of Illinois Press.

Flath, James A. (2005), "'This is How the Chinese People Began Their Struggle': Humen and the Opium War as a Site of Memory," in Marc Andre Matten, ed., *Places of Memory in Modern China: History, Politics, Identity*, Vol. 5, Leiden: Brill.

Fleetham, Deborah Lee (2001), "In the Shadow of Luther: The Reshaping of Protestantism in Berlin, 1817–1848", PhD dissertation University of Rochester.

Flint, Kate (2000), *Victorians and the Visual Imagination*, Cambridge: Cambridge University Press.

Flores Richard R. (2002), *Remembering the Alamo: Memory, Modernity, and the Master Symbol*, Austin: University of Texas Press.

Foote, Kenneth (1990), "To Remember and Forget: Archives, Memory, and Culture," *The American Archivist*, 53 (3): 378–92.

Ford, Caroline (2016), *Natural Interests: The Contest over Environment in Modern France*, Cambridge, MA: Harvard University Press.

Forty, Adrian and Susanne Kuchler, eds. (1999), *The Art of Forgetting*, Oxford and New York: Berg.

Foucault, Michel (1977), "Nietzsche, Genealogy, History," in *Language, Counter-Memory, Practice*, Ithaca, NY: Cornell University Press.

Foucault, Michel (1990), *History of Sexuality*, Vol.1, New York: Vintage.

Fournier, Eric (2008), *Paris en ruines. Du Paris haussmannien au Paris communard*, Paris: Imago.

François, Etienne and Hagen Schulze, eds. (2008), *Deutsche Erinnerungsorte*, Vols. 1–3. München: Beck.

Fraser, Lyndon (2012), "Memory, Mourning and Melancholy: English Ways of Death on the Margins of Empire," in Lyndon Fraser and Angela McCarthy, eds., *Far From Home: The English in New Zealand*, 105–9, Dunedin, NZ: Otago University Press.

Fraser, Lyndon (2017), "Death in nineteenth-century Australia and New Zealand," *History Compass*, 15 (7): 1–14, https://doi-org.myaccess.library.utoronto.ca/10.1111/hic3.12399

Frederking, Bettina (2008), "'Il ne faut pas être le roi de deux peuples': Strategies of National Reconciliation in Restoration France," *French History*, 22 (4): 446–68.

Freitag, Sandria B. (1989), "Popular Culture in the Rewriting of History: An Essay in Comparative History and Historiography," *Journal of Peasant Studies*, 16 (3): 169–98.
Freud, Sigmund [1891] (1953), *On Aphasia*, New York: International Universities Press.
Freud, Sigmund [1896] (1962), "Heredity and the Aetiology of the Neuroses," *The Standard Edition of the Complete Psychological Works of Sigmund Freud*, Vol. 3, London: Hogarth Press.
Freud, Sigmund [1898] (1962), "The Physical Mechanism of Forgetfulness," in J. Strachey, ed. and trans., *The Standard Edition of the Complete Psychological Works of Sigmund Freud*, Vol. 3: 289–97.
Freud, Sigmund [1899] (1962), "Screen Memories," *The Standard Edition of the Complete Psychological Works of Sigmund Freud*, Vol. 3.
Freud, Sigmund [1901] (1960), *The Psychopathology of Everyday Life, The Standard Edition of the Complete Psychological Works of Sigmund Freud*, Vol. 6.
Freud, Sigmund [1914] (1958), "Remembering, Repeating, and Working Through," *The Standard Edition of the Complete Psychological Works of Sigmund Freud*, Vol. 12.
Freud, Sigmund [1920] (1955), *Beyond the Pleasure Principle, The Standard Edition of the Complete Psychological Works of Sigmund Freud*, Vol. 18.
Freud, Sigmund [1927] (1961), *The Future of an Illusion, The Standard Edition of the Complete Psychological Works of Sigmund Freud*, Vol. 21.
Freud, Sigmund [1939] (1964), *Moses and Monotheism: Three Essays, The Standard Edition of the Complete Psychological Works of Sigmund Freud*, Vol. 23.
Friedrich, Karen, ed. (2000), *Festive Culture in Germany and Europe from the Sixteenth to the Twentieth Century*, Lewiston: The Edwin Mellen Press.
Fritzsche, Peter (2004), *Stranded in the Present: Modern Time and the Melancholy of History*, Cambridge, MA: Harvard University Press.
Fryd, V.G. (1992), *Art and Empire: The Politics of Ethnicity in the United States Capitol, 1815–1860*, New Haven: Yale University Press.
Führman, Rainer (1973), "Das Reformationsjubiläum 1817: Martin Luther und die Reformation im Urteil der protestantischen Festpredigt des Jahres 1817," PhD dissertation Eberhard Karls University of Tübingen.
Fulda, Daniel (1996), *Wissenschaft aus Kunst: Die Entstehung der modernen deutschen Geschichtsschreibung 1760–1860*, Berlin: Walter de Gruyter.
Funkenstein, Amos (1989), "Collective Memory and Historical Consciousness," *History and Memory*, 1: 5–26.
Furet, François (1981), *Interpreting the French Revolution*, trans. Elborg Forster, Cambridge: Cambridge University Press.
Gacon, Stéphane (2002), *L'amnistie. De la Commune à la guerre d'Algérie*, Paris: Editions du Seuil.
Garvey, Ellen Gruber (2012), *Writing with Scissors: American Scrapbooks from the Civil War to the Harlem Renaissance*, New York: Oxford University Press.
Gelber, Harry G. (2004), *Opium, Soldiers, and Evangelicals*, New York: Palgrave.
Georghallides, G.S. (1985), "The Management of Public Records Under the British Colonial Administration in Cyprus," *The International History Review*, 7 (4): 622–9.
Geppert, Dominik and Frank Lorenz Müller (2015), "Beyond national memory. Nora's *Lieux de Mémoire* across an Imperial World," in Geppert and Müller, eds., *Sites of Imperial Memory: Commemorating Colonial Rule in the Nineteenth and Twentieth Centuries*, 1–18, Manchester: Manchester University Press.
Geppert, Hans Vilmar (1976), *Der andere historische Roman: Theorie und Strukturen einer diskontinuierlichen Gattung*, Tübingen: Max Niemeyer.

Gerson, Stéphane (2003), *The Pride of Place: Local Memories and Political Culture in Nineteenth Century France*, Ithaca, NY: Cornell University Press.

Gerson, Stéphane (2012), *Nostradamus: How an Obscure Renaissance Astrologer Became the Modern Prophet of Doom*, New York: St. Martin's Press.

Gildea, Robert (1994), *The Past in French History*, New Haven, CT: Yale University Press.

Gillingham, Paul (2010), "The Strange Business of Memory: Relic Forgery in Latin America," *Past and Present* 206 (Suppl. 5): 199–226.

Gillis, John R., ed. (1994), *Commemorations: The Politics of National Identity*, Princeton, NJ: Princeton University Press.

Gillis, John R. (1996), *A World of Their Own Making: Myth, Ritual, and the Quest for Family Values*, Cambridge, MA: Harvard University Press.

Glassberg, David (1990), *American Historical Pageantry: The Uses of Tradition in the Early Twentieth Century*, Chapel Hill: University of North Carolina Press.

Goldhill, Simon (2012), "Revolutionary Politics and Revolutionary Aesthetics: Opera, Classics, and Popular National History" in Stefan Berger, et al., eds. *Popularizing National Pasts: 1800 to the Present*, London: Routledge.

Goldmann, Lucien (1967), *The Hidden God. A Study of Tragic Vision in the Pensées of Pascal and the Tragedies of Racine*, 17, London: Routledge.

Goldstein, Jan (2005), *The Post-Revolutionary Self: Politics and Psyche in France, 1750–1850*, Cambridge MA: Harvard University Press.

Görres, Johann Joseph von (1821), *Europa und die Revolution*, Stuttgart: Metzler.

Gossman, Lionel (1986), "History as Decipherment: Romantic Historiography and the Discovery of the Other," *New Literary History* 18: 23–57.

Grafton, Anthony (1997), *The Footnote: A Curious History*, Cambridge, MA: Harvard University Press.

Granquist, Mark A. (2016), "Martin Luther in North America," Oxford Research Encyclopedias: Religion. Available online: http://oxfordre.com/religion/view/10.1093/acrefore/9780199340378.001.0001/acrefo9780199340378-e-322

Grau, Oliver (2003), *Virtual Art: From Illusion to Immersion*, trans. Gloria Custance, Cambridge, MA: The MIT Press.

Green, Nicholas (1990), *The Spectacle of Nature: Landscape and Bourgeois Culture in Nineteenth Century France*, Manchester and New York: Manchester University Press.

Green-Lewis, Jennifer (2016), *Victorian Photography, Literature and the Invention of Modern Memory*, London: Bloomsbury Publishing.

Gretton, Tom (2015), "Industrialised Graphic Technologies in Symbiosis with the World of Art: The Illustrated London News and The Graphic, 1870–c. 1890," in Kate Nichols, Rebecca Wade and Gabriel Williams, eds., *Art Versus Industry: New Perspectives*, Manchester: Manchester University Press.

Gribaudi, Maurizio (2014), *Paris ville ouvrière. Une histoire occultée, 1879–1848*, Paris: La Découverte.

Grier, Katherine C. (1992), "The Decline of the Memory Palace: The Parlor After 1890," in Jessica H. Foy and Thomas J. Schlereth, eds., *American Home Life, 1880–1930: A Social History of Spaces and Services*, 49–74, Knoxville: University of Tennessee Press.

Guégan, Xavier (2015), "Transmissible Sites: Monuments, Memorials and Their Visibility on the Metropole and Periphery," in Dominik Geppert, and Frank Lorenz Müller, eds., *Sites of Imperial Memory: Commemorating Colonial Rule in the Nineteenth and Twentieth Centuries*, 21–38, Manchester: Manchester University Press.

Guenther, Katja (2015), *Localization and Its Discontents: A Genealogy of Psychoanalysis and the Neuro Disciplines*, Chicago: University of Chicago Press.

Guha, Sudeshna, ed. (2010), *The Marshall Albums: Photography and Archaeology*, London/New Delhi: Mapin Publishing.

Guha-Thakurta, Tapati (2003), "The Monument as Image: The Compulsions of Visual Representation in Colonial India," in Maria Antonella Pelizzari, ed., *Traces of India: Architecture, Photography, and the Politics of Representation*, 108–39, Montreal: Canadian Centre for Architecture.

Guha-Thakurta, Tapati (2004), *Monuments, Objects, Histories: Institutions of Art in Colonial and Postcolonial India*, New York: Columbia University Press.

Guillon, Albert (1897), *Les Maladies de la mémoire. Essai sur les Hypermnésies*, Paris: Baillière.

Guizot, François (1858–67), *Mémoires pour servir à l'histoire de mon temps*, 8 vols., Paris: Michel Lévy frères.

Gupta, Narayani (2003), "Pictorializing the 'Mutiny' of 1857," in Maria Antonella Pelizzari, ed., *Traces of India: Photographs, Architecture, and the Politics of Representation, 1850–1900*, 216–37, Montreal: Canadian Centre for Architecture.

Hacking, Ian (1995), *Rewriting the Soul: Multiple Personality and the Sciences of Memory*, Princeton, NJ: Princeton University Press.

Hacking, Ian (2002), *Mad Travelers: Reflections on the Reality of Transient Mental Illnesses*, Cambridge, MA: Harvard University Press.

Hagemann, Karen (2015), *Revisiting Prussia's Wars Against Napoleon: History, Culture and Memory*, New York: Cambridge University Press.

Hager, Werner (1989), *Geschichte in Bildern: Studien zur Historienmalerei des 19. Jahrhunderts*, Hildesheim: Georg Olms.

Haines, Robin (2003), *Life and Death in the Age of Sail: The Passage to Australia*, Sydney: UNSW Press.

Halbwachs, Maurice [1925] (1992), *On Collective Memory*, introduction and translation Lewis A. Coser, Chicago: Chicago University Press.

Halbwachs, Maurice [1950] (1980), "Collective Memory and Historical Memory," in Halbwachs, *The Collective Memory*, translated by Francis J. Ditter, Jr. and Vida Yazdi Ditter, New York: Harper Colophon Books.

Hall, Jacquelyn Dowd (1998), "'You Must Remember This': Autobiography as Social Critique," *The Journal of American History*, 85 (2): 439–65.

Hall, Melanie, ed. (2011), *Towards World Heritage: International Originals of the Preservation Movement*, Farnham: Ashgate.

Hare, J. Laurence (2015), *Excavating Nations: Archeology, Museums, and the German Danish Borderlands*, Toronto: University of Toronto Press.

Harris, David (1999), *Of Battle and Beauty: Felice Beato's Photographs of China*, Santa Barbara, CA: Santa Barbara Museum of Art.

Harris, Neil [1966] (1982), *The Artist in American Society: The Formative Years*, Chicago: University of Chicago Press.

Harris, Robin, ed. (1994), *The Eldon House Diaries: Five Women's View of the 19th Century*, Toronto: The Champlain Society, 1994.

Harman, Kristyn and Hamish Maxwell-Stewart (2012), "Aboriginal Deaths in Custody in Colonial Australia, 1805–1860," *Journal of Colonialism and Colonial History*, 13 (2):1–21.

Harrow, Susan, and Andrew Watts (2012), *Mapping Memory in Nineteenth-Century French Literature and Culture*, Amsterdam: Rodopi.

Hartung, Olaf (2010), *Kleine deutsche Museumsgeschichte von der Aufklärung bis zum frühen 20,* Jahrhundert, Köln: Böhlau.

Harvey, David (1990), *The Condition of Postmodernity: An Enquiry into the Origins of Cultural Change*, Oxford: Blackwell.

Haynes, Christine (2016), "Remembering and Forgetting the First Modern Occupations of France," *The Journal of Modern History*, 88 (3): 535–71.

Hazareesingh, Sudhir (2004), "Memory and Political Imagination: The Legend of Napoleon Revisited," *French History*, Vol. 18, No. 4.

Hazareesingh, Sudhir (2009), "Conflicts of Memory: Republicanism and the Commemoration of the Past in Modern France," *French History*, 23 (1): 193–215.

Headrick, Daniel R. (1991), *The Invisible Weapon: Telecommunications and International Politics 1851–1945*, Oxford: Oxford University Press.

Heathorn, Stephen J. (2007), "Angel of Empire: The Cawnpore Memorial Well as a British Site of Imperial Remembrance," *Journal of Colonialism and Colonial History*, 8 (3) DOI: 10.1353/cch.2008.0009.

Hebekus, Uwe (2003), *Klios Medien: Die Geschichtskultur des 19. Jahrhunderts in der historistischen Historie bei Theodor Fontane*, Tübingen: Max Niemeyer.

Herntrich, Hans-Volker (1982), "Ein deutsch-nationaler Freiheitsheld: Wie Martin Luther vor hundert Jahren gefeiert wurde," *Lutherische Monatshefte*, No. 21: 274–6.

Hess, Günter (1975), "Allegorie und Historismus: Zum Bildgedächtnis des späten 19. Jahrhunderts," in Hans Fromm, Wolfgang Harms, and Uwe Ruberg, eds., *Verbum et Signum: Beiträge zur mediävistischen Bedeutungsforschung*, Vol. 1, 555–91, München: Fink.

Hickford, Mark and Carwyn Jones, eds. (2019), *International Perspectives on the Treaty of Waitangi*, New York: Routledge.

Higgs, Elizabeth and Polly F. Radosh (2013), "Quilts: Moral Economies and Matrilineages," *Journal of Family History*, 38 (1): 53–77.

Hill, Jason E. and Vanessa R. Schwartz, eds. (2015), *Getting the Picture: The Visual Culture of the News*, London: Bloomsbury Publishing.

Hinrichs, Carl (1954), *Ranke und die Geschichtstheologie der Goethezeit*, Göttingen: Musterschmidt.

Hobsbawm, Eric (1962), *The Age of Revolution: Europe, 1789–1848*; (1975), *The Age of Capital, 1848–1875*; (1987), *The Age of Empire, 1875–1914*, London: Weidenfeld & Nicolson.

Hobsbawm, Eric and Terence Ranger (1983), *The Invention of Tradition*, Cambridge: Cambridge University Press.

Hochschild, Adam (1999), *King Leopold's Ghosts: A Story of Greed, Terror, and Heroism in Colonial Africa*, Boston: Houghton Mifflin.

Hoffenberg, Peter H. (2001), *An Empire on Display: English, Indian, and Australian Exhibitions from the Crystal Palace to the Great War*, Berkeley CA: University of California Press.

Holden, Robert (1988), *Photography in Colonial Australia: The Mechanical Eye and the Illustrated Book*, Sydney: Horden House.

Hollander, Stacey C. (2016), *Securing the Shadow: Posthumous Portraiture in America*, Dalton, MA: Studley Press.

Holzheid, Anett (2011), *Das Medium Postkarte: Eine sprachwissenschaftliche und medienwissenschaftliche Studie*, Berlin: Erich Schmidt.

Howard, Thomas Albert (2000), *Religion and the Rise of Historicism: W.M.L. de Wette, Jacob Burckhardt, and the Theological Origins of Nineteenth-Century Historical Consciousness*, Cambridge: Cambridge University Press.

Howard, Thomas Albert (2016), *Remembering the Reformation: An Inquiry into the Meanings of Protestantism*, Oxford: Oxford University Press.
Howard, Thomas Albert and Mark A. Knoll (2014), "The Reformation at Five Hundred: An Outline of the Changing Ways We Remember the Reformation," First Things, November 2014. Available online: https://www.firstthings.com/article/2014/11/the-reformation-at-five-hundred
Huhtamo, Erkki (2013), *Illusion in Motion: Media Archaeology of the Moving Panorama and Related Spectacles*, Cambridge MA: The MIT Press.
Huhtamo, Erkki and Jussi Parikka, eds. (2011), *Media Archaeology: Approaches, Applications, and Implications*, Berkeley: University of California Press.
Hull, Isabelle (2004), *Absolute Destruction: Military Culture and the Practices of War in Imperial Germany*, Ithaca, NY: Cornell University Press.
Hunt, Lynn (1984), *Politics, Culture, and Class in the French Revolution*, Berkeley and Los Angeles: University of California Press.
Hunt, Lynn (1989), "Introduction: History, Culture, Text," in Lynn Hunt, ed., *The New Cultural History*, 19, Berkeley: University of California Press.
Hutton, Patrick (1993), *History as an Art of Memory*, Hanover and London: University Press of New England.
Hutton, Patrick (2016), *The Memory Phenomenon in Contemporary Historical Writing: How the Interest in Memory Has Influenced Our Understanding of History*, New York: Springer.
Innis, Harold A. (1951), *The Bias of Communication*, Toronto: University of Toronto Press.
Ishiguro, Laura (2018), "'A Dreadful Little Glutton, Always Telling You About Food': The Epistolatory Everyday and the Making of a Colonial Settler," *Canadian Historical Review*, 99 (2): 258–83.
Ito, Mizuko (2008), "Introduction," in Kazys Varnelis, ed., *Networked Publics*, 1–14, Cambridge MA: The MIT Press.
Jacyna, Stephen (2000), *Lost Words: Narratives of Language and the Brain, 1825–1926*, Princeton, NJ: Princeton University Press.
Jaeger, Friedrich and Jörn Rüsen (1992), *Geschichte des Historismus: Eine Einführung*, München: Beck.
Jalland, Patricia (2002), *The Australian Ways of Death: A Social and Cultural History, 1840–1918*, New York: Oxford University Press.
Janet, Pierre (1889), *L'Automatisme psychologique*, Paris: Alcan.
Janet, Pierre (1914–15), "Psychoanalysis," *The Journal of Abnormal Psychology*, Vol. 9.
James, William (1890), *The Principles of Psychology*, Vol. 1, New York: Henry Holt.
Janney, Caroline E. (2013), *Remembering the Civil War: Reunion and the Limits of Reconciliation*, Chapel Hill: University of North Carolina Press.
Johnston, Anna (2001), "Antipodean heathens: The London Missionary Society in Polynesia and Australia, 1800–50," in Lynette Russell, ed., *Colonial Frontiers: Indigenous-European Encounters in Settler Societies*, 68–81, Manchester: Manchester University Press.
Jones, Kimberly (2008), "Landscapes, Legends, Souvenirs, Fantasies: The Forest of Fontainebleau in the Nineteenth Century," in Jones, ed., *In the Forest of Fontainebleau: Painters and Photographers from Corot to Monet*, 2–27, Washington, DC: National Gallery of Art.
Joschke, Christian (2013), *Les yeux de la nation. Photographie amateur et société dans l'Allemagne de Guillaume II 1888–1914*, Paris: Les press du réel.
Jussen, Bernhard (2002), "Die Liebig-Sammelbilder und der Atlas des historischen Bildwissens: Einleitung," in Bernhard Jussen, ed., *Bilder des Historischen Bildwissens 1: Liebig's Sammelbilder*, 2–15, Berlin: The York Project.

Kachun, Mitch (2003), *Festivals of Freedom: Memory and Meaning in African American Emancipation Celebrations, 1808–1915*, Amherst: University of Massachusetts Press.

Kammen, Michael (1983), "Moses Coit Tyler: The First Professor of American History in the United States," *History Teacher*, 17 (1): 61–87.

Kammen, Michael (1991), *Mystic Chords of Memory: The Transformation of Tradition in American Culture*, New York: Vintage Books.

Kanahele, George S. (1986), *Ku Kanak, Stand Tall: A Search for Hawaiian Values*, Honolulu: University of Hawaii Press.

Kansteiner, Wulf (2002), "Finding Meaning in Memory: A Methodological Critique of Collective Memory Studies," *History and Theory*, 41(2): 179–97.

Kaul, Chandrika (2014), *Communications, Media and the Imperial Experience: Britain and India in the Twentieth Century*, Basingstoke: Palgrave Macmillan.

Kelman, Ari (2013), *A Misplaced Massacre: Struggling over the Memory of Sand Creek*, Cambridge, MA: Harvard University Press.

Koselleck, Reinhart (1972), "Geschichte: Historie," in Reinhart Koselleck, Otto Brunner, and Werner Conze, eds., *Geschichtliche Grundbegriffe: Historisches Lexikon zur poltisch-sozialen Sprache in Deutschland*, Vol. 2, 647–52, Stuttgart: Klett.

Koselleck, Reinhart [1985] (2004), *Futures Past: On the Semantics of Historical Time*, New York: Columbia University Press.

Kroen, Sheryl (2000), *Politics and Theater: The Crisis of Legitimacy in Restoration France, 1815–1830*, Berkeley: University of California Press.

Kugler, Franz, and Adolph Menzel ([1842]1876), *Geschichte Friedrichs des Großen*, Leipzig: Hermann Mendelsohn.

Landry, Stan M. (2011), "From Orthodoxy to Atheism: The Apostasy of Bruno Bauer, 1835 1843," *Journal of Religion and Society* (13): 1–20.

Landry, Stan M. (2013), *Ecumenism, Memory, and German Nationalism 1817–1917*, Syracuse: Syracuse University Press.

Landsberg, Alison (2004), *Prosthetic Memory: The Transformation of American Remembrance in the Age of Mass Culture*, New York: Columbia University Press.

Lara, Oruno P. (2005), *La liberté assassinée: Guadeloupe, Guyane, Martinique et La Réunion en 1848–1856*, Paris: Harmattan.

Larcher, Silyane (2006), "Les errances de la mémoire de l'esclavage colonial et la démocratie française aujourd'hui," *Cité*, 1 (25): 153–63.

Larrowe, Marcus (1886), *Physiological Memory, or, The Instantaneous Art of Never Forgetting*, New York: Loisette.

Laschley, Karl (1950), "In Search of the Engram," *Symposium of the Society for Experimental Biology*, 4.

Laurent de L'Ardèche, Paul Mathieu (1843), *Histoire de L'Empereur Napoléon*. Illustrations by Horace Vernet, Paris: J.-J. Dubochet.

Lavabre, Marie-Claire (2013), "A propos de l'oubli dans les réflexions sur la mémoire collective ou sociale," in Edward Berenson and Denis Peschanski, eds., *Mémoire et mémorialisation 1: De l'absence à la représentation*, 11–24, Paris: Hermann.

Lawrence, Dianne (2012), *Genteel Women: Empire and Domestic Material Culture, 1840–1910*, Manchester: Manchester University Press.

Leerssen, Joep and Ann Rigney, eds. (2014), *Commemorating Writers in Nineteenth-Century Europe: Nation Building and Centenary Fever*, London: Palgrave.

Le Goff, Jacques (1992), *History and Memory*, New York: Columbia University Press.

Lehmann, Hartmut (1983), "Das Lutherjubiläum 1883," in Jürgen Becker, ed., *Luthers bleibende Bedeutung*, Husum: Husum Druck-und Verlagsgruppe.

Leonardi, N, and S. Natale, eds. (2018), *Photography and Other Media in the Nineteenth Century*, University Park, PA: Pennsylvania University Press.

Le Trocquer, Olivier (2006), "Mémoire et interprétation du 4 septembre 1870: le sens de l'oubli," *Temporalités*, 5, http://temporalites.revues.org/283 (accessed February 28, 2018).

Leys, Ruth (2000), *Trauma: A Genealogy*, Chicago: University of Chicago Press.

Lightman, B., and B. Zon, eds. (2014), "Introduction," *Evolution and Victorian Culture*, Cambridge: Cambridge University Press.

Linde, Charlotte (2008), *Working the Past: Narrative and Institutional Memory*, New York and London: Oxford University Press.

Linenthal, Edward T. (1993), *Sacred Ground: Americans and their Battlefields*, Urbana: University of Illinois Press.

Loisette, Alphonse (1896), *Assimilative Memory, or How to Attend and Never Forget*, New York and London: Funk & Wagnalls.

Lok, Matthijs (2014), "'Un oubli total du passé?': The Political and Social Construction of Silence in Restoration Europe (1813–1830)," *History and Memory*, 26 (1): 40–62.

Loraux, Nicole (2002), *The Divided City: On Memory and Forgetting in Ancient Athens*, trans. Corinne Pache and Jeff Fort, New York: Zone Books.

Lorcin, Patricia E. (2002), "Rome and France in Africa: Recovering Colonial Algeria's Latin Past," *French Historical Studies*, 25: 2, 295–329.

Lowenthal, David (1985), *The Past is a Foreign Country*, Cambridge: Cambridge University Press.

Lutz, Deborah (2015a), *Relics of Death in Victorian Literature and Culture*, Cambridge: Cambridge University Press.

Lutz, Deborah (2015b), *The Brontë Cabinet: Three Lives in Nine Objects*, New York: W.W. Norton.

Lutz, John Sutton, ed. (2007), *Myth and Memory: Stories of Indigenous-European Contact*, Vancouver: University of British Columbia Press.

Lydon, Jane (2005), *Eye Contact: Photographing Indigenous Australians*, Durham, NC: Duke University Press.

Lyne, Charles E. (1885), *New Guinea: An Account of the Establishment of the British Protectorate over the Southern Sores of New Guinea*, London: Sampson Low, Marston, Searle and Rivington.

MacKenzie, John M. (1984), *Propaganda and Empire: The Manipulation of British Public Opinion 1880–1960*, Manchester: Manchester University Press.

MacKenzie, John M., ed. (2011), *European Empires and the People*, Manchester: Manchester University Press.

MacLaren, I. S. (2006), "'Caledonian Suttee?' An Anatomy of Carrier Cremation Cruelty in the Historical Record," *B.C. Studies*, 149: 3–37.

Madison, James H. (2003), "Civil War Memories and 'Pardership Forgitting,' 1865–1913," *Indiana Magazine of History*, 99 (3): 198–230.

Magee, Gary B. and Andrew S. Thompson (2010), *Empire and Globalisation: Networks of People, Goods and Capital in the British World*, Cambridge: Cambridge University Press.

Maleuvre, Didier (1999), *Museum Memories: History, Technology, Art*. Stanford: Stanford University Press.

Margalit, Avashai (2002). *The Ethics of Memory*, Cambridge MA: Harvard University Press.

Marchand, Suzanne L. (2009), *German Orientalism in the Age of Empire: Religion, Race, and Scholarship*, Cambridge: Cambridge University Press.

Marchandiau, Jean-Noël (1987), *L'illustration 1843–1944: vie et mort d'un journal*, Paris: Bibliothèque historique Privat.

Marinetti, Filippo Tommaso (2009), "Selections from Le Futurisme (1911)," in Lawrence Rainey, Christine Poggi, and Laura Wittman, eds., *Futurism: An Anthology*, 84–105, New Haven: Yale University Press.

Marks, Lynne (2000), "Railing, Tattling, and General Rumour: Gossip, Gender, and Church Regulation in Upper Canada," *Canadian Historical Review*, 81 (3): 380–407.

Marty, Joseph (1844), *Promenades pittoresques au cimetière du Père Lachaise, de Montmartre, du Montparnasse et autres*, Paris: Fourmage.

Masco, Joseph (1995), "'It is a Strict Law That Bids Us Dance': Cosmologies, Colonialism, Death, and Ritual Authority in the Kwakwaka'wakw Potlatch, 1849–1922," *Comparative Studies in Society and History*, 37 (1): 41–75.

Mason, Randall (2009), *The Once and Future New York: Historic Preservation and the Modern City*, Minneapolis: University of Minnesota Press.

Matt, Susan J. (2011), *Homesickness: An American History*, New York: Oxford University Press.

Matthews, Samantha (2004). *Poetical Remains: Poets' Graves, Bodies, and Books in the Nineteenth Century*. Oxford: Oxford University Press.

Matsuda, Matt K. (1996), *The Memory of the Modern*, Oxford: Oxford University Press.

Matsuda, Matt K. (2005), *Empire of Love: Histories of France and the Pacific*, New York: Oxford University Press.

Maurer, Kathrin (2006), *Discursive Interaction: Literary Realism and Academic Historiography in Nineteenth-Century Germany*, Heidelberg: Synchron Verlag.

Maurer, Kathrin (2013), *Visualizing the Past: The Power of the Image in Nineteenth-Century German Historicism*, Berlin: Walter de Gruyter.

Maurer, Kathrin (2018), "The Paradox of Total Immersion: Watching War in Nineteenth-century Panoramas," in Anders Engberg-Pedersen and Kathrin Maurer, eds., *Visualizing War: Emotions, Technologies, and Communities*, 78–94, New York: Routledge.

Mayor, Adrienne (2008), "Suppression of Indigenous Fossil Knowledge: From Claverack, New York, 1705 to Agate Springs, Nebraska, 2005," 163–82, in Robert N. Proctor and Londa Schiebinger, eds, *Agnotology: The Making and Unmaking of Ignorance*, Stanford, CA: Stanford University Press.

McKenna, Katherine M.J. "The Role of Women in the Establishment of Social Status in Early Upper Canada," *Ontario History* 83, 3 (September 1990): 179–206.

McKenzie, Kirsten (1997), "'My Own Mind Dying within Me': Eliza Fairbairn and the Reinvention of Colonial Middle-Class Domesticity in Cape Town," *South African Historical Journal*, 36: 3–23.

McKenzie, Kirsten (2004) *Scandal in the Colonies*, Melbourne: Melbourne University Press.

McMillan, J.F. (1993), "Reclaiming a Martyr: French Catholics and the Cult of Joan of Arc, 1890–1920," *Studies in Church History*, 30: 359–70.

McNally, David (2011), Speeches and Letters of Toussaint L'Ouverture on the Haitian Revolution (1793–1800), http://davidmcnally.org/wp-content/uploads/2011/01/Toussaint-LOuverture-Proclamation-and-Letters.pdf

McQuire, Scott (1998), *Visions of Modernity: Representation, Memory, Time and Space in the Age of the Camera*, London: Sage.

Melman, Billie (2006), *The Culture of History: English Uses of the Past 1800–1953*, Oxford: Oxford University Press.

Merrill, Michael (1976), "Interview with E.P. Thompson," in H. Abelove, et al. eds, *Visions of History*, 20f, Manchester: Manchester University Press.

Metcalf, T.W. (2003), "Monuments and Memorials: Lord Curzon's Creation of a Past for the Raj," in Maria Antonella Pelizzari, ed., *Traces of India: Photographs, Architecture, and the Politics of Representation, 1850–1900*, 240–59, Montreal: Canadian Centre for Architecture.

Metge, Dame Joan (2013), "Whakapapa—New Zealand Anthropology: Beginnings," *Sites: New Series*, 10 (1): 4–29.

Mieszkowski, Jan (2012), *Watching War*, Stanford: Stanford University Press.

Miles, Pliny (1848), *American Mnemotechny: Or Art of Memory, Theoretical and Practical . . .*, New York: Wiley and Putnam.

Miller, J. R. (1996), *Shingwauk's Vision: A History of Native Residential Schools*, Toronto: University of Toronto Press.

Miller, J. R. (2009), *Compact, Contract, Covenant: Aboriginal Treaty-Making in Canada*, Toronto: University of Toronto Press.

Milloy, John S. (1999), *A National Crime: The Canadian Government and the Residential School System, 1879–1986*, Winnipeg: University of Manitoba Press.

Minardi, Margot (2010), *Making Slavery History: Abolitionism and the Politics of Memory in Massachusetts*, New York: Oxford University Press.

Mires, Charlene (2002), *Independence Hall in American Memory*, Philadelphia: University of Pennsylvania Press.

Moffatt, Kirstine (2009), "The Piano as Cultural Symbol in Colonial New Zealand," *History Compass*, 7 (3): 719–41.

Morgan, Cecilia (2004), "Turning Strangers into Sisters? Missionaries and Colonization in Upper Canada," in Marlene Epp, Franca Iacovetta, and Frances Swyripa, eds., *Sisters or Strangers? Immigrant, Ethnic, and Racialized Women in Canadian History*, Toronto: University of Toronto Press.

Morgan, Cecilia (2017a), *Building Better Britains? Settler Societies in the British Empire, 1783–1920*, Toronto: University of Toronto Press.

Morgan, Cecilia (2017b), *Travellers Through Empire: Indigenous Voyages from Early Canada*, Montreal and Kingston: McGill-Queen's University Press.

Morgan, Emily Kathryn (2014), *Street Life in London: Context and Commentary*. Edinburgh; Boston: MuseumsEtc.

Moses, Dirk, ed. (2004), *Genocide and Settler Society. Frontier Violence and Stolen Indigenous Children in Australian History*, New York: Berghahn Books.

Mosse, George L. (1975), *The Nationalization of the Masses; Political Symbolism and Mass Movements in Germany from the Napoleonic Wars through the Third Reich*, New York: H. Fertig.

Muckle, Robert J. (2004) "Potlatch," in Gerry Hallowell, ed., *Oxford Companion to Canadian History*, 497, Toronto: University of Toronto Press.

Müller, Harro (1996), "Historische Romane," in Edward McInnes and Gerhard Plumpe, eds., *Hansers Sozialgeschichte der Deutschen Literatur 1848–1890*, 690–708, München: Carl Hanser Verlag.

Mumford, Lewis (1961), *The City in History: Its Origins, its Transformations, and its Prospects*, New York: Houghton Mifflin Harcourt.

Murray, D.J. (1976), "Research on Human Memory in the Nineteenth Century," *Canadian Journal of Psychology*, 30: 4, 201–20.

Namer, Gérard (1987), *Mémoire et Société*, Paris: Méridiens Klincksieck.

Nash, Roderick Frazier [1967] (2014), *Wilderness and the American Mind*, 5th ed., New Haven and London: Yale University Press.
Nassar, Issam (2006), "'Biblification' in the Service of Colonialism", *Third Text*, 20 (3–4): 317–26.
Natale, Simone (2012), "Photography and Communication in the Nineteenth Century," *History of Photography*, 36 (4): 451–6.
Nelson, Megan Kate (2012), *Ruin Nation: Destruction and the American Civil War*, Athens, GA, and London: University of Georgia Press.
Newbury, Colin Walter (1980), *Tahiti Nui: Change and Survival in French Polynesia, 1767–1945*, Honolulu: University of Hawai'i Press.
Nietzsche, Friedrich [1874] (1980), *On the Advantage and Disadvantage of History for Life*, trans. Peter Preuss, Indianapolis and Cambridge: Hackett.
Nietzsche, Friedrich (1989), *On the Genealogy of Morals*, New York: Vintage.
Nietzsche, Friedrich (1997), "On the Uses and Disadvantages of History for Life," in *Untimely Meditations*, Cambridge: Cambridge University Press.
Nochlin, Linda (2004), "The Imaginary Orient," in Vanessa R. Schwartz and Jeannene Przybliski, eds., *The Nineteenth-Century Visual Cultural Reader*, 289–398, New York: Routledge.
Nora, Pierre (1989), "Between Memory and History: Les Lieux de Mémoire," *Representations* 26.1, 7–24.
Nora, Pierre, ed. (1984–92), *Les lieux de mémoire*, Paris: Gallimard.
Nora, Pierre, ed. (1996–98), *Realms of Memory: Rethinking the French Past*, Vols. 1–3, New York: Columbia University Press.
Nora, Pierre, ed. (2001–10), *Rethinking France: Les Lieux de Mémoire*, 4 vols., Chicago: University of Chicago Press.
Norman, Alison (2012), "'Fit for the Table of the Most Fastidious Epicure': Culinary Colonialism in the Upper Canadian Contact Zone," in Franca Iacovetta, Valerie J. Korinek, and Marlene Epp, eds., *Edible Histories, Cultural Politics: Towards a Canadian Food History*, 31–49, Toronto: University of Toronto Press.
Norvins, Baron de (1819), *Tableau de la Révolution française depuis son origine jusqu'en 1814*, Paris: Babeuf.
Nugent, Maria (2014), "Shellwork on show: Colonial history, Australian Aboriginal women and the display of decorative objects," *Journal of Material Culture*, 19 (1): 75–92.
Oettermann, Stephan (1997), *The Panorama: History of a Mass Medium*. Trans. Deborah Lucas Schneider, New York: Zone.
Oexle, Otto Gerhard (1986), "Historismus: Überlegungen zur Geschichte des Phänomens und des Begriffs," *Jahrbuch der Braunschweigischen wissenschaftlichen Gesellschaft*, 86: 119–55.
Oldenberg, Friedrich (1859), *Ein Streifzug in die Bilderwelt*, Hamburg: Agentur des Rauen Hauses.
Olick, Jeffrey (2003), *States of Memory: Continuities, Conflicts, and Transformations in National Retrospection (Politics, History, and Culture)*, Durham and London: Duke University, Duke University Press.
Olick, Jeffrey K., Vered Vinitzky-Seroussi, and Daniel Levy (2011), eds. *The Collective Memory Reader*, Oxford: Oxford University Press.
Oliver-Smith, Anthony (2011), "Anthropology in Disasters: Local Knowledge, Knowledge of the Local, and Expert Knowledge," in Mara Brandusi et al., eds., *Disasters, Development, and Humanitarian Aid: New Challenges for Anthropology*, 25–38, Rimini: Guaraldi.

Orange, Claudia (2011), *The Treaty of Waitangi*, Wellington, NZ: Bridget Williams Books.
Orosz, Joel J. (1990), *Curators and Culture: The Museum Movement in America 1740–1870*, Tuscaloosa: University of Alabama Press.
Osorio, Jon Kamakawiwoʻole (2002), *Dismembering Lahui: A History of the Hawaiian Nation to 1887*, Honolulu: University of Hawaiʻi Press.
Osterhammel, Jürgen (2009), *Die Verwandlung der Welt: Eine Geschichte des Neunzehnten Jahrhunderts*, München: Beck.
Osterhammel, Jürgen (2014) *The Transformation of the World: A Global History of the Nineteenth Century*, Princeton, NJ: Princeton University Press.
O'Sullivan, J.L. (1839), "The Great Nation of Futurity," *United States Democratic Review* 6 (23): 426–30.
Otis, Laura (1994), *Organic Memory: History and the Body in the Late Nineteenth & Early Twentieth Centuries*, Lincoln: University of Nebraska Press.
Oulebsir, Nadia (2004), *Les Usages du patrimoine. Monuments, musées et politique colonial en Algérie (1830–1930)*, Paris: Editions de l'EHESS.
Passerini, Luisa (2003), "Memories Between Silence and Oblivion," in Katharine Hodgkin and Susannah Radstone, eds., *Contested Pasts: The Politics of Memory*, London and New York: Taylor & Francis.
Paul, Gerhard, ed. (2011), *Bilder, die Geschichte schrieben: 1900 bis heute*, Göttingen: Vandenhoeck & Ruprecht.
Paulhan, Frédéric (1904), *La Fonction de la mémoire et le souvenir affectif*, Paris: Félix Alcan.
Peace, Thomas (2018), "Indigenous intellectual traditions and biography in the northeast: A historiographical reflection," *History Compass*, 16 https://doi-org.myaccess.library.utoronto.ca/10.1111/hic3.12445
Pelizzari, M.A., ed, *Traces of India: Photographs, Architecture, and the Politics of Representation, 1850–1900*, Montreal: Canadian Centre for Architecture.
Pelletan, Eugène (1840), "Troisième lettre à M. le ministre de l'lnstruction Publique. Des encouragements littéraires," *France littéraire*, 9: 162–8.
Peterson, Brent Orlyn (2005), *History, Fiction, and Germany: Writing the Nineteenth Century Nation*, Detroit, MI: Wayne State University Press.
Pfitzer, G.M. (2008), *Popular History and the Literary Marketplace, 1840–1920*, Amherst: University of Massachusetts Press.
Phillips, David (2016), "The 'Migrated Archives' and a Forgotten Corner of Empire: The British Borneo Territories," *Journal of Imperial and Commonwealth History*, 44 (6): 1001–19.
Phillips, Ruth. "Making Sense Out/Of the Visual: Aboriginal Presentations and Representations in Nineteenth-Century Canada," *Art History* 27, 4 (September 2004): 593–615.
Piehler, G. Kurt (1995), *Remembering War the American Way*, Washington, DC: Smithsonian Institution Press.
Piggush, Yvette (2009), "Fancy History: John Fanning Watson's Relic Box," Common-Place 10 (1), www.common-place.org
Pike, Martha (1980), "In Memory Of: Artifacts Relating to Mourning in Nineteenth Century America," *Journal of American Culture*, 3 (4): 642–59.
Pinney, Christopher (1997) *Camera Indica: The Social Life of Indian Photographs. Envisioning Asia*, London: Reaktion Books.
Pinney, Christopher (2003), "Some Indian 'View of India': The Ethics of Representation," in Maria Antonella Pelizzari, ed., *Traces of India: Photographs, Architecture, and the Politics of Representation, 1850–1900*, 262–75, Montreal: Canadian Centre for Architecture.

Piper, Andrew (2009), *Dreaming in Books: The Making of the Bibliographic Imagination in the Romantic Age*, Chicago: University of Chicago Press.

Pohlsander, Hans A. (2008), *National Monuments and Nationalism in Nineteenth-Century Germany*, Bern: Peter Lang.

Porter, Frances and Charlotte Macdonald, eds., with Tui Macdonald (1996), *"My Hand Will Write What My Heart Dictates": The Unsettled Lives of Women in Nineteenth-Century New Zealand as Revealed to Sisters, Family and Friends*, Auckland, NZ: Auckland University Press with Bridget Williams Books.

Price, Fiona (2006), "Resisting the Spirit of Innovation: The Other Historical Novel and Jane Porter," *Modern Language Review*, 101(3): 638–51.

Price, Leah (2012), *How to do Things with Books in Victorian England*, Princeton, NJ: Princeton University Press.

Proctor, Robert N. and Londa Schiebinger, eds. (2008), *Agnotology: The Making and Unmaking of Ignorance*, Stanford, CA: Stanford University Press.

Quinault, Roland (1998), "The Cult of the Centenary, c. 1784–1914," *Historical Research*, 71 (176): 303–23.

Rabinow, Paul (1989), *French Modern: Norms and Forms of the Social Environment*, Cambridge, MA: MIT Press.

Racette, Sherry Facell (2005), "Sewing for a Living: The Commodification of Métis Women's Artistic Production," in Katie Pickles and Myra Rutherdale, eds., *Contact Zones: Aboriginal & Settler Women in Canada's Colonial Past*, 17–46, Vancouver: University of British Columbia Press.

Rangan, Haripriya, Edward A. Alpers, Tim Denham, Christian A. Kull, and Judith Carney, "Food Traditions and Landscape Histories of the Indian Ocean World: Theoretical and Methodological Reflections," *Environment and History* 21, 1 (February 2015): 135–57.

Ranke, Leopold von (1884), *Zur Kritik neuerer Geschichtsschreiber*, Leipzig: Duncker & Humbolt.

Ranke, Leopold von (1975), "Idee der Universalhistorie," in Volker Dotterweich and Walther Peter Fuchs, eds., *Vorlesungseinleitungen*, 72–89, München: Oldenbourg Verlag.

Reid, Kirsty (2003), "Setting Women to Work: The Assignment System and Female Convict Labour in Van Diemen's Land, 1820–1839," *Australian Historical Studies*, 121 (34): 1–35.

Reynolds, Henry (1987), *Frontier: Aborigines, Settlers and Land*, Sydney: Allen and Unwin.

Ribot, Théodule [1881] (1906), *Les maladies de la mémoire*, Paris: Baillière.

Ribot, Théodule (1894), "Recherches sur la mémoire affective," *Revue Philosophique de la France et de l'Etranger*, 38, 376–401.

Richards, Thomas (1993), *The Imperial Archive: Knowledge and the Fantasy of Empire*, London and New York: Verso.

Ricoeur, Paul (2004), *Memory, History, Forgetting*, trans. K. Blamey and D. Pellauer, Chicago: University of Chicago Press.

Rigney, Ann (2012), *The Afterlives of Walter Scott: Memory on the Move*, Oxford: Oxford University Press.

Rigney, Ann (2014), "Scott 1871: Celebration as Cultural Diplomacy," in Joep Leerssen and Ann Rigney, eds., *Commemorating Writers in Nineteenth-Century Europe: Nation Building and Centenary Fever*, London: Palgrave.

Rigney, Ann (2016), "Cultural memory studies: Mediation, narrative, and the aesthetic," in Trever Hagen and Anna Lisa Tota, eds., *Routledge International Handbook of Memory Studies*, Abingdon, Oxon; New York: Routledge.

Roediger, Henry L., Yadin Dudai, and Susan M. Fitzpatrick, eds. (2007), *Science of Memory: Concepts*, Oxford: Oxford University Press.

Rosenstein, Leon (2009), *Antiques: The History of an Idea*, Ithaca, NY: Cornell University Press.
Ross, Robert (1999), *Status and Respectability in the Cape Colony 1750–1870: A Tragedy of Manners*, Cambridge: Cambridge University Press.
Roth, Michael S. (1989), "Remembering Forgetting: Maladies de la Mémoire in Nineteenth Century France," *Representations*, 26, Spring, 49–68.
Roth, (2012), *Memory, Trauma, and History: Essays on Living with the Past*, New York: Columbia University Press.
Ruchatz, Jens (2010), "The Photograph as Externalization and Trace," in Astrid Erll and Ansgar Nünning, eds., *Cultural Memory Studies: An International and Interdisciplinary Handbook*, Berlin: De Gruyter, 367–78.
Rupke, Nicolaas A. (2008), *Alexander von Humboldt: A Metabiography*, Chicago: University of Chicago Press.
Ruskin, John (1849), *The Seven Lamps of Architecture*, Project Gutenberg.
Rutherdale, Myra (2005), "'She Was a Ragged Little Thing': Missionaries, Embodiment, and Refashioning Aboriginal Womanhood in Northern Canada," in Katie Pickles and Myra Rutherdale, eds., *Contact Zones: Aboriginal & Settler Women in Canada's Colonial Past*, 228–45, Vancouver: University of British Columbia Press.
Said, Edward (1978), *Orientalism*, New York: Random House.
Salmond, Anne (1999), "Māori and modernity: Ruatara's dying," in Anthony Cohen, ed., *Signifying Identities: Anthropological Perspectives on Boundaries and Contested Identities*, 37–58, London: Routledge.
Samuel, Raphael [1994] (2012), *Theatres of Memory: Past and Present in Contemporary Culture*. London; New York: Verso.
Samuels, Maurice (2004), *The Spectacular Past: Popular History and the Novel in Nineteenth-Century France*, Ithaca, NY: Cornell University Press.
Santich, Barbara (2011), "Nineteenth-Century Experimentation and the Role of Indigenous Foods in Australian Food Culture," *Australian Humanities Review*, 51: 65–78.
Savage, Kirk (1994), "The Politics of Memory: Black Emancipation and the Civil War Monument," in John R. Gillis, ed., *Commemorations: The Politics of National Identity*. Princeton, NJ: Princeton University Press.
Savage, Kirk (2009), *Monument Wars: Washington, DC, the National Mall, and the Transformation of the Memorial Landscape*, Berkeley: University of California Press.
Schama, Simon (1995), *Landscape and Memory*, Toronto, ON, New York: Random House/Knopf.
Scheffel, Joseph Victor (1876), "Ekkehard. Eine Geschichte aus dem zehnten Jahrhundert," in Johannes Franke, ed., *Sämtliche Werke*, Leipzig: Hesse & Becker.
Schivelbusch, Wolfgang (2003), *The Culture of Defeat: On National Trauma, Mourning, and Recovery*, New York: Metropolitan.
Schlögel, Karl (2007), *Im Raume lesen wir die Zeit: Über Zivilisationsgeschichte und Geopolitik*, Frankfurt am Main: Fischer.
Schmidt, Nelly (2012), "Teaching and Commemorating Slavery and Abolition in France: From Organized Forgetfulness to Historical Debates," in Ana Lucia Araujo, ed., *Politics of Memory: Making Slavery Visible in the Public Space*, 106–23, New York: Routledge.
Scholz, Natalie (2010), "Past and Pathos: Symbolic Practices of Reconciliation during the French Restoration," *History & Memory*, 22 (1): 48–80.
Schwarz, Angela (2003), "Bilden, Überzeugen, Unterhalten: Wissenschaftspopularisierung und Wissenskultur im 19. Jahrhundert," in Carsten Kretschmann, ed., *Wissenspopularisierung: Konzepte der Wissensverbreitung im Wandel*, 221–34, Berlin: Akademie Verlag.

Scott, Ernest (1916), *A Short History of Australia*, Oxford: Oxford University Press.
Scribner, Robert (1986), "Incombustible Luther: The Image of the Reformer in Early Modern Germany," *Past and Present*, (110): 38–68.
Sears, John F. (1989), *Sacred Places: American Tourist Attractions in the Nineteenth Century*, Amherst: University of Massachusetts Press.
Seelye, John D. (1998), *Memory's Nation: The Place of Plymouth Rock*, Chapel Hill: University of North Carolina Press.
Segalen, Victor (1907), *Les Immémoriaux*, Paris: Plon.
Semmel, Stuart (2000), "Reading the Tangible Past: British Tourism, Collecting, and Memory after Waterloo," *Representations*, 69, Special Issue: Grounds for Remembering: 9–37.
Semon, Richard (1921), *The Mneme*, London: Ruskin.
Sen, Parajyna, (2013), "Gaur as 'Monument': The Making of an Archive and Tropes of Memorializing," *Journal of Art Historiography*, 8:1–23.
Sherwood, Topper (2008), "Lincoln Portraits Hide as Much as They Reveal," *Inside Smithsonian Research*, 22: 6.
Shevchenko, Olga (2016), "The Mirror With A Memory" in Trever Hagen and Anna Lisa Tota, eds., *Routledge International Handbook of Memory Studies*, Abingdon, Oxon; New York: Routledge.
Showalter, Camille and Janice Driesbach (1983), *Wooton Patent Desks: A Place for Everything and Everything in its Place*, Bloomington: Indiana University Press.
Siegel, Elizabeth (2010), *Galleries of Friendship and Fame: A History of Nineteenth-Century American Photograph Albums*, New Haven: Yale University Press.
Silverman, Debora L. (2015), "Diasporas of Art: History, the Tervuren Royal Museum for Central Africa, and the Politics of Memory in Belgium, 1885–2014," *The Journal of Modern History*, 87 (3): 615–67.
Singley, Blake (2012), "'Hardly Anything Fit for Man to Eat': Food and Colonialism in Australia," *History Australia*, 9 (3): 27–42.
Sinnema, Peter (1998), *Dynamics of the Pictured Page: Representing the Nation in the Illustrated London News*, Aldershot: Ashgate.
Smith, Bonnie G. (2003), *The Gender of History: Men, Women, and Historical Practice*, Cambridge, MA: Harvard University Press.
Smith, S.L. (2000), *Reimagining Indians: Native Americans Through Anglo Eyes, 1880–1940*, New York: Oxford University Press.
Sollier, Paul (1892), *Les Troubles de la mémoire*, Paris: Rueff.
Solnit, Rebecca (2006), "The Ruins of Memory," in Mark Klett, ed., *After the Ruins, 1906 and 2006: Rephotographing the San Francisco Earthquake and Fire*, 18–32, Berkeley, CA: University of California Press.
Spence, Mark David (1999), *Dispossessing the Wilderness: Indian Removal and the Making of National Parks*, New York and Oxford: Oxford University Press.
Stabile, Susan M. (2004), *Memory's Daughters: The Material Culture of Remembrance in Eighteenth-century America*, Ithaca, NY: Cornell University Press.
Stabile, Susan M. (2013), "Biography of a Box: Material Culture and Palimpsest Memory," in Joan Tumblety, ed., *Memory and History: Understanding Memory as Source and Subject*, 194–211, New York: Routledge.
Stafford, Fiona J. (1994), *The Last of the Race: The Growth of a Myth from Milton to Darwin*, Oxford: Clarendon Press.
Stammers, Tom (2014), "Collectors, Catholics, and the Commune: Heritage and Counterrevolution, 1860–1890," *French Historical Studies*, 37 (1): 53–87.

Stanard, Matthew (2011), "King Leopold's Bust: A Story of Monuments, Culture, and Memory in Colonial Europe," *Journal of Colonialism and Colonial History*, 12 (2).

Standage, Tom (1998), *The Victorian Internet: The Remarkable Story of the Telegraph and the Nineteenth Century's Online Pioneers*, London: Weidenfeld & Nicholson.

Staum, Martin S. (2003), *Labelling People: French Scholars on Society, Race, and Empire, 1815–1848*, Montreal: McGill-Queen's Press.

Stedman Jones, Gareth (1983), *Languages of Class: Studies in English Working-Class History 1832–1986*, 22, Cambridge: Cambridge University Press.

Steinberg, Ted (2001), "Smoke and Mirrors: The San Francisco Earthquake and Seismic Denial," in Steven Biel, ed., *American Disasters*, 103–26, New York: New York University Press.

Sternberger, Dolf (1991), *Panorama oder Ansichten vom 19. Jahrhundert*, in *Schriften*, Vol. 5, Frankfurt am Main: Insel.

Stiegler, Bernard (2010), "Memory," in W.J.T. Mitchell and Mark B.N. Hansen, eds., *Critical Terms for Media Studies*, 64–87, Chicago: University of Chicago Press.

Stillman, Amy Kuʻuleialoha (2001), "Re-membering the history of the Hawaiian Hula," in Jeanette Marie Mageo, *Cultural Memory: Reconfiguring History and Identity in the Postcolonial Pacific*, Honolulu: University of Hawaiʻi Press.

Stillman, Amy Kuʻuleialoha (2007), "The Hawaiian hula and legacies of institutionalization," *Comparative American Studies*, Vol. 5, No. 2.

Stoler, Ann Laura (2002), "Colonial Archives and the Arts of Governance," *Archival Science*, 2: 87–109.

Stoler, Ann Laura (2009), *Along the Archival Grain: Epistemic Anxieties and Colonial Common Sense*, Princeton, NJ: Princeton University Press.

Stoler, Ann Laura (2011), "Colonial Aphasia: Race and Disabled Histories in France," *Public Culture* 23, (2): 121–56, repr. in Stoler, *Duress: Imperial Durabilities in Our Times*, Durham and London: Duke University Press, 2016, 122–70.

Stradling, David (2007), *Making Mountains: New York City and the Catskills*, Seattle and London: University of Washington Press.

Strauss, David Friedrich translated by George Eliot (1972), *The Life of Jesus Critically Examined*, Philadelphia: Fortress Press.

Suckale, Robert (1999), "Menzels Querblick und die Ästhetik des Subjektivismus," *Jahrbuch der Berliner Museen*, 41: 19–31.

Swenson, Astrid (2013a), "The Heritage of Empire," in Astrid Swenson and Peter Mandler, eds., *From Plunder to Preservation: Britain and the Heritage of Empire, c. 1800–1940*, *Proceedings of the British Academy*, 187: 2–28.

Swenson, Astrid (2013b), *The Rise of Heritage: Preserving the Past in France, Germany, and England, 1789–1914*, Cambridge: Cambridge University Press.

Tagg, John (2009), "The Pencil of History: Photography, History, Archive," in Tagg, *The Disciplinary Frame*, Minneapolis: University of Minnesota Press.

Taithe, Bertrand (2001), *Citizenship and Wars: France in Turmoil, 1870–1871*, London and New York: Routledge.

Taithe, Bertrand (2003), "Slow Revolutionary Deaths: Murder, Silence, and Memory in the Early Third Republic," *French History*, 17 (3): 280–306.

Tebbe, Jason (2008), "Landscapes of Remembrance: Home and Memory in the Nineteenth-Century Bürgertum," *Journal of Family History*, 33 (2): 195–215.

Terdiman, Richard (1993), *Present Past: Modernity and the Memory Crisis*, Ithaca, NY: Cornell University Press.

Te Rito, Joseph Selwyn (2007), "Whakapapa: A framework for understanding identity," *MAI Review* (article 2): 1–10.

Thielking, Siegrid (2000), "Denkmal, Turm, Grab und Gruft. Orte der 'Memoria' und des 'Kultur-Bildlichen' bei Theodore Fontane," in Hanna Delf von Wolzogen and Helmuth Nürnberger, eds., *Theodor Fontane: Am Ende des Jahrhunderts*, Vol. 3, 15–27, Würzburg: Könighausen & Neumann.

Thompson, Krista (2011), "The Evidence of Things Not Photographed: Slavery and Historical Memory in the British West Indies" *Representations*, 113 (1): 39–71.

Thomson, John and Adolphe Smith [1877] (1969), *Street Life in London*, New York: B. Blom.

Thornton, Tamara Plakins (1996), *Handwriting in America: A Cultural History*, New Haven: Yale University Press.

Titchener, Edward B. (1915), *A Beginners' Psychology*, New York: Macmillan.

Tocqueville, Alexis de [1835/40] (1988), *Democracy in America*, ed. J.P. Mayer, New York: Harper Perennial.

Tocqueville, Alexis de [1841] (2001), "Essay on Algeria," in *Writings on Empire and Slavery*, Baltimore: Johns Hopkins University Press.

Tocqueville, Alexis de (1856), *The Old Regime and the French Revolution*, trans. John Bonner, New York: Harper Bros.

Todd, Zazie, Brigitte Nerlich, Suzanne McKeown, and David D. Clarke, eds. (2004), *Mixing Methods in Psychology: The Integration of Qualitative and Quantitative Methods in Theory and Practice*, Hove: Psychology Press.

Toews, John E. (1987), "Intellectual History after the Linguistic Turn: The Autonomy of Meaning and the Irreducibility of Experience." *American Historical Review* 92, 4 (Oct.): 879–907.

Tönnies, Ferdinand [1887] (2001), *Community and Civil Society*, ed. Jose Harris, trans. Jose Harris and Margaret Hollis, Cambridge: Cambridge University Press.

Travers, Len (1999), *Celebrating the Fourth: Independence Day and the Rites of Nationalism in the Early Republic*, Amherst: University of Massachusetts Press.

Treitschke, Heinrich von (1883), "Luther und die deutsche Nation," *Preußische Jahrbücher*, 52: 469–86.

Trouillot, Michel-Rolph (1995), *Silencing the Past: Power and the Production of History*, Boston: Beacon Press.

Trumpener, Katie (1997), *Bardic Nationalism: The Romantic Novel and the British Empire*, Princeton: Princeton University Press.

Tulving, Endel (1983), *Elements of Episodic Memory*, Oxford: Oxford University Press.

Turner, Frederick Jackson (1983), "The Significance of the Frontier in American History," available at: https://www.historians.org/about-aha-and-membership/aha-historyand-archives/historical-archives/the-significance-of-the-frontier-in-american-history

Van den Braembussche, Antoon (2002), "The Silence of Belgium: Taboo and Trauma in Belgian Memory," *Yale French Studies*, 102: 35–52.

Van der Kolk, Bessel A., Paul Brown, and Onno van der Hart (1989), "Pierre Janet on Post Traumatic Stress," *Journal of Traumatic Stress*, 2: 4, 365–78.

Van Grieken, Emile and Madeleine van Grieken-Taverniers (1957), *Les archives inventoriées au Ministère des Colonies*, n.p.

Van Toorn, Penny (2006), *Writing Never Arrives Naked: Early Aboriginal Cultures of Writing in Australia*, Canberra: Aboriginal Studies Press.

Varley, Karine (2008), *Under the Shadow of Defeat: The War of 1870–71 in French Memory*, Basingstoke and New York: Palgrave Macmillan.

Vellut, Jean-Luc (2005), "Regards sur le temps colonial," in Vellut, ed., *La mémoire du Congo: le temps colonial*, Gent: Musée royal de l'Afrique centrale.

Verret, Michel (1984), "Mémoire ouvrière, mémoire communiste," *Revue française de science politique*, 34: 413–27.

Vieregg, Hildegard (2008), *Geschichte des Museums: Eine Einführung*, München: Fink.

Victorien, Sophie (2016), "L'histoire du patrimoine lié au bagne en Nouvelle-Calédonie, du non-dit à l'affirmation identitaire," *Outre-Mer/Revue d'histoire pénitentiaire*, 11, https://criminocorpus.hypotheses.org/18816.

Wallman, Johannes (1987), "The Reception of Luther's Writings on the Jews from the Reformation to the End of the 19th Century," *Lutheran Quarterly*, (1): 72–97.

Walters, Krista (2012), "'A National Priority': Nutrition Canada's *Survey* and the Disciplining of Aboriginal Bodies, 1964–1975," in Franca Iacovetta, Valerie J. Korinek, and Marlene Epp, eds., *Edible Histories, Cultural Politics: Towards a Canadian Food History*, 433–52, Toronto: University of Toronto Press.

Wanhalla, Angela (2015), "Living on the River's Edge at the Taieri Native Reserve,' in Zoë Laidlaw and Alan Lester, eds., *Indigenous Communities and Settler Colonialism: Land Holding, Loss and Survival in an Interconnected World*, 138–57, London: Palgrave Macmillan.

Warner, Marina (2006), *Phantasmagoria: Spirit Visions, Metaphors, and Media into the Twenty-first Century*, New York: Oxford University Press.

Weber, Eugen (1976), *Peasants into Frenchmen: The Modernization of Rural France, 1870–1914*, Stanford: Stanford University Press.

Webster, Daniel (1825), "A Discourse, Delivered at Plymouth, December 22, 1820," in *Commemoration of the First Settlement of New-England*, Boston: Wells and Lilly.

Weedon, Alexis (2003), *Victorian Publishing: The Economics of Book Production for a Mass Market, 1836–1916*. Aldershot: Ashgate.

Weil, François (2013), *Family Trees: A History of Genealogy in America*, Cambridge, MA: Harvard University Press.

Wendebourg, Dorothea (2012), "Jews Commemorating Luther in the Nineteenth Century," *Lutheran Quarterly*, (3): 249–70.

West, Patricia (1999), *Domesticating History: The Political Origins of America's House Museums*, Washington, DC: Smithsonian.

Whitehead, Anne (2009), *Memory*, London: Routledge.

Widmer, Edward L. (1999), *Young America: The Flowering of Democracy in New York City*, New York: Oxford University Press.

Wiese, Christian (2003), "Überwinder des Mittelalters? Ahnherr des Nationasozialismus? Zur Vielstimmigkeit und Tragik der jüdischen Lutherrezeption im wilhelmischen Deutschland und in der Weimarer Republik," in Stefan Laube and Karl-Heinz Fix, eds., *Lutherinszenierung und Reformationserinnerung*, Leipzig: Evangelische Verlagsanstalt.

Williams, Carol J. (2003), *Framing the West: Race, Gender, and the Photographic Frontier in the Pacific Northwest*, Oxford: Oxford University Press.

Wilson, Colette (2007), *Paris and the Commune, 1871–1878: The Politics of Forgetting*, Manchester: Manchester University Press.

Wilson, L. Michael (2004), "Visual Culture: A Useful Category of Historical Analysis," in Vanessa R. Schwartz and Jeannene Przybliski, eds., *The Nineteenth-Century Visual Cultural Reader*, 26–33, New York: Routledge.

Wilson, R.G. (2003), "Monument Avenue, Richmond: A Unique American Boulevard," in Cynthia Mills and Pamela H. Simpson, eds., *Monuments to the Lost Cause*, Knoxville: University of Tennessee Press.

Winter, Alison (2012), *Memory: Fragments of a Modern History*, Chicago: University of Chicago Press.

Winter, Jay (1995), *Sites of Memory, Sites of Mourning: The Great War in European Cultural History*, Cambridge: Cambridge University Press.

Worden, Nigel (1994), "Between Slavery and Freedom: The Apprenticeship Period, 1834–1838," in Nigel Worden and Clifton Crais, eds., *Breaking the Chains: Slavery and Its Legacy in the 19th-century Cape Colony*, Johannesburg: Witwatersrand University Press.

Yablon, Nick (2009), *Untimely Ruins: An Archaeology of American Urban Modernity, 1819–1919*, Chicago: University of Chicago Press.

Yablon, Nick (2012), "'Land of Unfinished Monuments': The Ruins-in-Reverse of Nineteenth Century America," *American Nineteenth Century History*, 13 (2): 153–97.

Yablon, Nick (2019), *Remembrance of Things Present: The Invention of the Time Capsule*, Chicago: University of Chicago Press.

Yakubik, Jill-Karen (1997), *Archaeological Investigations at the Site of the Cabildo, New Orleans, Louisiana*, Earth Search Incorporated.

Yates, Frances A. (1966), *The Art of Memory*, Chicago: University of Chicago Press.

Young, James E. (1992), "The Counter-Monument: Memory against Itself in Germany Today," *Critical Inquiry*, 18 (2): 267–96.

Young, Linda (2004), "'Extensive, economical, and elegant': The habits of gentility in early nineteenth-century Sydney," *Australian Historical Studies*, 36 (124): 201–20.

Zantop, Susanne (1997), *Colonial Fantasies: Conquest, Family, and Nation in Precolonial Germany, 1770-1870*, Durham: Duke University Press.

Zaretsky, Eli (2015), "Reflection: Freud and Memory," in Dimitri Nikulin, ed., *Memory: A History*, Oxford: Oxford University Press.

Zeeden, Ernst Walter (1954), *The Legacy of Luther: Martin Luther and the Reformation in the Estimation of the German Lutherans from Luther's Death to the Beginning of the Age of Goethe*, London: Hollis and Carter.

Zierold, Martin (2010), "Memory and Media Cultures," in Astrid Erll and Ansgar Nünning, eds., *Cultural Memory Studies: An International and Interdisciplinary Handbook*, 400–7, Berlin, De Gruyter.

CONTRIBUTORS

Susan A. Crane is Associate Professor of Modern European History at the University of Arizona. Her research focuses on thematic issues of collective memory, historical consciousness, and historical photographs. Recent publications include "Photographs at/of/and Museums" in Gil Pasternak, ed., *Handbook of Photography Studies* (Bloomsbury Publishing 2020); "'Take Nothing but Photos, Leave Nothing but Footprints': How-to Guides for Ruin Photography," in Siobhan Lyons, ed., *Ruin Porn and the Obsession with Decay* (Palgrave 2018) and "The Pictures in the Background: History, Memory and Photography in the Museum" in Joan Tumblety, ed., *Memory and History: Understanding Memory as Source and Subject* (Routledge 2013). Her book, *Nothing Happened. A History* (Stamford University Press, 2020), considers varying uses of the word "Nothing" as an expression of historical consciousness.

Thomas Dodman is an intellectual historian of Modern France and an Assistant Professor in the Department of French at Columbia University. His first book, *What Nostalgia Was: War, Empire and the Time of a Deadly Emotion* (Chicago 2018), traced the history of how people used to die of nostalgia. He has co-edited *Une Histoire de la guerre du XIXe siècle à nos jours* (Éditions du Seuil, 2018) and is an editor for the journal *Sensibilités: Histoire, critique & sciences sociales*. As a member of Institute for Advanced Study in Princeton, he recently began working on a microhistory of a French revolutionary-era soldier.

Elizabeth Edwards is a visual and historical anthropologist who is currently Andrew W. Mellon Visiting Professor at VARI (the Victoria and Albert Museum Research Institute) in London. Until 2005 she was Curator of Photographs and Lecturer in Visual Anthropology at Pitt Rivers Museum/University of Oxford before leaving for academic posts. Now retired, she is Curator Emerita at the Museum, Emeritus Professor of Photographic History at De Montfort University, Leicester, and Honorary Professor in the Department of Anthropology, University College London. She was elected Fellow of the British Academy in 2015. Specializing in the social and material practices of photography, she has worked extensively on the relationships between photography, anthropology, and history. Her monographs and edited works include *Anthropology and Photography* (1992), *Raw Histories* (2001), *Photographs Objects Histories* (2004), *Sensible Objects* (2006) and *The Camera as Historian: Amateur Photographers and Historical Imagination 1885–1912* (2012).

Stéphane Gerson is a cultural historian of modern France, a professor of French studies at New York University, and the director of its Institute of French Studies. He has won several awards, including the Jacques Barzun Prize in Cultural History and the Laurence Wylie Prize in French Cultural Studies. His publications include *Disaster Falls: A Family Story* (2017), *Nostradamus: How an Obscure Renaissance Astrologer Became the Modern Prophet of Doom* (2012), and *The Pride of Place: Local Memories and Political Culture in Nineteenth-Century France* (2003). He also coedited *Why France? American Historians*

Reflect on an Enduring Fascination (2007), and edited the English-language edition of Patrick Boucheron et al.'s *France in the World: A New Global History* (2019).

Stan M. Landry earned his PhD in European Cultural History at the University of Arizona. His primary research explores how the religious divide between Catholics, Protestants, and Jews inflected the histories of the German-speaking lands, with a special focus on those sites at which religion, theology, and political culture intersected. In particular, he is interested in the "presence" of the Reformation in the modern world through memory, historical consciousness and commemoration. He has published in *Church History*, *Journal of Religion and Society,* and *Lutheran Quarterly*. His monograph, *Ecumenism, Memory, and German Nationalism, 1817–1917* was published by Syracuse University Press in 2013.

Matt K. Matsuda is Professor of History at Rutgers University-New Brunswick, where he teaches Modern European and Asia-Pacific global and comparative histories. He is the author of *The Memory of the Modern* (1996), *Empire of Love: Histories of France and the Pacific* (2005), and *Pacific Worlds: A History of Seas, Peoples, and Cultures* (2012). He is the founding editor of the Palgrave Studies in Pacific History.

Kathrin Maurer is Associate Professor of German Studies at the University of Southern Denmark (Denmark). She earned her PhD in German literature from Columbia University and worked as an Assistant Professor at the University of Arizona. She was awarded a Research Fellowship by the Humboldt Foundation in 2009, and in 2015 she became Dr. Phil. at University of Southern Denmark. Her research areas are nineteenth-century German literature, visual culture, representations of history, war studies, and surveillance technologies. She published the books *Visualizing the Past: The Power of the Image in Nineteenth-Century German Historicism* (Berlin: Walter de Gruyter, 2013) and *Discursive Interaction: Literary Realism and Academic Historiography in Nineteenth-Century Germany* (Heidelberg: Synchron Verlag, 2006). She is the co-editor of *Visualizing War: Emotions, Technologies, and Communities* (New York: Routledge, 2018) and has published many articles about German realism, historicism, visual culture, trans-national literature, and, most recently, on aesthetic representations of military drones.

Cecilia Morgan is a professor in the Department of Curriculum, Teaching and Learning at the University of Toronto. Her most recent books include *Travelers Through Empire: Indigenous Voyages From Early Canada* (McGill-Queen's University Press, 2017); and with University of Toronto Press, *Building Better Britains? Settler Societies Within the British Empire, 1783–1920* (2017); *Commemorating Canada: History, Heritage, and Memory 1850s–1990s* (2016); *Creating Colonial Pasts: History, Memory, and Commemoration in Southern Ontario, 1860–1980* (2015). She has just completed a manuscript on the careers of English-Canadian actresses on transnational stages, 1840–1940, and is starting work on a study of elite settler families in nineteenth-century Ontario. From 2008–2012 Morgan co-edited the *Canadian Historical Review* and at present is a Section Editor, Nineteenth-Century North America, for *History Compass*. She also is an Associate Editor for the *Journal of British Studies*.

Nick Yablon received his PhD in history from the University of Chicago and is associate professor of history and American studies at the University of Iowa. He specializes in nineteenth and early twentieth century US cultural history, with a focus on urban history, memory and monument studies, the built environment, material culture, photography, and the changing experiences of space and time in modernity. He is the author of *Untimely Ruins: An Archaeology of American Urban Modernity, 1819–1919* (University of Chicago Press, 2009), and *Remembrance of Things Present: The Invention of the Time Capsule* (University of Chicago Press, 2019). His third book explores the intersections between urban photography, historic preservation, and urban archaeology in Progressive-era New York.

INDEX

Aboriginal peoples 92 (*see also* indigenous peoples)
academic historicism 119, 123–4, 133
activism, indigenous 156
aesthetics, history writing and 119–20
affective memory 87, 88, 136
Africa, European imperialism in 92 (*see also* names of individual countries)
Age of Empire 30
Age of Revolution 22
Algeria 92, 165
American Antiquarian Society 6
American Civil War 44
American Historical Association 92
amnesia (*see also* forgetting)
    collective 92, 158–9, 160, 173
    legitimizing 35
    studies of 85–6
    term 46
amnesties, amnesia/forgetting and 35, 166
Anderson, Benedict 6, 122, 158
anniversaries 103–4
anthropology 19, 85
antiquarianism 101, 102, 132–3
anxiety(ies)
    cultural 46
    of memory 17–20
aphasia 169
Archaeological Survey of India 63
archaeology 7, 62, 63, 91, 133, 177n.5
architecture 15–16, 96
archives
    archival practices 57
    digital-historical photography archive 8
    the Great Forgetting and 168
    historical knowledge and 27
    inadequate 168
    photographic 9
    proliferation of 40
Arnaud, François-Léon 86
Arnold-Forster, H.O. 61
artifacts 41
arts of memory 21–2
Ascher, Saul 111

assimilation
    of indigenous peoples 150–3
    national 167
Assmann, Aleida 76
Assmann, Jan 55, 57, 112
association items 47
Atkinson, Maria 146
attachments, to places 136
Augsburg Confession 107
Australia
    Captain Cook's statue in Sydney 70–1
    death rituals and 149
    European imperialism in 92
    food in 137, 138
    women settlers in 140–1
authenticity, market for 12–13
authority 35, 36
authors, published work of 2, 6 (*see also* literatures)
autographs 48
Azam, Eugène 87

Bachelard, Gaston 51
Bal, Mieke 80
Bann, Stephen 5, 13, 96, 100–1
Bär, Adolf 128
Barker, Henry Aston 121
Barnett, Teresa 12, 47, 174
Barrias, Louis-Ernest 162
Barton, William 121
Bastille, storming of the 21, 30–1
Batchen, Geoffrey 48
The Battle of Sedan (painting) 121–2
The Battle of Waterloo (painting) 121
battlefield pilgrimages 12, 13
Bauer, Bruno 98
Beiner, Guy 173
Belgium 165, 168, 171
Benjamin, Walter 42, 49, 50
Berger, Stefan 89
Bergson, Henri 79, 84, 87–8, 103
Berlin Childhood around 1900 50
Bertillon, Alphonse 36, 37
Bettannier, Albert 89–90

Bewick, Thomas 125
biblical past, reimagining of 64–5
biblical texts, historical critique of 98
Bildersaal Deutscher Geschichte: Zwei Jahrtausende deutschen Lebens in Bild und Wort (*Gallery of German History: Two Millennia of German Life in Image and Text*) 128
Binet, Alfred 85
biological memory, of human development 64
biological sciences 64, 83
Black Eagle of Prussia 160
black people, forgetting and 166, 171
Bligh, William 21, 23
Blight, David 161
bodily memory 80–1, 87
Bolivar, Simon 34
Bonaparte, Napoleon 32–3, 91, 124–6, 160
Bonnet, Jean-Claude 104
books 6, 124–9 (*see also* literatures; novels)
Bougainville, Louis Antoine de 23
Bouillard, Jean-Baptiste 81
Bouillier, Francisque 174
Boukman, Dutty 27
Bounty, HMS 21, 22–3, 26
bourgeois class 36, 50
Bourget, Paul 15
Bourne, Samuel 63, 72
boxes 50–1
Boyarin, Jonathan 59
Brady, Thomas A. 111
brains, human 81
Brantlinger, Patrick 19
Braw, J.D. 5
Britain 28–30, 65–9
Broca, Paul 81
Brown, Gordon 28
Brown, Matthew 34
Browning, Robert 4
Brubaker, Rogers 35
Brundage, Fitzhugh 44
Büchner, Georg 130
Burckhardt, Jacob 98, 120
Burkhardt, Johannes 108–9
Bust of Voltaire 105, *106*
Butler, Samuel 83

Cabildo 33
calendrical memory 40
The Camera as Historian project 8–9
Canada
    food in 138

Hudson Bay Company 137
    indigenous peoples 149–50, 153, 154
    women settlers in 135, 137
capitalism 26, 45
Carlyle, Thomas 104
centennial anniversaries 103–4
Chaix, Gérald 108
change(s) 6, 45, 60
Charcot, Jean-Martin 87
Chateaubriand, François-René de 119, 157
childrearing, indigenous 154
children
    photographs of 10–11
    residential schools for indigenous children 154
China 28–30, 123
Christ, Catherine 157
Christian, Fletcher 21, 23
Christianity 25, 65, 98, 149 (*see also* missionaries)
"Civilization and Barbarism" 171
civilizing mission 91
Claparède, Edouard 90
"Clapham Common Industries" 10–11
class
    bourgeois 36, 50
    class-based identifications 162–3
    middle-class 49–50, 143, 156
    the transatlantic bourgeoisie 50
    working-class forgetting 174
Clavandier, Gaëlle 168, 173
Clench, Elizabeth Johnson 142
collective amnesia 92, 158–9, 160, 173
collective forgetting 157–8, 168–9, 173–4
The Collective Memory (Halbwachs) 117
collective memory
    collective efforts of memorializing 91
    forgetting and 158
    frameworks of 7
    historical fiction and 129
    illustrated history books and 128
    indigenous peoples and 154
    manufacture of 100
    monuments and 62
    photography and 60
    popularized and politized 123
    as a product of the late 1800s 92
    public collective memory events 17
    socialization, communication and 55
    spectacularizing of 122
    studies of 89
    visual 115

"Collective Memory and Historical
    Memory" 17
Colombia 34
colonialism (*see also* imperialism)
    administration and 36
    collective colonial mind-set 56–7
    colonial capitalism 26
    colonial communications development 71
    colonial forgetting 171
    colonial memorials and topographies of
        colonial action 65–74
    colonial memory 76
    colonial rituals 138, 143, 147–9
    colonial violence 92, 159, 165, 168, 171–2
    colonial wars 60
    historical panoramas and 122
    indigenous peoples and 156
    justifying 91, 123
    memorializing imagery of 69
    memory work of 24
    photography and 124
    photography and communicative
        technologies of Empire 59–62
    settler colonialism 24–5, 135–6, 136–49,
        149–55
Combe, George 81
commemoration 100, 103, 107–8
Communards 166–7
communication(s)
    colonial communications development 71
    communication imperialism 55
    communication revolution 55–6
    communicative memory 55, 112
    communicative technologies 57, 59–62,
        176n.3:2
    new forms of 55
communities of memory 56, 58, 75, 76
Condillac, Étienne Bonnot de 80
Congo 165, 168, 171
Connerton, Paul 167
Conrad, Sebastian 76
constucting memory 49
Copway, George 150
Cottias, Myriam 165
counter-memories 4, 25, 128, 129–32
Crane, Susan A. 118, 209 (*see also*
    introduction)
Craponne, Adam de 170
"The Crawlers" 9
Creighton, Margaret 166
criminal anthropology 85
crisis of historicism 98

crisis(es) of memory 1, 46, 80, 86–7
Critique of the Synoptic Gospels 98
Cubitt, Geoffrey 136
cult of personalities 104–7
cult of ruins 90–1 (*see also* relics and ruins)
cult of the centenary 103–4
cult of the historical relic 47 (*see also* relics
    and ruins)
culture(s)
    brush culture 138
    cultural anxiety 46
    cultural eradication 25
    cultural identity 53
    cultural memory 26, 55
    cultural politics 131
    cultural transmission 103
    of defeat 160
    eradicating Indigenous culture 154
    German high culture 119–20
    Greek and Roman 7
    high and popular 116, 119–20, 132
    historical consciousness and 101
    historical cultures of the nineteenth century
        4–7
    historicizing of 118
    of indigenous peoples 24–6
    mass reading 129
    material 11–14, 136, 140, 144
    memory culture 99, 115, 116–17,
        128–9, 132
    modern media 59
    political 31
    popular culture 65
    print culture 43, 59
    of remembrance 40
    Tahitian 25
    visual 126–8
    visual memory culture 115–16, 118,
        133, 134

Daguerre, Louis 85
daguerreotypes 17–18, 85
Danish-German Wars 133
Danish National Museum 133
Darwin, Charles 19, 83, 85
Dawkins, Richard 103
death rituals 147–9, 154–5, 158
Defense of Paris 162
déjà vu 86
Deleuze, Gilles 83
Denecourt, Claude François 14
Dening, Greg 23

Dessalines, Jean-Jacques 27, 28
Deutsches Kolonialmuseum (Colonial Museum) 122
Deutsches Museum (German Museum) 132
Diderot, Denis 23, 104
Diex, Elizabeth 152
digital-historical photography archive 8
Dilthey, Wilhelm 84
dîners Chez Magny 102
disasters, forgetting and 160–1, 168, 169
disconnectedness, from the past 53
discourse(s)
    memory 2
    of the self-exterminating savage 19
discursive practices 35
dislocation 6–7
dissociation theory 87
Dodman, Thomas 209 (*see also* chapter 4)
Döllinger, Ignaz von 111
domestic conflicts, forgetting and 161–5
domesticity, genteel 138–9, 140–1
Doré, Gustave 160
Dorigny, Marcel 160
Douglass, Frederick 171
Draaisma, Douwe 85
dress, indigenous peoples and 151–2
Droysen, Gustav 120
Du Bois, W.E.B. 171
DuPetit Thouars, Abel 23
Durkheim, Emile 89

Ebbinghaus, Hermann 84
Edison, Thomas 85
education
    European missionary 152
    expansion of 60, 89
    illustrated history books and 124
    museums and 12, 132
    role of memory in 90
Edwards, Elizabeth 15–16, 124, 209 (*see also* chapter 3)
Egypt 91
The Eighteenth Brumaire of Louis Bonaparte 7
Ekkehard: Eine Geschichte aus dem zehnten Jahrhundert (Ekkehard: A Story from the Tenth Century) 130
Eksteins, Modris 96
elites
    academic historians 40, 117
    elite forms of memory 5, 6, 100
    museums and elitist conservationism 132
    Reformation anniversaries and 108

Emancipation 40–1, 49
embodiment, as a site of memorial understanding 25–6
emigration 14–15 (*see also* immigrants; migration)
emotions 85, 88, 136, 169
Empire (*see also* colonialism; imperialism)
    Age of 30
    photography and communicative technologies of 59–62
engravings 59, 125, 126–8
environmental forms of violence 165–6
Erichsen, John 87
Erinnerungshorte (memory hoards) 117
Evans, Richard 36–7
event-centered memory 173
evolutionary biology 83
evolutionary thinking 64
exceptionalism 45
exile, memories of 14–15
experimental pedagogy 90
experts 36
exploitation, commercial and labor 27
extinction 17, 19

Fairbairn, Eliza 140
fake memorabilia 14
Falret, Jean-Pierre 85
families, as agents of historical continuity 44
family heirlooms 136
family memories 142
Fanon, Frantz 168
fear, of forgetting 137
Feuchtersleven, Ernst von 85
fiction
    historical 129–32, 134
    truth and 5–6
flag-raisings 65–8, 69–71
Fleetham, Deborah L. 108
Fontane, Theodore 130–2, 134
food, memory and 137–8
forgetting (*see also* amnesia)
    amnesties and 166
    black people and 166, 171
    collective 157–8, 168–9, 173–4
    colonial 171
    communicative memory and 112
    domestic conflicts and 161–5
    fear of 137
    the Great Forgetting 165, 166–73
    institutionalized 166–8
    local politics of 173

military defeats and 159–60
natural disasters and 160–1, 168, 169
politics of 159, 170–1, 173–4
prescriptive or conciliatory 167
to preserve grandeur 159
remembrance and 158, 172–3
rituals and 166
royal 170
strategic 101
studies of 158
women and 174
Forty, Adrian 158
Foucault, Michel 35
France
   domestic interior spaces 15
   Franco-Prussian war 111, 173
   the French Revolution 6, 7, 21, 27, 30–2, 97, 119, 157
   the French Terror 161
   imperialism of 23–4
   Louisiana Purchase 32–3
   memory crisis of 1
   the Pantheon 105
   personality cults 104–7
   state power in 32
   Third Republic 104, 106–7, 161, 167
Franco-Prussian war 111, 173
Francois-Champollion, Jean 103
François, Étienne 118
Fraser, Lyndon 155
Frederick II of Germany (the Great) 126–8
Freedom Day 41
Freud, Sigmund 88–9, 158
Friedrich, Karin 110
Friedrich Wilhelm IV of Germany 98
Frisch, Albert 124
Fritzsche, Peter 6, 17, 44, 96, 101, 102, 157
frontier thesis 92
Furet, François 31
furniture 15

Gall, Franz Joseph 81
gardens 138–40
Gauguin, Paul 24
Gautier, Théophile 15
gender, forgetting and 174
The Genius of Christianity 119
genocidal massacres 92
gentility, of women 138–9, 141, 143
geographic mobility 40
geology 7, 19
Geppert, Dominik 55, 59–60, 76

German History in the Age of the Reformation 99
Germany
   academic historicism and high culture 119–20
   Danish-German Wars 133
   historical fiction and 129–32
   historical panoramas 121–3
   identity 111, 112, 113
   imperialism of 113
   Jewish people 111
   Luther and the Reformation 98–100, 104, 107–13
   nationalism 111, 112, 122, 179n.18
   Prussia 121–2, 126, 131
   Prussian School 120, 130
   Roman Catholics and Jews 110–13
   visual culture of 126–8
Gernsheim, Helmut 9
Gérôme, Jean-Léon 122
Gerson, Stéphane 209–10 (*see also* chapter 8)
Gervinius, Gottfried 120
Geschichte der poetischen National-Literatur der Deutschen 120
Gettysburg, battle of 166
Gibraltar (painting) 121
Gildea, Robert 159
Gillis, John R. 2
Gluck, Christoph Willibald von 7
Goldhill, Simon 7
Görres, Joseph 111
Gosse, Thomas 23, 24
governance 35, 62–3
Goya, Francisco 123
Graetz, Heinrich 111
The Graphic 60, 63, 65, 67, 177n.8
Great Forgetting 165, 166–73
Greece, culture of 7
Greeley, Horace 166
Green-Lewis, Jennifer 17, 58
Greenwood, Agnes 147, 148
Greenwood, Sarah 147, 148
Greisinger, Wilhem 85
Guégan, Xavier 58
Guenther, Katja 88
Guizot, François 157
Gunkel, Friedrich 124

habit memory 88
Hacking, Ian 80
Haeckel, Ernst 83
Hagen, Mae 143–4

Hagenbeck, Carl 122
Haiti 27–8, 32, 159–60, 165
Halbwachs, Maurice 7, 17, 55, 89, 95, 117, 118, 158
Hare, J. Laurence 132–3
Harris, Amelia Ryerse 135, 146, 147, 156
Harris, Sophia Ryerson 146, 147
Hawaiian islands 25, 26
Haynes, Christine 160
Hazareesingh, Sudhir 32
Heath, Lizzie 140
Hegel, G.W.F. 101, 108, 119
Heine, Heinrich 130
Herder, Johann Gottfried von 108, 119
hereditary taints 83
Hering, Ewald 83
heritage, monumental 62 (*see also* monuments)
Hermannsschlacht (painting) 124
Histoire de L'Empereur Napoléon (*History of the Emperor Napoleon*) 125–6
histoire, *mémoire* and 117–18, 122, 128, 133, 134
historical associations and societies 91, 101
historical consciousness
    the emergence of 96–7
    mass 99, 100–1, 102
    the nineteenth century and 1, 21, 42, 90–1
    post-Napoleonic 17
    reading and 6
    remains and relics and 13
historical copying 15
historical fiction 129–32, 134
historical memory 28, 117–18, 133–4
historicism 98, 100
    academic 119, 123–4, 133
histories, professional and popular 100–2
history
    as an academic profession 40, 117
    literatures and 96
    memory and 3, 95–6, 100
    willful disavowals of the past 45
History of Frederick the Great (*Geschichte Friedrichs des Großen*) 126
History of Photography 9
Hobsbawm, Eric 2–3, 22
Hochschild, Adam 159
holdouts 45, 46
Hollander, Stacey 17–18
Holmes, Oliver Wendell 8
homes, as a refuge and retreat 49–50
homesickness 44, 85

homomateriality 47
Hong Kong 29
Houdon, Jean-Antoine 104, 106
Hübsch, Heinrich 15
Hudson Bay Company 137
Hugo, Victor 107, 166
Huhtamo, Erkki 59–62
hula dance 26
human development, biological memory of 64
Humboldt, Alexander von 14
Hume, David 80
Hunt, Leigh 6
Hunt, Lynn 31
Hutton, Patrick H. 100
hypermnesia 46
hypnosis 88
hysteria 88

Ideen zur Philosophie der Geschichte der Menschheit (*Philosophical Ideas about the History of Humankind*) 119
identity(ies)
    changing 2
    class-based identifications 162–3
    cultural 53
    German 111, 112, 113
    Haitian 28
    history and 96
    of indigenous peoples 25
    multi-layered collective 173
    narratives of 91
    national 2–3, 41–2, 132–3
    self-respect and 15
    social 163
The Illustrated London News 60, 65, 66, 67, 70, 72, 73, 177n.8
illustrated press 59–60
images
    of colonial monuments 63
    historically-coded 100
    image theories 118
    imperial and militarist 60
    mass-dissemination of 59
    mass production/consumption of 124, 134
    proliferation of 115
    wood engraving 126
imagined communities 89
Les Immemoriaux 25
immigrants 167 (*see also* migration)
imperialism (*see also* colonialism)
    communication imperialism 55
    European in Africa/Australia 92

of France 23–4
of Germany 113
historical panoramas and 122
illustrated history books and 128
indigenous peoples and 92
the justification of 91
new 22
Independence Day 40
India 63, 71–4, 177n.19
indigenous peoples (*see also* names of individual indigenous groups)
 activism of 156
 assimilation of 150–3
 Canada 149–50, 153, 154
 colonialism and 156
 culture of 24–6
 death rituals 154–5
 dress and 151–2
 eradicating Indigenous culture 154
 European imperialism and 92
 the food of 137–8
 identity of 25
 indigenous knowledge 150, 152, 154
 marriages 152–4
 memories of 149–55
 New Zealand 149–50 (*see also* Maori people)
 North America 150
 photography and 155
 the salvage paradigm 19
 settler colonialism and 136
individualism 134
industrialization 96, 162
information superhighways 56
Innis, Harold 43–4
The Instantaneous Art of Never Forgetting 174
institutional memory 35–6
institutionalized forgetting 166–8
interior design 15
involuntary memories 86–9
Irene 104

Jamaica 26–7
James, William 79, 84, 88, 158
Janet, Pierre 86, 87
Janney, Caroline 170
Jarvis, Hannah Peters 143
Jefferson, Thomas 13, 32–3
Jewish people, Germany 111
Jones, Eliza Field 135
Jones, Peter 150, 152
judicial sovereignty 28

Jussen, Bernhard 115
justice 28, 36

Ka'ahumanu, Queen of the Hawaiian islands 26
Kalakaua, King of the Hawaiian islands 26
Kammen, Michael 40
Kansteiner, Wulf 59
The Keepsake 6
keepsakes 6, 12
Keltische Knochen (Celtic Bones) 130
knowledge
 creation of 12
 dissemination of 44, 61
 indigenous 150, 152, 154
 management of 35
 from the past 4
 power and politics of historical 27
Koselleck, Reinhart 44, 119
Kraepelin, Emil 86
Kugler, Franz 126–8
Kwakwaka'wakw people 154

labor
 exploitation of 27
 servants 139, 140, 156
 slavery 11, 23, 26–7, 139, 165, 166, 167, 171–2
 unfree 139
 working as a photographic subject 11
Lacassagne, Alexandre 36
Lagresille, Alfred 36
Lamarck 83
Landry, Stan M. 210 (*see also* chapter 5)
landscapes 14
Langlois, Jean-Charles 121
Langton, Anne 138–9, 155
Langton, Ellen Currer 135, 155–6
Lanney, William 19
Larcher, Silyane 170
L'Ardèche, Paul Mathieu Laurent de 125–6
Laschley, Karl 81, 83
Latin America, gaining independence from colonizers 33–4 (*see also* names of individual countries)
Lavisse, Ernest 89
Le Goff, Jacques 75
Le Roy, P. 36
learning memory 89–92
Leclerc, Charles 160
The Legacy of Luther 107
Leo X, Pope 107

Leopold III of Belgium 165, 168
letter-writing 152
libraries, public 60, 129
Liebhaber (dilettante) 132
Liebig, Justus 115
life masks 47–8
Life of Jesus 98
Lin Zexu 29
Lincoln, Abraham 48
Linde, Charlotte 35
literatures
    the academic disciplines of memory and 5
    historical fiction 128–32, 134
    history and 96
    illustrated history books 128
lived memories 27
Locke, John 80
Loftus, Elizabeth 35
Lombroso, Cesare 83, 85
London Missionary Society 67
loss 6–7
Lost Cause mythology 166
Loti, Pierre 24
Louis XVI of France 21, 161, 170
Louis XVIII of France 161, 170
Louisiana Purchase 32–3
Lovell, Julia 30
Lowenthal, David 5, 15
Luther, Martin 98–100, 104, 107–13
Lyell, Charles 19
Lyne, Charles 67, 69

Macdonald, Charlotte 136–7
MacKenzie, John M. 58
Madame Tussaud's wax museum 96–7
Magny group 102
Maleuvre, Didier 15
Mao Zedong 30
Maori people 25, 152, 154–5
Margalit, Avashai 4
Marie-Antoinette of France 170
Marien, Mary Warner 9
marketing, mass 41, 115–16
markets
    for authenticity 12–13
    for memories 2
    memory driven 10
    for reading materials 60
maroons 27
marriages
    colonial 145–6
    indigenous peoples 152–4

Martinique 172
Marx, Karl 7
Masco, Joseph 154
material cultures 11–14, 136, 140, 144
materialism 81
Matsuda, Matt K. 103, 210 (*see also* chapter 1)
Matt, Susan 44
Matter and Memory 79, 87, 103
Matthews, Samantha 13
Maundrell, Eliza and Frederick 147, 149
Maurer, Kathrin 210 (*see also* chapter 6)
media
    circulation of explicit memorialization 72
    development of mass media 124
    historical memory as a multi-media phenomenon 133–4
    mass-media-cultural imaginary 74
    media technologies 41, 56
    modern media culture 59
    photography 55, 59
    temporal blindness and the 43–4
melancholy of history 96
Melo, José María 34
membership, memory and 4
mementoes 157
memes 103
mémoire, histoire and 117–18, 122, 128, 133, 134
memoirs, printed 26–7
memorabilia, fake 14
memorial architecture 96
memorial entrepreneurs 168
memorial monuments 12, 65–74
memorial practices 17, 173
memorialization
    media circulation of 72
    practices of 55, 58, 71–2
memorization exercises 90
memoro-politics 80
memory
    abnormal 85
    assertion and disruption of 24–5
    individual 46
    as knowledge from the past 4
    the measurement of 84–6
    memory-as-slogan 4–5
    memory construction 55
    memory disorders 85
    memory-history 25
    memory objects 13, 50, 60
    memory practices 1, 14, 53, 59, 76
    memory studies 1–2, 57, 79–80, 89

memory traces 87, 88, 93
memory wars 93
new forms of 42, 44–5
popular forms of 5
the proliferation of 42
mental illness 85, 86, 87
Menzel, Adolph 126–8, 179n.12
Mestorf, Johanna 133
Michelet, Jules 103
middle-class 49–50, 143, 156
migration, black 40–1 (*see also* emigration; immigrants)
military defeats, forgetting and 159–60
missionaries 23, 25, 26, 67, 149, 150, 152–5
mnemonic practices 25, 27, 35, 40
mobility, geographic 40
modernity 3, 7, 17, 52, 71, 107, 159, 169
Möhler, Johann Adam 111
Molloy, Georgiana 148
Mommsen, Theodor 120
monuments
    Captain Cook's statue in Sydney 70–1
    collective memory and 62
    historical fiction and 130–2
    images of colonial 63
    India 63
    to Luther 110
    memorial monuments 12, 65–74
    origins and 62–5
    photographs as 58
    public 12, 17, 40, 42
    spatial contexts of 49
    Walter Scott Monument, Edinburgh 96–7
    Washington Monument 42, *43*
Morgan, Cecilia 210 (*see also* chapter 7)
Morgan, Emily 9
Mosher, Charles D. 41
Mosse, George 12
Mount Vernon estate 48
mourning 12, 17, 47, 173
Müller, Frank Lorenz 55, 59–60, 76
Mumford, Lewis 45
museology 132
museums
    the age of the 132–3
    Danish National Museum 133
    Deutsches Kolonialmuseum (Colonial Museum) 122
    Deutsches Museum (German Museum) 132
    education and 12, 132
    elitist conservationism and 132
    historical copying and 15

memory objects and 13
Museum of Arts and Trades 107
natural history and anthropology museums 56
Niagara Historical Museum 143–4
Opium War Museum, Humen town 29–30
parlors as 50
Philadelphia Museum 40
photography and 8
proliferation of 11–12, 40
public 91
the Smithsonian 13

Nahneebahweequa 135, 152, *153*, 156
naming, as a a memory practice 14
Napoleon III of France 165
narratives
    of identity 91
    national 89–90
Nassar, Issam 64
nation-building 89, 92
nation-states 2–3, 42 (*see also* states)
national history 115
national holidays 40–1
national identity 2–3, 41–2, 132–3
national memory 14
national narratives 89–90
nationalism
    Germany 111, 112, 122, 179n.18
    historical fiction and 134
    historiographical 89–90
    illustrated history books and 128
nationalization, of memory infrastructure 41
nations, memory and 35–6, 37 (*see also* states)
Native Americans 92
natural disasters, forgetting and 160–1, 168, 169
natural landscapes 14, 49
nature, commodification of 169
Naubert, Christiana Benedikte 129
Necker, Madame 104
networked publics 56
networks of Empire 61
neuroscience 92–3
New England Society 40
New Guinea 65–9
New Guinea: an account of the establishment of the British Protectorate over the Southern Shores of New Guinea 67, 69
New Orleans 33

New Testament 98
New York 45, 46, 165–6
New York Daily Tribune 166
New Zealand 25, 136, 149–50, 152, 154
newspapers 43
Niagara Historical Museum 143–4
Nietzsche, Friedrich 15, 45, 86, 101, 159
Nochlin, Linda 122
Nora, Pierre 57, 65, 95, 117, 118, 175n.1
Nordic mythology 133
North America, indigenous peoples 150
Norvins, baron de 170–1
nostalgia 7, 44, 46, 85, 96
Nostradamus, Michel de 169–70
novels (*see also* books; literatures)
    historical 128–9
    historical fiction 129–32
    Professorenroman (academic novel) 130

objects, memory 2, 3
L'oblio: saggio sull'attività selettiva della coscienza 158
oblivion 159
O'Brien, Mary Gapper 147
Oceanian island groups 25–6 (*see also* names of individual islands)
Oexle, Otto Gerhard 118
official memory 100
The Old Regime and the French Revolution 31
Oldenberg, Friedrich 115
Olick, Jeffrey 35
On Aphasia 88
"On Heroes, Hero Worship and the Heroic in History" 103–4
"On the Uses and Disadvantages of History for Life" 101
opera, as a global phenomenon 7
Opium Wars 28–30
oppression, memories of 172
oral histories 152
oral traditions 43
organic memory 80–1, 83–4
organology 81
orientalism 91, 122
Orientalist School 122
origins, monuments and 62–5
The Origins of Contemporary France 120
Osorio, Jonathan 26
Osterhammel, Jürgen 4, 7, 117
Other(s)
    constructing the cultural 124

historical panoramas and 122
the past as 103

paintings
    historically themed 7, 40, 123–4
    panorama paintings 120–4
    posthumous paintings 17–18
Panama 34
Panorama oder Ansichten vom 19. Jahrhundert (Panorama or Views of the Nineteenth Century) 122
panoramas, historical 120–4
Pantheon, Paris 105
paramnesias 86
parlors, as memory spaces 50
Passerini, Luisa 159
The Past Is a Foreign Country 5
pasts, popular 5
paternalism 61, 62
Paulhan, Frédéric 87, 158
Peale, Charles Willson 40
Pelletan, Eugène 157
performances, of mourning 12
personality cults 104–7
personality disorders 86
Philadelphia Museum 40
Phillips, Ruth 151, 152
philosophy, historicist 101
Philosophy of Right 101
phonographs 85
photographic memory 85
photographs
    of children 10–11
    as historical evidence 8
    iconic 9
    as monuments 58
    portrait photographs 16–17, 47
    slavery and 11
photography
    battle site 124
    collective memory and 60
    colonial photographers 63
    colonialism and 124
    communicative memory and 55
    and communicative technologies of empire 59–62
    emergence of 4, 56
    half-tone 69
    historical painting and 124
    history, memory and erasure in 8–11
    indigenous peoples and 155
    media 55, 59

memory and 56
museums and 8
portrait 47
post-mortum 148
the printed press and 59
surveillance and 36, 37
telegraphy and 176n.3:4
truth and 60
Photography: A Cultural History 9
"Photography on the Common—Waiting for a Hire" 10
photomnemonics 59
phrenology 81, 82
Piehler, Kurt 42
Pigalle, Jean-Baptiste 104, 105
pilgrimages 12, 13, 48, 106
Pioneering in New Guinea 67
Piper, Andrew 6
places
　attachments to 136
　historical 49
　mnemonic power of 48
Plessy v. Ferguson (1896) 33
Plymouth Oration (1820) 49
politics
　archaeology and 133
　colonial 24–5
　cultural 131
　of emotion 169
　erasure of political unrest 165
　of forgetting 159, 170–1, 173–4
　of historical knowledge 27
　local politics of forgetting 173
　memorial counter-politics 171
　memoro-politics 80
　memory and 21–2, 26, 90–1, 124
　nostalgia and 7
　political culture 31
　political topography of colonial action 65–74
　power and 26, 30–1
　of a revolutionary era 28
Polynesian islands, *ariki* 24
popular culture 65
popular history 41
Porter, Frances 136–7
Porter, Jane 129
Portman, Helen 147
portraiture
　portrait photographs 16–17, 47
　posthumous 17–18, 148
Portugal, colonies of 33–4

Posso, Camilo Gonzales 34
postal network 61
postcards 56, 123
posthumous paintings 17–18
postmortem photography 148
poverty 9
power
　of historical knowledge 27
　institutional archival power 57
　institutional memory and 35–6
　memory and 21–2
　micro-power and bio-power 35
　mnemonic power of place 48
　politics and 26, 30–1
　resituated into professional and expert roles 35
　state 31–2, 122, 126
presence, memory and 103
Present Past 1
preservationist movement 48, 63
primogeniture 44, 176n.2:4
print culture 43, 59
printed press 59–60
printing 41, 59, 129
Prior, William Matthew 18
private domestic space 49–50
privatization, of memory 174
professionalization of history 101–2, 109–10, 118
Professorenroman (academic novel) 130
Progressive era 49, 52
prospective memory 52
Protestant Reformation 99, 107–9, 112
Proust, Marcel 19, 87
　À la recherche du temps perdu 19
Prussia 121–2, 126, 131
Prussian School 120, 130
pseudoreminiscences 86
psychiatry 85
psychic trauma 87
psychoanalysis 88
psychology 79, 81, 83, 84
public commemoration 40
public memory projects 42, 50, 57
public monuments 12, 17, 40, 42
public urban spaces 49
published work, of authors 2
publishing 59
pure memory 87

The Queen's Empire 58, 60–1, 62, 69, 72, 74
Quensel, Paul 128
Quinault, Roland 103

Raabe, Wilhelm 130, 134
race memory 64
racism 19, 33, 83, 123
Ranke, Leopold von 5, 98, 99, 101, 102, 119, 120
Rauch, Christian Daniel 126
reading 6, 60, 129
realms of memory 3
The Realms of Memory 95
recapitulation theory 64
reconciliation 34, 170
reconciliationist memory, of United States 161, 166
relics and ruins 6, 12–13, 47–9, 90–1
religion
    challenges to religious authority 19
    Christianity 25, 65, 98, 149 (*see also* missionaries)
    commemoration of religious conflict 107–8
    Roman Catholicism 110–13
remembrance
    colonial 61, 71, 142
    culture of 40
    forgetting and 158, 172–3
    human 44
    material 148
    social function of 53
    subterranean world of 172–3
Renan, Ernest 158
repetition, memorization through 90
representations
    history as a medium of 101
    of revolutionaries 7
    of workers 11
repression, of memories 88, 158, 167
resistance 4, 25
Revolution, Age of 22
Revolutionary Armed Forces of Colombia (FARC) 34
Ribot, Théodule 46, 83, 85–6
Ricoeur, Paul 80
Rigney, Ann 3, 13–14, 104
rituals
    colonial 143, 147–9
    of colonial dining 138
    death rituals 147–9, 154–5, 158
    forgetting and 166
Roman Catholicism 110–13
Roman culture 7
Romantic historians 103
Romantic period 100
Romanticism 6, 7, 12, 96, 119, 129

Roosevelt, Theodore 167
Rosenthal, Joshua 34
rote memorizing 90
Roth, Michael S. 85
Rousseau, Jean-Jacques 106–7
ruins, cult of 90–1 (*see also* relics and ruins)
Rüsen, Jörn 120
Ruskin, John 17

Saint-Simon, Henri de 35
salvage paradigm 19
Samuel, Raphael 8, 9
Samuels, Maurice 126
San Francisco earthquake 169
Sarkozy, Nicolas 28
Savage, Kirk 17
Schama, Simon 14
Scheffel, Viktor 130
Schiller, Friedrich 119
Schivelbusch, Wolfgang 160
Schlegel, Friedrich 130, 132
Schlögel, Karl 134
Schoelcher, Victor 167
Scholten, Frederik von 165
Schulze, Hagen 118
sciences
    biological sciences 64, 83
    locating memory 80–4
    of memory 79, 80, 87, 88, 92–3
    in the nineteenth century 19
Scott, Walter 13–14, 96, 129
The Scottish Chiefs 129
scrapbooks 47
Scribner, Robert 107
secularization 99
Sedan, battle of 121–2, 160, 173
Sedan Panorama 121–2
Segalen, Victor 25
Selwyn, George and Sarah 144
Semmel, Stuart 4, 12, 13
Semon, Richard 83
servants 139, 140, 156
settler colonialism 24–5, 135–6, 136–49, 149–55
Shaikh, Akmal 28, 29
Shepherd, Charles 63, 72
Short History of Australia 92
Silverman, Debora 171
Simpson, Frances Ramsay 137
Simpson, George 137
sites of memory 3, 55, 89, 95, 175n.1
slavery 11, 23, 26–7, 139, 165, 166, 167, 171–2

Slavery, Abolition and Emancipation: Black Slaves and British Empire, A Thematic Documentary 11
slogan, memory as 4–5
Smith, Adolphe 8, 9–11
Smithsonian, the 13
social calling 143
social changes 60
social Darwinism 83
The Social Frameworks of Memory 89, 117
social function, of remembrance 53
social identities 163
social inequalities 162
social memories 136, 150, 155
social regulation 143
Society Islands 23–4
society, mass 43
Society of the Friends of Jean-Jacques Rousseau 106
Soufflout, Jacques-Germain 105
souvenirs 12, 13, 14–15, 47
sovereignty 31
spaces
    memory 50
    private domestic 49–50
    public urban 49
Spain, colonies of 33–4
spatial practices, of memory 49
split personality 87
Spurzheim, Johann Gaspar 81
Stafford, Fiona 19
Stanner, W.E.H. 92
Stansell, Christine 161
states
    institutional memory of 36
    nation-states 2–3, 42
    political power and 31–2
    state historical societies 40
    state memory 67
    state power 32, 122, 126
statue mania 17 (*see also* monuments)
Steinberg, Ted 169
stereotypes, racist 123
Sternberger, Dolf 122
Stillman, Amy Ku'uleialoha 26
storytelling 26, 43
Stranded in the Present 102
strategic forgetting 101
Strauss, David Friedrich 98
Street Life in London 8, 9–10, 11
Studies on Hysteria 88
superstition 170

surveillance, photography and 36, 37
Sutton, William 135
Swann's Way 87
Sydney Morning Herald 69

La Tâche noire 89–90
Tahiti 22–4, 25
Taine, Hippolyte Adolphe 120
tangible memories 13
tattoos 13
technology(ies)
    cameras 8
    communicative 57, 59–62, 176n.3
    measuring memory and 85
    memorial practices and 17
    new media 41, 56
    phonographs 85
    photography and communicative technologies of Empire 59–62
    printing 41, 59, 129
    technological disasters 168
    telegraphic technologies 56, 61, 176n.3:4
    of vision 5
    visual technologies 56
telegraphic technologies 56, 61, 176n.3:4
temporal blindness, the media and 43–4
temporal rupture 44, 45
temporality 42
Terdiman, Richard 1, 157
Thanksgiving 40
Theatres of Memory 8
The Third of May 1808 (painting) 123
Thomas, Richard 36
Thompson, Krista 11
Thomson, John 8, 9–11
Thoreau, Henry David 14
time 43, 44, 45
time capsules 51–3
Time Regained 87
Tissié, Philippe 87
Tocqueville, Alexis de 31, 44, 92
Tourgée, Albion W. 171
tourism 12–14
Toussaint L'Ouverture 27, 160
trading cards 115–16
traditions 2–3, 89, 95
The Transformation of the World: A Global History of the Nineteenth Century 4
transnational memories 41–2
trauma 87, 88, 128, 172
trees, ancient 49
Treitschke, Heinrich von 111, 112

Trouillot, Michel-Rolph 27, 159
Trumbull, John 40
truth 5–6, 60
Tsimshian people 151, 152
Turner, Frederick Jackson 92
Tussaud, Madame 96–7, 104

Über das Gedäcthnis 84
Über die ästhetische Erziehung des Menschen in einer Reihe von Briefen (Letters on the Aesthetic Education of Man) 119
unconscious memory 83
United States
    1904 World's Fair 33
    American Antiquarian Society 6
    American Civil War 44
    American Historical Association 92
    Hawaiian islands and 26
    Louisiana Purchase 32–3
    Luther in 113
    New England Society 40
    New Orleans 33
    New York 45, 46, 165–6
    proliferation of mnemonic sites 40
    reconciliationist memory of 161, 166
    San Francisco earthquake 169
    slavery and 171
    Westinghouse Electric Corporation 51–2
    Young America movement 45
urban spaces, public 49
urbanization 45

Varley, Karine 173
Vernet, Horace 125
Victoria, Queen of Great Britain 61, 152
violence
    colonial 92, 159, 165, 168, 171–2
    environmental forms of 165–6
    in Europe 6
    the Great Forgetting and 165, 168
    white 172
vision, technologies of 5
visual cultures 126–8
visual media, new 41
visual memory culture 115–16, 118, 133, 134
visual technologies 56

Völkerschaus (painting) 122
Voltaire 104–7
Voltaire Nude 104, *105*
Voyage of the Beagle 19

Wanderungen durch die Mark Brandenburg (Wanderings through the Mark Brandenburg) 130–2
war(s)
    American Civil War 44
    battlefield pilgrimages 12, 13
    colonial wars 60
    Danish-German Wars 133
    Franco-Prussian war 111, 173
    memories of 12
    memory wars 93
    Opium Wars 28–30
Wartburg festival 109
Washington, Booker T. 172
Washington Monument 42, *43*
Watson, John Fanning 47, 50
Waverley 129
Weber, Eugen 42
Webster, Daniel 49
Werner, Anton von 121, 122
Wernicke, Karl 81
Westinghouse Electric Corporation 51–2
Wette, W.M.L. de 98
White, Hayden 45
wilderness 166
Wilhelm II, Emperor of Germany 123
Williams, Carol J. 155
Williams, James 26–7
Wolfers, Philippe 171
women
    forgetting and 174
    gentility of 138–9, 141, 143
    settler 135, 136, 137, 140–1
wood engraving 125, 126–8
Worsaae, Jens Jacob Asmussen 133

Yablon, Nick 210–11 (*see also* chapter 2)
Yates, Frances 80
Young America movement 45

Zeeden, E.W. 107